Daniel Berrigan

Poetry, Drama, Prose

Daniel Berrigan

Poetry, Drama, Prose

Edited with an Introduction by
Michael True

ORBIS BOOKS

Maryknoll, New York 10545

The Catholic Foreign Mission Society of America (Maryknoll) recruits and trains people for overseas missionary service. Through Orbis Books, Maryknoll aims to foster the international dialogue that is essential to mission. The books published, however, reflect the opinions of their authors and are not meant to represent the official position of the society.

ISBN 0-88344-444-5
ISBN 0-88344-274-4 (pbk.)

To the brothers Berrigan
Thomas, John, James, Jerome, Philip
and to John Deedy
Dear companions on the way

Contents

Part Eight: Celebrations

Preface

In forty years of writing (and almost as many books), Daniel Berrigan has had a significant influence on U.S. cultural and religious life. In several awards, beginning with the Lamont Poetry Award of the Academy of American Poets in 1958, his literary achievement has been acknowledged by his peers. In recent years, however, public attention has focused on the activities of the public figure — the war resister and political prisoner — rather than on the achievement of the writer.

Such a circumstance is understandable given the urgency of the questions raised by Father Berrigan's persistent challenge to militarism and the nuclear arms race. He has given "meaning to his words by his deeds," as his brother Philip has said, working among the poor, being exiled in Latin America and jailed during the Vietnam War, traveling to Hanoi for the release of captured U.S. fliers and to Hamburg on behalf of nuclear disarmament. As teacher, priest, and orator, he has influenced both individuals and institutions and helped to initiate movements for social change.

Daniel Berrigan is first and foremost a writer, however, a man drawn repeatedly to the power of art in conveying his sense of the world and his relationship to it. In poetry and prose, as well as in one very successful drama — translated and performed around the world — he unites art and message in a manner that is sometimes unique and sometimes traditional in U.S. history.

From the time of the publication of a poem in *America* magazine in 1942, through the turbulent 1960s, to the present, Daniel Berrigan has recorded his experience with more than a casual attention to craft and with a faith in the regenerative power of art. "I sing / the star whose light my song makes steady," he wrote in an early poem and, later, art "cries reality! / like a mordant, blinded god." In notes scribbled while sitting on the floor of an Erie County jail in 1970, he spoke of writing as "in essence a form of life itself." And in moments of discouragement, in a Connecticut federal prison, he wrote that art seemed the best way to name "the miracle of rebirth." Similarly, in his late sixties, one of his favorite ways of knowing he is still on the move "is to reflect that, after thirty-five years of writing poetry, I am still at it."

The present volume is a selection of Daniel Berrigan's writing over four decades, most of the works previously published in books and periodicals. It includes also the text of his one play, *The Trial of the Catonsville Nine*, as well as a letter that was privately circulated and previously unpublished poems and essays. The introduction and brief chronology of the writer's life at the front of the book, as well as the list of publications by and about him at the back, provide background information and further references related to his work.

The organization of the material, under eight headings, calls perhaps for some explanation. Although the arrangement is somewhat arbitrary and roundabout, the general plan has been to call attention to persistent themes and preoccupations. Within the individual parts, writings appear in the chronological order in which they were published.

Part One, "Beginnings," assembles items in which Daniel Berrigan has written directly about his family, his early life and times. Included among these poems and memoirs is "Open Sesame," my favorite account of his "education": a moving description of his journey to Catonsville, shortly before he began a prison term in Danbury federal prison in 1970. Had his life ended at this point—and it very nearly did, as a result of a medical mishap—this might have been his epitaph. Twenty years later, it provides still one of the best reflections on the major preoccupations of his life.

The title of Part Two, "The Church," indicates the central place of Roman Catholicism in his upbringing and vocation, a factor without which his life is unexplainable. It is a fate he shares with two very different writers of his time, Dorothy Day, a convert and one of his teachers, and Thomas Merton, a friend and admirer, six years his senior. The institutional church gave him a powerful rationale and rhetoric, as well as a way of understanding himself and of explaining himself to others. The sense of paradox at the heart of Catholicism suited his temperament as a writer, and, working from within that paradox, Berrigan gave resonance to a language grown slack in the speech and writings of church professionals.

Part Three, "Guides and Witnesses," includes portraits of secular and religious figures who have provided inspiration and encouragement in good times and bad: an Old Testament prophet, poets, a pastor in El Salvador, and close associates, including his brother Philip, about whom Daniel wrote in 1969: "upon this single relationship has been built every other one in which my life rejoices."

Part Four, "Scriptures," indicates his wide reading and eclectic taste and reveals influences and texts that were important at critical points in his life and writings: the Gospels, Dante's *Divine Comedy*, European theology after the Second World War, as well as the writings of previous apostles of nonviolence, especially Gandhi and King, the worker priests in France, and fellow resisters at home and abroad.

Parts Five, Six, and Seven might all be contained under the one heading, "Encounters and Confrontations" (the title of Part Five). But obviously being on trial (the subject of Part Six) and being in exile, prison, or underground (Part Seven) are special cases—offering times of reflection and isolation following acts of civil disobedience. What is often impressive about all these writings is the careful attention Berrigan gives to new factors, as his life moves along. Has anyone, in fact, been more attentive to the signs of the times than he? In this, he resembles that writer whom Henry James once described as "a person on whom nothing is lost."

"Celebrations," finally, is a group of writings about Berrigan's many enthusiasms, conveying a sense of joy that sustains a life both involved and purposeful. They include such diverse affections as friends, tulips in spring-time, his home base (Manhattan), the poetry of Ezra Pound, the writing and life of Kim Chi Ha, and "the grandiose, grotesque" Book of Kells. Here, his awareness of the importance of celebration and his sense of liturgy reflect again the "Catholic" character of the writer. Suffering is central to the religious tradition, but so is celebration.

Anyone familiar with Daniel Berrigan's extensive writings may find that I have omitted certain favorites. Some attracted to his prose or poetry have reservations, at times, about work in other literary forms. The purpose of this volume is, however, to suggest the extent of his ability in several genres, an achievement that has been recognized on occasion, but seldom attended to as seriously as it should have been—a loss not only to readers, but also to the writer himself.

For anyone who has published so much, the quality of the writing will often vary, and in previous reviews of his work I have mentioned that Daniel Berrigan needs an editor, not knowing that I would eventually wind up in such a position. My hope is that I have served him and his readers well in calling attention to his best work and in rendering "the grammar of a life" (in Stanley Kunitz's phrase) that continues to inform, challenge, and enrich the culture of his native country.

MICHAEL TRUE

Acknowledgments

In preparing this volume, I have benefited from the suggestions and encouragement of several people, including Michael Carlisle, who suggested the idea, John Deedy, as well as Robert Ellsberg and especially Hank Schlau. I am grateful also to Richard A. Oehling and Michael O'Shea, Assumption College, and to the Committee on Faculty Development, for time and support along the way; to Nancy Scott, for invaluable secretarial assistance; and to librarians Philippe Poisson and Priscilla Berthiaume, for bibliographical help. Mary Pat True made useful changes in the Preface and Introduction. Anne Klejment, College of St. Thomas, responded generously to bibliographical questions, and James Tyler has been invariably helpful through his care of the Berrigan collection at Cornell University. Daniel Berrigan cooperated in various ways, during several years of preparation. He served, in fact, as a kind of co-conspirator in the project; any indictment for shortcomings, however, should be leveled at me.

MICHAEL TRUE

Chronology

1921, b. May 9, Virginia, Minnesota, the fifth of six sons of Frieda Fromhart and Thomas Berrigan.

1926, Family moved to a farm near Syracuse, New York.

1926–39, St. John the Baptist Academy, Syracuse, New York.

1939, August 14, entered the Society of Jesus, St. Andrew-on-Hudson, Poughkeepsie, New York.

1942, A poem, "Storm Song," published in *America* magazine (June 13).

1946, B.A., St. Andrew-on-Hudson.

1946–49, Taught at St. Peter's Prep, Jersey City, New Jersey.

1952, June 19, ordained a priest; M.A., Woodstock College, near Baltimore, Maryland.

1953–54, Study and ministerial work in Europe, especially France.

1954–57, Taught French and philosophy at Brooklyn Prep, Brooklyn, New York.

1957, *Time without Number*, which received the Lamont Poetry Award.

1957–62, Taught New Testament at Le Moyne College, Syracuse, New York.

1963–64, Sabbatical leave in Europe, including Czechoslovakia, and Africa; co-founder of Catholic Peace Fellowship.

1965, Assistant Editor, *Jesuit Missions*; co-founder, Clergy and Laity Concerned about Vietnam; November, exiled to Latin America by Francis Cardinal Spellman, then recalled the following March.

1967, In Colorado and California; fall, to Cornell University, United Religious Work; arrested at the Pentagon.

1968, February, to Vietnam with Howard Zinn; May 17, burned draft files with others, including his brother Philip, at Catonsville, Maryland.

1970, Lived underground; August to federal prison, Danbury, Connecticut, as prisoner #23742–125. *The Trial of the Catonsville Nine*, which received an Obie Drama Award for distinguished production in 1971 and the Los Angeles Drama Critics Award. Other awards: the Thomas More Association Medal and the Melcher Book Award. Film, *The Holy Outlaw*.

1972, February, released on parole from Danbury federal prison.

1973, *Selected and New Poems*; *Prison Poems*; October, addressed Association of Arab University Graduates, Washington, D.C.; arrested at the White House.

1974, *Lights On in the House of the Dead*.

1976, Arrested at the Pentagon, the United Nations, and various arms manufacturers; taught, lectured, gave retreats in the United States and Europe.

1979, Worked at St. Rose's Cancer Home, New York City; taught at Yale University and College of New Rochelle.

1980, September 9, arrested with the Ploughshares 8 at GE missile plant, King of Prussia, Pennsylvania; visited Northern Ireland.

1982, Ploughshares 8 trial; *Portraits — Of Those I Love*; film, *In the King of Prussia*; in Germany and Ireland.

1984, June–July in El Salvador and Nicaragua; taught at Loyola University, New Orleans.

1985, *Steadfastness of the Saints*; April–July, making a film, *The Mission*, in South America; in Australia.

1987, Taught at Berea College, Kentucky; *To Dwell in Peace: An Autobiography*.

Introduction

George Orwell once named four motives for a person's becoming a writer: (1) the wish to seem clever; (2) a delight in the sound and rhythm of language; (3) a desire to find out true facts; and (4) an impulse to push the world in a certain direction. These motives exist in different degrees in every writer, he said, though the proportions vary from time to time, "according to the atmosphere in which he is living." Had he lived in a less tumultuous age, Orwell confessed, he "might have written ornate or merely descriptive books, and might have remained almost unaware of . . . political loyalties." Living in an age of revolution, of total war, he was forced into becoming "a sort of pamphleteer."

Daniel Berrigan, eighteen years younger than Orwell, may be regarded as a person who came of age in a similar context, in a tumultuous era and at the height of empire for his native country. Further, both writers grew to manhood in the service of an "imperial army": Orwell as a British policeman in Burma, Berrigan as a Jesuit on the Hudson River. Both were censored by their bosses, Orwell by his socialist editor during the Spanish Civil War, Berrigan by Francis Cardinal Spellman, who sent him into exile during the Vietnam War. Both have had considerable influence on the language of their time—Orwell through his critique of political language "that makes lies sound truthful and murder respectable," as he wrote in "Politics and the English Language"; Berrigan through his critique of religious language that invokes God's blessing on "more of the same. More of war, more of war preparation, more of socialized death," as he wrote in "The Speech Defines the Style." In spite of their obvious differences, the English socialist and the North American priest share certain motives as artists. Recognizing these similarities is useful, I think, to anyone wishing to understand Berrigan's distinctive character as a writer.

Reading his early poems, one might imagine for Berrigan a very different career as a writer from the one he has followed, perhaps as the author of ornate, religious verse or of conventional, artful sermons. From the beginning, the various impulses named by Orwell—egoistic, aesthetic, historical, and political—were there. In the early work, the aesthetic impulse was obviously strong, including a delight in metaphor and image and a conscious effort to shape the performance, whether poetry or prose.

The same may be said for Berrigan's recent writings, also. But since 1965, the political purpose is often dominant, using the word *political* as Orwell did, meaning a desire "to alter other people's idea of the kind of society that they should strive after." Knowing about Berrigan's early development tells one something about the impulses that made him a writer and that sustain him in that commitment, even now. A brief survey of his publications from the 1940s to the present — and of the main currents of his aesthetic — may be useful, also, in understanding the later "pamphleteer." That gradual evolution reflects changes in his relationship to the culture that nurtured him as well as certain tensions at the center of his aesthetic. Changes in style and subject matter accompany the development of the literary radical.

•

Berrigan's earliest writings, all poems, center on the natural world and on matters close at hand. This is true of "Storm Song" and "You Vested Us This Morning (for four soldier-brothers)," both published in *America*, the Jesuit weekly, in 1942 and 1943 respectively. One section of "The Innocent Throne," a long poem dedicated to his brother Philip, recounts scenes from childhood, describing games that they played together and their re-enactment of adventures out of the knights' tales.

Another section of the poem concerns the gradual estrangement between son and mother during Daniel's early years as a member of the Jesuits (to join the order he had had to leave home at eighteen):

> A son's identity can startle
> even the mother, upon whose limbs, whose life
> this child has clung. He has stepped out of her
> as image from its mirror. . . .
>
> Then on a day, that subdued and smiling pulse
> grows brutal, grows tragic, snatches his heart away.
> What has befallen? *Thy father and I*
> *have sought thee sorrowing.* A stranger suddenly
> stands at her door.

In these and similar verses about his family, such as "Aunt" and "The Coat," the statement is direct and clear, a combination of personal feeling and precise description. In the latter poem, one hears the willful voice of the rebel who, much later, took an independent stand on religious grounds: "I am more kin of him than hers," one stanza concludes, "who cut and seamed me til her body bled."

After the first magazine publications, however, the poet gradually moved away from simple, direct statements toward a rhetorical language and tortured syntax that make many of the poems almost inaccessible. Among the latter group, subsequently gathered under the subheading "The Gospel According to Me," the author's religious life and vocation dictate the subject matter. One hears echoes of Gerard Manley Hopkins, the nineteenth-century Jesuit; of John Donne and George Herbert, metaphysical poets of the seventeenth century; as well as of T.S. Eliot, the metaphysicals' principal twentieth-century disciple. Eliot's *Four Quartets* and Berrigan's early poems were published during the same decade, and the young writer did not escape the influence of Eliot's lapses into moralizing and philosophizing in verse. Also, from Eliot's contemporary, Marianne Moore, Berrigan apparently learned a highly personal style and a tendency toward preachiness, as in her "What Are Years?," which contrast with the directness and economy of her (and his) better poems.

Berrigan's religious verses from this period often combine a conventional religious statement with an idiosyncratic, almost impenetrable style. Some are rhetorical, in the pejorative sense of the term, where the reader is "told" rather than "shown" the implications of a scene. The obvious is made difficult, so that the point of a poem seems merely academic, rather than strongly felt. "Biography: Christ," for example, begins

> Who you are
> let astounded midnight say
> that saw itself flooded with day
>
> or springtime that came around
> subtly on the world's wheel
> and saw you, small and larger, walking its ground

The form of such poems appears arbitrary, as if the speaker were unsure about what he wishes to accomplish by the metrical pattern or sound of the words.

Some of the early writing is characterized, nonetheless, by a clever turn of phrase or an arresting metaphor, and there are fully realized poems — reasons enough, certainly, for Marianne Moore and the other judges to regard Berrigan's collection *Time without Number* as the best first book of poems for 1957, with its promise of things to come. This recognition by the Academy of American Poets, to be followed by a National Book Award nomination, was important to Berrigan. It meant, at thirty-six years of age, easy access to publishers, who "would now take almost anything I chose to compile; the quality was largely in my own hands and my own sense of things," he wrote later.

Within two years, Berrigan published his first book of prose, a selection of essays on the church, based upon writings that originally had appeared in another Jesuit publication, *Modern Humanist*. By 1959, a pattern had been set that would be repeated over the next three decades, with books of poetry and prose being intermixed: by 1988, thirty-six books in all. In the first fifteen years, 1958–73, eight of twenty-one books were poetry, ten were prose, one was drama, and two were "conversations." In the second fifteen-year period, 1973–88, only one of fifteen books was poetry, thirteen were prose, and one was "conversations."

Anyone interested in Berrigan's prose will find his first two prose
collections, *The Bride* and *The Bow in the Clouds*, fascinating for several
reasons, but especially because of the marked contrast in attitude and tone
between them and his religious writings after 1965. *The Bride* (1965),
appropriately subtitled "Essays in the Church" and dedicated to Philip, then
a Josephite priest, and *The Bow in the Clouds: Man's Covenant with God*,
dedicated to his aunt, a nun, are almost wholly predictable within the
context of U.S. Catholicism before the Second Vatican Council. There is
little suggestion in them of things to come either in the lively debates on
church issues during the Second Vatican Council or in the priorities and
preoccupations of the later pamphleteer. Through these early books, in
fact, runs a note of conventional piety, complacency, and self-satisfaction
characteristic of writings by Catholic clergy in this period.

Although significant changes were occurring within the Catholic church
elsewhere in the United States, including liturgical reforms in the upper
Midwest and innovative theological writings by fellow Jesuits Gustav
Weigel and John Courtney Murray, Berrigan seldom criticizes the status
quo in *The Bride* or *The Bow in the Clouds*. Perhaps only in his mention of
John Henry Newman, in "Catholicism and the Intelligence," from the latter
book, is there any indication that Berrigan was aware of significant
theological stirrings in the development of Christian doctrine. Although he
apparently read modern theologians and even spent a year in France in the
1950s, neither of his books reflects the theological turmoil in Europe after
the Second World War that would flare out in the debates during Pope
John XXIII's Council in the 1960s.

Both of these early prose works preceded Berrigan's sabbatical year from
Le Moyne College, in 1963. In leaving the community of Jesuits, who own
Le Moyne College (as they did the seminaries, schools, and colleges where
Berrigan had studied and taught for the previous twenty-four years), he
became more closely associated with members of the Catholic Worker
movement and the Fellowship of Reconciliation, as well as with other
individuals committed to nonviolent social change. Eventually regarded as
a leader and spokesman among Catholic war resisters, Berrigan was
learning from and responding to a community which had been involved
with these issues some time before they were to exercise a significant
influence on his own writings. The impact of his sabbatical year abroad,
first in France and, more importantly, in Czechoslovakia in 1964, where he
attended the Christian Peace Conference, was "ineradicable upon my
spirit," he wrote later.

Of the two books that grew out of the European experience, *No One
Walks Waters* and *They Call Us Dead Men* (both published in February
1966), the first book, a collection of poetry, renders the ensuing change in
the writer more dramatically. In a collection prior to that, *The World for
Wedding Ring* (1962), the memorable poems dealt with the speaker's
concerns as an artist (in "The Poet as Observer," for example, and "To

Wallace Stevens"), while those on religious subjects ("Teresa of Avila" and "Saint Peter Speaks") seem distant and abstract. The identification between writer and subject appears forced, and the portraits of the saints read like summaries learned from a book, on topics that a clergyman is expected to write about.

In *No One Walks Waters*, by contrast, the poems center on immediate experience, including his journeys to Prague and Dachau, and vividly convey the personal impact of that pilgrimage. They reflect the consternation that accompanied Berrigan's first acquaintance with Eastern Europe and his growing concern about U.S. intervention in Vietnam. The diction and syntax of the poems are simpler than those of the earlier religious poetry, less self-conscious and mannered.

"The Divided Man Celebrates His Birthday," a poem on his forty-second birthday, for example, reveals his obvious personal turmoil in the midst of change and a certain dread about venturing deeper and deeper into troubled waters.

> man lives
> neither caught up in Danae's cloud
> nor taking joy of some fierce sacrifice;
> but sodden, unlovely,
> half murdered or born, dragged to his hour.

These lines resemble Dorothy Day's remark that she seldom involved herself in public controversy unless she were dragged into it by others (usually by Peter Maurin, Ammon Hennacy, or Karl Meyer). In theme, Berrigan's *No One Walks Waters* looks toward later writings that center on the trials and tribulations of a life in resistance.

In prose, Berrigan's change in attitude is reflected in his questioning of priorities, first, of his church and, later, of his native country. A chapter in *They Call Us Dead Men*, "The Priesthood of the Laity," calling for changes in church governance, concludes, for example, with this admonition to the hierarchy: "to refuse the church the best energies of its own members, out of a false sense of proprietorship or clerical egoism, is to wound the church at its very heart." This challenge to clergy and laity would be leveled with ever-increasing intensity in the books that followed. The subtitle to *They Call Us Dead Men*, "Reflections on Life and Conscience," and a final chapter, "New World, New Forms of Faith," reflect a commitment to social justice that informs everything Berrigan has written since then. "From that period in my life I gained new courage, new resources, new evidence," he wrote later. Responding to that "cry of despair," as he called the Vietnam War, he began responding to a vocation "thrust into our hands, . . . to bind up the wounds of humanity, to place the gifts of creation where indeed they belong—in the hands of the poor of the world."

Various people had a hand in Berrigan's redefinition of his vocation during this critical period of the mid-1960s. Their names appear in dedications to his books, as well as in his essays and interviews between 1964 and 1967. Of the various "guides" who might be mentioned, three were especially important in shaping his thought: his brother Philip, to whom Daniel had already dedicated various writings and whose own book *No More Strangers*, criticizing segregation and militarism, appeared in 1965; Thomas Merton, the Trappist monk and prolific writer, with whom Berrigan maintained an extensive correspondence over several years; and William Stringfellow, a lawyer, Protestant theologian, and close friend. Each of these figures has played a role in Berrigan's life and work, but Merton's influence was particularly crucial in the mid-1960s, both in supporting Berrigan's commitment to nonviolent social change and in his remaining a Jesuit, in spite of the repression he endured by the order and from the Catholic hierarchy.

In November 1964, Daniel and his brother Philip had participated in a retreat with Merton on "The Spiritual Roots of Protest." At that gathering—attended by A. J. Muste, a long-time peace activist and clergyman, John Howard Yoder, a Protestant theologian, and several Catholic clergy and laity who went to jail for war resistance within the next four years— Merton spoke about the need for "total personal renewal, as a prerequisite for valid nonviolent action" and about the role of sacrifice and suffering in "redemptive nonviolent protests." These themes appear repeatedly in Berrigan's writings ever since.

Equally important to the development of the writer were Berrigan's public activities, including demonstrations on behalf of civil rights and protests against the Vietnam War. In 1965, he participated in the civil rights march in Selma, Alabama, with Martin Luther King, Jr., and later joined several leading Protestant and Jewish clergy in founding Clergy and Laity Concerned about Vietnam. That same year, Berrigan was exiled to Latin America by Francis Cardinal Spellman, an event that generated public support for Berrigan's social protest and helped to confirm him in his vocation as a social critic and resister. Suffering exile served a function for Berrigan that going to jail had served for Eugene Victor Debs in the late nineteenth century; for Dorothy Day during the First World War; and for other Americans in the 1930s and 1960s. It intensified his understanding of earlier resisters such as Gandhi and Bonhoeffer and deepened his fundamental opposition to the imperial policies of the U.S. government.

The public reaction to Berrigan's exile also brought his writings to the attention of a larger audience, including many Catholics who arrived late to the civil rights movement and to resistance against the war in Vietnam. From that time on, his books and pamphlets, coming from the press with increasing regularity, had a large readership. Although records on the exact number of copies published for each of his books is scanty, those that are available suggest a dramatic increase in the number of readers in the period between the early 1960s and the early 1970s.

The initial hardcover edition of *The Bow in the Clouds* (1961), for example, was 5,000 copies, while that of *No Bars to Manhood* (1970) was 7,500; for *The Dark Night of Resistance* (1971), written "underground," after his sentencing for the destruction of draft files at Catonsville, Maryland, the initial run was 15,000. Paperback editions provided much larger circulation of his writings including 195,000 copies of *No Bars to Manhood* and probably about the same number for *The Dark Night of Resistance*. Even his poetry, whose sales are often limited among the general public, enjoyed surprising popularity. A small press published 3,000 copies of *Prison Poems* (1973), followed by another edition by a commercial press and, ten years later, a second printing of the original. Cloth and paperback editions of *New and Selected Poems* (1973) numbered 12,000 copies, again unusual for poetry. Equally significant was his increasing influence on other writers — both in the United States and abroad — through individual and communal statements regarding the Vietnam War and the arms race.

Although more could be said about the style and content of Father Berrigan's work since his emergence as a well-known writer, it seems clear that the principal characteristics and themes were well established by the early 1970s. Other related issues would provoke him to thought and reflection regarding his eventful life or would serve as the occasion for his numerous poems, essays, reviews, fables, meditations, letters and journals since then. But the basis for his political and moral attitudes and his way of being a writer were set by this time. And an appreciation for his distinctive contributions in prose and poetry inevitably centers on this earlier work.

A strong case can be made, in fact, for regarding three books from the early 1970s, *No Bars to Manhood* and *The Trial of the Catonsville Nine* (both 1970) and *Prison Poems* (1973), as his principal publications and best writing. In each book, there is a close correspondence between form and meaning, as the pamphleteer conveys his truth with immediacy and tact, without excessive moralizing or preaching. The man stands before us as memoirist and social critic in a way that seems self-evident. In much of this work, also, the style has immediacy and power.

Two essays from *No Bars to Manhood*, one an autobiography covering the years up to the Danbury prison term and the other a statement on language, illustrate the point. The first, "Open Sesame: My Life and Good Times," appears, on first reading, as merely linear, like any brief autobiography. Yet on closer reading, it resembles a kind of *apologia pro vita sua*, or a history of the writer's religious opinions, emerging, as it does, quite naturally out of his life and experience. The presentation, historical in context and unassuming in manner, resembles similar autobiographical statements by previous North American radicals, from Henry David Thoreau and Emma Goldman to Dorothy Day and Martin Luther King, Jr., as testimony of their behavior in confronting injustice. "If I must go to prison (and go I undoubtedly must)," Berrigan concludes, "I shall go neither in a spirit of alienation, or bitterness, nor of despair. But simply in the hope that has sustained me in better and worse days up to now."

In another section of the book, "The Speech Defines the Style," he turns to a theme that has haunted many writers since the Second World War: the way in which truth becomes a casualty of political language and the imperial state. Orwell addressed the theme in an epilogue to *1984*, as well as in "Politics and the English Language," as did Thomas Merton, shortly before his death, in "War and the Crisis of Language." In his essay, Berrigan makes important links between politics and religion, including the complicity of church and the state in the corruption of language. "I hear a rhetoric from the White House, from the Cathedral, from the new leadership and the old," he says. "A leader of my own Church returns from the latest Christmas visit to our troops, camped like marauding buccaneers on the promontories of the world. This gentleman returns to invoke our greatness, to assume God's blessing on—what? on more of the same. More of war, more of war preparation, more of socialized death."

In making connections between his aesthetic and religious concerns, between his literary and priestly vocations, Berrigan explains that he is here "concerned with so simple a thing as language." And in the name of the gospel, he condemns "the speech of power politics, the speech of military murder, the language of religious mystification, all language that indicates the death of the mind, the studied obscenity, the speech that pretends to human dignity and truth while in fact it brings down the world." Because the literary radical relies on language as well as action in imaging a saner world, one may rightly regard this essay, along with a related one, "The Word as Liberation," as central to his work. In examining the interconnectedness between his religious sensibility and language, he comes as close to a detailed vision of a new society as he ever does in his writing.

Elsewhere, in *No Bars to Manhood*, Berrigan focuses on other concerns and themes that will occupy him in his later work (though often less directly and succinctly than he does here): the example of the Old Testament prophets; the relevance of the Book of Revelation to the present predicament; the challenge of Gandhi and Bonhoeffer, as religious persons who confronted the war-making state. Berrigan returns to these two figures in various writings that deal with his direct action against the Vietnam War and, later, against the manufacture and deployment of nuclear armaments.

Because it fleshes out his theories of being and acting in the midst of a violent culture, *The Trial of the Catonsville Nine* also deserves a special place among Berrigan's writings. In the play, eight men and women, in addition to the author, speak for themselves, giving a variety of perspectives on the unjust social structures that prompted them to burn draft files in

Catonsville, Maryland, on May 17, 1968. Although their language reflects their common Christian background, they speak from broad concerns and experience: Thomas and Marjorie as former Maryknoll missionaries in Guatemala; George Mische as a former worker with the Alliance for Progress; Thomas Lewis as a civil rights activist in the inner city. The testimonies of Brother David Darst and John Hogan serve, in their simplicity, as counterpoints to the sophisticated statements by the previously-named participants. Quotations from Sophocles, Camus, Pablo Neruda, and the court record, interspersed throughout the text (and, when acted out, flashed on a screen above the stage), provide historical and political perspective on the action.

U.S. history of the past and present, essential to an understanding of the tradition of nonviolent resistance, is provided by Philip Berrigan's testimony. In the play, as in his writings, Philip gives a context to the action against the government. As the first "defendant" in the drama, he describes his own conversion, from his enthusiastic participation in the Second World War, to his civil disobedience against the Vietnam War. As usual, the text suggests, Philip Berrigan has done his homework and provides hard evidence for the more abstract statements of the other characters: "There have been times in our history / when in order to get redress / in order to get a voice   vox populi / arising from the roots / people have so acted / From the Boston Tea Party / through the abolitionist and anarchist movements / through World War I   and World War II / and right on / through the civil rights movement / we have a rich tradition / of civil disobedience."

In the introduction to the play, Daniel Berrigan, making an association between his drama and the new "factual theater," says that its one purpose is "to wind the spring tighter." As a success both in the U.S. and abroad, translated and performed in thirty countries, the play not only made a case for the Catonsville action, but also dramatized the issues surrounding the incidents involving "the ultra-resistance," as Francine du Plessix Gray called the movement. Two decades later *The Trial of the Catonsville Nine* is still an effective theatrical rendering of self-evident truths that have informed the radical tradition in the United States, from the movement for independence, articulated in the Declaration of Independence, through the abolitionist and civil rights movements, given voice in Thoreau's "Civil Disobedience" and King's "Letter from Birmingham Jail."

In a different way, *Prison Poems* argues the case for dissent, while conveying the anguish of the writer over the consequences of his protest. Although occasionally marred by a self-conscious rhetoric and arbitrary form that characterized his earlier religious writings, the poems are often artful and concrete in conveying the absurdity of the life of a political prisoner. In an eloquent elegy to his father and in similar works included in the present selection of Berrigan's writings, the poet pays attention to the integrity of individual stanzas and their relationship to the whole poem. In the works contained in *Prison Poems*, there are few throwaway lines or pointless asides interrupting the feeling and direction of the argument. The poems, including "Skunk," are also quite witty, as in this vivid picture of a mammal entering the prison yard: "He crept in under the full moon / like a moon thing, eyes / dazed, moonstruck. Limped along unhandily, as though / on 5 feet or 3, footsore." The poem ends with the speaker recruiting the skunk—a reluctant prisoner, in black and white—for the resistance movement. The speaker pleads: "O skunk, raise / against lawnorder, your grandiose / geysering stinking NO!"

As a collection, *Prison Poems* may remind the reader of the importance of poetry in forming a consciousness about a nation at war, as did Wilfred Owen's poems during the First World War; or Randall Jarrell's and Karl Shapiro's poems during the Second World War; or Denise Levertov's and Robert Bly's poems during the Vietnam War. For Berrigan, in loneliness and discouragement, poetry provided consolation and inspiration for the work in prison and beyond. As a journal from jail, *Prison Poems* represents a special gift to the movement for social change, whereby Berrigan conveys a message of nonviolent resistance as effectively in verse as he had previously in prose and drama.

In Berrigan's writings since the early 1970s, one can find similar acute reflections on his experience, heavy with metaphor and meaning. But with the exception of occasional passages in prose and poetry, the argument is not as sustained or as clear as it is in the three books I have just discussed. Instead, one gets a recounting of experiences, in meditations, journals, sermons, notes, letters: working in a cancer hospital, in *We Die Before We Live* (1980); traveling in Central and South America, in *Steadfastness of the Saints* (1985); or advising and appearing in an award-winning film, in *The Mission* (1987), for example.

In such books, the writing appears casual, meandering at times, with little conscious effort to accomplish a clearly defined task or to give the material a form commensurate with its insight or feeling. Many of the later books, in fact, appear to be "spoken" rather than "written," with little revision on the part of the author or editor. For that reason, it is difficult to plot any clear development of the writer, in these occasional writings, though, as in the past, the more controlled, descriptive, and narrative statements of the pamphleteer shine, at times, in the cryptic and thought-provoking prose.

In spite of this wide variation in style and the unevenness in execution, readers are understandably drawn to Berrigan's books by the subject matter, by the noble causes he has advocated, and by the insights into his personal pilgrimage as a war resister. And although standard anthologies seldom make room for his poems, his writings find their way to a sizeable readership, frequently reprinted in movement publications. Quotations from his essays and poems provide appropriate texts for fliers, posters, pamphlets, and broadsides, and fulfill a function similar to that of graphics by Käthe Kollwitz, Fritz Eichenberg, and Corita Kent, in conveying the message of resistance.

A long poem, *Block Island* (1985), also adds something new to the canon, in its lament for what might have been. In longing for the peace and beauty of a United States uncorrupted by avarice, war-making, and conquest, Berrigan conveys his affection for a country gone wrong. Dedicated to his late friend, William Stringfellow, the poem is an elegy for that "city on the hill" that might have been, rather than a jeremiad against what it has become. Written, appropriately, in the literary form that Berrigan employed in his first published works, it contrasts with the mood of much of the recent prose.

In other recent writings, Father Berrigan returns to earlier enthusiasms and to his traditional concern for language. The appreciation for the poets Ezra Pound and Denise Levertov, as well as for Manhattan, underscore his delight in "the only world we have." These writings may remind the reader, once again, of Orwell, who said that even in his polemical books, he included material that many would regard as "useless information," unsuitable to the political purpose that provoked a book or essay. As with previous North American radicals, also, such as Henry David Thoreau and Paul Goodman, Berrigan's sense of justice is grounded in an abiding affection for the physical world and a wish to ensure its survival. A look at this native tradition, below, suggests his relationship to these and other pamphleteers in the American grain.

•

In Berrigan's work, a central preoccupation—religion—underscores the peculiarly American character of his radicalism. In England, William Morris and the Fabian socialists had prepared the way for a writer on the left like Orwell, who worked from a practical and naturalistic perspective. In the U.S., a mixture of Catholicism and Puritanism pushed Berrigan in other directions—symbolic and apocalyptic. From the roots of this peculiar, God-haunted culture have sprung a number of political rabble-rousers and social militants with similar characteristics.

Thomas Paine, for example, gave equal time to rallying the colonists to rebel and to purging Christianity of superstition and ignorance. William Lloyd Garrison, a generation later, turned from evangelical Christianity to militant abolitionism with equal fervor, as did several feminists of that period. Later, Eugene Victor Debs, in preaching socialism during the early decades of this century, sometimes borrowed the rhetoric of the prophets. In the speeches of Martin Luther King, Jr.—and, indeed, the writings of Daniel Berrigan—that U.S. tradition has flourished in recent times.

Yet in the diversity of his writings, averaging over a book a year since 1957, and in the range and variety of his concerns, Berrigan extends the boundaries of the tradition in a special way. From the beginning, his identity was decidedly Roman Catholic, rather than evangelical Protestant, and from the roots of that ancient church (including the history of the religious order to which he belongs), he brought particular gifts, some of them useful to the task, others perhaps not so appropriate to a "political" writer. Or so one might argue after any careful reading of those writings that deal with fundamental social issues, such as the relationship between the individual and the state, the conflict between human and divine law, and the violence of the status quo.

Initially, the institutional church gave Berrigan a powerful rationale and rhetoric. Through the Catholic church and the Jesuits, the largest male religious order, a wide range of associations and perks, one might call them, were available to him: encouragement to excel, a ready audience, international associations, and a community of believers whose language he spoke (and altered). Although its demands, including the cold-shower years in seminary, were harsh and his early years lonely and isolated, the Jesuit education appears to have served him well in the long run. He lived among people to whom his skill as a writer mattered, and Jesuit magazines, *America* and *Thought*, published his early poems. Even in his roughest moments, in exile and prison, the Jesuit tradition of martyrs and writers (Edmund Campion, Robert Southwell, and Gerard Manley Hopkins) sustained him.

In waging a battle against the state since 1965, Berrigan has inevitably had to take on the church and the religious order, bound up as they are with the status quo, including the adventuresome, interventionist policies of the U.S. government. Although his principal audience and support are probably Catholic, several of his severest critics come from that community as well, as he tries to make a place for pacifism, for nonviolence, in a religious tradition that has long provided philosophical and theological justification for the most brutal wars. Berrigan the Catholic is the persistent critic of Catholicism, much as Orwell the socialist was the perpetual hair shirt of British socialism.

In evaluating Berrigan's achievement as a writer, including the main currents of his aesthetic and argument, one must keep in mind that his life as a literary radical is still very much in process, as productive and persistent as ever. He remains as attentive to the signs of the times as any North American literary radical past or present. Although he may not always succeed in making "political writing into an art," as Orwell put it, Berrigan has been effective in appropriating religious language to the major social issues of his time. And while the rhetoricians of the Cold War have tried to disentangle political and moral issues, Berrigan has dramatized the close association between the moral and the political.

Within his own religious tradition, he has contributed to a subtle transformation, also, symbolized by the shift in leadership from the autocratic Francis Cardinal Spellman (who sent Berrigan into exile in 1964) to Joseph Cardinal Bernardin (who co-authored the North American bishops' pastoral on nuclear disarmament, *The Challenge of Peace*, 1983). And behind the headlines about Catholicism's institutional commitment to disarmament and economic justice are the lives and writings of Daniel Berrigan, his brother Philip, as well as Dorothy Day, Thomas Merton, Gordon Zahn, and the communities they have helped to initiate. In various pastoral letters, policy statements, and liturgies, one is likely to find phrases, images, and metaphors first heard in the writings that appear in this book.

Taken as a testament, Father Berrigan's writings are important additions to a long list of books — sermons, poems, essays, novels — appropriately named by Sacvan Bercovitch as the American jeremiad, "a mode of public exhortation that originated with the early Puritans and continues to inform American letters." In joining social criticism and spiritual renewal and in many other aspects of his writing, Daniel Berrigan is characteristically American, as he has said on several occasions.

Describing his life, in 1969, Berrigan even acknowledged an indebtedness for having "enjoyed all the fruits that America offers those fortunate enough to make it within her system," adding that if he mourns for the death of that system, "it is as one who has enjoyed its cup to the depths. If that same vintage has now turned bitter as gall in my mouth, it is because I have seen the society that might have been great, according to its own rhetoric, turn murderously against those throughout the world to whom it had once offered the fairest of hopes."

In the two decades since that statement appeared, Daniel Berrigan has continued to work, as previous North American radicals from Thomas Paine to Paul Goodman did before him, to alter the priorities and direction of his country. In prose and verse, he has suggested also how it might sustain, rather than repress, those hopes that it now finds "too revolutionary or too untimely to be borne with." In his late sixties, he lives at the center of events, with pen in hand and with that awareness essential to a writer, as Orwell said, "in a tumultuous, revolutionary age like our own."

MICHAEL TRUE

Daniel Berrigan

Poetry, Drama, Prose

Part One

BEGINNINGS

Credentials

I would it were possible to state in so
few words my errand in the world: quite simply
forestalling all inquiry, the oak offers its leaves
largehandedly. And in winter its integral magnificent order
decrees, says solemnly who it is
in the great thrusting limbs that are all finally
one: a return, a permanent riverandsea.

So the rose is its own credential, a certain
unattainable effortless form: wearing its heart
visibly, it gives us heart too: bud, fulness and fall.

THOUGHT, SUMMER 1957

1961

I summon my parents, a jubilee morning.
When in gold vestments I came down
to kiss them where they stood, their tears and mine

were a clear pressing of the eighty-year vine.
I touched their faces, a gentle unweathered grain
the blind might visualize, as of green leaves
up from exposed ground.
                    What winter fury
that moment tempered, they and I know.

THE WORLD FOR WEDDING RING, 1962

My Name

If I were Pablo Neruda
or William Blake
I could bear, and be eloquent

an American name in the world
where others perish
in our two murderous hands

Alas Berrigan
you must open those hands
and see, stigmatized in their palms
the broken faces
you yearn toward

you cannot offer
being powerless as a woman
under the rain of fire—
life, the cover of your body.

Only the innocent die.
Take up, take up
the bloody map of the century.
The long trek homeward begins
into the land of unknowing.

NIGHT FLIGHT TO HANOI, 1968

Open Sesame:
My Life and Good Times

My brother Philip and I were two of six brothers. We were depression babies, all of us. My father used to say that in the 1930s he had lost everything but his shirt. If that was so, we must also recall with a certain wry humor that he only had one or two shirts to lose.

We lived most of our lives in a sixty-year-old house on the top of a hill, surrounded by ten not very fruitful acres. I remember vividly that we housed and fed a continuing number of homeless men during those dark years of loss. Even those neighbors who would not themselves feed or clothe or house the poor would always tell them that they could find something at our place.

Our schooling was mediocre at best. But it was augmented by constant reading. My mother deserves an eternal reward for the constant tonnage of books she carried home by streetcar from the city library.

Our life was frugal and untidy, with regular cleanups on my father's part to reassert his iron brand of authority. But it was always something like a roundup of colts. The fact is that he was not home a great deal of the time, and we generally ran free.

I entered the Society of Jesus in 1939. I was acquainted with no Jesuits, so it was a matter of an act of faith on both sides. Not a bad arrangement.

As with any young person of eighteen entering upon an entirely new form of life, the memories of my first years are particularly vivid. With regard to present convictions, I think they gave me a deep sense of the presence of God in the world, and most especially in human community. I must say too that I fell in love immediately and incurably with the Jesuit style, although prior to my entrance I had practically no knowledge of it firsthand. But it appealed to me immediately as a ground for my boundless idealism; and I found in the talents and youth and drive around me a constant spur to make my own life count.

When I entered upon my studies it became clear that I had a great deal of ground to catch up and win. Practically all of my classmates had graduated from Jesuit schools in the New York or Buffalo areas. They were invariably far ahead of me on almost every criteria that counted for achievement in our Bruderhauf.

I passed three miserable years at Woodstock College studying philosophy. It was simply not my dish. So I languished like an unhappy three-year freshman, trying with varying degrees of desperation and moodiness to find myself in a thicket of logic and metaphysics. I finished that period with enormous relief and almost entire lack of distinction.

I taught high school for three years, 1946–49, in St. Peter's Preparatory School, Jersey City, New Jersey. As I recall, I taught French, Latin, English, and what was fondly called, at that time, "religion." Everything I had believed or hoped about myself, by way of being a contributory creature in the real world, began to come true. I struck out in every direction, like a belated flower child. And this at the hands of some three hundred rough and tough Jersey kids. It was indeed the first of many miracles.

With some misgivings, I undertook theological studies at West College, at Weston, Massachusetts, in the autumn of 1949. I was then twenty-eight years old, ten years away from my initial decision to enter the order; three years awaited me until ordination, five years until the completion of the ordinary Jesuit regime of studies. So it was as a kind of ageless elephant that I lumbered into this other phase and began anew. There is nothing of distinction to report of those next years. The courses were in the main mediocre, with some exceptions in scriptural studies. I was finally (and from my point of view miraculously) ordained to the priesthood on June 19, 1952. Another year of theology and rustication in the same green acres. And a year later, in July of 1953, I departed for a year of studies in France.

Although I did not realize it for the space of several months, my real mind was being implanted, the future was being furiously sown. It was a tumultuous and even catastrophic year for French society and the French Church. Pius XII was bearing down heavily upon the worker priests; he finally suppressed the movement entirely in February of 1954. The French were living through the dying spasms of Dienbienphu. The end of the Indo-Chinese colonial adventure was at hand, and the republic was stricken at the heart, to a degree it had not known since the crisis of occupation and Vichy. It was a year of national humiliation and turmoil.

Our house of studies near Lyon was as poor as any church mouse dwelling. But we had a sense of sharing in something extraordinarily painful in France at large. Many of my compatriots were survivors of German exploitation, and had worked in labor camps and factories under the occupier. Almost everything I experienced was being experienced for the first time. I felt in many cases as though I had landed upon a new planet, and was being asked to operate in an entirely new way, to rebuild my senses, my very soul. It was not merely a matter of fumbling about with a new language and slowly gaining confidence in it. The truth was that the language offered new ways into the world of other human beings — and that these others, penetrated and formed by a thousand-year history expressed in their lucid and vivid language, were also new beings, into whose community I was invited to enter. The invitation was austere but irresistible.

What I discovered in France for the first time in my long experience of

Catholic community was so simple a thing as personal freedom. It was an invitation to become a human being by way of others, immersed as we all were during that year in the tradition of our scripture, as well as the experience and history of our order.

In retrospect that year is bathed in a glow of idyllic personal light. The actuality was somewhat more gritty. It must be confessed that in February of 1954 I sojourned into West Germany and became party to our vast military complex there. I served for some two months as an auxiliary chaplain; thoughtlessly and with a naïve acceptance that had nothing to do, as I look back, with the cruel realities of that land and time. I preached and heard confessions and counseled innumerable soldiers—and never once brought up, or had brought up to me, the question of modern war, the question of why we were in Germany at all. I do remember writing home from Germany that the endless expenditures and installations, including the first nuclear installation in Western Europe, reminded me ominously of the advance of the Roman Empire. In order to come up with such a thought, I must have entertained at the time rather serious misgivings about the whole adventure. But I cannot claim an acuity of conscience that was only to come to me much later. The fact is that at the time I enjoyed those months; I thought the soldiers who crossed my path and with whom I dealt were unusual and delightful fellows. As undoubtedly they were.

More germane to what I can only call the retardation of my development was the influence upon me of the chaplains I was assisting. I remember that every one of them, without exception, was totally militarized. They wore their uniform not solely upon their frame, but upon their soul. It was a symbol of the state of their spirit. They were as military as their colleagues in the Officers' Clubs, and in church on Sunday. Indeed, it seemed to me even at the time that several of them made an especially severe push to project themselves as military men to the core—especially the head chaplain, who was a Jesuit of the New York area, fitted this mold to the very cap. He was a lieutenant colonel, a tireless worker, and had an astonishing influence over the young soldiers. He used to drive all night to a mountain retreat with groups of them to preach a retreat that many of them declared had brought their lives to rebirth. He would drive back with them through the night following the close of their spiritual exercise. Alas, he died later of overwork, and I have no doubt that the judgment upon him is merciful. But it seems to me also that he was a captive of the military system, that his life never once raised the questions that lie at heart of the gospel.

I returned to New York in the autumn of 1954 and began to teach at Brooklyn Preparatory School. For three years, I undertook work with teams of students among the Puerto Ricans of Brooklyn, and on the Lower East Side of Manhattan. We also instituted an honors system of studies in the school, which later won some distinction as the students went on to university work.

In the autumn of 1957 I reported for teaching at Le Moyne College in

Syracuse, New York. In a sense I felt that now my life was beginning on an entirely fresh and exciting basis. I was teaching college classes for the first time; the college was only eleven years old, and we were, in a rather innovating way, making go as we went. I was assigned to teach New Testament classes.

The following six years were an intense, even incandescent continuum— between the classroom on campus and the communities in rural Mexico, between my work in Syracuse and the work of my brother Philip in New Orleans. I cannot remember when I was more hardily tested or more blessedly renewed in spirit. For six long years I was riding the crest of a wave toward a shore that continually receded and expanded, showing now its reefs, now its populated and noisy centers, now the human faces upon its shore, inviting or threatening.

I think I had the reputation of being a very demanding teacher. I think too that my mind was still in a kind of mind-set. I know I always resented being referred to as a teacher of "dogmatic" theology. But the fact was that I was still, in many aspects, quite dogmatic. And that is the one regret that I have when I ponder those years. For the rest, I continued to grow, still very much in my own nest, with all the possibilities both of befouling and of building it.

In 1957 I won the Lamont Prize for my first book of poetry. This was an enormous stimulus upon work that up to then had been wrought mainly in darkness. With the publication of my first book my mind exploded. The poems went into three printings, were a nominee for the National Book Award, and established me in the publishing world. Publishers would now take almost anything I chose to compile; the question of quality was largely in my own hands and my own sense of things.

Of interest with respect to the tumultuous years that were to follow is the fact that David Miller was one of my students. At least one thousand students passed through my classes in those six years. But it is not to be wondered at that I remember David quite vividly. The question of war had not yet occurred; Vietnam was still a remote and obscure event. David, however, was part of whatever social action was occurring off-campus, or being planned on-campus.

His was a poor family; as far as I can recall his parents were separated. The family lived in public housing, and David eked out his college career with state loans. My name has been associated with him in the years that followed, and I am indeed proud of whatever that may be construed to imply, even of guilt by association. The fact is that we never discussed war and peace; we often discussed civil rights and tried to do something about the horrendous ghetto conditions of downtown Syracuse. I can only reflect upon the mystery that has since become a little more apparent. That is to say, David's life was fertile soil upon which the good seed fell and flourished.

Toward the new year of 1962 I was granted a go-ahead with a project of living off-campus with fifteen students who would prepare themselves for Peace Corps type of work in rural areas of Mexico. We got the house off to a flying start, built a simple chapel in the basement, and settled into the chancy business of making ourselves into a community. It went well. By the time I left Le Moyne for Europe in the summer of 1963, things were proceeding well, and the first team had already gone south.

I come now to the discussion of another watershed in my life. According to all plans, I was to lead a rather stereotyped year abroad in a Jesuit house, reportedly finishing a book and undertaking another. Those well-laid plans!

After some two weeks of searching for housing in Paris, I finally was able to find a student hostel and a job as chaplain.

By Christmas I had decided that Western Europe was no longer my cup of tea, and that if I was to get anything out of the year I had better launch southward and eastward. And so I did. At Christmastime I visited Czechoslovakia and Hungary for periods of about one week each. It was my baptism in Marxist society. I was particularly moved by the evidence that the churches in those countries, especially the Protestant communities, were finding ways of survival in most difficult circumstances. I returned to Paris by way of Rome, in order to report to the Vatican on what I had discovered in Eastern Europe. It amounted to a very strong recommendation on the part of the Protestant communities that the Vatican begin to take a more practical interest in the religious and social situation in Marxist Central Europe. I reported to Cardinal Bea's assistant, a man who later became a bishop. He gave me a sympathetic hearing. I was trying to interest the church officials in the idea that I should be appointed a Vatican observer at the Christian Peace Conference to be held in the summer of 1964. Alas for those great hopes.

However, I did get to Prague in June of 1964, and proceeded with a group of American theologians into the Soviet Union, by invitation of the Orthodox and Baptist communities there. The impact of that trip is ineradicable upon my spirit. I was discovering for the first time, and at firsthand, the radically different social forms by which other decent men and women were living. I was discovering peaceable communities of faith, surviving and even thriving in most difficult and trying circumstances. I was seeing at firsthand the damage wrought to the human spirit in the West as a result of the Cold War.

At Prague, I met with Christians from both Marxist and Western societies, and gained some inkling of the role that the churches could play in the ongoing struggles for human peace and survival. Along with my American companions, I was also exposed to the full glare of world Christian opinion with regard to our part in the Vietnam War. From Japan to Cuba, Christians were assailing us, extremely embittered at the course that even then seemed to be written in our stars.

At the conclusion of that trip, I traveled to Africa, the second extended trip I had made during the year. This time it was western Africa, to Nigeria.

(Toward Eastertime of the previous spring, I had gone along the coast of eastern Africa to the Republic of South Africa, at the invitation of an archbishop there.)

I returned to the United States in the autumn of 1964 convinced, as I now recall, of one simple thing. The war in Vietnam could only grow worse. The course we had set at the initiative of John Kennedy, and more remotely by Dulles' brinkmanship and by the nuclear fervor of Truman—all of this was about to turn in the direction of a war which we were in no mood to limit or to abandon. From one point of view, it struck me that we were about to repeat the already bankrupt experience of the French, with a new provocation and a new rhetoric. From another point of view, we were altogether masters of our own method. We had nothing like the colonial interests that France had had in Southeast Asia. But we were determined, justified as we were by the course and momentum of the war itself, to prove our manhood and to put to the test our formidable military machine. It is extraordinarily difficult, even years later, to attempt to unravel the tortuous symptoms and motivations that edged us even deeper into that remote morass. But the unraveling of that tangled and tightened skein is not to my purpose here.

I am attempting merely to record that, for me, the course of the future was made plain by everything I had experienced in Europe and throughout other continents. That is to say, I began after my return to the States in the autumn of 1964, as loudly as I could, to say "no" to the war. It is always, of course, an extremely difficult and risky business to try to relive things, from the point of view of one's life, once events have been lived through. But I am still near enough to those decisions, and still enduring their consequences, so I have a realistic hope that I can convey these experiences with reasonable accuracy. I remember being afflicted with a sense that my life was being truly launched—for the first time—upon mortal and moral seas that might indeed overwhelm me, as the tidal violence of world events churned them into an even greater fury. And even in those years, when we were speaking hypocritically of "military advisers to the Vietnamese," I had a sense that the war could not but get worse. I felt that we were even then launched upon a suicide course; we were spoiling for a fight; we were determined not to yield before a poor and despised people, whose "underdeveloped, non-white status" made them prime expendable targets. I felt (and I believe I shared this conviction with my brother Philip) that this war would be the making or breaking of both of us. There would be simply no turning back upon the initial serious moves we were making at that time.

I was even then signing statements of complicity, and opening myself to the kind of prosecution that Benjamin Spock and William Sloane Coffin were later to undergo.

Within a year's time, I had taken part in the forging of those methods of protest against the war which, from our present vantage point, we perhaps are justified in calling conventional. We fasted, marched, picketed, sat in, followed every step of escalation as well as we could with our halting methods and means; at least we were dogging the iron heel of Mars. We never succeeded, and we never quite gave up. That is the best that can be said for us. We must be content if it is to be our obituary.

Of course, the ground was shifting under my feet. My conception of history and of moral action was being altered, even as I strove to act. The old, tidy, well-arranged box of the universe was flying open, and the seven plagues were loosened upon the world. There would be no closing that box again. There could only be an attempt to follow the course of evil and the death with whatever trail mercy and compassion might blaze.

Nor could I convey the electric and terrifying quality of the times merely by saying that my relationship to my church and my order were being profoundly reordered. The fact is, two cents plain, that we were helping to create a new church, and a new order. American Catholics had never before, in the history of American wars, been found wanting. They were doubly patriotic because they were Catholic, and once had been commonly branded as somewhat less than American. The epitome of this older Martian spirit was of course the cardinal archbishop of New York, then alive and flourishing. It was entirely predictable that he and I, coming from backgrounds that were interesting in their common aspects, he exercising enormous authority in the same area in which I was saying "no" to the war, should come into conflict. The fact that the conflict would be scaled down to my size in no way put off the conflict. My "no" was being heard despite the sound of his immensely more powerful and permeating "yes." So it came to pass that only one year after my return to New York, I found myself faced with the most severe crisis of my life up to that time. It is almost impossible, even at this date, to unravel the many threads that were weaving my shroud. The suffocating descent of that shroud about my head and body came about, I am certain, as a result of my peace activities. Among these, and evidently a source of great friction, was the fact that I had helped found Clergy and Laymen Concerned about Vietnam during the previous summer.

Then there was the mysterious affair of the death of Roger La Porte. He was a boy whose face I remember remotely at the edges of the crowd of young people on the Lower East Side who were resisting the war. He had recently left a monastery upstate and was seeking to discover his own soul among the young Catholic workers. He had said to someone, as I recall, that he wished to get to know me better. But we had scarcely even spoken, apart from greeting one another on occasion. Then without warning, he immolated himself, in early November, before the United Nations buildings in New York early one morning. He lived for about three days. Within a week or two, the most atrocious rumors were linking his death to his friendship with me. It was not to be wondered that a time of growing national madness was also infecting us, on our own scene.

In any case, about a week before Thanksgiving, I was ordered out of New York and within a week was aboard a jet for Mexico City, bound for indefinite exile.

I spent about five months in Latin America. I traveled throughout ten countries, observing and writing. The story of those months is told in a later book, *Consequences: Truth and. . . .* In the meantime, opinion in my behalf in the Catholic community had become so unified and pressing that my superiors were forced to recall me. An ad appeared in the *New York Times* challenging the archdiocese of New York and the Jesuit community as to their reasons for my hasty exit. The protest was effective. I was able to return, held a large press conference to announce the publication of two new books, and say that beyond doubt I would continue with my peace work as usual.

Which I did. The war had worsened. My brother had been evicted from the seminary where he was teaching in Newburgh, New York. He had published his first book, which had been well received, we had marched in Selma, heard the President announce on television "We shall overcome." I had returned to the work of building a community of alternatives in New York and throughout the country. The éclat surrounding my exile had stimulated a number of invitations to address campus groups throughout the country, and I responded as well as I could. I was writing and being published, finding that a great deal of imprisoned space in my psyche had been released through the dark experience of the previous year. It was, all in all, a time of great anguish and great exhilaration.

In the summer of 1967, I went to Pueblo, Colorado, to teach in the Upward Bound program. I had been associated with poverty programs at the national level before this, but I wished to ground myself in immediate work with a small number of young people. Previously, I had journeyed throughout California and met with perhaps ten or twelve examples of diverse communities which the Office of Economic Opportunity was trying to help. If I bring in this aspect of my experience, it is only to underscore my growing disillusionment with national programs to "help the poor." Also my growing sense, expressed to Mr. Sargent Shriver on many occasions, that his program would get nowhere as long as the war was on. It seemed to me spiritually absurd and suicidal to be pretending to help the poor at home while we bombed the poor abroad. This seemed to me the deepest reason for the forewritten doom of the OEO.

In any case, uncertain as to what the next year would bring, I taught some fourteen young Mexican Americans from a poverty-stricken area of the town. My success was at best mixed. I gained additional fuel for my conviction that serious involvement in the poverty program was an inevitable source of alienation for the poor themselves, as well as being a money and land grab for the bureaucrats. Neither in Pueblo nor anywhere else in the country had I ever seen a poverty program whose leadership were part of the community of the poor. Once they began to draw a federal salary, the "leaders" inevitably were cut off from the best of their own community, and appeared, at least to the radicals and activists among them, as simply copouts. Thus for the dreams, liberal and unattainable, of the OEO.

I finally was invited by Cornell University in the autumn of 1967 (the first Catholic priest in the history of the university) to take a position in the United Religious Work. I left New York with trepidation and many second thoughts. It appeared to me a choice of the utmost seriousness, to decide to leave the peace community, which was in perennial need of all kinds. But I decided to come, because Cornell was a new scene to me, and because the university had changed so rapidly in the previous two years. I must say that I have never had a serious regret for the choice I then made.

But the war was going from horrendous to intolerable; it was devouring more and more of the energies of our lives.

My brother Philip was working in the inner city of Baltimore; a community man, he drew the community around him like a magnet. The facts of life were his daily bread. He saw in his prophetic bones that our support of the student resisters was a game the government would tolerate indefinitely. So in November 1967 he and three friends decided to take their peaceable war into the enemy camp. As is by now well known, they poured blood into draft files in Baltimore.

I was at the time very far from their understanding of things. But I was shaken into reflectiveness. I had gone to Hanoi, I had experienced American bombings and brought home prisoners of war. So when Philip approached me in early May with a new action into which I was urgently invited, my immediate reaction was one of bewildered sympathy and shaken readiness. I was faced with the evidence of intransigent courage on the part of those who were already in legal trouble up to their very necks. Imagine Philip and Tom Lewis, men already under threat of several years of imprisonment, calmly repeating the same action that had brought them into jeopardy!

Like a shipwreck or a person sucked into quicksand or drowning, one to whom almost every resource of friendship and ingenuity is lacking, and yet who somehow emerges alive, I say simply that I was saved at the last moment.

In speaking analogically, I mean to speak no less rigorously. I was saved at the last moment. My brother and his friends were planning a new assault upon a new draft center. They visited me at Cornell toward the middle of May 1968. There, over a long evening of eating and discussion, they made their proposal to me. Would I join them? I was still wedded to the idea that in standing with the resisting students I was doing all that was possible, or indeed helpful. But after the others had left, Philip opened before me the facts of the case, which he had so often outlined in correspondence with me. That is to say—it must be evident by now that the government would allow people like myself to do what we were doing almost indefinitely; to sign statements, to picket, to support resisters in court. Even if people from the government did pick us up, it was they who were choosing the victim and the time and place of prosecution. The initiative was entirely in their hands. But in the plan under discussion, the situation was entirely reversed. A few people were declaring that the initiative of action and passion belonged to the peaceable and the resisting.

Toward dawn, I can remember seeing the light. I told Philip that I was with them. They should allow me some twenty-four hours to subject my decision to possible change of mood, but if they had not heard from me within that period, they could assume that I would be a member of the Catonsville group. And so, as the Book of Genesis says laconically, it was done.

We nine invaded the draft office, took out hundreds of 1-A files, and burned them with homemade napalm in a macadam parking lot nearby. I remember so well the heat and fury of that afternoon, and the sense of almost crushing relief with which we faced one another after it was done.

I remember also, when we had been apprehended and put in temporary custody, the expressions on the faces of the F.B.I. men as they entered and saw us clerics under arrest, the familiar face of Philip, previously apprehended in a like cause. How their jaws dropped! One of them turned in disgust to a companion and exclaimed, "I'm going to change my religion." Which was, I would think, entirely to our point; we had invited men and women to a change of heart, so that in the case of this officer, to have changed from a conventional Catholic to a Christian, might portend the first success of our efforts.

We spent eight days in Baltimore County jail in Towson, Maryland. We fasted and prayed and rejoiced — and waited.

I remember with special gratitude the warden, Stephen Foster. He was consistently good to us, puzzled as he was by our action, and of a curious integrity, which drove him to question and discuss with us why we had placed our lives in the breach.

I remember also that on the final day we decided to break our fast with a Eucharist. Someone had brought us in a loaf of freshly baked bread. We asked the warden if we might have a bottle of wine. He acceded on condition that he himself might be present for our Eucharist. Of course he might. Whereupon, around that board table, began one of the simplest and most moving of communal actions. "Do this in memory of me." Which is to say; "In remembering me, re-member yourselves. Put your lives and your souls together again."

The unpredictable savagery of a federal marshal is also vivid in my mind. One day, as we were being taken handcuffed from the jail for a court appearance, a young nun who was a dear friend reached out her hand to mine in solidarity as we issued from the jail. One of the marshals came forward in a swift, reptilian move. He crashed down between our hands with a karate blow. "Don't touch!" It was the epitome of the system; he had said it all.

Don't touch — make war. Don't touch — be abstract, about God and death and life and love. Don't touch — make war at a distance. Don't touch your enemies, except to destroy them. Don't touch, because in the touch of hand to hand is Michelangelo's electric moment of creation. Don't touch, because law and order have so decreed, limiting the touch of one person to another, to the touch of nightsticks upon flesh. . . .

It must be evident by now, that the most powerful and immediate influence upon my life has been that of my brother Philip. Indeed, his incarceration for some seven months after Catonsville, placed my own spirit in bondage. It was many weeks before I could realize that being free was also a way of allowing a larger freedom for him. But I must say also that upon this single relationship has been built every other one in which my life rejoices.

Another weight upon the decision to go to Catonsville was my voyage to Hanoi in February of 1968. I went with Howard Zinn of Boston University, to repatriate the first American fliers freed by the North Vietnamese. I will not linger over particulars here; they are told in some detail in my book *Night Flight to Hanoi.*

I have referred elsewhere to another event that occurred in the course of our federal trial and that shook my existence in those months. It was the self-immolation of a sixteen-year-old boy in front of the Syracuse Cathedral in the spring of 1968. I visited him as he lay dying in St. Joseph's Hospital. And I smelled, for the first time, and yet again not for the first time, the odor of burning flesh, evidence of which I had seen so often in North Vietnam. The boy died, but not before he had brought something to birth in me. Perhaps it is that day, that youthful dying face, whose wordless intimations I am still undergoing and undoubtedly shall for years to come.

I am, in this autumn of 1969, under federal sentence of three years, for destruction of draft files in May of 1968. So my life enters upon its middle course. These many beautiful years cannot be lived again. But they are compounded in my own flesh and spirit, and I take them, in true measure, with me toward whatever lies ahead.

I have by now had published thirteen books on a variety of subjects, have written numerous articles and poems and plays, and have enjoyed all the fruits that America offers those fortunate enough to make it within its system. If I mourn for the death of that system, it is as one who has enjoyed its cup to the depths. If that same vintage has now turned bitter as gall in my mouth, it is because I have seen the society that might have been great, according to its own rhetoric, turn murderously against those throughout the world to whom it had once offered the fairest of hopes. I could no longer drink the fruit of those grapes that had turned to wrath against the majority of humankind; the murderous vessels of death were even now tipping upon victims in North Vietnam, ready elsewhere to deal the same death to other women and men whose hopes were too revolutionary or too untimely to be borne with.

If then I must go to prison (and go I undoubtedly must), I shall go neither in a spirit of alienation, of bitterness, nor of despair. But simply in the hope that has sustained me in better and worse days up to now. May this offering open other alternatives to official and sanctioned murder, as a method of social change. May men and women of power come to a change of heart, confronting the evidence and quality of the lives we offer on behalf of our brothers and sisters.

KATALLAGETE, WINTER 1968–69

My Father

1.
All bets were on; he was dying
back in '62; found by mother 2:00 a.m.
on the john floor, bleeding end to end mightily.
Toward dawn I was summoned;
A jungle of tubes and bowls; going out big,
the symbols of mortician culture
blooming around like fungi.
He lay there weak as childhood.
They were filling him, an old sack,
with new wine. He took it darkly.
"When the wheat's ready for harvest,
draw it in," all I remember.
Strong enough behind his milky cat's eyes
to spin a trope about death, strong enough to live.
Foul January dawn
beetled down upon us, he lay there like a switchblade
awaiting the spring, awaiting death
like a palmed blade. No takers . . .

2.
Phil goes in chains to Harrisburg today
I sit here in the prison ward
nervously dickering with my ulcer
a half-tamed animal
raising hell in its living space.
Time to think once more of my father.
There were photos, brown, detailed
tintypes. You had only to look
(30, 40, years ago)
for the handsomest bucko present.
It was uncanny.
A head of burnished locks, a high brow
a cynic's sidelong look.
Boyo! You kept at center eye
the eye of storms.
In a mad Irish way "all there." Whole apple, one bite.
The mouth reminds me of a whip;
sensual and punishing.

Tasting the world, sexually alive,
calling the tune, paying the piper.
He was chaste as an Irish corpse,
Mother-maidensister-haunted.
We 6 were as much emblems of expiation
as of seasonal bedding
each of us sponsored by the church
like a first class relic or a nun's goody.

3.
I wonder tonight in Danbury Prison
in the damned off-season of human beings
an ulcer kicking at my groin
like the sour embryo of Nixon's next brainchild
I wonder—
the Jesuits staring 'round like frogs of the Nile
at baby Moses—
I wonder if I ever loved him
if he ever loved us
if he ever loved me;
an undersized myopic tacker
number 5 in pecking order
pious maybe, intelligent I guess
looking for corners where half in, half out
he could take soundings,
survive, emerge; protective coloration.
Not enamored of the facts of life
i.e., sledgehammers, chicken little,
the cracking muscles of the strong.
As a child you expect violence; the main issue
somehow to clear away
space and time
to survive in. Outside the circle, who cares?

He exacted performance, promptitude,
deference to his moods
the family escutcheon stained with no shit.
The game was skillful (we never saw it so well played
elsewhere), he was commonly considered
the epitome of a just man.
We sat on our perches blinking like six marmosets.
There were scenes worthy of Conrad,
the decks shuddering;
the world coming to end!

He is dead now.
The conduct of sons and priests
is not grist for news-hawks and kites.
When my mother (who surely
suffered most at his hands) read one account
served up by an esteemed scribe
she wept for shame and loss.
There is more honor, more
noblesse oblige, more
friendship with reality, more unconscious graceful wisdom
in the least gesture of her
little finger, than in
the droppings and screams of the whole preening profession
of whooping cranes.
The office of charity, of classic
Pietàs, fills the vacuum
around that absent figure
with the presence of compassion. My father —
when in '39 I braced and dug in
for the great leap, I was one
of 38 candidates for priesthood.
All excelled me
in arts, language, math,
self-assurance, the golden number of
the Jesuit dance. 32 years later
I sit in Danbury Prison for illegal
acts contrary to war.
Father
I close my eyes, conjure up
like a deaf-mute mimic
your ironic ghost. How convey
my gratitude, my sense
of the delicious rightness of things?
Whatever you denied us, you
gave us this, which enemies name
distemper, madness; our friends,
half in despair, arrogance.
Which I name, denying both — the best of
your juice and brawn, unified
tension to good purpose.
Prosit, requiescat.
The bad news drones on
plague after seventh plague
hypnotic, futile as an argument
for God's existence. . . .

5.

. . .

My father, asked what crop he grew
on the old farm outside Syracuse (depression
sour clay and drought); laconically:
boys! One year, an old mare dragging a harrow
through the sparse corn rows, with the perfect timing
of senescence
reached a drain ditch
near the roadside, stepped down daintily
as a duchess, lowered her backside,
lowered her long face to her knees (harness
jangling like rude jewelry) lay there
saying from her eyes; next move, yours.
Tonight under a paschal moon, I mimed
a Goya etching in the
prison yard
3 shadows coming, growing
came, grew, vanished like footpads —
Jesus, Satan, that interdicting
third, weaving, bargaining, up to his ears
in bloody Friday; Lord, is it I?
Under the shrewd exhalation of the moon,
I bundle up to throat; no
horse thieves, poachers,
informers in our blood! Nicked by his razor Dado
mutters in the mirror; *the blood of Irish kings*!
Mother at the stove, turns up her eyes to heaven . . .

7.

Dado's classical bent
left none unstigmatized. A white billy-goat
was marvelously misnamed, to fanfare
from the dog, faint horselaugh from the mare;
Ursus. He knocked the postman for a loop,
scattered mad Mamie Powell, chewed up,
in the side yard, until chased by sticks,
the shirt the '29 depression spared.
Crimes multiplying, stink
offending, he was sold off, reversing
the Judas trick, to metamorphose in paschal stew
in Little Italy, down country. We mourned him —
hooves, pride of blood, horns of
neighborhood dilemmas, nattering mouth, pirate's eye,

the uncouth unreconstructed thieving
alter ego of six boys.

1930; Dado decreed a mercy death.
A splay-legged spavined nag
bit the dust, under an orchard tree,
Tom firing point blank. Laziness
our virtue in common; we dug a shallow grave
heaped the cadaver over, like a
prairie cenotaph. One week later, mother,
stringing the laundry from tree to tree
was shaken to tears and flight. A colossal
long drawn fart issuing from the grave,
a strange unnatural
convulsion; earth heaved, ground opened,
a great equine rear leg shot up skyward.
The resurrection of the dead?
Weeks passed, sweet seasonal process
grounded the upstart sign, grounded my father's
Jovian lightnings . . .

8.
      In the old fables
   jays   macaws   jackals
cowardly   inching forward careening hobbling jeering
   surrounded the mysterious firebird.
  The figure and form of the age.
Philip; the little blond boy with lowered eyes
    in a blue fluted sweater
      stands to the left of me in a faded kodak film, 1927.
  You threw stones like a demon
hid your windup locomotive in the old grey immigrant trunk.
In one year your limbs telescoped out
   a poet's brow, those commanding utterly blue eyes
a sapphire intensity, precision instruments taking
    the world's size.

  I do not know when the wager was first struck
I see another photo, a windy June day
   outside Washington Shrine, the family smiling,
a single-minded triumph; its ordained priest!
   war years, depression years   decently buried in albums
then that "stampede into religion"
     (John's sneering phrase)
   the church's chased cup

continuity, rounded latinate
     breaking up   breaking up

Dado,
your sons
close kept in Danbury Jail
keep Maundy Thursday.
You lie close too
after the 90 year uphill climb.
Pompey graveyard, a "sylvan close"
(your phrase) of trees and mounds
slopes westward, gentle, sunny.
Are you proud of your 2 priests
plucked by the sovereign state, for crimes
against war crimes? The children of My Lai
like Fra Angelico's angels, make sport of death;
with instruments of harmony
keep green, for us, your grave.
Children—those natural buds
those nodes of process, rose red, snow white
first fruits of blood and semen, fallen rosy and white
to the spread aprons of women, fruits
of energetic love. Who strikes them— . . .

10.
    Winters we chugged two miles to Sunday Mass
in a model-T snowbucker, old the year
    it was born. Like a sailing fish it sported
flapping gills of isinglass and canvas.
    We bedded down like Peter Rabbit's litter, crowded
in the hold, eyes, cold noses, Dado
    pumping and worrying us along. Spread over all
6 boys, a 7 foot square Buffalo robe
    gamey, coarse as porcupine. Arrived, dismounted
at St. John Baptist
    we made an obedient huddle, awaiting
disposition of the steed. The robe, pulled from the rear seat,
    made a splendid radiator noseguard
against deep freeze.

    We sat at the children's Mass
singing from 5¢ notebooks the hymns
    we murdered all week to Sister's beating stick
Mother dearest Mother fairest; to Jesus' heart all burning.
    Monsignor McEvoy, our ample prophet, out of his
workday overalls (teacher, lawyer, builder)

splendid as an iconostasis, humble as Nazareth
gave us a children's gospel. Not bad; religion
   stuck to our Sunday bones . . .
If we went mad, it was
for sweet reason's sake;
to wish all children well; to make of the world's breakup
cup, loaf, murder, horror, a first (or last) communion.

   Aunts Aggie, Maggie, Elizabeth, Mollie, Bird the nun,
Uncle Johnny, Ned the priest, Dado,
   held Sunday pow-wow in the family long house
on Matson Avenue. Mother, born German
   never quite made the caucus. Al Smith, Father Coughlin
were house penates. Once a year
   New Year's Day, Mom and "the gang"
(Maggie's put-down) were summoned
   to state dinner. I remember
straight chairs, straight talk, kids
   frozen to our seats by the old maids'
steely looks; indifferent food, Maggie
   dispensing into shirt pockets, on the hour
with a teaspoon, her stony pacifier, "Loft's Hard Candies."
   They were straight out of Port Royal, Maynooth,
Oneida, pure as angels, proud as devils.
   My father's marriage stuck in the throat of virtue.
Upchuck or swallow; the discreet dilemma
   was audible for years, burp, cover up.

Grandmother Berrigan's portrait
   looked down in mild wonderment,
a queen above a nest of bickering kites
   she, troubled, questioning
the trick and treat of time's outcome—11 children, a widow on
   Christmas day
   of '74. Grandfather, bleeding
from immigrant's lung,
   A daughter ran outside
to break the ice on the rain barrel, plunge a chunk
   into his mouth. His body hauled
up scoured December hills in a democrat wagon
   to lie where my father would lie.
Dado slept that day, a child
   in a farm woman neighbor's arms . . .
I set this down
   in Danbury Jail; Philip and I

priests, first (for all we know) to break
   trust of the clan, trust
again and again, like Jansenius'
   first rule of order; first pass-fail;
no one, not one of the
   family, ever in jail.

11.

In old Assumption church on Salina Street
a phony dungeon on the dark rear stair
kept con Jesus under lock.
We crept down
during the long noon hour,
Lucifugae, sprats, beguiled
by darkness and vigil lights, prayed there
some better outcome for the man, caught in the twin
pincers of church and state. Would Pilate
dash the bowl to ground, would Caiaphas convert? . . .
Holy Saturday I set this down
by courtesy of the twin powers, doing time.
Jesus, lift head tonight from the foul grime
of churches. Thorns like bees
drone at the skull; does sacrifice bring in
straight on a beeline, honey, money, honor?
The dull eyes focus under a full moon
outside my window, resplendent
to frame a face in the informer's kiss. Who knows? Who knows?

a bargain struck
in silver, brings it down; rain, ruin
piece by piece, indictments on the 6
Harrisburg peacemakers, Berrigan et al
versus United States . . .
My grandmother's head
turns side to side, dubious as a ghost.
We teased mother.
Tom, Tom, the farmer's son,
why did you ever marry that one? —
(she blushed)
Indeed? He was considered quite a catch!

12.

November dawn, 1969, your jaw dropped, a semaphore
   the last train out of ghost town.

We gathered in 2 brown sacks
    everything you owned, an immigrant pauper's bundle

I leaned over the bed, breathing for you
    all that night long
    (somebody else was there)
    2 shadows over a fish tank
    helpless as men watching the death
    of the fish from whom
    all men, fathers and sons, ad infinitum, come

A fish metamorphosing
    into a father before our eyes —
    hands, feet, blue as a fish

I could not take you in my arms, give you back
    wits, volatile energy
    confounding moods, appetite
    the farm, drought, depression years
    the scythe that whistled
    like a wood plane across hard earth

Did you want it all back anyway?
    Think. 6 sons, 5, 4, 3, 2, 1, —
    then nothing, a wedding night, a bride
    life awaiting doing all again?

You hated like hell that necessity
    we lived by — your scant love
    the stigma
    it took years to heal; making do,
    fear, damnation, fury.

Well we made it; some deep root of sanity
    we sucked on. Above,
    the idiot thrashing storms you made

Maybe it was your face dropping its mask
    asleep over a book,
    Irish intelligence; now and again
    a piercing stab of virtue; a boy
    kneeling beside you at Mass; a 6 yr. old
    rocking-horse Catholic.

Thank you old bones, old pirate
    old mocker and weeper.

Could have lived to a hundred. But contrary passion
set in hard; falling downstairs
that last time, into your own
unconscious. To hell with it; bag it all.
a bloody act of the will, a fever nursed by rage. Sons
no longer mitigating presences, who
now and again had been;
      has been now. You turned to the wall.

And I have no recourse except
hatred and love, your hand
breaking through earth
nightmare or miracle;
your face
muffled in its shroud
a falcon
disdaining
the dishonor nailing
us here
like stinking fish
(ancestors, sons)
to the world's botched cross

Landed, boned, buried in Pompey yard . . .
To see the performance, was scarcely
to believe it. One summer night
he tipped
the kitchen table, set for supper, up on end
for some supposed infraction. He fought sons
to a sullen draw, told enchanting children's stories
of summer nights, wrote poetry
like a flaring Turk, absurd, byronic,
battled the land to a dust storm,
prayed, slept stertorously in the big
leather rocker, ate like a demon,
exacted instant "yes sir! no sir!"
died like a sword swallower choked on
his breath's long blade . . .
The old house breathed relief
in his absence. None of us could, those years,
were screws turned on our thumbs, confess
to love him.
Was it that dearth of love
turned us to the long tragic way
on and on? What measure

of that irascible spirit, lodged unappeased
in us, bears, endures, survives—even Danbury? One virtue awaits
the arresting fist of death.
Until: Walk on, Take breath, Make do.

In blinding Minnesota winter sun
one of the older brothers
would hoist a kid up, pick-a-back, and run.
I was 3 or 4; John trundled me round the yard
ducked suddenly into a dark wood shed
striking me blind. Against my face
some rough pelted thing swayed frozen.
Recovering sight
screamed, screamed like a banshee, a child
gone mad for terror;
a frozen timber wolf's death-head
hung by a thong from the rafters, eyes open
bloody mouth—

  The stuff of nightmares or of dental chairs.
  In Danbury Clinic
I urge the wary inmates; *open wide now*; a superannuated
  paraclete, all in white
for the liturgy; needles and drills
  needles and drills. Domestic policy, we juice
America's pain to sleep. . . .

In the wink of an eye, graves shall open
the dead arise. Easter morning
I write: dearest mother, many friends
bring flowers to your bedside, smiles
from Danbury. We are well, our thoughts
are thanks. Thanks to you, the instrument
of truth, who plucked us by the hair
harebrain and all, from false peace. Alleluia.

PRISON POEMS, 1973

My Mother

It occurred to me long after my mother's death (and perhaps the thought was salutary, removed from self-esteem or raw grief) that such a woman might safely have been entrusted with the fate of the world.

Can this be considered sensible, a reflection whose danger is drawn like the sting of a nettle, by long grief subsided?

Let me say it. She could be entrusted with the world. She was providential, foreseeing, compassionate, a woman who without self-aggrandizement had a weather eye out for virtually all weathers. And modest; she had no great interest in her own repute or stature, the difference her life might be thought to make. Knowing her place in a scheme of things; a place larger, not smaller, than she knew.

Six children, boys. A husband. Take from her all modern conveniences, devices, accouterments. Except in late middle age, when she, like any modern woman, could turn a switch and her hard work was relieved.

Before that, it was labor and labor — in more senses than one. The labor of bringing children into the world. Each, we learned, had been a wrenching agony. And each child, once born, made another mouth at table, another to clothe and house and nurse and love and worry over. Each different, each calling into play ingenuity, wisdom, a different language, to persuade, cajole, urge into self-sustaining humanity, pride. "The way we live, or try to live, is the way you're invited into. Come along."

Philip and I were the two youngest. If her body had given up, if she had said in the teeth and glare of the family and their priest and nun, "I've had it," then of course we would not be here — to tell, to raise hell. Thank you.

Take away her work, take away her house, her garden, the wash-day steam and chaos, the stove to be poked into a flare — like stripping a rich ear of corn, intent only on the husks.

This describes her extreme old age. But not the great early and middle years, when she literally created a future for so many.

Yet we never thought of her as extraordinary or spiritually gifted. Such simply did not enter into the equation of childhood. One had parents; the parents were good, bad, or indifferent.

In our neighborhood, we had quite a spectrum: portents, horrors, smilers, punishers, softies, gorgons, everything. It didn't occur to ask, to remark, "Isn't our mother really something!" Or taking measure from some other, "Look at Ms. Sonso, she sure isn't up to momma." Though it could be said justly, turning 360 degrees in our neighborhood, any Ms. Sonso you could mention sure as hell wasn't.

The judgments of children are primitive, cruel, and allowing for wooden and puddin' heads and much selfishness (or self-interest), are strangely right. Or so it seems to me.

If I can put on a six- or ten-year-old head once more and look on that farm of ours — what homesickness, loathing, longing wells up! A deep vein is set pulsing, like a tube that branches out to nurture the body.

I find myself there once more; child of a landscape I open, like a hinged album drawn from some secret place.

I see the gray weather-scoured house, already old in my childhood, set on its meager hillside, windows grudging and narrow like eyes sizing up their world, disliking what they see, morning to night. The barn leans on its haunches like a tired beast. Outhouse and chicken house out back, to the east the orchard where we buried old Maj (senile, dragging his neck to doom, the nag stood in his shallow grave and the boom! of the bullet sprayed his dim brains on the sod and clay). Beyond, eastward, fields stretched, nine or ten acres of corn and potatoes and berries, the kitchen garden south of the house beyond two wormy pear trees.

My mother, her gaze hemmed in by those windows. My mother's life, hemmed in by that house. A damp, floorless cellar underfoot, a cold set of bedrooms overhead. And on the third floor, an unfinished attic, three tiny windows, not so much offering light or cheer as spreading thick shadows meagerly. And above that thankless dungeon, like a cap on a dunce, a cupola; reached by a stair like the stair to a scaffold. Those two top enclosures smelling of dead bats and trapped birds. Eerily, once or twice in my boyhood, a bat or bird crossed my eyes in the perpetual dusk, terror on terror.

My mother's house. That inert, comfortless dwelling, which custom, religion, ceremony, the imposed myth that is crueler by far than plain fact — all these would conspire to insist: This is a home. My mother was, so to speak, no nominalist. My father was. This is one way of putting the hurt, the conflict. When my mother was absent, the "home" froze in its bones. It went rigid; it became a house of blocked ice, of will, of myth. A former home. Which is to say, a house.

A house that my father, aided and abetted at all times by his chorus of sisters (those nominalist fates and furies), insisted on calling a home. "Home!" they would exclaim. "You boys must be grateful for so good a home!" They did protest too much. And we sat there and endured, or disappeared from sight and endured. Awaiting her return.

For your absence was, to a small boy, the hugest hole in the universe. When you went to town, disappearing down the road in the old teetering streetcar, the boy turned disconsolately indoors, closed the door, strove with his small brother to be brave and good, to wash a few dishes and sweep a floor. Then the home dropped its jaw and stopped breathing. You were not there. It made little difference that you were less than three miles distant, that you would return before sundown. What difference did such mitigations make, against what were time and distance measured (three hours, three miles)? They belonged properly to those twice one's size and thrice his years! They did not signify, any more than if one were told, "Your mother is dead, but be comforted, sweet bye and bye, on that beautiful shore . . . " Such wrong strokes, such dumping of straw in the void! It falls, falls in a dead well of loss.

She was gone from the house, she was gone from the world. With no exaggeration, this is what I remember. If the father came in from work and she had not yet returned, his presence added nothing of recourse or consolation. Indeed, because he was feared and she was loved and lacked, his coming made one want to flee for dear life. A voice whispered, "She is gone." Then it added, "Flee." It was sound advice, and the boy obeyed.

I look back on that child (yet I do not look back, he is here before me). He is studious and owlish, goes by a nickname both contemptuous and affectionate—"Four Eyes." He is known to disappear for hours, crouching in some out-of-the-way corner, wrapt in a book.

Not to be deceived. It is a ploy, his way of keeping out of sight, buried as his spirit is in a more or less constant wretchedness. Behind a book, the boy is out of ear and eyeshot of the father, that anger against a nonconforming, maladroit specimen.

My father lived through fifty-four years of marriage, handsome and complete in frame, an exiled Irish king among yahoos. So he saw himself.

A question arises: How did I see him?

A missing part; a hole perhaps in the heart, or a hole where a heart should have been. An essential lack; something that could not be "cosmetically corrected."

Yet it must be understood that he was neither a drunkard nor a common brute, nor was he unfaithful in the strict sense. To his credit must be set down, in all fairness, his hard, bruising labor, a near religion of labor, the most un-Catholic ethic in this matter; self-punishment, ineptitude for repose. Settle in a comfortable chair? He shrank from comfort as from a bed of nails or coals. Thus even his love of work, if it could be called that, turned sour, turned against others. Uneaseful tension sprang from his frame like an emanating leap, a reproach to the longed-for repose of my mother. He kept things on edge; his presence was like the whirr of an emory wheel on a blade—it set off sparks.

He loved good talk; but it had to turn on his topic, pursued at his sweet will. The method veered about; now it was a snarled ball of monologue, again a kind of Socratic bark and bite. You kept trying to follow the yarn (literally), to unknot, disengage. You showed the best will in the world. After all, this wayward game was preferable to his other one, an appalling icy silence. . . . After which you were brought up short as he barked out a question meant, one presumed, to engage your wits, to bring light on some matter or other.

In my case, it did exactly the opposite. It was as though he seized a length of the yarn and effectively tied up my tongue. I remember to the hour one of those barks, gone off like a firecracker in the face. I was reduced on the spot to a mute for some fifteen minutes, at the end of which period, evidently convinced that nothing further was to be expected from the dummkopf, he resumed his yarn snarling.

Had there been two such parents instead of one, had my mother been cursed with the temperament of any one of his sisters, then it would have been all up with the six sons. In the tundra of upper Appalachian clay that surrounded us, an unpromising, poverty-ridden waste of isolation, bitter winters, and often fruitless summers, there dwelt families driven insane by such parents, in tandem working their worst on one another and on their hapless children.

We were saved from that. Whatever substance has accrued to our lives, whatever goodness, must be laid at our mother's feet. Tardily, with an aching sense of the lateness of the gift and of her loss, I lay it there.

He worked like a demon for years and years, at a series of humiliating, paltry jobs that could have been filled by a lout.

His religious life requires a word, as does hers.

My mother's was a practical German piety, unselfconscious, a matter of yea and nay, intellectual only in the sense of being firmly held and consequential. She knew what she believed; she saw no reason either to parade her belief abroad or to inflate its scope. The "day of worship" brought in its wake no contrary or competing rhythm; only an enlarged, refined, slowed sense of her life. Sunday descended on her like a shekinah; she arrayed herself in her poor best; she appeared with a hardly won majesty before the Lord.

And her family too; they were summoned on Sunday to their best conduct and costume, for thus was it written.

We became, over the years, whether in the old Model T Ford or the streetcar or bus, or on foot, or hitchhiking, or in the later grandeur of an Olds—we became the indefatigable, the redoubtable, the church-goers supreme; a family whose arrival in the Holies the Almighty might have set the clocks of the universe by, with a nod of satisfaction and a slight adjustment of the mighty stem of things.

However. The sabbatarian rest by no means appealed to my father. A command to slow down? A far different voice sounded in my father's bones, twitched him like a goad. Often as not after mass, in summer, he beckoned to himself spirits more restless than he, ordered one or several of the sons out of doors with him, in prospect of something offhandedly anounced as a "look around the place." Which cursory look, soon dispensed with, was followed oftener than not, by the appearance, as though conjured out of thin air, of tools of trade, hammers, saws; and then, of stooped bodies over the furrows, above the workbench. "A plain scandal to the neighbors," my mother would cry. All in vain.

Religious matters could be summed up in the simple, unchanging quality of a face. Which is to say, my mother took on no special "Sunday look." If at mass she seemed remote, even wrapt, still the cast and coherence of her features were intact. When she turned from prayer to attend the rambunctious child at her side, and gravely shook her head in disapproval, and turned back to the altar, there was a sweetness and suavity, even an elegance in the gesture. It impressed itself, that turn of the beautiful head from profile to full face and back. The universe was attending to me. The motion met the soft wax of the child's mind; the wax was cast in the metal we name memory; it rests there to this day.

The sixty-year-old public man consults the child, that owlish undersized one, big glasses tilted on his button nose—and he finds no clue.

The man ponders, consults himself. Mother and father are long dead, the argument of these pages perhaps better buried with them. But he cannot bury it. Pressing, haunting as the question of unknown parentage, is the question of his mother's survival, her clues, coloration, the springs of her soul; these cling to him. He would rather be mistaken than be ignorant. He senses that in reaching longingly toward her ghost as she recedes on time's waters—in that gesture, though a mess of shadows mock his tears; still the effort strangely suffices. He touches her; if he merely touches the hem of her garment, the odor of memory.

She was lonely, lonely. But so, I reflect, were most country wives; with the added sting, in her case, that she refused the common devices that bonded country women: card playing and gossip.

Lonely. I write the word and write it again. The word is forged in the ice and fire of maturity. We children were never, as I recall, lonely. That corrosion began later, under rejection and contumely.

I do not want to dramatize her plight, an injustice to the sweetness of spirit she fought for, in the teeth of the world, and finally attained. She was no stoic; she had no armor against the world. She was supple, free, a contemplative, an inward-looking spirit. This was her secret, and her salvation.

Granted, she was out of her element, in furious seas; granted, the skiff was unseaworthy. Once she had pushed off from shore and the voyage formally blessed, a course set; if things went awry and ruin impended — what then was she to do? Was she perhaps to step out of the boat and walk on waters?

There is no untangling things, except in memory, that fusing force and healer.
There was no untangling things, when life was knotting and tightening, and in every way open to perversity and ill luck, going wrong. It was only to be borne; a passive role in grammar but, in reality, a life that, like impeded streams, found its own way — around, under.

She is by far the more difficult of the two to conjure up. My father is fifteen years dead, but his ghost still stalks us — his sardonic, inspired, Irish-Yankee lingo, his wit and witlessness, the moods that made us cringe. He pushes into the mind, jostles for a place there.

Her ghost lies still, or sits, or moves about, always quietly, claiming no attention: a great listener, one whose life is a moving light. Her face is averted; she is like a Strindbergian emanation; her face is veiled from us.
She sits at a kitchen table in winter, reading; always alone. And if she is interrupted by an importunate child, she may suddenly erupt in wild despair, "Leave me alone, leave me alone!" (The day has been too much, the years too much . . .)
Why recall such things, her tears, we standing there dumb and helpless?
In memory there is healing.

No private faces in public places. All photos of the family, including the fresh-faced, dog-collared clerics, were placed in rooms off bounds to any but the immediate family.
This was a strict rule of hers. The family was one thing, friends and acquaintances another. There was no mixing the two; of that would come only confusion of mind and divided loyalties and frivolous pride. Her house was not an inn, nor was her mind. On such matters she never yielded.

The elemental things of the world exclude tragedy and comedy. Water and fire know nothing of conflict, desire; they go their own way. And when we borrow these elements for the sake of human analogy, we enter a kind of Zen world, in which simplicities are restored; as though we too, rendered perfect as water and fire, were "beyond" anguish and farce.

These elements of creation make no history; at least in the Western sense, where history is inevitably the record of ruthless winners, warriors and liars, duplicitous diplomats, bloodshot juntas and shahs and their clerical clones; leveling adversaries, creating lost peoples, slaves, and victims.

My father was voracious after a name, a history. He sought fame as a shark scents its meat. But fame is more than a prey; something he never learned. Not idly the ancients called fame a woman; in the subtle arts and arena of courting and enticing and winning love—in this he was no subtler than a shark, shooting toward its prey. Alas, for him, he hungered and hunted in vain.

My mother made no history; women commonly make no history. Is it because they have other, less sharklike appetites?

She was very like the woman at the well whom Jesus encountered. For a short time, this woman made a little noise, a small tumult. She was the occasion of his committing a scandal; he, a rabbi, attentive to her, a woman and a Samaritan, double indemnity.

And this is very nearly all we know of her. She ran to tell her village about the strange man of the mountain who, in her crude phrase, "told me all I had done." In her eyes, he seemed a kind of Magian, a necromancer; but strangely merciful too, beyond her experience of men (which, we are informed, was considerable).

The townsfolk came running, half in bored excitement, half in good-natured contempt for "her type." This is the last we hear of her, a woman who occasioned one of the deepest epiphanies of the Fourth Gospel. She is nameless. Can one imagine a male occasioning so long and important a discourse of the Lord—and remaining nameless? She does a very great thing and disappears into it.

A nun said to me, discussing this passage, "She's like all of us. What do we count for?"

It is important for me to ponder why this is so, why women are of less account. But also this: What is the countering strength, the countervailing truth? On the one hand, the "apostles," "disciples," "friends" are given a name, a history, an exalted, specific task in the world; while the women are left shadowy, anonymous, mere messengers, intermediaries.

In my mother's life, commonly esteemed things like money, ego, a mighty fortress of a God, a bloodletting bloodline—these were forbidden, taboo. They could not confer beatitude, in this world or any other. She went another way. And God, who is commonly merciless to the merciful, tested her fiercely. Her life became a desert. And living that life, which is the common life and calling of Christians, she became what she was called to: a resplendent ikon of that *aurea media* praised by the ancients, Christians and others.

There could have been, God knows, a better marriage; there could also have been less contentious, clamorous offspring.

Her life could have been less dreadful, less routine-ridden and work-ridden — and her life would, by modern standards, still qualify as moderately awful.

All this is true, according to modern measure. And yet I remember also, for this is the chief point of her story, its commendation — her life struck others as gentle, a rhythm of peace and spiritual plenty.

Talk about an achievement!

Her life: comedy, tragedy, farce, tragicomical farce. It was all there, the meld and mix of our condition. And it was written and choreographed (and largely staged) by my father.

Her face changed. It was not merely that she grew older. She bore too much; she grew ashen, weary, a look of bare endurance appeared.

They were married in a little country church in northern Minnesota, by a priest whose sepia photo, dignified and old-fashioned, hangs on my wall. He sits there, his long beard and broadcloth coat and big clerical book in hand; an impassive yet tender face, a look of sacrifice in the patriarchal eyes. And then two great, outsize hands: the left easeful and horizontal, holding his book erect on its spine; the other downward-pointing, resting on the chair arm. An Abraham at peace, a Moses on watch.

This priest has fame and holy repute among the Catholics of that region, having lived for many years the harsh life of the plains Indians, dwelt in their bark cabins in scorching and icy weathers, talked their language, eaten their food. His life is published; among many he is considered a saint. His bishop honored him in old age as "one of the two or three greatest missioners to have come to our shores." And by all evidence, deservedly.

In my boyhood, the picture of this priest was in our home for as long as I can recall. Was it an unconscious irony of the fates that his face should be the guardian saint of that union, blessed in the beginning by his laborer's hands; that the blessing should have brought us in the next generation — to this? Prison, the courts, near expulsion from my order, public contention, honor, dishonor? Surely he reached deep in the well of history, of early Christians, of the heart of Christ, to dredge up such a blessing.

We were the only family I knew, before or since, who in the course of some twenty years had no event in our midst to celebrate or mourn. No birth, death, marriage; no funeral or baptism. We traveled hardly at all, once we had made the west-east trek from Minnesota to New York State and dug in. Only one of us ever saw a stage play in New York. Our exposure to the great world was, in sum, roughly that of the Appalachian poor: few wants aroused, fewer satisfied. Our father saw us as he saw himself: workhorses, in harness or out.

Out of harness, the pleasures were mitigated, spartan. A movie was a rare delight; we hardly ever ate out, even in the most modest emporia.

This was an interesting anomaly. We were poor; we dwelt in a wide circuit of families in like plight or worse. We were poor, and for years we did not even know it. There were, in fact, few if any ways to test those words: *poor, nonpoor.*

I suppose we were simply part of what came to be known later as the "culture of poverty." Stuck in it, among the stuck. Such a conclusion a learned study would undoubtedly have come up with.

And yet I have little memory of unhappiness. That circle of ours, tightly drawn as it was, and stifling perhaps, inductive of a kind of naiveté, also had its compensations: We grew up as something more than appetites on the hoof. You had a few nickels in your pocket; more often than not, you had nothing. But the pockets of your brothers and your friends up and down the country road were similarly unburdened. So the coins made no great difference; what you had you were taught to share; there was little envy in the air.

Then, time passing, we started trekking to the parochial school, some two miles distant from home. There, a few yard-sticks stood up, to take our measure. The country mice met the city mice; and here and there a son of the new rich or the near rich bumped or shouldered us out of the way. Thus we were instructed in their inalienable right to the right of way. Few specimens in the world are more arrogant, we learned, than the younger mandarins cast, for a time only (before Notre Dame or the College of New Rochelle), among swine and swineherds.

One winter night, my mother was grouped with three of the younger children in the kitchen. It was bedtime; she was about to shepherd us up the dark back stairs to the attic room. Bitter, that upstate cold that had the grip of a wolf upon a frozen shank.

She, who was normally uncomplaining and resilient of spirit, turned toward someone in the family (I do not know how the subject got broached). She said something that, all at once, in a tone I recall to this day, revealed the scalding grief that dwelt behind her eyes, her lonely gambit in the ugly, barren house, children to be fed and clothed and somehow kept alive and kicking. (And himself grandiose, above these petty concerns, wrapped in his ego.)

Exactly what she said I cannot recall, but I read her sense as though I were reading this moment the lips of her mind, or had heard her speak once more among the speechless dead. Something about the bitterness of poverty; what it cost, the bread and beans and macaroni and meat loaf. As though these must be dredged up from the center of the earth, dragged by main might across a continent, doled out, portion by portion, day after day, against odds beyond measure. This is the sense I keep: the burden of it, the dead weight of a poverty that was inexorable.

She turned and beckoned and we followed her up the stairs.

She grew ill.

There was something obscurely shameful about it, a contagion referred to ambiguously as a "spot on the lung." She was taken off to St. Joseph's Hospital (it was there, some fifty years later, the FBI were aided and abetted in their pursuit of me and their shadowing of her by the nuns in charge).

On Sundays, we three youngest were brought in to her bedside for a viewing. My father would trumpet our arrival: prize exhibits of his and the aunts' buffeting care. And my mother, pallid, gray as the linen of the bed, broke down in weak tears at sight of us; so skinny and underfed we were, she mourned later.

And came home from hospital before her cure was accomplished, to be ensconced in a bed just off the kitchen, so she could direct the older boys at cooking operations. "To get rid of his sister, that hellcat," she said with satisfaction, "to get her out of my house."

Back on her feet, she would board a senile streetcar, an hour's voyage each Monday, to mend clothing at an orphanage. There she gained a circle of friends, women her age or older. It cost next to nothing, and it extricated her for a space from the blank box of her life. And, oh, how it was resented, this mild excursion.

Like Mother Courage, willy-nilly, knowing that she could neither make wars nor unmake them, she dragged her cart through the hideous carnage of the century. All those wars, which finally are one war!

Unlike Mother Courage, she had neither the wit nor the flamboyant, easy conscience to make a buck where she could, to con victors or victims. Neither did her religion come wrapped in a flag. I see her as a kind of holy drudge, never quite broken; her gifts pressed hard, ground under; the lost chance, the bad luck she put on with her wedding ring, the sacrament: thou shalt, thou shalt not. And there she must stand: outside the circle she could not take a stand. It had been taken for her. Truly, possibility had been taken from her.

But not all. To hem her in too closely is to do her injustice, just as to "make her an example of Christian womanhood, etc." is to do her an injustice.

Let me do her justice, take the measure of that circle in which she must live and grow old and die. And in which, covertly, and without an ear to attend to her, she may yet dream.

She sent four sons off to World War II, that virtuous, blood-sodden threshing floor. Four sons to war, a fifth incapacitated, myself in seminary. She hung the four stars in the window; most days, my father put out a flag. The house, with only the two of them, was vacant as a ghost's eyes, shadowy with voices and memories.

Comely is a word that occurs.

This is a boy's inarticulate awe of his mother. His life is raw and incomplete. He must look upward, see what the world and time make of that other, that improbable friend and mentor.

She was comely. I choose the old-fashioned word with care. It bespeaks an aura, a worldly style and verve, tart opinions, a mind of her own.

And otherworldly too, a woman of devotion.

A scene sticks in the boy's mind. In the cold northern bedroom of the house stood a portent of note, a five-foot statue of the Blessed Virgin. It had been deposited with us on the basis of some vague loan ("until required") by a local convent of nuns.

My mother, who abominated all display, including the religious pavane of the Irish, commonly made her devotions before this image. But only after the boys had been dispatched to school, and my father departed for work.

The memory of her, kneeling on the floor, in the winter cold, her shoulders draped in an ugly, maroon shawl — the memory is a grace, a mere accident (the boy at home ill, wandering into the room where she knelt).

The boy knew nothing of beauty, conventional or otherwise. People around were as alike as a bundle of sticks: short, fat, tall, sticks with faces. He knew, however, something about function, conduct, rhythm, holding and withholding. And what he saw in his mother, what he understood without a word to back him up, or the need of a word, was an effortless (he thought it effortless) overflow of soul, brimming over the body like water over a limestone sheer; forming as it flowed. Hers was something of that "too much" that makes of the normal and good too little. This is why, to the boy, other women, mothers of his friends, paled before her.

Hers was the beauty of imbalance, dissonance, the soul that overflows, all but overwhelms.

This is a strange thing, that the soul should be so in command: "A terrible beauty is born." Captive, reconciled; but unreconciled too, and free.

There was a Christmas ritual.

A skinny tree, a few lights and trinkets, a gift or two. To the boy, what a miracle!

On that morning a great to-do arose surrounding small matters. Dining plates had been set out the night before, around the living-room table, a name beside each place. Sometime during the night, the mother, helped by one of the older boys, placed on each plate, meagerly or generously, depending on the current state of the exchequer, the following items: a handful or two of hard candy, three or four chocolates, an orange. Beside, a toy or an article of new clothing.

A clamor arose on Christmas morning at sight of such wonders! (No containing oneself; nor, indeed, any effort worth speaking of to contain us.) Our own portion, slice, the edible, delightful world! The boy enchanted, astray in his wits; why, the world itself was made of rock candy! See, a morsel of that world falls to his hands!

The round plate from which he has eaten, day after dull day, his dull portion; now a few trifles are heaped on it: colors, smells, the very marrow of happiness!

The world cheats, ever-larger portions, stakes, enterprises, Pyrrhic conquests. Other Christmases, better gifts, we weigh what lies in our hands; our eyes take on the narrowed meanness of those who know a pennyweight of gold from a pound of feathers. And all is lost.

One Christmas there arose a bustle and hurry like that of all previous Christmases. An older boy was awakening the others: Hurry! What gifts, what wonders lay in store. . . .

We knew, we did not know. Tactile, sweet-smelling Christmas awaited.

Then the mother appeared in the doorway. She wore a different face, a grave and steady and searching look. Not her Christmas face by any means; a suffusion of sweetness unfeigned and warnings only half-purposed.

She shook her head sorrowfully. What could this mean?

Children, she murmured, this year there are no gifts. We have no money for gifts. I want you to be grateful instead for what we have—a good Christmas dinner. . . .

She had little to say about the early years of her marriage, especially as those years touched on my father. I suspect it was in reaction to the Irish, their keening for the "good old days." In any case, the past was a closed book whose text might, in accord with scripture, be sweet on the tongue; but it was also bitter as gall in the guts.

She lived too long not to be glad at times that most of living was over. Now and again, rarely, the boy was granted a glimpse of her young years; how sorrow and loss had lodged themselves, gross grains or fine, in the tissue of her life.

We loved to twit her, a mild form of harassment. Would inquire, in mock astonishment, "How did you ever come to marry *him*?"

Once (he still alive), she drew herself erect like a myna bird confronted with an offensive odor: "I'll have you boys know your father was considered a *great catch*!"

Again, in her old age, and he having departed this vale, we dared put the same question, malice aforethought. She turned away, paused for a long time. Then she turned on us, that candid, devastatingly direct look: "You know, someone should have knocked me in the head!"

Depression years, and the drought. At the bottom of the heap (where our family dwelt, our appointed place in nature), whatever goes wrong hits hardest. I believe I have referred to us as northern Appalachian poor. My father, kicked out of his job, was taken on finally by one of the Works Projects Administration crews in the neighborhood. They set about creating a park on the shores of Onondaga Lake, including a salt-spring swimming pool.

We were at the bottom of the economic heap, but the bottom was made of good earth. We raised our own food, and enough to spare: an austere regime, but never a stingy one. With, often as not, one, two, or three strangers included at table.

And there was the famous three-wheeled cart. It became as near a part of Clay Farm existence as, on a loftier sabbatarian plane, did the galloping Model T, the latter strictly reserved, so to speak, for formal wear and tear.

But that cart! The aforementioned Mother Courage pushed or hauled about the stage of the world no more adaptable, high-spirited, splay-backed instrument of basic economy and appropriate technology and etcetera!

Consider its burdens and glories over those years. Fresh strawberries and Colombia berries and tomatoes, hawked with varying success in the neighborhood. Or, with a small, adjustable, lightweight rack placed on this excellent wooden nag, a round load of golden hay would arise, bumping from meadow to barn. Or a stash of shucked corn ears. Or on return voyages from here, there, anywhere, the two side wheels careening along at the bidding of hands at the crossbar: Behold our cart, liberated in spirit and fact, no longer a mere, mangy, woebegone beast of the poor. Now, more in the nature of a circus car or a rodeo bronco, possessing the tar road, hill and dale, motor traffic seldom intruding; the burden of the transmogrified cart being now simply—a boy! A starry-eyed, windy-haired, uneasy rider. He clung to the wooden flanks for dear life; he sat there like the Buddha in an earthquake. The more his vehicle shook him, wildly testing his faith in the God of the crossroads, why, the more loudly he flung abroad his laughing challenge to the shaman of storms. A laughing Buddha!

But the foregoing is no more than the economics of the red pushcart, the ecstatic progress of the cart, the celebratory bacchic cart.

There was quite another side to this mobile marvel. Therefore it shall be referred to hereafter as the Cart of Compassion. And it is at this point that the mother enters the scene, her spirit possessing, animating, revving up this remarkable chameleon chariot.

During those years of my childhood (as is far more terribly and universally true at present), food was a bitter question for many. Survival. The less-than-likely next meal. Surrounding us in the neighborhood were families for whom the cornucopia had dried up (the drought), or to whom it turned only its small, sealed, hind end (the depression). There were the ashamed poor, the aged poor, the shiftless poor, the unemployed and incapacitated and zonked, the country characters and ne'er-do-wells.

On these the skies, habitually beetling and overbearing, had quite brutally fallen. In little, tacky houses and hovels, off the main roads, in unnamed dead-end cinder paths where no cars ventured, among a few chickens and weeds and a dog and a rusty auto cadaver or two, dwelt such families or solitaries, eking out an unutterably miserable existence—the country poor, forsaken by God and humankind. Snot-nosed, bony kids, blank-eyed women, a nameless, ignored grandmother in some dank corner, the slack-shouldered, defeated men.

There were horrors, too, in those shanties and sheds: madness, violent spasms, wife beatings, murder, the raw ache and agony simmering in August heat, crouching indoors through the battering winters.

This is where the famous cart rolled in. Where this endlessly adaptive creature transmogrified once more. It became a kind of food bank on the move, a celebration of that promised land where all would be free and easy and the mystical goose hang high.

With regularity, we boys were dispatched by twos, to deliver free provender from the cart. To wit: in all seasons, tin pails or half-gallon bottles of fresh milk. And in season, all sorts and varieties of fresh produce from the garden: corn, spinach, potatoes, carrots, beans, berries; also apples, plums, prunes from the orchard. Also dairy products: fresh butter and cottage cheeses. These severally to Ms. Zapp and Ms. McDermott, who were bed-ridden; to the Bodys, who were purse-proud and brought low; to the Smiths, the most colorful and outrageous of all the colony of the lost; to Mamie and Oliver Powell and their snarling shepherd bitch (to Oliver because he was old as a fence post, a Civil War veteran; and to Mamie simply because she was mad and mean-spirited and terrorized the neighbors in fervent pursuit of both destinies).

Thus, my mother's largesse, which extended and widened the domestic table, was not exhausted at our board. How wickedly comparative a thing it is, I reflect, this little or much; how those scales marked "more" and "less" teeter madly in the chaos of America!

We scraped the unpromising land, and with a few domestic animals and labor that included all, we made it through some of the leanest years since Pharaoh turned out his seams.

My mother. She threaded many through the gospel's needle eye: ourselves and others. Convinced as she apparently was that others than the family must be gotten through such times; that, indeed, unless those others made it also, our own passage would be much impeded or summarily halted.

An example. Through her urging, there sat at our table frequently, among many others, a misfortunate clan whom I take even today as emblem of the abused human lot. The mother was a sour exile from obscure grandeur and mysterious wealth frequently invoked, with nose aloft and the wobbly eye of the born martyr. Her marriage, by her oft-rehearsed account, had brought her low. The guilty husband, paying in her uxorious swath for the sin of daring to exist, looked habitually bewildered and defeated, as though the fates had, at her hands, delivered him a blow intended for an ox. A truck driver, he had an even worse fate in store than his marriage.

One awful day, his vehicle killed a child in the streets, by account of witnesses, through no fault of his. And in mad shock or remorse, seeing the child fall under the wheels, he abandoned the truck and disappeared for months into the nearby swamps.

Ill luck multiplied and compounded. A baby had fallen from their second-story window, hovered for months between this world and a better. An older offspring, in concert with two other drifters, undertook to rob a country bank; and in the process, inept and edgy at their first heist, they shot and killed an old bank clerk who had not leapt to obey them quickly enough. The employee, it transpired, was stone deaf. The three gained not a cent and were captured in hours.

Ill luck, the bottom, the law, ill fortune kneaded grittily into the very dough of creation. Such families as these sat at our table or received food at their own door. The women among them stopped for hours at our kitchen, reciting their litanies of malice and woe. At our house, their children were counseled, reprimanded, praised—and fed. Talk about extended family!

Our family was lacking almost genetically in what is vulgarly known as American smarts. It was not that, from some Olympian motive, we disapproved of the theory and practice of the Great Upward Scramble. (I remember devouring the nincompoop novels of Horatio Alger, junk food for the mind, and finding, to say the least, nothing morally repulsive in those propulsive creations of low wit, flummery, and swerve.)

We were afflicted, so to speak, with the bad luck that saves, innocent as bumpkins in Shylock's clutches. We had no idea of what makes cash registers sing, what makes families get on top and stay there.

There were, in my father's background, any number of Irish who had gone from tidy little farms nearby, amassing their tidy little sack, to become petit bourgeois merchants in the city—of coal and ice, of hardware and dry goods and groceries. He rehearsed such wonders by the hour.

We used to speculate on this: why he never got anywhere in any of the numerous areas where his luck or skills might be applied. He worked the railroad, the assembly line, the steel mills, the power company. He was also an experienced farmer, mechanic, plumber; in his old age, he constructed a table for a Jesuit chapel. It was a piece of cunning, a wonder.

Then there was the writing: poetry, prose, reminiscences, humor, reams and reams, most of it written out in his hieroglyphic longhand—practically all of it worthless. But he kept it coming, like the great salt machine at the bottom of the sea.

My parents lived in a war-ridden world. They died, and nothing eased in the world.

Were they to return, they would find nothing eased in the world. War is still the universal coin; many are beggared; a few grow rich. There is less of the earth for most; there is war and threat of war and preparation for war and waste and rapine in service to war. The mad momentum gains ground every hour.

Only now, war would be claiming their grandsons instead of their sons.

They and we are thus caught in a warp of the unnatural. It leaves us with desperately narrowed choices, as it did them. To go with the horror named war; or to resist.

But either choice is, in a sense, unnatural. Silence is complicity, resistance is the task, perpetually repeated and set at naught, of Sisyphus the absurd.

This is a bitterness beyond telling. My parents bore us into a cultural and political and moral compact as to means and end. The compact was proclaimed as binding on all. Yet we spend our lives resisting the violation by highly placed authority (men and women beyond accountability or recourse) of that same compact.

My father died in 1969. My mother lived on for another decade, grew older in the cross fire of war. Through her whole life, up to (but not including) the Vietnam War, she had no instructor, no moral map. On this question of war, the first question of all, the question in comparison with which all others pale—on this question she, who was devout as a Teresa or Joan, had not even a church. She was simply one with the millions who perished, the millions who begat sons who perished, the millions whose sons returned. She raised no questions; no one suggested there were questions to raise. She hung out the stars; he put out the flag. And who was to help them do otherwise?

In her world, the modern world, war was like one of those public bouts between two brutes, an old-time-champ free for all. They stood toe to heel for fifty or more rounds, beating one another barefisted to death. The best the giants could expect was an interlude, a few minutes' recovery, water splashed on the bruised limbs, dazed eyes briefly focused. Then back to the mauling. Ding dong, next round.

The round named Vietnam spun my mother about, a weather vane in a tornado. She was now in her early seventies, entitled by every canon of the culture to a conventional fading, a sepia grandmother image, slipped between the pages of a Bible.

How we let go of them, the aged (how we let ourselves go)! To the attic, closed like a musty book, the trunk lid lowered, then off to the city dump. We deny them the grace of pain and freedom; we want them warehoused, disposed of. This is how we go, especially the men, those who survive the battlefields only to die, lumpish of mind and empty of eye, having paid their debt to biology and nothing at all to the fierce and sacrificial heart of reality.

She was denied that curse, that graceless ending. She was presented, at seventy, at eighty, with choices that burned in the hand like coals. Her sons heaped coals of fire and offered them; and she took them up and was burned to the bone.

Priests? Priests were conventional darlings of the nursery of heaven. Dolls, part of the cultural décor. Their powers, once formidable, were shrunken. Only here and there, among the young and the very old, were circles of belief; in them, priests could still shine. They forgave sins and comforted the ill and baptized infants. In sum, they were allowed to celebrate life, to mime it. All this, as long as they did not insist on living.

Her sons stepped down from that high, nearly foreclosed estate, two of us. We said our no as best we might, to the latest round of the bloody bout. We told her, gently as we might, of a fait accompli—our fate being, by then, all but determined by both church and state.

This was the great honor, the crown we put on her head, a crown of thorns. We did not want her to die, this unconventional, unbroken spirit, of a vapid moral decline, a melting of the ice, a fire that perished for want of fuel and air. We poked the fire, we breathed on her. And all this toward the end of her life, when she was weakened physically, when everything in the mad, frivolous culture would have her cosseted, cosmeticized, a corpse in a tufted box.

This was our gift to her, these last years. This is what draws the sting of regret or remorse. I know neither regret nor remorse toward her. What is there to regret? We offered her a place at the table of sacrifice, a place of honor, the honor due old age, no wasting game, no folderol of reverence.

She was ill. Philip was in prison. I was walking gingerly underground, shortly to be captured and shipped to prison. She was attended night and day by Jerry and Carol. These are the bare bones of that time. And we made it. All of us. No one perished, no one was harmed. No one of us, as far as we know, harmed others. Thus are the losses and gains of peacemaking totted up; in contrast, as may appear, to the losses and gains of war, which require no accounting here.

We came out of prison; there was a great reunion, then another and another. And eventually, in the course of nature, full of days and love, she died. No moral husk, but bursting like a pod with the seeds of eternity.

How describe that face, the face that bent over a first-born child, the face that turned to me in boyhood and manhood, that in her sublime, unrelenting old age, turned to me?

I was summoned from New York by the word, low-pitched with grief: "Come, she has just died."

With two brothers I entered her room. Her slight form had been arranged decently; bedclothing folded back, hands joined. Her jaws were toothless, face waxen, empty. The slate wiped clean; stillness, humiliation, mystery. We stood there, three of us, the clock of the universe stilled. We prayed a while; I bent over, kissed her cold forehead. Amen, alleluia.

PORTRAITS, 1982

Part Two

THE CHURCH

Catholicism and the Intelligence

Catholicity is one of the marks of the church, as the church itself has always agreed. And it is true to say by way of corollary that the same quality is also a mark of the intelligence of the believer.

St. Thomas is a good authority in this matter. He wrote that "God has imparted his goodness to created things in such a way that each of them could transmit to the others what it had itself received." And his conclusion is at once a summons and a reproof: "Consequently, those who withdraw from things their own operations, do wrong to the goodness of God." Such people, Thomas implies, offend in fact against justice, since they refuse to God the glory that belongs to him precisely through his creation—a glory that is destined to be formalized by the minds of men and women.

"To do justice to God in the order of nature." The saying implies an entire vocation. The Christian, Thomas would seem to say, is summoned to investigate and synthesize the reality which faith and human beings' nature and the universe open before them.

In regard to this task it would perhaps be helpful to contrast the mind of the Old Testament believer with the Christian mind, as both face their universe. It seems clear, first of all, that the Christian view of the mind has expanded the working area which has been granted to women and men of the Old Testament. Formerly, certain aspects of truth were forbidden to human beings because of specific danger to their religious life. We have only to think of the deliberately imposed insularity of the old law, of the restrictions it imposed on humanity's intellectual and cultural life. The law, issuing from a priestly hegemony, legislated the whole of people's lives; it regulated not only specific religious life, but social, economic, and political life as well.

But the Incarnation has broken the jealously guarded vessel in which the truth had formerly been placed, immune and untouchable. The intelligence of humankind is now, in St. Paul's phrase, "in Christ." It has a vocation to the world of reality, and this vocation has its center in the vocation of the Son of God to humanity, in such wise that he is the Master Image of intellectual maturity and catholic generosity of mind.

And this relationship of the intellectual task of humanity to Christ, the early church seems to have sensed rather quickly; a Christian statement expressive of it was coined by Augustine. He wrote that "nothing is secular save sin"; and the formula of the Middle Ages echoed him. *Valde ama intellectum*: "love the intelligence with a kind of passion."

In the light of the entrance of God upon the human scene, Christians conceded no force to the ancient warnings which had protected Israel.

Those warnings had taught in effect that to touch "the outsider" was to be lost. But with Christ, this period of self-protection and isolation is declared ended. The early Fathers of the church set their faces in another direction. "Welcome the truth," wrote St. Augustine, "wherever it be found, for the truth remains always itself, whatever its source." The sign which had forbidden Israel to enter the Gentile world was removed by the arrival of God among human beings. When the catholic Christ is present, all such things as fear, exclusiveness, a failure of intellectual sympathy on religious bases—these are once and for all anachronistic.

Instead, as the church becomes more conscious of itself as destined to welcome all people to Christ, it announces from age to age a universalism of mind and heart. And in this view of the world, it is simply being itself and summoning the mind of humankind to become itself, in the church.

It would seem to follow, then, that intellectual iconoclasm is not a Christian pastime. It belongs rather to a provisory order of things which preceded the church; to a period when men and women were children on the earth, and defense was the key to their survival. But mere survival can never define humanity's adulthood; and a survival psychology can never bring humanity to maturity.

But the church, which was the adulthood of humankind, understood that it had the power of inducing adulthood in its sons and daughters. By way of dramatizing this power, Paul and the Fathers of the early church loved to speak of the foundation of the church as the climax of sacred history. . . .

It need hardly be said that the struggle of the church continues today. And its present situation invites us not so much to a tallying of gains, as to a simple and dolorous hope.

For to say the least, the march of events cannot be called favorable to the church. It is sufficient to recall the last four or five hundred years of history in order to realize the truth of this. Those years saw three stages of effective opposition which have succeeded in reducing the body of ancient "Christendom" to a more or less ineffectual minority. The first stage was the destruction of inner unity. The second tended to cast doubt on the relevance of religion to society. And the third, accepting this state of affairs in its turn, was inclined to reject even the idea of a private witnessing in religious life.

And along with these changes we note the break-up of the organic components of human life: science from culture, politics and public life from morality, and as if by implicit agreement, all of these together from the life of humanity in God. In this way, not only the relevance of faith but its very right to exist have become matters for sober debate.

It requires a great deal of vitality, one would agree, for the religious spirit of humankind even to exist under such a situation. But to press the public claim of religion, no matter how acutely these are felt, would seem to be folly. Yet the pressing of this claim, in season and out, remains a substantial part of the Christian task.

The believers' sense of their times moreover will forbid them, with regard to the state of their faith, to name the times incurably hostile or irreparable. The terms are unrealistic and simply unhistorical. The fact is that there have been better times, and there have been worse times, and probably the most deceptive judgment on any period of history comes from those who are within it. The Christian historical sense suggests rather that the present is by no means as evil as it appears, nor is the past as attractive as our remoteness from it would make it seem.

Knowing history, Christians can regard their own times with the detached love necessary to them if they are to work effectively in those times. Their faith tells them that the only reality promised and indefectible life within time is the church itself. The promise of Christ is extended to nothing else; neither to forms of government nor to treaties made with the church, nor to cultures favorable or inimical to it, nor even to special forms of the religious vocation. All forms and groupings of humankind are by nature subject to change and to death; no matter what philosophy of history one prefers, the fact is clear, as theology tells us. For Christian adults, these facts are at once sobering and encouraging.

Their sense of history gives a fine edge of discernment to their view of life. They know the difference for instance between serving the church and trying to make it, even with the best will in the world, acceptable to this or that age. They are strong in a sense of mystery, as they are strong in the sense of their life's task. So they can see the ambiguities which are bound to be present when the church is triumphant within time, just as they can live equably in an age when the church is in a minor role or must submit to persecution.

And if they are Christians living today, they find in the church's contemporary struggle the greatest stimulus to their loyalty and zeal. They know that defeats are not irreversible, as though the church were a victim of some blind circle of time or were bound to a Will that allowed no free play to the will of human beings. Christian theology is agreed that the onset of modern paganism can be turned back by holy and zealous men and women; and turned back on the same three stages of its apparent triumph — humanity's conscience, public life, and the unity of the nations. The moment when public life lost its roots in religious life is reversed by the moment when a viable religious life communicates its spirit once more to the life of humanity.

Again, we have our lesson from history. It is instructive that the modern break-up of religious unity began not from without but from within the church. The church had shown in a hundred previous crises that its vitality could summon resources to meet its enemies. But at a point of time, it was unable to put to good use the reforming zeal of some of its own members. The spirit of reform was embittered, and broke away. This is an aspect of the historical truth which Catholics have not often dwelt upon; but as Pope John has said, Catholics must bear a part of the blame for the loss of religious unity. The Catholic spirit, a welcoming of the truth even when the truth is unpleasant and insistent, has not always been part of the equipment of Christian men and women.

A simple sense of history will tell us that the modern religious situation is at least partially the historic outcome of this Christian failure. The church of the sixteenth century had refused a hearing to believers who were reacting against selfishness and clericalism and worldliness. We are not forbidden, then, to see the beginnings of the revolt as a profound religious reaction to abuses within the church. In many of its first aspects the reform had been admirable and holy.

It remains true nonetheless that the Reformation came eventually to a principle, not of reform, but of division, and that it set in motion the beginnings of a debate whose progress went somewhat as we have indicated. First, the public worth of religion was called into question; then the intelligence of men and women began seriously to doubt the very worth of religion to human life.

The theological doubtings of men and women, in one form or another, go on. Analyzed and psychoanalyzed and elaborated in symbols, they are the source of much of the greatness of modern literature. It would not be far from the truth to say that one who does not understand the power which religious doubt exerts in the spiritual life of modern men and women will have little understanding of them at all. One thinks almost at random of Newman, Claudel, Rouault, Lorca, Brunner, Greene, de Foucauld — of those whose religious and ideological and literary judgments have shaped the human spirit today. It is through this fearless and agonized inner debate, in which the meaning of existence itself was sometimes placed in the balance, that their achievement was formed.

And what draws all men and women irresistibly toward them is something much more than the triumphant outcome of their struggle. It is rather the vitality of their struggle itself, the power and honesty with which its terms are illuminated. It is modern humanity's fascination, not for goals and victories, but for "the way," for struggle and the ironies of combat.

If there is anything in all this that remains regrettable, it is not a debate which has given modern history so many of its great spirits. For this, we can only be grateful. But the truly regrettable fact is that the debate is conducted in many instances so unfairly. The state of the question in regard to the nature and value of religious faith is weighted with half truths and fables and prejudices, and the burden of historical Christian failure. The debaters show a genius for the peripheral, for ignoring what is central. They disinter buried issues, substitute rancor for human feelings, and call it religious conversation.

Still, at the heart of these failures lies a Christian opportunity. Christian intellectuals, that is, accept as their task the restoration of an atmosphere of life in which the claims of the faith may win a hearing. The task rightly understood is a public one and an intellectual one. One cannot be true to it and cast about to affect one or another individual while his or her environment, with its many complicated structures, remains untouched. Neither is one stating the terms of the task with any accuracy by viewing it as some kind of intellectual violence. The task is rather to give a quiet and persistent evidence of the great idea that the sacred is not a threat to humankind, that the truest victories of the human spirit are consonant with belief, and that modern men and women lose neither their claims nor their ambition nor their honor before humanity, by an act of faith.

THE BOW IN THE CLOUDS, 1961

The Sistine Chapel

Illusory, a maelstrom of wrong purpose.
I would whitewash the whole.
Then, in favor of religion,
place there
for a poverello's sake
for his gospel eye, Cezanne's *Card Players*, say.

See, the painter cries, *God*
is that meditative peasant
or the watcher brooding over; He is
like us, all said.

Divine things
need only look human. The cards deal and fall
fair as leaves or creation; we are in good hands.

SPIRIT, MAY 1964

The Priesthood of the Laity

The tradition of the church agrees that the nature of the priesthood, whether possessed by clerics or by the laity, is essentially social. One could mention many biblical sources here, among the most remarkable of which is surely the Letter to the Hebrews. The letter speaks with a majestic sustained rhetoric of the priest Christ, a being of divine power and of human compassion, doing the Father's work of reconciliation in the world. This Holy Priest is turned totally toward the Father and toward human beings; he is son and brother (Heb. 8:12). His acute sense of the Father's honor is verified on a human scene. He has taken the very shape of humanity to himself and raised it to the dignity of priesthood in order to accomplish the work of restoration and peace in the human community (Heb. 5:14).

And the mystery of priesthood also has special emphasis in the writing of St. John. John formed his image of the Savior from the point of view of a Jewish liturgy that still awaited fulfillment. Humanity awaited its Priest. In Christ, women and men awaited their own destiny. Year upon year, century upon century, the long file of believing pilgrims made its way across history; the Exodus, the periods of prophets and kings extended the theme. Life was a religious venture, and sacrifice marked its great stages; sacrifices of burning and bloodletting formed a constant call upon the community to acknowledge its guilt and awaken its hope. In all these centuries, Jewish communities remained bitterly conscious of a double loss in humankind, a loss of daughter- and sonship and of sister- and brotherhood.

These realities—sonship and daughtership, brotherhood and sister-hood—were of the essence of men and women's lives; these realities made them human. In the first days of existence, human beings had stood at that living intersection where they rejoiced in the dignity of being both child and brother and sister—child to God, brother and sister to their neighbor. This was the gift that God had offered humankind at the beginning of sacred history (Gen. 2).

But human beings had ruptured that bond. They had sinned and hidden away in the thicket; and when they were called, their answer already was redolent of arrogance, slavish fear, and double-dealing. "I was naked, and I hid myself" (Gen. 3:10). No longer child and neighbor, they had declared themselves rebel and murderer.

The stain that infected humankind's dealing with God very shortly broke out into a universal human plague. Those who were rebels against God could not be friends to human beings. Rather, since they were God's enemy, their hatred of God corrupted the human community; it made them murderers of their brothers and sisters. Cain committed a heinous crime against nature and against blood, effectively resigning his human love because he had already rejected his sonship in God. The murder of Abel was humankind's declaration of that war against men and women and God, the sin called original. "And the Lord said to Cain: Where is thy brother Abel? And he answered, I know not: am I my brother's keeper?" (Gen. 4:9).

The savior would answer that question—and in blood. He had come to stand at the intersection of life, that place where humankind had struggled against God and murdered its brother. Christ had come to restore humankind at the crucial point of life where they had rebelled. He died and arose and left to humankind the effective commemoration of his love for them.

And in the Mass, God verifies once more the love which is older than humankind and which insists not only that human beings must love God but that without love of their brothers and sisters, they are unworthy of the name human.

Human history reveals the truth again and again; the Mass dramatizes it in an entirely unique way. History insists on the unity of humankind, in its recurrent rhythms of anarchy and of harmony, of war and of peace. And it is to this history, to its tragic struggle and deferred hope, that the Mass summons believers. Through words and action, women and men are reminded constantly of the community task that awaits their hands and heart.

They gain a true historic and human sense at the Eucharist. They are invited to contemplate a history that the Incarnation made sacred, once and for all. In his death and victory, the Son of God submitted to a process of life which human beings had profaned but which divine love had made sacred in the gift of Christ's life. The profane memory of humankind, stained with a history of revolt, has been cleansed by the action of Christ the Priest. "Having loved his own who were in the world, [Jesus] loved them to the end" (John 13:1).

Men and women learn most vividly who Christ is by recalling what Christ has done. And they learn also in Christ's death and victory who they themselves are and to what they are called. So we recall, at the *memores* prayer immediately after the consecration, "the blessed passion of Christ our Lord, His resurrection from the dead, and His glorious ascension into heaven."

The prayer summons women and men to a new understanding of what has been brought to pass upon the altar. The death and the Resurrection of the Savior, made present under the banquet symbols, are dwelt upon in a sacred stillness, in gratitude and inner recollection. And the truth of this moment is not merely that our human memory is recalled to a past event, however noble and great. The Eucharist is not a mere memorial. Rather, by the power of God, our memories are immersed in a present happening—the celebration of Calvary and the Resurrection of Christ—at the sacrificial banquet. "We your servants and with us your holy people, recalling, making present your death and victory, do now offer you these holy gifts."

A view of life is opened before men and women here. It corresponds to history, to God's word, and to humanity's deepest instincts. Humankind is one in its members; humankind has fallen in one person, all have arisen in one Person, all go to God with one Person. So it is eminently true that to speak of the "social" character of the Mass is a pleonasm; it is like adding "social" to "Catholicism." It is as superfluous as adding "people" to "priesthood."

The priestly work of the people is in essence a work on behalf of a community. Christ had verified this. He was son and brother (John 8:29). And his blood cried out to God more eloquently than the blood of Abel (Heb. 12:24). His blood was, in fact, creative of a race of sons and daughters and brothers and sisters. It bestowed a new reality on human beings; it gave them a new name in the Hebrew sense, in which a name strictly conforms to the reality and destiny of the person.

Their new name would be adopted children of God. "Behold what manner of love the Father has bestowed upon us, that we should be called children of God" (1 John 3:1). And human beings are also newly named as brothers and sisters to others. "For this is the message that you have heard from the beginning, that we should love one another" (1 John 3:11).

Now this work of reconciliation, the work of priesthood, is a work of God and a work of women and men. It is the very opposite of automatic or magical. It implies, rather, all the ironies and contrasts of a living historical process. Christ had finished the work, yet he had left it unfinished. He had assured its victory, yet he had placed it in the breach. Peace and unity are both accomplished in him, yet they are left in continuing crisis. Reconciliation is possible, but for many it is not yet actual. The gift of God has been offered to humankind; it has not as yet been welcomed by all men and women (Heb. 2:11-17). The sorrows and difficulties that the church is experiencing, and will always experience, in announcing the word of God to the nations bear witness to the essentially dynamic and temporal nature of salvation.

One must understand redemption as a continuing and unfinished work — as the work of the whole Christ. Certainly this was the understanding of St. Paul. Christians are mysteriously summoned by Christ to undertake a work that the divine plan for humankind has left unfinished. "What is lacking of the sufferings of Christ I fill up in my flesh" (Col. 1:24). And, again, "I bear the marks of the Lord Jesus in my body" (Gal. 6:17). The Savior has willed that the redemption of humanity be a vortex of a struggle that would mysteriously continue until the last day. In this way, the baptized are summoned, not to be static dispensers of formulas or the heralds of a victory that is finished with. To conceive of Christianity in such terms is to do injustice to its grandeur and challenge; it is to miss the human and historical substance of its work. It is to substitute a closed and magical system of salvation for an entirely open and unfinished history whose outcome still waits upon women and men's response to love as humanity struggles toward its fulfillment.

May we not say, then, that a biblical and eucharistic view of humankind implies all this—that the history of salvation is still open and that the Christian is still the shaper of humankind's history as Jesus was the shaper of history?

These are large words, and yet they express something extremely simple and lucid. We are suggesting that there is no substitute for the believer who is an unusual human being, permeated deeply with a sense of the life of human beings as they exist here and now. And this sense of sharing and shaping human life comes to focus on the two great realities that are central to human existence—daughter- and sonship, and sisterhood and brotherhood. Christianity is, in fact, the elevation and perfection of these crucial relationships of existence. The believer is by definition son or daughter of God and brother or sister of others (Rom. 8:5).

This is the gift of God. What Christians are empowered to announce and accomplish for others is already effectively conferred on believers themselves. As adulthood brings them new experiences, every human instinct assures them that they are children and neighbors of others, that they are relational beings. Further, their baptism has intervened to bless and elevate these relationships, to make them children and neighbors in an entirely new way.

So through their human nature and through the gift of God, Christians have entered into new relationships; their hope now is to introduce others to the same realities. The human being, who is rebel and sinner, may look to Christians and be healed, for Christians are children of God. The solitary human being, the one who stands outside community for whatever reason, may look to Christians in hope, for Christians love their neighbors, are neighbors to all, and wear their humanity with a sense of power and weakness, of compassion and strength.

In their deepest hearts, do men and women seek anything else than a hope of healing and reconciliation? Let us suggest that the Christian is God's answer to the millennial search of humankind—a search for humanity and for God, a search that modern life has complicated and delayed to the point where men and women themselves can scarcely tell upon what road their feet lie. An analysis of modern literature shows the breadth and purpose of this search. Human beings seek their brothers and sisters even in the denial of them. Graham Greene has probed the disease whose symptom is social refusal. One of his powerful and mordant short stories, "The Destructors," concerns a gang of London teenagers. Under the leadership of an architect's son, Trevor, they have decided on the destruction of a beautiful old house originally designed by Christopher Wren. The owner is absent; the destruction is in progress:

"Come over here," Trevor said, "and look." Out of both pockets he drew bundles of bank notes. "Old Misery's savings."

"What are you going to do? Share them?"

"We aren't thieves," Trevor said. "Nobody's going to steal anything from this house. I kept these for you and me—a celebration. We'll burn them; one by one." And taking turns they held a note upwards and lit the top corner, so that the flame burned slowly toward their fingers. The gray ash floated above them and fell on their heads like age. "I'd like to see old Misery's face when we're through," Trevor said.

"You hate him a lot?" Blackie said.

"Of course I don't hate him," Trevor said. "There'd be no fun if I hated him." The last burning note illuminated his brooding face. "All this hate and love," he said, "it's soft, it's hooey. There's only things, Blackie," and he looked around the room crowded with the unfamiliar shadows of half things, broken things, former things. "I'll race you home, Blackie."

E. M. Forster and Aldous Huxley have seen the process of depersonalization as continuing at an accelerated rate, until humankind can no longer stomach itself. In the world of the future the machine has won, and men and women are reduced to its image of impersonality and indifference. In Forster's short story "The Machine Stops," a woman is summoned to a television set to speak with her son in a far-distant country:

"Be quick here I am in the dark wasting my time. . . ." ". . . Mother . . . I want you to come and see me. . . ." She watched his face in the blue plate. "But I can see you," she exclaimed. "What more do you want?" "I want to see you not through the machine," he said, "I want to speak to you not through the wearisome machine. . . . I see something like you in this plate, but I do not see you; I hear something like you through this telephone, but I do not hear you. That is why I want you to come. Pay me a visit, so that we can meet face to face, and talk about the hopes that are in my mind." She replied that she could scarcely spare the time for a visit. "The air-ship barely takes two days to fly between me and you." "I dislike air-ships." "Why?" "I dislike seeing the horrible brown earth, and the sea, and the stars when it is dark. I get no ideas in an air-ship!" "I do not get them anywhere else." "What kind of ideas can the air give you?" He paused for an instant. "Do you know four big stars that form an oblong, and three stars close together in the middle of the oblong, and hanging from these stars, three other stars?" "No, I do not, I dislike the stars. But did they give you an idea? How interesting. Tell me." "I had an idea they were like a man." "I do not understand." "The four big stars are the man's shoulders and his knees. The three stars in the middle are like the belts that men wore once, and the three stars hanging are like a sword. . . ." "It does not strike me as a very good idea, but it is certainly original."

But even in practical agnosticism, in desperate paganism, in the cult of pleasure and pride, there is a certain moral hope at work. It is the kind of recognition of illness that always wins mercy.

And let us not be overly pessimistic. The human situation is always saved by the few who retain conscience, hope, and a sense of humanity. It is of these Charles Williams speaks in *Descent Into Hell* (a poet, Stanhope, speaks to a troubled girl):

"Haven't you heard it said that we ought to bear one another's burdens? . . . When . . . Christ said 'bear,' I think he meant . . . carrying a parcel instead of someone else. To bear a burden is to carry it instead of.

". . . If you insist on making a universe for yourself . . . if you want to disobey and refuse the laws that are common to us all, if you want to live in pride and division and anger, you can. But if you will be part of the rest of us, and live and laugh and be ashamed with us, then you must be content to be helped. You must give your burden up to someone else, and you must carry someone else's burden. I haven't made the universe and it isn't my fault; but I'm sure this is a law of the universe, and not to give up your parcel is as much to rebel as not to carry another's. . . . When you are alone, remember that I am afraid instead of you . . . and go on. Remember it is mine. . . ." Deliberately he opened himself to that fear. . . . The body of his flesh received her alien terror, his mind carried the burden of her world. The burden was inevitably lighter for him than for her, for the rage of a personal resentment was lacking; he endured her sensitiveness, but not her sin; the substitution there, if indeed there is a substitution, is hidden in the central mystery of Christendom.

. . . We spoke of Christians as marked by a strong sense of the present and of their world. We must make our terms quite clear. There is no question here of the man or woman whose sense of the present is a rather crude involvement in the affluent life and its gadgets and games or in intellectual childishness. A Christian's sense of the times is nothing so flimsy or artificial as this. We are thinking, rather, of a sense of this world that is like Paul's. Such a sense of the times takes its lead from the Incarnation of the Son of God. It may be called an affective and intellectual friendship with the world of men and women. This sense of reality is a conviction that the divine is friend to humankind, that grace is the immersion of human life in the life of God.

In speaking this way, one must be conscious of a full sympathy for differing temperaments and views of life. The heart and mind of the church are as ample and generous as the heart of Christ; it accepts all women and men, as he did. And it is true that conservatism is fostered by many elements of modern life. Many Christians, materially fortunate, live and die with the implicit belief that the life they have known is the common lot of humankind. No least suspicion is aroused in them that their lives have been highly special in a material sense, that they have been favored in ways that most never experience.

It is not to be thought wonderful that such people will also have a restricted experience of the faith and will tend to conclude that their experience of the church coincides rather exactly with reality. Their lives, so safe and protected, encourage them to think that the faith is finished, academic, a matter of formulas and of legal observance. Such persons will consider themselves as certainly obligated to God and only possibly obligated to humankind. And they will think of faith and the human order as necessarily separate realities.

We note in many Christians, as a result of such influences, a certain remoteness from life, a tendency toward indecision, a distrust of individual opinion except if it is official opinion, a strong bias toward the prudential, a quick skill at detecting the vagaries of modern life and a corresponding blindness in regard to its values, a strong sense of the dogmatic and a correspondingly weak sense of the pragmatic, a tendency to enlarge the areas of clerical competence and to restrict areas of lay competence.

Let us reflect on this remoteness from life, especially one aspect of it that seems particularly regrettable today—the lack of sympathy in the minds of priests for a truly adult social apostolate. It is an indifference to life's forms perhaps related to the conviction that the sacred must be kept immune from the issues of this world. So most sermons preached in the modern church stress the dogmatic or moral or personal formation of laypersons but leave them with hardly any cause to reflect on public life and Christian involvement.

There is something more here, one would think, than an unrealistic view of the layperson's powers of thought. It is not simply a question of priests remaining silent on public moral issues because they think laypeople ought to draw their own conclusions within their own lives. To speak bluntly, the social order is sometimes neglected in the public speech of the church because to draw social conclusions from Catholic moral teaching would be uncomfortable and disturbing and because in the minds of many priests, prudential judgments rule almost any given circumstance. It is thought somehow unworthy of holy church that it should mix in conflict; it disturbs good order, disturbs good women and men, and awakens ugly local feeling and controversy. It puts the church in the breach; it makes the church, the mother of peace, a source of friction and hatreds. For all these reasons, in many dioceses of the South, for example, the patent conclusions of the doctrine of the Mystical Body are ignored. Priests walk a gingerly path around local and obvious facts. Prudence wins out. It wins out not only against unwise zeal and extremism but also against charity, against public scandals, against the feelings and consciences of black Catholics, who are in many cases left to fend for themselves when faced with a conspiracy of silence or procrastination. In such a way, public and personal wrongs perpetuate themselves within the church.

And to speak of the North, the situation is not startlingly different. From the silence which up to recent times has veiled many pulpits in regard to social questions, northern Catholics are free to draw many conclusions. One of them would say, "We of the North have no problem with blacks; if we did, the priests would speak of it." Giving the lie to this are northern black slums and Catholic real-estate owners and employers who draw as hard and fast a line across the path of blacks as was ever drawn in the Deep South, forbidding them areas of housing and work.

This failure of courage in facing one's own times, this lack of a full-blooded sense of history, inevitably harms the church's efforts in many ways. Let us speak of two forms of that harm. First, from the point of view of conversions, the clear apologetic always evident in a body of vigorous, honest men and women is blurred into an ambiguous picture of Catholic safeness, of false peace, and of jargon. And people today are unerringly aware of this; especially aware are those who would make the best Catholics. They are simply not drawn to a church that seems to dwell with unfeeling detachment in the midst of turbulence and injustice, a church that assures itself and its believers, by implication or silence, that all will be right if we keep our heads and stay clear of messy conflict. Such thinking, or such a presentation of what the church is, stands as far from the gospel as it does from the thought of men like Leo XIII and Pius XII and John XXIII. Such cowardice is, in effect, a bargaining for a false peace that has no place in the war for humanity's soul.

And in consequence of our failure to be true to the peace of Christ and to bear with him the cross of public, courageous action, it often happens that valuable men and women remain outside the church. Such men and women do not see in Catholics that fire which the Savior came to light upon the earth. Rather, they find in us a stereotype of some of the least valuable qualities of those who claim no faith at all; we are, they say, safe and institutionalized and predictable.

And failure of social action in the church performs still another disservice to it. It is a commonplace to hear priests mourning that Catholics are apathetic in regard to the whole Christian pattern of life. Our parishioners can hardly be persuaded to reflect, to pray, to read, to converse with any degree of seriousness. The sensory life of the world seems to swallow them whole. They largely pursue the same values as others, they love and hate with the loves and hates of this world. And even when they are persuaded into some form of Catholic Action, it is often in a childish or protesting or moralistic way.

Now, this situation of the church will be part of the lifelong struggle of good Christians. Their church will never be free from the lax, the indifferent, even the scandalous. But let us add that when one has agreed to a truth, he or she is still far from the whole truth. The whole truth about the sterility and neutralism of much of modern Catholic lay life must include the priest in its picture. And the priest's part in all this brings us back to our reflections on a truly Catholic sense of life, a sense of vitality, an understanding of women and men today, a passion to reach and affect other lives. It remains true, for good or for ill, that laypersons take their lead from their priests, that they are men and women of wisdom or of blindness in general accord with the vision of life held out to them by their priests.

One reason, surely, why laypersons are somewhat childish in understanding the faith is that many priests are dogmatists. The faith is often preached as though the congregation were made up either of theologians or of children. So laypersons fail to sense the meaning of Catholic life or to understand their part in its processes. And this remains sadly true because the form in which they receive the faith is sometimes neither adult nor human. It is rather consistently abstract, moralistic, and apart from their lives.

But the human being, as St. Thomas says, is both *mens et manus* — human beings have intelligence and hands. If we give their hands nothing to do, their minds fall to sleep or grow bored or are reassured in their worst assumptions — that the Christian has no task, no responsibility to grow or to love, that the mind can be Christian and the hands remain idle.

We are forced by the nature of things to conclude that priestly courage is the father of lay courage, that a sense of life in the pulpit engenders a layperson's sense of life in public. Further, it is clear that when people's thinking does not engage their hands, two things tend to happen — their hands soften and lose their skills, and so does their thought.

And this brings us to our final reflection on modern lay life as it relates to the life of the priest. The fact is that many priests continue to remain at a distance from adult lay life and its growing capabilities for serious Christian action. There are many signs that this is true, and one can do little more than point to them and leave conclusions to those who seek a change. One thing that strikes many observers is the rather constant rate at which the apostolic ambitions of college graduates tend to level off five or ten years after graduation from college. Active, zealous men and women, highly trained and presumably ready for parish leadership and community work, are simply never heard from during their adult productive years. It is being said by many adult Catholics with increasing bluntness that parish organizations are lifeless, that they offer no intellectual or spiritual formation, that the tasks they undertake are merely appendages of the clerical will.

Another straw in the wind is the undeniable truth that some twenty-five years after the lay apostolic movements began in this country, they are still waging an uphill battle for clerical approval and help. This is true of the Catholic Family Movement, the Young Christian Workers and Students, the Legion of Mary, the revitalized sodalities. And the fault cannot be imputed altogether, or even primarily, to laypersons; it lies in largest measure with priests who have shown small understanding and will to work with the adult energies of the baptized.

As a result of these conditions, a twenty- or thirty-year gap has opened in the ecclesiastical life-span of average laypersons. They are strongly supported by their church throughout childhood and adolescence. They are schooled, given the sacraments, counseled, shriven, and confirmed in their faith. But from the ages of twenty to fifty, years that from both the human and the Christian points of view must be considered as a person's most productive period, laypersons are usually adrift as far as their church is concerned. They are not heard or welcomed or put to serious work; they go about their own business. Finally, they reappear again, usually domesticated and set in their views, to join a parish organization geared to the onset of old age. But their best and most creative years, what of them? They are, by and large, a story of loss, of leakage, and of compromises. They are also years that from the point of view of a person's life in God have been lived at subsistence level, without serious help or challenge or direction from priests.

And this situation continues in spite of the great varieties of lay apostolates today. Given the better education and human opportunities of Catholics, our laypersons are prepared to take on great burdens and handle them with dispatch and professional skill. These burdens would include the social needs of humankind both at home and abroad, the great political challenge of the emerging nations, the needs of the poor, the educational needs of Africa and Latin America and the East.

In the face of these evident worldwide needs, priests continue to act and think as though parish life, continued in a deadly traditional way, could awaken the intelligence and competence of Catholics. Such thinking can only engender bitterness and disillusionment in the Body of Christ.

The solution would seem to lie in the general admission that no parish today can be itself without going beyond itself. The parish produces greatness in its own people by enlarging their horizons to the point where they embrace the world in its truth, complexity, need, and hope. In the process, the parishes of the developed nations contribute human greatness to the church at large, to the lay missions, to the intellectual world, to the many forms of the extraparochial apostolate.

Another interesting aspect of our present situation is the fact of the layperson's status symbols. One notes how priests and laypersons alike have created and maintained them; views of lay prestige, subtly reflected in the attitudes of priests, help or hinder laypersons to understand themselves and to be themselves. By and large, as contemporary life shows, clerical response to lay status coincides nicely with the attitudes of our culture. Priests respect those professions that are rewarded and respected by Americans today. And this is not necessarily a bad thing; doctors, lawyers, Catholic professionals have done admirable work for their communities. One can admit this and still insist that to defer to professional men and women — as always and everywhere the first to be heard, to be worked with, or to be given responsibility in the church — is at best a restrictive view. One is allowed to doubt whether such an attitude corresponds to the needs of the church here and now. Laypersons who are heard from and whose attitudes prevail in the church should not primarily or automatically be those who have "arrived" in a restricted material or professional area of life. Otherwise, the church risks nothing and attains no breadth; it reflects only the social attitudes and methods of people who tend to be self-protective, ruggedly individualistic, and resentful of change.

It is becoming more and more evident that the layperson's development simply will not occur without the priest's help. If such development does occur on its own, by main force of lay conviction, it does so at the price of balance. Isolated lay life is marked by defensiveness; it loses the sense of peace, acceptance, and achievement that is its right. And if we have cause to mourn the fact that some lay movements are not as Catholic as they might be, that laypersons are more critical than helpful, that they see only fault and defect in the church, our own criticism sticks in our throats. The question is, rather, why was priestly influence lacking at the beginning and all along the course of lay development?

One could pass many instructive hours considering papal documents in this regard. They invariably converge on a rather revolutionary but very old and deeply Christian idea. Over the past four hundred years, an untapped reservoir of intelligence, courage, enterprise, and action has been allowed to rise, slowly and mightily. This reservoir is the energy of millions of baptized men and women. No one, or almost no one, thought to tap it, to canalize it, to channel it to its mighty potential. One is tempted to ask, considering the centuries of Christian loss and conflict from the Reformation to the First World War, why these laypersons' energies were not put to use. Why were no laypersons on the foreign missions? Why were they not conducting universities and schools? Why were they not writing theology and philosophy and apologetics? Why were they not instructing the ignorant? Why were they not articulate in public life, in politics, in writing, in the social and political upheavals that have shaped humankind?

And the answer would be, possibly and clumsily, that history was not ready for them. The church was not ready. Perhaps even the laypersons themselves were not ready. And the answer would stand as long as the question was cast merely in historical terms and left at that.

But alter the question and the answer is valueless. Put in present terms, the question "Why are laypersons not taking their adult, responsible place on the church's team today?" cannot be simply put off with "Because the church is not ready" or "Because the times are not ripe."

The times are ripe to the point of falling to the one who will reach and pluck them. And the times have for their spokesperson all our recent popes. According to them and according to the ground swell which is rising daily and yearly in the church and which anyone gifted with sight can see, laypersons are ready. They are ready in impressively large numbers and with even more impressive capability and zeal. It is no longer a matter of the pioneering effort of a few, of this or that voice in the wilderness. History has reached flood tide. The opportunity is at hand today for both priest and layperson to ride and harness the crest.

Priests today who have a sense of the church know that the church is fully itself only when the layperson's adult voice is heard. Such priests will labor to bring laypersons to adulthood, will encourage them to speak, will bear with their fits and starts, their clumsiness, the mistakes that always accompany awakenings. The enterprise we speak of is surely one for people of unusual love and of unusual capacity for courage and suffering. Such people, priests and laypersons both, "will be forgiven their mistakes," Cardinal Suhard assures us. They will be forgiven because all their mistakes, reckoned over a lifetime at compound interest by their harshest critics, still will not equal the one error that alone is mortal and final—the error of inaction, somnolence, and false peace.

Those who resist change in the church become the enemy of the church they serve. We may be willing to pay any price to prevent mistakes in the church, but the price we pay for peace may be the costliest mistake of all. The peace we cherish may be a false peace; if it is, its outward signs will be sterility and stagnation. To cherish this false peace is to violate both nature and grace. A law common to both realities decrees that to neglect the development of life energies or to forbid their development to others is to court personal and social ruin. And to refuse the church the best energies of its own members, out of a false sense of proprietorship or clerical egoism, is to wound the church at its very heart.

THEY CALL US DEAD MEN, 1966

Death and the Bishop: A Parable

Once, a bishop was accosted in public by Death.

My lord, would you have a minute to spare?

The Bishop, who was a hearty man in public, thought he would.

Would you by any chance have a smoke on you? The Bishop who was a chain smoker, but not in public, handed one over.

And Bishop (Death's skinny hand was now on my lord's coat), could you spare the price of a cup of coffee?

The Bishop thought he could, but less heartily. He strove to end the interview, and to pass on. His day was a busy one.

Death clung to him. My lord, he whined, a poor man needs a coat. The winds are chill, even to an unbeliever.

This was pushing a bit hard. But they were in public, and a crowd was gathering. The Bishop, who was not beyond a gesture, had heard of St. Martin of Tours, though he had no ambitions in that direction. He took off his coat. Death put it on. The Bishop's hat as well. And his shoes. And his socks. And his ring. And Death went on his way, humming the "Alleluia" from Handel.

In the days that followed, Death had cause to marvel at his improved situation. People kissed his ring with fervor, his public relations warmed. Indeed a religious revival began to make itself felt.

And a small matter, heretofore thought unpleasant, took a visible turn for the better. Instead of violence and long wasting and absurd eventuality, Death adopted the paternal liturgy of a bishop. Men and women came to him willingly. And a slight blow on the cheek, a gesture of confirmation, sufficed. Things ended satisfactorily for many. There was talk of a larger See, a more ample scope for this promising and adaptive person.

THE CRITIC, APRIL-MAY 1967

Inside and Outside the Church

This conversation with Robert Coles, psychiatrist and author of Children in Crisis, *took place in July 1970, two weeks before Daniel Berrigan was captured by F.B.I. agents on Block Island, after his being underground for four months.*

Coles: I'd like to ask you how unique you consider your experience as a fugitive priest? We are now being told on radio and television and in newspapers and magazines that this is the first time that a Catholic priest has been a fugitive from justice. As I read and listen to those accounts I find myself thinking of our past, our history. What do we in fact know about our history? Who teaches us the history we learn? What don't we ever find out about our past? A teacher of mine when I was in fifth grade used to say, "history, twistory," and I've never forgotten that—because it's quite clear that what we learn about our past is determined by those who have their own reasons to notice this, ignore that, write about one thing and omit mention of something else. We are only now beginning to realize how distorted our history books have been so far as blacks and Indians are concerned. The issue often is one of blatant misrepresentation by historians; but more subtly, a certain tone or shade of emphasis can also lead readers far along into an ideological position which they confuse with a statement of "fact." So, I wonder about the history of the underground in America and other countries. I wonder how unique and surprising and unprecedented your behavior is. I have the impression that this country was founded by people from England who had been in the underground. Not only were many of our first settlers in the underground in England, but in addition they fled, they became exiles; so it was exiles and ex-members of a religious underground who started the United States of America. And then one wonders, apart from the underground railroad in the nineteenth century, whether there isn't a tradition in this country of dissent similar to yours, a tradition whereby people not only say controversial things, but take action that challenges the society in a more significant way, a more comprehensive or unnerving way—and do so without immediately surrendering themselves to sheriffs and judges. I am thinking of the South and Appalachia and the Southwest, where the needs of "justice" as well as "banditry" have prompted men and women to defy authorities believed to be corrupt, or worse.

Berrigan: I do believe very much that what I am doing has a tradition behind it. As for what you now hear about me, I believe in this country one constantly has to contend with the ahistorical and sensational aspects of our news media. We see every day how a "folklore" of sorts is created, how the words and acts of particular individuals are written about and talked about wildly, uncritically, hysterically, romantically, foolishly. And certainly in our culture, religion and the words or deeds of religious men and women are just more grist for the mills that the media run. I mean, every breakaway from the so-called "norm" is going to be a headline for the media, who obviously are interested in all kinds of *grotesquerie* and deviation. I really don't know whether it's useful any longer to consider my status or that of my brother in the light of the Roman Catholic segment of the population. It seems to me that it's much more useful to consider what I am doing in relation to a broad spectrum of dissent that goes back, as you just said, to the act of leaving Europe and settling here, then waging a revolution against England, a colonial power.

While we were in jail in Catonsville I learned about the career of an eighteenth-century American priest whose real name is not even known; evidently he used the alias John Urey. Very little is known about him except by hearsay and by reports and comments written about him after his death. He was executed and his execution was not recorded; his trial was blacked out, and the very disposition of his body was never revealed. But during those years before the American Revolution, when we were well into our terrible and brutal treatment of blacks, this man (who as far as I can piece it together was an émigré from Ireland) landed in Manhattan and shortly thereafter launched himself on a career of harboring fugitive slaves from the West Indies, and getting them North through Manhattan. He is said to have settled in the back room of an Irish pub in the lower East Side of Manhattan, and operated by night out of there. When runaway slaves were caught they were drawn and quartered, burned and lynched. And eventually he, too—after some six years of "illegal activity"—shared the fate of the slaves; he was swiftly killed. So there was an inspiring, mysterious figure out of our national mists for us to think about when we were in jail. At our sentencing I had composed a poem in his honor and read it that day; I hoped to link our fate with his, even though we had not been tested as he was, or shown his degree of lonely courage—and yes, willingness to defy the established "law and order" and the "tradition" of his day.

But in general, alas, one can't make very great claims about the heroism of religious figures in American history. I think especially the Catholic church has been very late in catching up with anything that remotely might be called its own tradition. Catholics in large numbers came to this country relatively late and came as large "ethnic" groups, each impoverished and frightened and essentially oriented toward winning its own place in the sun; for these reasons I think social and political radicalism could not take root. Up until very recently, say five or ten years ago, not only the hierarchy but the overwhelming majority of the church's intellectual and theological leaders were intensely loyal to American's foreign policy. I think in this regard the death of Cardinal Spellman was particularly significant. For a quarter of a century Spellman stood loyally, arm in arm, with the John Foster Dulleses of this nation. Spellman's international prestige, his connection with figures like Churchill and Pius XII and Roosevelt—all of that militated against anything very powerful rising from beneath. And of course I had a firsthand taste of his ideas and his power. He exiled me from New York and from the country.

Coles: You had a personal encounter with him?

Berrigan: It was personal in the sense that he found even so unexciting an organization as Clergy and Laymen Concerned About Vietnam a very personal affront. He and his subalterns were outraged. It was simply intolerable that a priest in his own diocese would make a beginning like this with Jews and Protestants. So I was very quickly got rid of. On the other hand, one can point to the fact that there has been, at least since the twenties, through the Catholic Worker Movement especially, a very solid tradition of biblical dissent from war; and one can also reflect that the first symbolic draft card burnings were centered in the Catholic community, and that as protest advanced into assaults upon draft boards it was in the beginning also a Catholic enterprise. So, I guess one might remember, as Francine Gray has noted, that out of the worst something very new and inspiring can emerge, such is the irony of history. Of course our Protestant communities have never been under the type of suppression that Catholics have on these social issues; whereas we Catholics have been subjected to the iron hand of authority. Again and again we have heard the church speak— on an astonishing range of subjects; and we have been told that once the church has spoken, one must bow one's head and say yes, yes, yes. As an American Catholic, an American priest, you could always point to the fine and progressive statements that have come out of Rome on social issues; but the church here for decades and decades never really responded to those papal encyclicals.

I guess that's a long way of saying a very simple thing: more and more Catholics, a distinct minority but still a significant minority, are finally able to see their place in the tradition of Christianity, and able to gain a much wider and more enlightened perspective on their place, and able to go ahead and work at what *they* believe right (rather than obey blindly the Spellmans of this land) and do that work with their brothers and sisters from other faiths. So in the last five years of this war we Catholics have been able to offer a certain leavening, a certain direction, to the peace movement. Not that Protestants and Jews haven't also had their moral and ethical struggles. Even recently one would hear in only half jest that churches like the Episcopal church could be depended upon to lend us their real estate for actions like Catonsville, but they were often unwilling to *participate* in an effort like Catonsville. In any event, in spite of the tremendous hold on Catholics that the church has, and in spite of the tight discipline of the priesthood and of religious orders, something was evidently gathering, some waters of human passion and concern were rising—were reaching a boiling point—and then, suddenly (it seems to me concurrently with Pope John's whole breakthrough) the kettle tipped over, the brew spilled, and—well, things will never be exactly the same again.

But, to answer your question a little bit more exactly: it seems to me that Roman Catholic identity as such is unimportant, given the times and the real issues. My brother and I have no continuing interest whatsoever in what you might call the internal questions of the Catholic community, whether that be the question of parochial schools or the question of birth control or the question of celibacy; we look upon such matters as in essence retarded questions of a community that still has to catch up with Christ's invitation that all men and women come join him, and be with him—in all their variety. And how sad it is that in the face of the terrible, terrible issues which face this planet's two billion human beings, some in the church, priests and bishops as well as laypersons, continue to be so utterly self-centered, so narrow, so uninterested in others, so aggrandizing—in the name of Jesus Christ! So let the church "catch up" through the efforts of others; and I say that not to be arrogant, but to emphasize how urgent are the tasks that all too few of us are taking the trouble to attend. My brother Phil and I are interested in a kind of raw fundamentalism that has to do with the stance of the church before humankind; we want to help the church make that stance, we want to do what we can in *that* direction. We will join with other communities, Catholic or non-Catholic, religious or thoroughly secular—so long as their seriousness and passion are manifest.

Coles: But you are loyal to the church, which is, after all, an institution.
Berrigan: I hope so.

New York Review of Books, April 8, 1971

We Will Now Hear the Word of God from Each of Our Beloved Chaplains

1.
Rev stump is   believe it or not   for real
as a stump to a grown tree
so he to the verdant gospel
this corpulent burgher   this fictitious
rubbery stamp   Stump
a huckster's   a hack's gospel
Stump   wormwood   miles of smiles

2.
the priest   an irish caricature   wheels up
in his cadillac each a.m. an alderman
to a cobbler's funeral   we   the dead faces
his asperges hisses on   have yet
like Lazarus in hell
one cold Christian curse
bestowal, blessing

PRISON POEMS, 1973

Of Priests, Women, Women Priests, and Other Unlikely Recombinants

They seemed so macho, self-assured, American. They come at me in public like members of a prosecutor's team. I was a suspect in the Matter of the Jesuits v. Berrigan, a case as hopeless of outcome as Jarndyce v. Jarndyce, as unwinnable, a stalemate. Within the club, one had betrayed the rules.

Brothers in Christ? Well, sort of. But it went otherwise when the Jesuit novices appeared in the audience of a public lecture. During the discussion, they took over with a vengeance. "Hadn't I written the following . . . ?" "What were my current views on the church, and the Jesuits?" The tone was high and mighty, they were sniffing out a heterodox, possibly a heretic.

It was chilling, it was educative. One knew at such a time, and winced at the knowledge, that the future was the past. They would go their way, I would go mine. There was no point in dreaming of a new generation, new outlook, culturally free, on the move. This had not been born, it had not even been imagined.

•

The Jesuits are masters of invention. They come out of the culture, they know how to take its pulse, try its winds and trim their sails. Nothing extravagant, nothing ahead of its time, nothing too fast. Consensus, consensus!

And then, of course, the institutional connection. We're not running the Little Brothers of Jesus, we're not running the Catholic Worker. Manifestly. We're running Georgetown University, the School of Foreign Service, we're a nursery for the State Department, only the brightest and best get born here. So connections are everything, dollars are nearly everything. The Shah of Iran, Kissinger, are good dollar connections. Therefore . . .

•

The only Jesuits who look me up or want to talk seriously are by and large third world types, beats, people in personal turmoil at the misdirection, misfirings, injustices, concrete impasse of things. I can't offer them much except a certain wry skill in surviving the Sillys on Stilts. I'm still around; not much more.

73

•

Priesthood? One could huff and puff about mystery, sacrament, sign, moments of grace. These I take to be realities. I am also consoled that they are out of our grasp, control, consuming.

•

We do well in a bad time not to multiply the "bads." Men I respect in the priesthood aren't particularly happy in thinking male. They feel miserable under the weight of life today, just as women do. That "just as" needs, of course, to be treated carefully; women are outside, men in, and the difference is not slight.

At the same time, it's worth saying that spite gets us nowhere. And on the question of priesthood, the "in" male and the "out" female meet on a ground that's fairly familiar to each; one barely making it meets another not making it.

•

In such matters, it helps to stay with a few simple ideas, and see where they lead. But some critics make history (in this case, male history, a bad start) into an obstacle against a better human arrangement. They also mistrust people, including their fellow Christians; the majority of whom do not sit in endowed university chairs announcing the facts of life to those "below." (A little like lifeguards scanning the beaches from chairs the height of the Empire State building.)

Would Christians accept the ministry of women alongside men? My experience is that good will is available; people adjust quickly, even with excitement, to new arrangements, especially when these are presented as forms of requital, righting of wrongs. "How sensible, I never thought of that before" is a common reaction in such matters, from the pew or the church door. But in the pulpit or podium, the process is infinitely more tortuous, the minds out of touch.

•

The healing of the woman bent double, in Luke 13. Nuanced and delightful. I cannot, for the life of me, find anyone who treats it adequately; so here goes a try.

She was bent over, Luke says (and he ought to know) by a diabolic spirit. Could it be that she was fated to dramatize in her frame, the fate of women in that culture (in every culture)? No one says so. Males write history, generally; then to place things beyond reasonable doubt, they write a male commentary. But Luke steps aside from all that; or better, Jesus does. In freedom, he walks over those puerile taboos. He takes the initiative with the woman; "he called her" to him when he saw her condition. Then he "laid his hands upon her." And simply announced her cure. She straightened up. And "she praised God." How sublime! A woman bent double (bent doubly) under the burden of hideous culture and worse religion, is healed of this evil spirit. For "a spirit" is at work in her, not a disease; more accurately, a diseased spirit. The culture, the religion, are rightly regarded by Jesus as demonic. The woman must be exorcised, of culture, of religion. Then she stands upright, then with all her wit and will, she responds to God. Can you see her face at that moment?

The keepers of the status quo are, of course, outraged. If we know anything, we know why. The miraculous is of no account to them. Religion is business. The rule is business as usual. Business is good.

But something deeper than this is in question; the healing of—a woman. Her face, alight with hope and joy, is an affront to their consecrated gloom, the atmosphere of a sanctuary which is no more than a counting house.

Would they have struck back with such irrational fury had a man been healed under the same circumstances? One is allowed to doubt it. In any case, Jesus is at pains to note that he has liberated, not a man, but a "daughter of Abraham." This is her dignity. He refers to it, against all custom. A daughter of Abraham stands, upright; stands up, as we say, for her rights.

In the gospel the title is unique, where "sons of Abraham" abound. In the Jewish Bible, the title is unthinkable. But no commentator notes these things, as far as I can find.

•

To make it in radical circles in America you're supposed to carry about an annotated list of correct attitudes and causes, conformed to stereotype. Thus, toward the end of the Vietnam War, one was "supposed" to be anti-war. At that point it was a position that could hardly be called radical or threatened. It was plain chic. You were (are) also supposed to be pro-abortion; supposed, that is, in the expectation of the left. Your ethical choices are rather presupposed than supposed; that is to say, prepackaged and pushed by social pressures.

I well remember the fury that greeted me when I broke this mold, suggesting publicly that one was required to defend and foster life along its whole spectrum, prebirth to last gasp. Clearly, this talk is intolerable. A whole thicket of misunderstandings arises. In the above case, one is immediately tarred with the brush of bad faith; of a church which is certainly in bad faith; madly anti-abortion, madly attached to war.

You start extricating yourself, as best you might.

Then there are the iniquities of a social system that refuses abortion monies to poor women, while the rich may cut and slice in perfect or near perfect safety, anonymity. You try to make clear the injustice of that. You try, moreover, to point out the horrors of a system that can do no better for its citizens than grant equal access to the death of the unborn. Even as the same machinery moves, with icy singleness, to plan the death of practically everyone.

But who grasps the unity of social method here, the linkages? Death is the solution to every human impasse; death and more death.

•

Women have always washed corpses and prepared them for burial. Women are in charge of delivery rooms — in more ways than one. A metaphor for today? Women make the death decent and the birth possible.

•

Sunday at St. Stephen's in Washington. This is one of very few parishes that take in street people during the cruel winter months, house and feed them. They also welcome the peace community from Jonah House, offer a place to pray and plan the continuing presence there. So it was quite natural and moving and befitting that I be invited to preach; a homecoming.

The Eucharist was conducted by women. And they invited me to serve Communion, along with several others. Black, white, young, old; and women orchestrating, setting the tone, announcing with authority, reverence, and verve, the Lord's body and blood.

It was overwhelming. (Most worship today is crashingly underwhelming.) It was like a quiet expedition of a few friends to the other side of the moon from this clamorous and polluted side. *Solvitur ambulando.* The absurd sexist knot of the centuries, tightened by macho muscle and muddle, was cut.

And all so naturally. The children wandered quietly about, folk prayed, talked up, sang, took Communion. No one seemed to think that anything of moment, beyond the sublime faith and hope that were on the air, was taking place. I wondered if a big stir would have gone through us if Jesus had walked through the chancel door. I doubt it.

How did all this come about, how did great changes get proposed, accepted, even rejoiced at? One could note the absence of hyper-psychologizing, expertise, sensitivity sessions, expensive gurus, hot and heavy breathing, shrinkification, touchy feely follies, inflations of spirit — that plague of self-indulgence. No, the people met with their pastor, they prayed together, struggled, things were worked through.

One notes something else. Liturgy here is no fetish or idol; the god is not fed on the hour or enshrined. The same parish that welcomes women ministers feeds and houses the homeless and hungry. The same parish also blesses and helps those who prepare for nonviolence at the Pentagon, in defense of life. The main business of the parish is not maintaining a nest, womb, space station, esthetic cave for the middle class. It is stewardship and service, up close, day-after-day, blow hot, blow cold. Such conduct, I think, accords with, and confers sanity.

Thus, what might be considered audacious or innovative elsewhere, is taken for granted here. People had the look of those who work at their faith, sweat it out. And the media were absent. Two good signs.

•

I believe we were created for ecstasy. And redeemed for it, at considerable cost. Certain vagrant unrepeatable moments of life tell us this, if we will but attend. Such moments, moreover, are clues to the native structure and texture of things. Not merely are such glorious fits and starts meant to "keep us going," a fairly unattractive idea, but ecstasy fuels and infuses us from the start, is our proper distillation and energy of soul. One could dream the world, the poet says, and one could even dream the eye; but who can imagine the act of seeing? We will never have enough of this, we will never have done with it.

TEN COMMANDMENTS FOR THE LONG HAUL, 1981

Cassocks

I've waited a long time
in and out of jungles
for—I know not what—
"that this mortal body
put on immortality"?

We donned the shabby moth-eaten robes
that so resemble the body, its wear and tear.

This might be the cassock
they gave me on entrance day
forty and more years gone.
Now it most resembles
a second aged skin.
And what trump or season
will see it laid aside?
And what on earth
will I look like then?

THE MISSION, 1986

78

Part Three

GUIDES AND WITNESSES

I Am Renewed

          to rising by that sun
sets courage like a summer round my roots
and welcomes me to stature.

I am renewed to breathing by that bread
sent like a sunrise to my dark
bringing me somehow morrow.

My blood that walks as sullen as a millstream
trumpets the joining of that wine of His.

My life that folds to burial grows bold
and hobbled in its windings climbs the grave.

My ashen words puff up in flame
infused with four winds of word *arise*.

My hollow breast takes heart at hearing Him
sing like a star above its broken roof.

My feet clear gardens in the greying snow:
my winters die for mention of His name.

O let these words remind His wounds of me.

MODERN HUMANIST, OCTOBER 1950

To Wallace Stevens

In each of us you live on, the lodged seed
of empiric imagination
from a great pod blown on death's virile wind.

Credo, we said, *credo*, mirror
to mirror, an inhumanity
before no god.

You are our puzzle. You, naked as we
amid the poverties of our world
— flowers, donkeys, angels meek as water —
cunningly
surpassed us in an hour. Refusing our credo
your marvelous method
made dawn, made a world, made marriage of light and flesh

without God, you said. But is decree of absence
final, when the imagination yields
like a god's brow
godlike men, armed, passionate for their world?

THE WORLD FOR WEDDING RING, 1962

82

A Bit of History

Those Jesuit fathers (wrote Isaac Jogues from New France)
who purpose volunteering for these wilds
   and the service of their Indian brothers
      had best leave behind all regret for
university degrees, honors, prerequisites.
The questions raised by their clients will be other
   than the subtleties their minds
      sharpened and shone on, elsewhere.
TO WIT: can they bear heartbreaking portages
   survive on sour pemican
live under intense extremes of heat, cold, solitude?
The times mitigate the questions, never quite stilling them.
   As I learn, my middle cast cranium
      bending to the intricacies, simplicities
         of a new a b c.

PRISON POEMS, 1973

Living in the Shadow of Egypt: Reflections on Isaiah

I'd like to offer a few thoughts from the Book of Isaiah. I hesitate to use the word "politics" about one of the prophets, but the prophets do seem to be passionately concerned about human justice. And that doesn't seem to be a bad definition of politics. Many of the so-called oracles of Isaiah are embarrasingly political in this sense. It probably comes as a salutary shock for American church people that the deepest roots of Jesus and the prophets have to do with a commonality that is never quite achieved and is always in danger. So I'd like to reflect with you on one of these oracles and consider whether we can see something about ourselves. It's the thirtieth chapter of Isaiah.

It says, "Woe to the rebellious sons and daughters," says the Lord, "who carry out a plan, but not mine"—a certain delightful irony to start with. "And who make a league, but not in my spirit, that they might add sin to sin; who set out to go down to Egypt without asking for my advice." Well, as far as I understand it, the word *rebellious* sets the tone of the oracle in a way which I personally find very unsettling. The word evidently is addressed to a group of so-called "believers" who have side interests involved, having nothing to do with the prior agreement that they have made with the Lord. So on that agreement evidently there was a great deal of invisible writing which had to do with their wheeling and dealing with the Power of this world, symbolized by the phrase "to go down to Egypt." Egypt being, of course, that perennial symbol of empire. I would submit as a strictly minority opinion that the first fact about American Christians is that they go down to Egypt rather than up to the Lord.

They "set out and go down to Egypt without asking for my advice to take refuge in the protection of the Pharaoh and to seek shelter in the shadow of Egypt!" When some of us stand in protest on the porticos of the Pentagon, I think we have a new understanding of what it is "to take refuge in the shadow of Egypt." When you see the thousands of Americans passing into that building for what is commonly called "making a living," I think again the full import of this kind of oracle comes home to you in the swift transformation of consciousness that has occurred within our own lifetime in the direction of absolute violence as a way of life. The going down of the national community into Egypt includes anonymously but rather purposefully the religious community. It includes writing an entirely new and blasphemous pact with powers of this world. This pact is symbolized day after day and year after year by good lock-step citizenship and the payment of taxes for death and the silent consumerism and the ignoring of the covenant of God to the point where, it seems to me, the religion itself is Egyptian. So I take it that the oracle had to do with an irreversible process whereby, after a while, we all really identify ourselves—first of all as Americans, and number twelve or fifteen as Christians—somewhere down the line where it makes no difference anyway. But in every decision, let's say every important decision or non-decision affecting life or death in the world, we are first of all Americans.

I don't know whether any of you have been outside the country for any significant length of time, but coming out of prison, for example, back to America, one is appalled by the truth of this kind of oracle. There has been a swift acculturation of the religious community to the inevitability of violence as a way of life, the inevitability of a way of death. In two years away one traverses something like ten years of degradation in consciousness. It's very difficult to assess the climate of spirituality in which we are being asked to live while we are being asked to breathe it. But if you are outside it and return to it the whole thing is lethal, and you find that either you have lost touch with decent human hope or others have around you, or maybe you have retained it, and that's what sets your head spinning. Well, anyway, on to Egypt.

So they "set out to go down to Egypt, . . . to take refuge in the protection of Pharaoh and to seek shelter in the shadow of Egypt." And this, of course, is without consulting the Lord, which is to say without taking stock of their own (our own) landmarks, our own scripture, our own tradition, our own wisdom which I submit is 360 degrees around from the way of Pharaoh, the way of the empire. Now we have a rather ironic and even bitter conclusion: "Therefore shall the protection of Pharaoh turn to your shame and the shelter in the shadow of Egypt to your humiliation."

It seems to me that the question for Christians is not merely that Pharaoh's method is not working in the real world. I don't think that's what the oracle is getting at at all, as though we have, somehow, a better tactic to offer the world than the world's—a better way of getting along in the world, or a better diplomacy, or a more humane paganism. I think that the point here is something completely other than that. The humiliation involved according to the Word of God here, and the shame, have to do with the sense of the betrayal of the Covenant. That is to say, having defined ourselves in effect and in truth as Americans and having abandoned the way of resistance, the way of nonviolence, the way of fidelity, we ourselves are brought to shame before our children, before our community, before the world, before God. And, as far as my experience goes, the mark of all that shame and humiliation is a loss of hope. It is a loss of that sense that we have something to offer which is not the world's offering, and that we have not joined the ranks of despair which are also the ranks of violence.

This is what strikes me most often these days in those Christian communities which have taken on the coloration of the whole scene and gone with it. There is a dreadful loss of what we commonly call the Christian resource of hope. The sense of going somewhere or of standing somewhere or of being able to say something is gone. It's very difficult to put into words because it's a matter often of atmosphere. But it is nonetheless real as far as I'm concerned. And maybe we would like to question one another and question ourselves about those resources, whether we have a sense that they're still available. Do we have a sense that our communities and our families and our work have something to say which is a powerful "No" to the death game, the game of Egypt?

I'll skip a little here, down to verse seven: "For Egypt's help is worthless and empty; therefore, I have called her Rehab, who sits still." It's a kind of term of contempt for Egypt offered by the God of purported believers. The method of Egypt is to "sit still"; it's a stalemate in the world. It's basically ahistorical. "And now, go, and write it before them on a tablet and inscribe it in a book, that it may be for a time to come a witness forever, for they are a rebellious people and lying sons and daughters who will not hear the instruction of the Lord." And so evidently the prophet has been told, "Look, there's not much really that can be done." And one comes to believe that; there's not a great deal that can be done; there's only a little that can be done. That's one way of putting the stalemate—not that a little is to be despised, but that we don't even see the little because we either have a notion that only a lot matters, that is to say big change, or cheap change, or sudden change. Or perhaps we've given up on the whole thing.

In that kind of stalemate, the prophet first of all knows the extraordinary modesty of the real job and that the people won't accept it by and large. He's told them, "Look, at least take some notes for the future. Maybe your children will come on them. But meantime it's very important to have the truth on record in some real way so that the truth is not entirely lost. They won't hear it so write it down. Put it away in a diary. Put it on a shelf, put it in the bank, put it somewhere. Put it in a bottle and throw it over a cliff. Someone will pick it up." I thought that it was a marvelous piece of irony in a kind of implied image there: "Don't act as though the truth doesn't exist because it doesn't get heard." And if it can't be spoken, then write it down. Write it down somewhere. And if it can't be shouted, then whisper it to a friend. But don't despair to the point where you think that because illusion and fantasy and lies and deception and violence are the public order of the day that that is reality, or that that is truth. After a while, of course, one can become persuaded that it is the only thing available. Go write it on a tablet or inscribe it in a book so that it may be a witness forever, "for they are a rebellious people, lying sons and daughters, who will not hear the instruction of the Lord. They say to the seers, 'See not'; and to the prophets, 'Prophesy not to us what is right; speak to us smooth things; prophesy illusions, leave the way, turn aside from the path; let us hear no more of the Holy One of Israel.' "

I would suggest that the Greeks were right, that the first casualty in the time of violence is truth. Furthermore, we, and possibly our children, will not live in a different world or atmosphere than that, given the fact that they are to have any world at all—which is a big given. That is to say, our lifetime is not a transition between, let us say, all war and peace. There is no peace. We are living our lives in the uneasy feverish twilight of hot war and cold, and there is no peace. Yet somehow the truth must be heard and spoken and accepted, first of all, by ourselves. And in the meantime, of course, the whole public scene, at least since the 1960s, is polluted, and public religion and public violence have joined hands, whether at the White House or the Pentagon, and we have smooth seers all over the place.

And in that scene, which is one of astonishing religious capitulation, we are asked to believe and to resist. One of the most dreadful phenomena, it seems to me, of the American public scene today is that religion has become another ingredient of the empire. But in my experience, what is new is the extent of it all. And then the fallout is the notion that the first covenant is with America, and that is the only one worth talking about, the only one worth paying tribute to, and the only one worth dying for.

The whole thing is very powerful and disturbing. But I did want to point out that toward the end there's a pattern in these oracles; the promise is always renewed. If the public word is bitter and shattering it doesn't end there as though the oracle is just giving us the bad news. So we have verse 18, way down at the end: "Therefore the Lord waits to be gracious to you; therefore the Lord exalts himself to show mercy to you. For the Lord is a God of justice; blessed are those who wait for him."

Well, it's extraordinary. You know all the bad news has ended in a "therefore," which is most ironic, because it's most illogical. Why should the Lord look upon such a terrifying scene of moral disarray, and then say, "Therefore, I am with you"? Isn't that amazing? So the promise doesn't depend upon our performance, which, of course, is our only hope. God help us if it did! But it's marvelous in that it doesn't say, "In spite of all that—in spite of everything you are not, in spite of everything you have done and have not done—I will be with you." No, it says "Therefore I am with you." So, evidently, in some awful sense, the bottom has to be reached before the promise becomes really apprehensible. And I submit that we're very near the bottom—if not in it.

This is something gracious and unexpected that we should dwell upon in our hearts: "The Lord exalts himself to show mercy to you. For the Lord is a God of justice; blessed are those who wait for Him." Well, I love the word "justice" there, because the whole oracle has been about our injustice, and there's a subtle reminder that he's a little different than we are, another reason for gratitude.

The final verse says, "Blessed are [you] who wait for him." This is not just a common, gentle conclusion. I think sometimes there's no deeper expression of belief and of life than to say, "We're waiting for him." There's not a great deal that we can do in the world; there's something we can do, but the deepest thing is to wait for him. Simone Weil said she's waiting on God. We're told throughout many of the parables in the New Testament to be alive and to be awake and to be vigilant and that "he comes like a thief," and so on and so on. It's a beautiful way of putting the kind of ethical resistance which is recommended elsewhere. The deepest thing, I would think, is not that we counter the ways of the world, but that we are standing somewhere. Amen.

RADIX, SEPTEMBER-OCTOBER, 1977

Thomas Merton

Well over a decade ago, the long sea trek of Thomas Merton culminated in his death in Bangkok. The facts of his death are so simple, so well known. Yet even at this long remove, they stop the heart in its tracks. Everyone knows how he died; a decade later, who can be resigned to such a death? Who has gotten used to his absence? We bear it because we must.

We were not sure, when he set out across country and into the East, what he was thinking—especially about us (the "us" in this case being the nine who in May of 1968 invaded the draft board at Catonsville, Maryland, and burned draft files). How did Merton take all that? The question was on all our minds. That summer, he wrote a kind of reaction in a Catholic weekly, *Ave Maria*. The clearest impression I have of his mood is a mix of alertness and bewilderment. He was stirred, fearful, didn't know where such acts might lead. He trusted us, but his trust was tested hard. In any case, he seemed to need more time to make up his mind.

We had been through this before. Tragedies, new directions connected with the war, set him rocking. Isolated as he was, he had no chance to be in on the sweat, discussion, prayer that went into an act like Catonsville. And when catastrophe struck, as in the case of the self-immolation of Roger Laporte at the United Nations in 1965, he tended to panic. One or another of us would thereupon go down to the monastery to help put things in focus. He simmered down, thought things over, and went on with us, at his own measured pace.

But after Catonsville, from May to December of 1968, there were no more visits to the monastery. I don't remember quite why, except that neither side pushed for a meeting. I can only record the impression that he was tired, fed up with a war that seemed to go on forever, that had no sense, no outcome. More, Merton was finding that even the solitude of his Kentucky eyrie was not immune against crazies. They kept coming around, like crows to a feeding station.

Then a breakthrough. A new abbot was elected at Gethsemane. Merton's hopes, deferred for years, welled up. He planned a pilgrimage into the world, some twenty-five years after he had left it, on a new basis indeed, seeking out a possible place for himself, a new setting.

His life had been a long patience, a long loneliness. There is no point in going over once again all he had suffered during the monastic years. The story has been told in part; someone will tell it more completely in good time. When the news came that he was setting out, we rejoiced because his hopes, so long put off, so arbitrarily squelched, were about to spring. One phase was over; it had seemed at times like the fate of those stuck at the base of Dante's original seven-story mountain:

> *colui che mostra se piu negligente*
> *che se pigrizia fosse sua serocchia . . .*

Always with the difference, of course, that Merton had put in his time, not as a time server, but simply as a patient, hard-wrung, gracious monk, a kind of long-distance runner in place, a master of hangman's humor. And to me, a friend peerless among friends, a gift given once or twice in a lifetime.

We had endured a few things together. There were crises and good times on both sides, things to laugh and weep about. The late fifties and the sixties plunged us into a scene where sanity at times looked like madness, where the highest art possible to the artful was simply hanging on.

In his case, the art followed the old classical norm: It hid itself well. To the world at large, he was the immensely productive author, book upon book, a large audience assured. He had the industry of a beehive, the discipline. More, he had a mandate from the community: "Keep at it." The scope of his interests grew apace; he began to take seriously the world he had shrunk from with the fastidiousness of the new convert. At first, that world had seemed manifestly bad; then gradually (maybe because he met specimens like us, hot from the hot spot), not so bad. Then the facade of fallen hopes, fallen loves, fallen kingdoms — it fell away. The world showed him its tragic bloodshot face.

By then he was getting somewhere.

I mean on his own terms, as he came to understand them: a monk, a man of prayer, a worldly man on the qui vive, a recluse for the kingdom's sake, a lucid, cutting mind that in a hundred ways helped us stand somewhere, mainly by standing with us. In entering the monastery, he had taken a large step backward from our world, a tactic the French proverb commends "in order to leap further." The leap was not long in coming, a mighty one indeed, a world record.

He leapt, and yet he stayed put. Rumors came and went; he was leaving the monastery, he was gone, he had returned to New York, he had left the church. It was all slightly dotty, or more than slightly; malice lurked in some of it. But such effluvia meant little to him; he issued a good-humored denial of this or that account of purported backsliding and kept plugging away at his own life. He was moving into more responsibility, an elder by now, in charge of the novices of the community.

By and large, the early sixties were good times. He brought people of all kinds to the monastery; his spirit was ecumenical; now he had scope to try out his instincts. Protestant seminarians came from Louisville; a rabbi from Canada; Catholics such as Philip, myself, many others. Merton wanted the young monks to learn something of the currents then riding fiercely across the church and the world. As usual, he put things bluntly: There would be no monastic prayer worth talking about without such exposure, grounding. One noticed changes in the novitiate—vitality, good art, good books, clippings from newspapers. It was worlds apart from the musty sacristy religion that would drive even a mouse berserk with boredom. Dignity, lucidity, gracefulness, clean air—I remember it well, with a pang. And I wonder about the pang those young monks must feel now, years after, wherever life has borne them.

I forget time and years; it must have been around 1965 that he brought friends together for a retreat. (Gordon Zahn wrote of it at some length in *Another Part of the War*, published in 1979.) Some ten or twelve of us were invited to discuss and pray together, according to his suggestion, on the subject "roots of protest." There was a Mennonite theologian, an aged revered minister (he ought to be invoked rather than named: A. J. Muste, pray for us), Catholic Workers, a friend from Hutchins's Center for the Study of Democratic Institutions in Santa Barbara, a few priests, my brother Phil, myself. Those two or three days have, in retrospect, the charged aura of a myth; practically all who took part have by now either died or undergone prison.

One delicious episode stays with me. Philip and another priest had arrived late. As things transpired, a liturgy had been proposed; it was to be ecumenical—but within limits. Merton passed the word to us Catholics: By instruction of the abbot, only we were allowed to take communion. (What seems barbarous now was then fairly standard practice. The separated brethren [*sic*] were still being "separated out," a quite active verb for Catholics.) We agreed. In fact there was nothing else to do; we were guests. Besides, the prohibition was no great departure from standard discourtesy. In any case, Philip careened in, just as communion was under way. Not having had the law read to him, and burdened with few native inhibitions, he simply passed the communion to whomever was in his vicinity. In the vicinity of course were several Protestants. They took communion. *Sic solvitur*. One of them said to me later, "If only I had known things were so simple! What are we waiting for?"

On another occasion, a Baptist minister and I visited Merton. On the way to the monastery, he told me of a nightmare he had sweated through the night before. He dreamed he was at the monastery chapel, taking part in a Catholic Mass. Shock, cold sweat indeed. We arrived at the monastery somewhat late in the evening and were shown to rooms. The next morning, when Merton came to greet us, he proposed that we take part in the community liturgy. A "Catholic Mass" if ever there was one! I stole a sidelong look at my friend; his eyes held a look seldom seen on land or sea. Merton had that way with him—face the incubus, exorcise it. *Sic solvitur*. . . .

I remember him as quintessentially a modern man to his fingertips: his slang, his ironies, the bravery that kept him on the move, his skepticism about big claims and names, his mind's cat prowl in the long night of the world, his skill at putting a finger on a sore spot, an illusion, a put-on. He was a monk; he was in touch. He was never, not for a moment, *relevant* or *efficient*, those catch basins for waste and want. Indeed, he would shoot fire when such words came up, on monastic lips or others. He met phoniness in high places with a barely controlled fury whose second phase on good days was hilarity and mockery. On bad days, there was no second phase. Then he simply lived with what he was forced to, knowing bad days do not last forever.

He was complex; but he was more than a grab bag of great talents. Complexity went deeper; he had lived several avatars before the monastery years, was instructed in the mad modern dance, which had spun him through Europe and New York, through Marxism, hedonism, agnosticism, into church and monastery. Integrating all that into a life of personal truthfulness, sanity, could not be easy. There always shone through the radiant, disciplined face that subdued soul light.

He hadn't, to change the image, gotten found by leaving a trail of debris behind. He brought along on the mountain of purgation every bone conviction, love unfeigned, courtesy, a sardonic sidelong glance. It took years I think, before he could trust himself to be himself, something perhaps usual in tumultuous converts. Then in the last years, everything came together; he was engaging, noncombative, listening, graceful, utterly warm of heart, even naive and gentle. He had no fetishes; he had nothing but the truth to defend, and that was a light burden. I remember his soul force, in the Gandhian sense, his strength, the plain talk you could expect from him. When he saw something, he said what he saw and stood by it. And he expected the same of his friends, that we would pay up.

What life exacted of him there is no need of totting up here. For perhaps the final ten years, tragedy entered his life. Severe limits were put on his writing and publishing; he was censored, reproved, forbidden to write on nuclear arms or modern war. He began to see the contradictions and follies that make ecclesiastical structures into secular traps. He was denied half of his soul, that half that was newly afire with the mad truth of the times: that the times were death ridden, that the society was hell-bent on a suicide run. He saw it, and he could not say it. A new vocation was flowering in the shell of the old: peacemaking. They said nay, they blessed their nay. And the act drew blood.

There was a kind of crazy consonance to all this. It was the mid-sixties; if you were in the church, in his circumstances, it made sense (so we were preached to also) to make no sense. Blood was being shed in prodigious draughts by Americans, the Draculas of war. Some few thought it was time, past time, to staunch the flow, given the skills of healing that the church was purportedly in possession of. Nothing of the kind, or better, for a very long time, a time of random, needless death, very little of the kind. In my case, the big guns of obedience were wheeled out, wondrous statements were uttered as to the inadmissibility of serious action. Like this one: "Such actions [as Catonsville] are Christian; they are not however Jesuit." Things could hardly have been put more damningly by the worst traducer of the order.

Merton's case was roughly parallel. Juggernaut and judgment, the war went on; it was declared off limits to the conscience of monk and Jesuit. The monks' role was prayer; mine was—what? Anything, as long as it remained ineffectual, law-abiding. (Gospel-abiding? The question seldom arose.)

It was the law, not the war, that threatened to destroy us both. The irony once stated (an irony I find almost unbearable even today), one can leave it at that. The law did not destroy him or me. We survived the law, including the law of the church. Whether the law should ever have been invoked, whether its invocation was not rather an incanting of the gods of war, or whether, on the other hand, his order and mine should have encouraged and blessed our work, our attempt at being faithful (peacemaking instead of complicity)—these are painful matters indeed. Today it must be added that such matters remain largely unresolved in the church, as indeed they are unresolved in the secular kingdom of the blind. They hover on the air, a nuke of Damocles. What was unlearned (better, plain rejected) in the sixties is still rejected. The brave protests of popes John and Paul against nuclear adventuring and genocidal tradeoffs—these cries wander like landless doves over the flood, return without relief to the beleaguered ark.

Still my friend suffered and did what he could, kept messages coming, stuffing them in bottles and casting them on the tide. He never gave up; he stayed put. If he cried Armageddon, he did so largely in the teeth of a wind that all but knocked him flat. His was, I think, the purest kind of truth telling, the kind that endures even in the empire of the deaf.

My mind returns often to this—he stayed put. It was not that he hid out, or vegetated, or gave up, or joined the officers' club, or hardened, or softened, or shrugged away his plight or ours. It meant that he had a place, a center, convictions that held, a sense of himself, wary and troubled as he was.

He reminds me of one of the Vietnamese Buddhist monks he so loved and learned from: Say, a monk of Hué dragging his altar into the streets and sitting down there to protest the mad war. The tanks arrive; the monk stays put. Because the monk stays put, the tank is confounded. What does a tank do when a monk refuses to "move when so ordered"? The tank has choices, but they are not large. Can we imagine a tank rubbing its iron skull in puzzlement before the immovable monk? The "it" has met the "he." It is a confrontation worth pondering; the implications are both millennial and hotly contemporary.

The impasse comes to this: The monk is more ready to die than the tank is to kill. And that is the rub indeed, for the tank is built to kill, only to kill. But the monk is not "built" at all, in order to do anything at all. If he is "for" anything, if he serves any purpose, if he has any goal in life, it quite surpasses the understanding of the tank (which is not quite equal to the prognostications of, say, a think tank). Indeed, the monk would also rub his skull in bewilderment at talk of "goals," "efficiency." For he serves no purpose, he has no goals, he is not "for" anything.

If he were to put the matter in words (and that also is unlikely), the monk might say something like this: He is called to be a pure and truthful expression of life itself. Of life. To be. Neither to strive, to gain, to lose, to earn, to spend, to be skilled, to be a pro, to ideologize, to make a mark, to be honored, to be dishonored, to survive, to perish. . . . It is all beside the point. The words befit the iron tread, the steely skull of the tank; they are not the words of a monk at all. Indeed, the words could imply a profound spiritual malaise, jaundice, disenchantment, disarray, even violence, thirst for blood. They imply a "come hither" to the tank. They offer a clue as to why tanks are thought necessary, are assembled, move in packs, why they do so well what tanks are made to do: kill.

But what has all this, this charade of force, this huff and puff, to do with the monk? He has something else to do: to stay put, to be. Especially to be, in places and times where life itself (his gift, his only love, his bride)—where life is endangered, put to naught, despised, obliterated. Then, oh, then he knows what must be done, he does what must be done!

And at that point something akin to the miraculous occurs. This solitary, foolish, exotic one, this silent refuser, this stubborn sitter, brings something to pass. Alive or dead, he brings it to pass. It being a matter of supreme indifference to him whether the tank stops short of him or rolls over him. He brings something to pass. He does something no other can do, because he stays put when all prudence, all legitimate self-interest, all logic, all casuistry unite in crying, in warning, "GET UP, MOVE IT, GET THE HELL OUT, THE TANKS ARE COMING!"

No, he stays put. He knows what he knows. What he knows is, he is called to stay put—an ecological rightness, nice to the hair's breadth—there in the path of the tank. This is his native ground; dangerous, they cry, they warn, flat out uninhabitable. No matter; where he belongs.

What does the monk offer us—the future, the unborn, the jaded, fed-up resisters, the makers and drivers of tanks? All of us, that is, whose destiny in one way or another converges on this unlikely distant scene: the tank and the monk? Who will prevail? Shall mere flesh and blood prevail? Shall spirit prevail? Shall death be robbed of its victory, its sting?

We long to know. I think the monk knows.

PORTRAITS, 1982

Merton

The years
pouring out
mick & mock & this & that

like a horn of plenty
in the hot hands
of the rich bored

& a friend maybe or even 2
but Christ only
1 you

UNPUBLISHED, CA. 1982

Dorothy Day

Dorothy Day's pilgrimage must surely be accounted an extraordinary life and accomplishment.

Writing as I do shortly after her death, any evaluation must be modest and tentative; the gestation of her memory is barely under way. Yet her place in the history of the century would seem already secure. It begins with those who loved her, lived with her, worked and wept with her, and both feared and faced her death. With them, as with thousands of others, there could be no doubt that Dorothy now belongs to history—as exemplar, mystic, lover of life, fighter of the good fight.

She is gone from us; the work of iconography so stoutly resisted by her (and her church) can get under way. As can those cooler and equally important evaluations of Dorothy from the point of view of culture, political aspiration, sociology, secular ethic. In this respect she was much like her great friends Merton and Maurin; she can be understood only as a Catholic Christian. But unlike them, she was no cosmopolite; her grip was on the American idiom and style and mental workings, the continental insularity, both liberating, and petrifying, of this country; it seems fair to say that such a phenomenon as Dorothy Day could have burst on no other scene than ours.

More of this later. But in calling her American to the marrow, I am not thinking merely of her marxist idealism, her pragmatism, the way she exasperated ideologues and gurus by joining issues to lives, her passion for freedom to the point of waywardness, her star performance in the jungle market of journalism, her life of gyrovague, disturber of mordant peace. Her sense of being daughter of this time and place went beyond; it brought her into the Catholic church.

There she found the basis, ground, for her adversary style: the signs, the "social doctrine," the ideology, the sacred she so yearned for, transfiguring the struggle, giving it scope, purpose, a final day. She found, so to speak, the Book from whose pages, warnings, frowns, threats, promise she could look up and shout aloud, in terror, anger, justice outraged.

In Catholicism she came not so much to her own place (too static a term), but to her true self, in natural setting—and motion. Herself, embattled. But never alone, never for once deprived of a "cloud of witnesses." A struggle now against forces clearly identified, a longer more enlightening history of life as drama; all this, and a larger vista of hope. She wrote that she had nothing to regret or leave behind in becoming a Christian. It was a strange, wonderful statement, for she had indeed lost much. But what she had lost (her lover and friend) she measured against all she had gained; a terrible beauty was born. And perhaps in such a disclaimer she was thinking not so much of her great renouncement as of the feckless, bohemian episodes that preceded it. In any case, all that is done with.

Those of us who knew her only in her later years were tempted, I think, to regard her rather thoughtlessly. That is, we saw her as a phenomenal presence whose greatness and goodness had descended full blown in our midst, easily won and as easily dispensed abroad. She seemed always to have been as she was: serene, graced with her aura of piety and pity.

Perhaps this sense of her, wrong as it was, was inevitable. For she was the soul of reticence about her past—or, indeed, about her present estate. Except for a few revealing passages in *The Long Loneliness*, her brisk mind was at home, so to speak, outside itself. Her ordinary grist was the stuff of life: work, faith, friends, hope, the poor, rent and food, work strikes, cupidity and injustice, and above all the skeletal leer of war mocking our days and nights. These were the rub, the horror and hope—of her life, of the lives of those who wished to join up and walk to her beat. These must be argued through, acted upon. She banged out her praxis on kitchen tables, in buses, before audiences of every kind, in every corner of the land.

An American woman came of an American family; a touch, no more, of Eugene O'Neill or Arthur Miller. In Dorothy's childhood, Day senior roamed the country, East Coast to West, someone called a "newsman," perpetually on the spoor of something called a "story." Whatever it was, it was to make their fortune. It was the quintessential American dream; the children were caught up in it—a hit-and-miss education, fat days and lean, life on the road. And amid it all, drinking it in, this wide-eyed, intensely observant child.

It was a good family, recalled with affection. The parents were never dull or demeaning: warm at the center, a bit chilly at the edges. The child loved books, read like a demon: Jack London, Kropotkin, Upton Sinclair, Frank Harris on the Haymarket anarchists, Vincent Sheean, Eugene Debs. There was an infant brother whom she loved boundlessly. All considered, hers was a lucky start. She tasted love, a first taste of nature.

Her first crisis was a religious one. She tells it vividly, as though turning a single page, a memory thin as membrane. On the one hand, she was studying everything from the anarchist history of America to the New Testament, a regime unrefined and chaotic.

Then she would look outward, into her poor Chicago neighborhood. She saw violence, injustice, strikes, police flailing away, political martyrs. She saw America: a brutalizing, defacing, death-dealing machine. Many years later she was to refer to it in disgust and anger as "this filthy rotten system."

She read Jesus' words, the words of the early disciples, found them dovetailing her vision of the way the world should go. She looked for Christians, and she saw something else. The Christians were like everyone else.

In recoil, one thinks, she joined the Socialist party in her first year of college.

Children look at things very directly and simply. I did not see anyone taking off his coat and giving it to the poor. I didn't see anyone having a banquet and calling in the lame, the halt and the blind. . . . I wanted, though I did not know it then, a synthesis. I wanted life and I wanted the abundant life. I wanted it for others too. . . . I wanted everyone to be kind. I wanted every home to be open to the lame, the halt, and the blind. . . .

Only then did people really live, really love their brothers. In such love was the abundant life, and I did not have the slightest idea how to find it.

She is now a college student, winner of a scholarship. She is reaching out, for affection, concordance of minds. She has also undergone a kind of preconversion; and though she is nowhere within shouting distance of the church, she has taken its measure, she knows where to find it. She knows what the church looks like; or, infinitely more to the point, she knows what it should look like.

There is a mutuality here worthy of note. What the church is, or will be, to her is analogous to what she is, or will be, to the church. I mean something extremely simple. When Dorothy enters its portals, the American church will undergo momentous changes, as though at a signal, a trumpet blast from a baroque ceiling. She will speak of Peter Maurin, her friend and mentor, as a "one-man revolution." But we are not to be fooled; there is a slight correction to be made. The revolution was in fact hers, a woman's. It was she who grounded Peter's lightnings, in long travail and patience, in planning and scrimping, she who got the Catholic Worker houses going and kept them going, who instructed and guided the young, bore with the foolish and ne'er-do-wells.

It was she who kept insisting: There is no mercy without justice. Kept insisting: The most dreadful injustice of the modern world is the crime of war.

It is here, I would judge, we touch on her great gift to the church. She saw the world wobbling perilously; its axis was the tip of a blade. The hand holding the sword that upheld the world, that whirled it crazily, belonged to a very ape of God. It was the hand of Mars, god of death. And until he was deprived of his prey, not by political means or military means, but by the hands of the Crucified, the world would never again move in its proper orbit and light. It would fall, literally and from grace.

Further, the saving hands must be our own, the hands of believers. Thus, she restored to our hands their proper function and anointing. But this was far in the future.

I was happy as a lark at leaving home. I was sixteen and filled with a great sense of independence. I was on my own, and no longer to be cared for by the family. . . . It was experience in general that I wanted.

I did not think in terms of philosophy or sociology. I continued the same courses I had been taking, Latin, English, history and science. . . .

She was, as she tells, quite pragmatic about college, and is unabashed in the telling. She lazed about, soaking up her neighborhood, skipped classes that held no interest, seemed to find in friendship her real awakening. Officially speaking, she turned in a tolerable performance; but like so many of her tribe (who were to make of her style a hallmark of a later decade), she kept her distance from straight academe; worked, so to speak, her own side of the street.

Then she came to New York, and the second broad phase of her life got under way. She began work as a newspaper woman, much in the way of Emma Goldman, a liberal among the Greenwich Village playwrights and poets. She moved among bohemians, serious artists, workers, theorists, parasites.

To Dorothy it was as though she were shot from the mouth of a cannon. From a relatively staid and sequestered campus of the Midwest, she was thrust into a volcano: O'Neill, Eastman, *The Masses*, Terry Carlin, Michael Gold. "No one ever wanted to go to bed," she writes (surely a hyperbole), "and no one ever wished to be alone."

With her suffragist friends she took to the streets of Washington and was arrested. That time, the ordeal was relatively brief. The second arrest was a different matter entirely, a taste of savage American justice, involving a hunger strike and a punishment cell.

She did a year's stint as a nurse at King's County Hospital. Then she left for an extended stay in Europe (with whom and for how long she does not say). She passes that year over with the cryptic remark that, after all, she never intended to write an autobiography, but only to "tell of the things that brought me to God and that remind me of God." Evidently her trip, and her companion, did neither.

Her state of soul at the time remains a puzzle—most of all, one senses, to herself. She oscillates between disbelief and—something, a country dimly perceived, then lost to her, a mirage. In yet another mood she draws apart in some church; but the stillness is a pit; she sits there trapped. Where does she belong, what is she to do with her life?

Hers was, among other things, a crisis of imbalances, of gifts misused, neglected, taken for granted. She was a person of great stamina, carrying a load that she shifted from right hand to left, but never without deep discomfort, a sense of being off center. How is she to manage her journey less painfully, how attain balance? She can perhaps carry everything on her head, or on her back—or in her heart. She could drag her possessions, gifts, insights, the pain of the world, behind her. But these are temporary appeasements, respites. She tried them all. And each and all, after a time, were unavailing. Everything of her life, her loves, skills, writings, friendships, family, social passion—things she admired and envied in others, emoluments, radiances, gifts—in her hands they turned to stone.

For all her reticence, the suffering of those years comes through, a suffering that soured the honey of life. By any worldly standard, which is to say, by any standard available to her and her circle, her life was all success and solid achievement. Who could fault her? She had courage, a sharp mind, a tongue to match. She had nursed the ill in a great urban hospital, worked on the staff of respected papers. She had been arrested and jailed, the ultimate honor among her kind. And so on, and so on. What more was she asking of life?

> The man I loved, with whom I entered into a common law marriage, was an anarchist, an Englishman by descent, and a biologist.

This was the "more." After much tumult and storms that never seemed to clear, Dorothy's life touches shore, "out of the arm of the sea." Her prose grows idyllic, characters wander in and out, hilarious, feckless friends, unclassifiable fauna of sea and land, crawling, sidling, running to her side. The figure is doubly tempting, since she and her lover set up a rickety household on the Staten Island shore. There the tides, moon changes, days and nights washed ashore practically anyone imaginable. She has total, vivid recall. The island saga is perhaps the most detailed and delightful period of her life, as the woman of mid-fifties recalls the woman of twenty-four. Forster is by no means her first love, but he is the last, all that matters. Sasha, Freda, the beachcomber Lefty and his lobster pot, the leaky old cottage bobbing in autumn storms like a badly anchored buoy, Peggy Cowley and her furs and cosmos and "highbred nose," Dorothy supporting herself and her lover by pounding out potboilers; the hilarity and innocence, the pearly glow before the dark, before the dawn; something of both, something beyond either. Dorothy conceived a child.

It was the child's birth, she says, that brought her faith to term. An old story but a new one, too. She was to develop it masterfully, not only in the pages of her "nonautobiography," but in New Masses, for which she wrote an account of Tamar's birth that was to become a classic.

The baby was born; it must be baptized. The imperative lay as strong on her as the child had weighed within her. And immediately another crisis was under way. She was already, at least in spirit, a Catholic; the child would shortly be baptized in the church. And her lover, the father of her child, came down hard; he was irrevocably opposed to religion: hers, the child's, anyone's.

The wonder here is not that Forster, enigmatic, solitary, watery dreamer, ineffectual pure spirit, who despised, distanced himself not only from the tin-can culture of America, but from any attempt to clean up the social debris—the wonder is not that he stood against the Catholicism of that day. As a measure of his world, an expression of its logic, ethos, conscience, concordance with the evidence available (an evidence by no means exciting or evangelical), his animus, his sense of loss and pain and resentment — all these make considerable sense.

He raised very hell with her purpose. And his anger had a deeper source than an infant's baptism; he was intelligent enough to sense that things would by no means stop there, an aspersion cast over a child. The mother who thrust the infant into magic and the unknown would surely and shortly follow. And how right was his instinct, in more ways than one.

I think of this man, this survivor, the one left out, the one from whom, like a Graham Greene protagonist, she must tear heart and destiny and child. Her decision to convert cut clean as a death stroke; not only her death, but his as well. A double indemnity it must have been: Catholicism laying claim to her, and just as ruthlessly disclaiming him.

She read the words of Jesus, austere and uncompromising, concerning a faith that sunders families, breaks blood ties, violates nature at its marrow. All for the sake of a higher calling, the call of Christ, arranger and wrecker of lives. She heard the call, and Forster did not. And, in justice, it must be added that the voice of Christ, summoning her to leave her lover and friend, was filtered through a "law of the church," which she, with every fiber of her soul, identified with the voice of the gospel harrower.

In another time, after Vatican II, one is led to speculate on a far different outcome. Need their tie have been broken so cruelly, her beloved set adrift?

In any case, Dorothy stated simply and finally the choice before her, a choice that at that time, and according to her lights and the law, allowed of no leeway.

> To become a Catholic meant for me to give up a mate with whom I was much in love. It got to the point where it was the simple question of whether I chose God or man.

The decision entered her being. For the rest of her life, it colored her attitude toward marriage, remarriage, divorce, sexual conduct — and the church. A time would come when priests and religious would marry, despite the law, when lay men and women would divorce and seek other partners. In every case her reaction was unyielding; her crisis, its cost, welled up. If she (and he?) had made a choice that by every criterion must be accounted heroic, why was less to be expected of other Catholics, at any time, under whatever impulse?

On social issues she was a furious innovator. She found the church a tabula rasa, and with great pain and the controlled nicety of genius, she inscribed the texts, lost or defaced or simply erased by cultural banality: Thou shall not kill. Turn the other cheek. Walk a second mile. . . .

And all the while, in matters sexual and marital, she conserved, controlled, broke friendships, tossed free-loving hippies out on their ears, forbade Catholic deviants access to her paper. A tempting analogy occurs:

When the chips were down, Tamar was *her* child, not Forster's and hers. And when other chips were down, *The Catholic Worker* was *her* paper, not hers and the other editors'. There on the masthead stood the redoubtable words for some thirty-five years: Publisher and Editor, Dorothy Day.

Only after a long time did she give place once more to her native tenderness. In old age, she began to inquire with feeling about those she had once loved and named her friends, then written off. She confided that she was visiting her husband, now old and ill, in hospital. She inquired after Philip and Elizabeth and others, wrote them letters, sought news of the children.

Her Catholic conversion remains a wondrous mystery. Why did Dorothy, in the maturity of her gifts, rejoicing in the fruition of her body, why did this agnostic and anarchist, veteran of jails, marches, fasts for justice, soul mate of a man who was, as she confessed, the very half of her soul, the Dorothy of strikes and prisoners and the condemned of the earth, this woman whose natural habitat was the underworld of the victims, the excluded, the urban poor, this woman so sensual, worldly wise—why did she renounce, against all sound reason, her only love, cut her past, anger and bewilder her friends?

She did this momentous thing, and more. She cast her fate, not toward some fashionable creed, one of worldly promise, a church vibrant with social passion, whose flame would invigorate and intensify her own. By no means such a church.

Nonetheless, she converted. Because—she believed. If the statement is illogical, so much the worse. So was she. She became a child again. An aged, rather ignorant nun was her instructor. Dorothy's memory stuck in its groove; sister's tongue often descended like a ferule, as the neophyte struggled to give back by rote the uncompromising truths of Baltimore Catechism Number One.

And Dorothy cannot believe her good fortune. Her head swims with the glory of it all, the gift. By anticipation she meets the objections of her friends. She is certainly not led by unhappiness into the church; indeed, she is in a very stupor of joy for having borne her child. Nor is Christ, she writes, a panacea against the travails and emptiness of the world.

> I wanted to die in order to live, to put off the old man and put on Christ. I loved, in other words, and like all women in love, I wanted to be united to my love. . . .
> I loved the church for Christ made visible. Not for itself, because it was so often a scandal to me. . . . There was plenty of charity but too little justice.

Did she enter the church like a queen of a hovel, gracing its squalor and ignorance with her radiant intelligence, her noble sensibility, her passion to set the world right? Did she enter, lamp in hand, crowned with her gifts, crowned above all with the grace of a great denial? The image is a tempting one; it has much to commend it. Except that it is a violation of her sense of herself.

Let others see her in somewhat this way, understanding as they must that this is by no means the way she saw herself. Her conduct bespeaks a far different image. What one can only call, for lack of better words, humility, a sense of rightful place and scope; what Paul Goodman names "creatureliness." And with respect to the church, a sense of having entered a mystery infinitely surpassing human gifts, talents, grasp of reality. This is her tone, her style; it is fraught with ironies, humor, grim conflict. She bows before the priest; she acknowledges his power over the invisible. But she reserves to herself the right to excoriate the church for playing whore, Judas, Cain; for playing the worldly game of power and money and institutional glory.

These are the ironies she both embraces and helps create and intensify. And withal, in her style and tone, she is herself, as she always has been. Her distinction and dignity are drawn from poverty, not possessions. She wears plain cotton dresses chosen, like any poor woman's, from the racks of hand-me-downs. There is a faded kerchief about her crown of hair. Her language is direct and lucid, utterly free of pietism. Her heart is unresting as ever; compassion racks her frame.

So the future hovers, an eyelid upon an eye, half-closed against too great a light. The worst is over; she has made a clean break, has reached a haven.

And now what? She went one day, in the course of a news assignment in Washington, into a shrine to pray. Her prayer, she tell us, was disarmingly specific. She wanted someone to cross her path, which was, she mourned, no path at all, but a stalemate. She prayed for someone to enter her life, to show her a way.

And thereupon she returned to New York, to her apartment. And there, a doppelganger, an unlikely answer taking shape before her, stood, or sat, or ambled about (the accounts vary) — one Peter Maurin.

And now her true life gets under way. Peter struck a match to her combustible heart. He offered her both a theory and a persuasive and patient example, a Christianity at once worldly, matter-of-fact, intensely personal, a method and means. Peter was what might be called today, in the best sense of that mutilated term, an evangelical. Which is to say, he took the intent of Christ seriously: the neighbor, the call to labor and sacrifice, the drudgery that made the kingdom possible.

Indeed, though Peter was twenty years her senior, the main outlines of his life had run parallel to her own, in a quite startling way. By temperament and grace and sheer dogged will, he was fitted for the great work he had set himself. And so, as he sized up this neophyte, as he was to insist day in and out, so was she. Or if she was not, if she doubted herself, he would so fit her.

Which he proceeded to do, with a persistence at once fascinating and irritating. He declared that her education was deficient in Catholic under-standing. But it was not too late, since he, Peter, was at hand and would correct the defect. He would introduce her to the great thinkers of the century, and beyond: Mauriac, Maritain, Gilson, Péguy, Dostoievski, the social writings of the popes. He would elaborate this doctrine, synthesize it, for her and others.

This hardy tumbleweed, blown hither and yon by the winds of the spirit, finally lodged in her door. Peter was at the mercy of those winds, which also had their eye, a center of mystery, a peasant's faith. What a man he was! She groaned and gloried. If a saint were to appear in her lifetime, would it not be in some such guise as Peter's, the truth bursting from his seams, the word ready on his tongue, no fear, no second thoughts, only that hardy, single-minded frame of obscurity and poverty, speaking the truth for the truth's sake?

How alike they were, Dorothy and Peter, and how complementary. A similar genius, at once dogged and rugged, a grasp of essentials, a linking of theory and practical love. Peter knew the world, a world of blind waste and want and war. And he remained serene, unafflicted by fatalism. Granted the evil, it was a world to be won; people need not die as they had lived, the world of salvation, the daily bread, all were at hand. And this was the task: Bread and truth must make the rounds.

He taught her to look on the world this way. Bread and truth, truth and bread, making the rounds. Today's food would yield, short of death (the death of the soul), to tomorrow's hunger; the task would never end. But let tomorrow take care of itself; it was today's hunger that must be met. Let us meet it. Let us multiply ourselves, in the youth, the workers, the poor, the street people, the excluded. All have the truth to offer; all can multiply the bread, bake it, break it, pass it on.

They started a newspaper; and the rest is history.

They started a house of hospitality; that too is history. Peter was forever talking about something he called "agronomic universities." They started one, on the land; and that is something rather less than history.

The paper grew like mad. Peter's timing, and Dorothy's as well, was impeccable. Not all American Catholics, it developed, were wired to a party line. Not all priests; wonderfully, not all bishops. The depression, the Spanish war, World War II swept over the flock, brimstone and cloud-bursts. The sheep were rattled and voiceless, surcharged with discipline and dogma, fed windily on abstraction. And downwind sailed an omen and landed at their feet: this cheaply printed broadsheet, bold, uncompromis-ing, reminiscent of something outrageous and familiar at once, black on white, a penny a copy. Month after month, through thick and thin, take it or leave; proworker, antiwar, prostrikers and prisoners and the down and out. Drawings by Eichenberg, Ade Bethune, Rita Corbin; art bold as a sandwich board, a clamor of forms, figures rough-hewn, stature and sanctity. And here and there and everywhere, within the crude art and text, like honey in a dead jaw bone, dwelt an enormous tenderness and compassion.

Dorothy was in her glory. She had found a master, a way. Peter? He had found a disciple worthy of his mettle.

Disciple, master; an interesting arrangement; but, to right thinking, one to be dispensed with as soon as might be. A rule, one might add, not universally honored in that time or ours.

In Dorothy's case, the rule was upheld—to the honor of both parties. There came a day, the date by no means certain, when Peter was no longer master, Dorothy no longer neophyte. Dorothy had begun to see things with her own eyes, judge with her own mind. And more, on occasion she judged differently than Peter; and he, having stated his case, accepted her judgment.

Dorothy tells the story, without dwelling on its implications, or perhaps even grasping them. Twice, she tells us, Peter was ready to give up. Once, when opposition had arisen against their using slim resources to feed the poor. The money, so the objection went, was better spent for propaganda, printing, and the support of editors of the paper. The language of the young Turks was interestingly, and typically, loaded: Substance was being wasted on "bums, derelicts, dead wood."

And Peter could bear it no longer. He stood up, beckoned to Dorothy: "Come, let us leave the house and paper to them." And she sat there, not budging. The tempest passed; so did the malcontents, who left to start their own paper on their own turf. Which shortly thereafter folded.

On another occasion, Peter was shaken by the outcry against their pacifist stand. "Perhaps," he confessed, "it is time to be silent; they are not willing to listen." And, again, Dorothy withstood him. Granted a hearing or lost on the wind, the truth must be spoken. In season and out. Hot war and cold, false peace and true. In face of the deadly drum beat of the nations, the wars crowding one after another like bloody lock-stepping squads—no matter. *The Catholic Worker* must go on, in her words, "opposing war and upholding the stand of the conscientious objector, and the absolutist who advocated nonpayment of taxes and nonregistration. . . . "

It was a dead-serious game; she was playing Paul to her Peter, "withstanding him to his face."

I am led to reflect, without attempting to blow the matter out of proportion, how often the coherence of a social movement, its moral substance, the possibility of offering an example to the immature, even the unborn—how often the chancy future rests on such moments, such speaking up. Seizing the occasion, not only to vindicate a truth here and now, but to guarantee as far as one can (it is not very far) a decent outcome.

How stunningly right she was to hang on, to endure. And yet she did not know if she was right or wrong and confesses to nagging thoughts:

> Peter may have been right on both occasions, silence may have been better. . . . But I do not know. God gives us our temperaments, and in spite of my pacifism, it is natural for me to stand my ground, to continue in what actually amounts to a class war, using such weapons as the works of mercy for immediate means to show our love and to alleviate suffering.

This strikes me as a triumph, modest, but a triumph nonetheless. The dove devouring the serpent.

I am conscious, too, of a kind of relief, perhaps mingled with selfishness; of gratitude also, remembering all that Dorothy's "withstanding" has meant to me and mine. When William Miller's history of *The Catholic Worker* was published, I had just come out of prison during the Vietnam years. I stayed up all night, unable to put the book aside. What held me in thrall was an absolutely stunning consistency. No to all killing. Excusing causes, invasions, incursions, call of the blood, summonings to the bloody flag, casuistic body counts; just wars, necessary wars, religious wars, needful wars, holy wars—into the teeth of the murderous crosswinds went her simple word. *No.*

Thus a large matter arose out of small, like a great and growing pyramid, reversed, steady on its apex. If Dorothy learned anything from Peter, even by opposing him, it was the power of that single monosyllable, turning her away from every enticement to compromise, to come to terms, to make it big, to institutionalize, to play god, to cotton up to the monied and powerful.

It was an unforgettable example; some of us never forgot it.

A moral premise had been examined, discussed, held up to light and darkness, exposed to public and ecclesiastical scrutiny, undergone objection and obloquy even—then a fully formed, conscientious position emerged, a light to a whole generation.

Her no to war was ultimately as simple as a newborn lisp. But it came out of much travail and searching and converging experience. In this, as in all serious matters, Dorothy took the long route to the center. Somewhat in this way. She resolved to taste the violence of American life, dreadfully apparent in marginal and expendable people. She would become, like Peter before her, a kind of holy *vaga*, a wandering scholar and worker. Thus the stigmata of her people dug deep in her hands and soul. She came to see that, in America, human devastation was by no means fortuitous; it was embedded in the scheme and texture and finality of the social contract, like rods of steel reinforcing, prestressing the dead weight of life.

One scholar, a refugee and former prisoner, queried her, "How close are you to the workers?" It was, she said, a pertinent question; and she answered it with a lifting pride:

> Going around and seeing such sights is not enough. To help the organizers, to give what you have for relief, to pledge yourself to

voluntary poverty for life so that you can share with your brothers is not enough. One must live with them, share with them their sufferings too. Give up one's privacy, and mental and spiritual comforts as well as physical. . . . Yes, we have lived with the poor, with the workers, and we know them not just from the streets, or in mass meetings, but from years of living in the slums, in tenements, in our hospices in Washington, Baltimore, Philadelphia, Harrisburg, Pittsburgh, New York, Rochester, Boston, Worcester, Buffalo, Troy, Detroit, Cleveland, Toledo, Akron, St. Louis, Chicago, Milwaukee, Minneapolis, Seattle, San Francisco, Los Angeles, Oakland, even down into Houma, Louisiana. . . .

We have lived with the unemployed, the sick, the unemployables. . . . Going to the people is the purest and best act in Christian tradition and is the beginning of world brotherhood. . . .

A mystic, she was blessed and burdened with a very thirst for reality. But the prior synthetic gift is withheld from her (another mark of her American soul). She had to see and touch and listen—and then cry out. She had perpetually to be "on the road." The country was seething with anguish and discontent; it was, as she said wearily, "always something": strikes or unemployment or war or the dispossession of those on the land, or civil rights crises. She had to be on hand, protesting such evils, going to jail.

And hers was a further burden: She must report back to her readers, the beloved "larger family" of *The Catholic Worker*. They winged it along with her; they saw America through the courage and vision that bore her along.

"On Pilgrimage" became her letter to the world, a column that ran for some thirty years in her paper, up to the month of her death. She wrote from Cuba, from Rome, from jail, from the farm fields of migrant workers, from coal-mining areas, from the reservations of the West. In her travels, she lived with, talked with, ate with, walked miles with, marched with; she became the guardian angel of the unangelic, a very angel of "with." It was her way, as she announced, literal as ever, of not separating Jesus from his cross.

In the course of a bitter winter in the early seventies, a group of California farm workers crossed the country in an unheated coffin of a van. They were hoping to undertake a grape boycott on the East Coast. They arrived in New York and showed up promptly at the Catholic Worker. Dorothy received them like long-lost brothers. And it was there, on the first floor of East First Street, as I arrived to offer Mass on a cold February day, that I and others first met the people of Cesar Chavez and his movement. Dorothy introduced the knot of dark, apparently unthawed folk, huddled on benches along the wall. Above them hung a new symbol, the farm workers' flag, black eagle on red; it has hung there ever since.

Meantime, Dorothy had written about, defended, explained the following: cotton pickers, braceros, prisoners and ex-prisoners, families of every condition, the unemployed, priests and nuns, scholars, Native Americans, monks, alcoholics, addicts, slum folk, auto workers, coal miners. Among others.

She stood with them. In the current jargon, and venturing the understatement of the century, she had "a point of view." She had long before recovered from the malaise of her profession, which she described more properly as its curse: the inability to sort things out, the reeling head, the condensed brain, the eye that, seeing everything, sees nothing. She became, that is, a reporter with a conscience—a phenomenon that daily grows rarer.

The Vietnam War erupted. Dorothy stood at the side of those who refused to "serve," which is to say (as she would say) refused to kill.

I well remember the first draft-card burning. We arranged for a Mass at the apartment of one of the men who was resolved to put the torch to his odious hunting license. I was permitted by superiors to lead the Mass, but not to appear in company with potential felons in Union Square (the kind of order that was corrected, in measure, as the war went on). Dorothy saw the young Workers go off to court and jail; she was proud as a mother of heroes; they were doing the truest "alternative service," she declared. She wrote of them and their wives, praised their courage, pledged that the Catholic Worker would sustain the separated families.

Our best and truest memories are invariably suffused with gratitude. I am grateful beyond words for the grace of this woman's life; for her sensible, unflinching rightness of mind, her long and lonely truth, her journey to the heart of things. I think of her as one who simply helped us, in a time of self-inflicted blindness, to see.

At length all was said and done; no more needed saying and doing. So she stood there, or sat down, like Christ, like the Buddha. This is the image of her last years. Her life passed over, into passive voice. Now she was served, reverenced, cherished, protected. Her flame was failing; her memory glimmered and guttered; "On Pilgrimage" became a barely audible murmur of space and silence as she struggled to say her farewell to the world.

I dare speak finally for eight Christians, the Plowshare defendants. The best tribute we could offer Dorothy is that we too would stand somewhere, or sit down. In any case, somewhere. In any case, in trouble. In our case, indicted, tried, convicted, and jailed for having destroyed, in September 1980, in King of Prussia, Pennsylvania, two nuclear warheads. It was the first nuclear disarmament, we proudly proclaimed, in thirty-five years. Without Dorothy, without that exemplary patience, courage, moral modesty, without this woman pounding at the locked door behind which the powerful mock the powerless with games of triage—without her, the resistance we have offered would be simply unthinkable. She urged our consciences off the beaten track; she made the impossible (in our case) probable, and then actual. She did this, first of all, by living as though the truth were true.

All honor to you, Dorothy! You dwell now in that place where the revolution has come true, perpetually renewed, perennially green.

Be with us, in our saying and doing. In our standing somewhere and our sitting down.

PORTRAITS, 1982

Pastor Medardos Gómez
of El Salvador

In 1984 Berrigan traveled through Nicaragua and El Salvador. In Salvador he was accompanied by Gene Palumbo, a journalist.

On a remote side street, led by Gene's infallible nose, we entered a modest Lutheran church; green paint of faintly nauseous hue, straightback pews, linoleum floors. We were seeking out the pastor, Medardos Gómez. He was, Gene said, not to be missed among the resisters in Salvador; imprisoned and tortured, he refused to leave the country, returning instead to his flock, and awaiting what, by common report, would be almost certain death.

Nothing grand here, no evidence of a church rewarded or furbished by the likes of Somoza. No plenipotent baroque, no cassocks, surplices, antependia, gorgeous saints in wood and ocher. No power, no trappings, no echo even of former power. We were at the heart of stern reformation.

A voluble woman aide received us. She too had been in prison, and undergone its rigors. *Sicut pastor sic grex.* We walked the length of the little church, toward the chancel. Beyond, an office, scarcely larger than its incumbent.

Pastor Gómez welcomed us with dignified gravity. A large man, and subdued. The look of a prisoner in his eyes; a look of those throughout the world, forced into a darkness laid like a coffin cover upon the living. A look of endurance, of patience wrested from unspeakable nights and days. (In Hanoi, a young communist guide and translator said to me, in a rare moment of candor: "I know the Christians. I can point them out in a crowded street." I asked astonished, "How?" He confessed not to know. It was something of "another world," something "different from our faces . . . ")

But how do you talk with the tortured? What topic, tone, will not trivialize their great torment, its memories and ghosts? I felt a kind of shame and confusion, forbidding that I lightly inquire of those who have been there, and somehow returned, the typography of hell. . . .

I once spent an hour in an Irish pub with a young religious brother who had been tortured in Argentina, and finally released and expelled. There were marks of cigarette burns on his arms and wrists. One did not poke about in the shadows of such infamy; rather I was grateful for the small talk at which the brother, being Irish, was adept. Thus did we keep the hounds of hell at bay.

But the brother had had great advantages, not available in Salvador. He had had two years to bind his wounds, as well as the help of psychiatrists. He was also a member of a group of the once tortured. And perhaps most important of all, he had been separated from that monstrous regime, once and for all.

No such relief for Pastor Gómez. He had returned, so to speak, from his grave, against all laws of nature, presumably also against conventional good advice. He sat here, welcoming us, at the scene of his crime. Indeed, in his case a plumb line could be laid down, crossing his brows, from crime to punishment—to intentional repeated crime.

Was he not a fool? (Conventional wisdom, the voices heard in the dungeon of Thomas More and Dietrich Bonhoeffer and Franz Jagerstatter and Dean Hammer and Elizabeth McAlister and Vernon Rossman.) Have such as these no thought for their children, the families whom their stubborn austerities, their intransigent virtue, are imperiling? . . .

The family, the children! How seldom, I thought, do we test them (and ourselves) against the steel of adult decisions—decisions which, come folly or right judgment, are at least our own, and even perhaps, now and then, deserve the name Christian. I look in the face of Pastor Gómez, remembrance numbs me. A recognition scene once more. Christian faces: let the world beware them!

There is no great point, I thought, in elaborating psychological theories about such people as the pastor. He is explained neither as simpleton nor extremist nor masochist. Given his world, his government, given religious faith and secular coercion—he is simply a criminal. He is infected from birth; he has the double indemnity of genetics and circumstances. Does he not issue from a long line of malcontents and protesters, does not his congregation ratify every disobedient instinct that arises in him?

Let us attempt to define the pastor's crime; it bears uncommon interest for us also.

It is this: he dares lead the common life of Christians. He opens his Bible; he reads there certain instructions and commendations. And then he proceeds to act, in the breach as he is, to act in the manner in which Christians throughout history have acted. He breaks through the smog of pseudonormalcy; he speaks out against unjust laws; he objects to murder. And worse still, he invites others to do likewise.

No wonder he is in trouble! For he exhibits openly before the world those characteristics extolled in his tradition and defamed by the state: courage, imagination, tenacity, solidarity with others.

Such virtues, it goes without saying, are available from the "treasure hidden in the field" of this world.

The common life. A life being led, in Salvador and throughout the world, often in equally unpromising situations, by multitudes. Therefore to canonize the pastor only isolates him, even as it dispenses others from the same calling. He is "doing his job," in the inelegant phrase, with a Christian twist. And in consequence, and with iron inevitability, the world is proceeding to do its job, which consists in impeding, by whatever means, his pastoral work. Removal, torture, threats against life—all to be taken in account beforehand, all part of the job.

The monotone went on; he spoke, for the large part, not about himself at all, but about the work at hand, the difficulties, the consolation. He never once raised his voice, or showed large emotion. Let the government indulge itself—flamboyant manifestoes, glitter, and glare. He was something else, a Lutheran, a reformer. He and his flock were called, not, God help us, to reform those as irreformable as D'Aubuisson and his squads. They must simply stand where they stood.

Might that not be the only hope—for D'Aubuisson also and his monstrous bullies? a mere sign? A sign that big government, the government that eats, lives, and excretes polity, the government of ringmasters and of jackals, this bloody circus and bloody bread—this, though it pretend to be all, was not all. Not by a long shot, or even a short one. He was there, after prison, with his flock, to say so. Indeed he had no need to say it; he was there.

And as long as he was there, and those of his flock who were in prison knew he was there—why, the government was not all! It was as simple as that, and as final.

Something over against. Pastor Gómez and his people were the church. An upstart church, a transplanted one, a church poor and assailed, denounced as a gringo stronghold, a mere import. And yet, and yet—the church, the humiliated remnant, ridiculous, powerless, irrelevant. . . .

For all sorts of reasons, including the sanctioned frenzies of Salvador, Pastor Gómez's story is exceptional only because he is a pastor, therefore, at least in measure, visible. But for that, he would of course be lost in a vast international "method," a maze whose entrance and exit are everywhere and nowhere. The politics of megadeath barely pass him by; the method tried and true against Armenians and Jews and Palestinians and how many others whose removal from the earth would purportedly improve the lot of all.

The pastor finished his story of prison, release, return. He might have been recounting an average day in a farm parish in Iowa; something of statistics, births, marriages, deaths in safe beds, of old age and tired hearts. He was a very connoisseur of understatement, the dispassion of the survivor whose world must, for sake of sanity, be presented as bound by fairly normal routine.

A question. Was there not an ecumenical advantage working in his favor in Salvador? Which is to say, did not his imprisonment and torture occasion a public response, as would befall a Catholic priest in like crisis? After all, priests had been imprisoned and even murdered; and their deaths were a cause of international uproar. . . . His answer was that, no, unhappily these events are not perceived in the same way. When a priest is imprisoned, you must understand that the culture is shaken. He is part of a vast and ancient communion. So the death of a priest, let alone an archbishop, is a blow struck at the heart of history and of selfunderstanding; even to the unchurched it is seen as a kind of insult. But we Lutherans exist in a corner, out of the public gaze. We are not part of the culture, the history. Consequently we can be dealt with quite as they decide, and with impunity. . . .

When form is the object, the poet says, more is always less.

Pastor Gómez's words—the "less" of dispassion and gentleness and resolve; the "more" of suffering. I asked him if he would not pray with us, something from the Bible, the Beatitudes perhaps? He opened his testament and began, in Spanish. The same dry tonality, his pulpit tone, an all-purpose tone; of use, if not of distinction. A tone of exposition, counsel, mild reproof. It was a voice that could turn with his people to God in prayer; and beyond doubt had, for a lifetime. And whether in dungeons or courtrooms or interrogation centers or vans of death squads, I thought, this is the tone in which the church uttered its no; subdued, all but inaudible, but unshaken, unmistakable.

A voice of embodiment. You don't announce the Beatitudes as though they were a virtuous formula worthy of mere admiration. You embodied them; then your body was in your voice. As in the first instance, Jesus simply lived the blessings, before commending them to us. They flowered in spirit before they entered his flesh, in ways we know of. A right order of things. So simple, and yet how rare. . . .

We said our goodbyes.

But how does one say farewell to Lazarus, after the event, so to speak? We mumbled something, fell back on the old Christian premise and promise; when all else fails, pledge a prayer.

The remembrance of this man, his family, and his people floods back. He is someone recalled without recourse to a heroic image. A nondescript figure, anonymous in his rumpled suit, somewhat overweight (do the saints overeat, out of dread?). A shabby room, cheap religious oleographs on the wall, everything ordinary to the point of bathos. No metaphors, no myths; the human, in abundance and solidity, only that.

When in prison, Bonhoeffer wrote, there is little to be done; tell the truth and say your prayers. Indeed.

(And I ask myself, Is there a great deal more to be done outside prison, given the times? and presuming that "telling the truth" is one with living the truth?)

STEADFASTNESS OF THE SAINTS, 1985

Part Four

SCRIPTURES

Each Day Writes

                in my heart's core
ineradicably, what it is to be man.

Hours and hours, no sun rises, night sits
kenneled in me: or spring, spring's
flowering seizes me in an hour.

I tread my heart amazed: what land,
what skies are these, whose shifting weathers
now shrink my harvest to a stack of bones;
now weigh my life with glory?

              Christ, to whose eyes flew,
whose human heart knew, or furious or slow,
the dark wingbeat of time: your presence give
light to my eyeless mind, reason to my heart's rhyme.

THE NEW YORK TIMES BOOK REVIEW, NOVEMBER 10, 1957

Prayer

I left Cornell
with half a wit; six mismated socks
ski underwear, a toothbrush,
passport, one hundred good
green dollars, their faces
virtuous as ancestors,
the chamois sack
Karl Meyer gave me years ago, handmade
by dispossessed Georgia blacks.

Later, dismay; no Testament.
I must construct, out of oddments, abrasions,
vapor trails, dust, pedicabs
three crosshatch continents, Brooks Brothers embassies
their male models dressed to kill—

all He meant and means. I touch
shrapnel and flesh, and risk my reason
for the truth's sake, an ignorant hung head.

Man of one book, stand me in stead.

LIBERATION, MARCH 1968

Socrates and Jesus

DANBURY (CONN.) FEDERAL PRISON

September 4, 1970

"A man . . . ought not to consider his chance of living or dying; he ought only to consider on a given occasion whether he is doing right or wrong" (Socrates).

To allow such a principle to rule one's life, how many other considerations have to be swept aside; and how few are ready for such extraordinary detachment of heart. We think we are living—for God, for an ideal, for our brothers and sisters, for principle; and we end up at Mass on Sundays, as "warden of the wretched" for a livelihood—for our whole lives. And beget children, and love them, and keep our job, in despite of what we are doing in public. . . . How cruelly such a life weaves its net—and how all the interstices cunningly join; an admirable life, after Gogol or Mauriac! A rabbi tells of the Catholics in Poland who ran an extermination camp near his home and bused to Mass on Sundays. The horrors that a single life can "make sense of" are almost beyond belief, given the stupefying effect of habit, inheritance, routine.

To break through the net.

To be the occasion of a fresh start for humanity, because one has made it for himself or for herself.

To stand with others even while he or she consciously walks a few paces ahead of them.

The gift of Philip and of my family—that "gift of unhappiness" Socrates and Weil speak of, the supreme gift of grace, habitually. We seem to be among the few who have had their family with them on the exodus from slavery.

The "long haul" of patience, in the course of which we not only prepare for the next stage of things, but actually have it "revealed" to us—as did the Jews in the desert.

September 5

Sounds of gunfire outside the compound; ominous from here, all day, for two days cold. Federal employees here obliged to practice up once a year. Now I know what it feels like to be in the gunsights of the law. . . .

"If I were to desert my post through fear of death or any other fear, . . .

I might justly be charged in court with denying the existence of the gods. For I had disobeyed the oracle in fear of death."

I find this a wonderfully concrete statement of morality.

It admits a mystical, nonverifiable basis for living in an imperfect world; i.e., the "oracle" can no more be verified than may the divinity of Christ. Both are taken on the word of the "interested party" in order to interest "other parties" in the truth of existence. A wizened, rationalized, scientifically bedazzled culture always demands a sign—i.e., submit before our criteria of proofs—come into our courts. But Jesus and Socrates counter by offering a very different sort of sign—the sign of death. This is their staggering, absurd act of faith and hope in human beings—that they will be able to read the sign.

Atheists are practically speaking those who renege on a genuine vocation. (*Sic* Socrates.) They have turned their backs on the incarnate aspect of the *mystery*.

" . . . The God who is with us is the God who forsakes us" (Bonhoeffer).

September 6

Jesus and his friends, Socrates and his friends. Two methods; in John's Gospel especially, the warmth, the human commingling, the passage from servanthood to friendship. That baring of the heart of God. Socrates is stern with the assimilated principle—the truth of life above the perdurance of life. He insists that the word of God to humankind is that they are called to be human—in a plenary sense—at the hour of death; but also over the long haul of the dialogue, irony, riposte, in which the truth might emerge. It is a Greek mind at its quintessential, filtered through the lucid systematic prose of Plato; the old man dies supremely well, surpassing death by his calm assumption of immortality; the robbery of death's sting by the native virtue of being human.

In Jesus: tenderness, majesty, and above all, personalism. The certainty of one who is not only familiar with the human scene and its range of experience, but with the transcendent life as well: "We testify to what we have seen. I give my life, as the Father commands me. . . . " It is this double life, hypostatically joined, marrow, mind, fiber, heart—the infinite One, radiant and humiliated in our flesh. Prison is a new chance to test that faith: as one would seek, not added "evidence" of truth, but that apparent counter to truth which lends the truth substance in conflict. . . .

They say so often here: it makes no difference whether he is God or not, we find him a real human being. One rejoins *sotto voce*, to his own spirit: it makes all the difference, as a clue leads to a hidden truth. Why this probed and approved humanity, whose stature even the worst sins of Christianity has been unable to diminish? Because he is God, he can command such constant historic respect, even from enemies, even from Christians.

I know for certain that deprived of this faith I could not for a single day endure the rigors of this jungle, keep myself from a destructive, exhausting, corrosive hatred. With him, I endure. I believe, help my unbelief.

LIGHTS ON IN THE HOUSE OF THE DEAD, 1974

Gandhi

February 14, 1971

Reflections on reading Gandhi's autobiography for the *n*th time:

Truth as *experiment* (title). The search for the truth of existence is as rigorous as a scientific experiment. I.e., it requires that the soul of the seeker be an analogous laboratory—freedom, rigor, purity of soul, readiness for suffering, respect for others. These seekers prepare their lives for experiment as they prepare a specimen, a complex of equipment, an organism of tissues. They are as rigorous in undergoing, in evaluating, in welcoming the new and unexpected. They are, in sum, imaginative. They realize that the original hypothesis, i.e., "human beings are creatures capable of the truth," remains a pious sentiment to be mouthed by the worst charlatans, killers, manipulators of power—until it is embodied in a personal and social style.

They call on the powers of the universe, embedded in a religion or culture, in deference to this quest. The *numina patrum* of Virgil; they take their gods with them. On this score, people from the West are at odds. They want to go it alone; like the waiters for Godot. Or they want not to win the gods to their side, but literally to steal their fire, like Prometheus. The result is technological catastrophe as a fact or a threat.

They wish also that the quest be a social one. The truth is not the possession of the seeker, after a loner's journey. Relations to others are the field on which one determines both means and end, judges their impurity or validity. The seekers are also the liberators—they release (vacate) fields of force in others, unsuspected, latent resources of heroism, new directions for the enslaved.

Circumstances may make the English, in possession of the land, into the "enemy." But the seeker knows the enemy lies much nearer; the will to enslavement, the dismembered consciousness of the enslaved; the willingness to give life over to impersonal fate; to die as one was born. Laziness of soul.

We are free to sneer at cultural childishness in a great or holy man or woman. The question remains, what made them great? or: how did they see themselves emerging from childhood, family, into the world, a gigantic leaven of an immovable mass?

(1) Sexual taboos; (2) dietary taboos; (3) betrayal of father in his death.

Interesting that these three also trouble the process of breakaway from old culture (Slater) to new consciousness in young America.

The unacknowledged, boiling connection between sexual codes (monogamy, puritan marriages) and public violence (cf. L.B. Johnson's metaphors about Vietnam War, as told in "Tuesday Cabinet"). Also my conversation with federal marshals on way to Rochester . . . "degenerates, against war, yelling, 'give us your daughters.' " Also: geography of allowable sex — violence; whites long looked on blacks as an open reserve for sex and violence. Daniel Lang's account of rape slaying in Vietnam War declares open season *perpetually*; contrast with the *qualified* open season at home on nonwhites. Mylai declares the unlimited time and place allowed to such incursions.

In light of this, Gandhi's quest for sexual control emerges as a healthy sign. He declares himself as unbearably lustful toward his child bride. We would easily pooh-pooh such scruples. Our culture, the new one, allows for an open season on others. But considered as violence toward others, sexual urges that take no account or little account of the other person often become another symptom of the permeating violence of the culture. Hyperdelicacy, on the other hand, can be a sign that a general conquest of oneself, including one's will to violence, is under way. One has identified a concrete obstacle to humanity, and is in process of facing it. Gandhi said later: only the violent are capable of nonviolence. It is in light of so profound a truth that one can understand the right reason under his rather jejune narrative.

Attitude toward women, specifically his wife. Like many strong men, he paid a mere lip service to the full humanity of others. He wanted her to learn to read and write, and mourns righteously that she showed little interest or progress in letters. . . . Her life was a footnote to his own ego. He awakened her, to make love to her, the night his father died: and he mourns the failure of his love (but only of his love for his father . . .).

LIGHTS ON IN THE HOUSE OF THE DEAD, 1974

The Psalms

I carry around a dog-eared paperback edition of the Psalms, in French, dated 1961. Given the temporal journeys of David's poems, the lives moved, the music put to memory, the monks and their dawn and twilight susurrations, seventeen years is indeed but a drop in a bucket of the well of that fountainhead. Still, in a dry time on earth, it is a joy to return again and again to the Psalms. Their waters hiss on the tongue, as though laid against hot metal, or seared flesh. A dry time indeed.

So dry, we ask our souls, are we already in hell, like the rich man who scorned Lazarus? Not yet; we are only on earth, though the distinction between these terrains may someday utterly vanish. Indeed, given the lethal union of violent technology and ruthless diplomacy, the distinction hell–earth may at almost any moment be declared not only irrelevant, but (along with ourselves) obsolete. One thinks in this regard of the sublime triumph known here and there as the neutron bomb, together with the blind pieties which assure us that our arsenals require yet another tinker toy. No matter, if you and I must for some reason perish, our property will survive us intact. On formerly Earth, though the meek will not be around to inherit, the property will be there to testify: who we are, what consummate folly made us the architects of our own doom.

These are somber reflections, admittedly. I can only plead that I did not induce them. The world did, "the way it goes," in Macbeth's phrase. Years and years ago, when I was first introduced to the Psalms, my love for them took root in a more or less common assumption: that the world made sense, that lightheartedness and joy were our patrimony, that over and above mere survival life was a concert, a very conspiracy of hope. That, in consequence, poetry ought to be the ordinary prose of life. And further, that we were to live as long as God does, that death was an interruption, a hiatus, a rude but by no means prevailing wind, knocking us down indeed, but out never.

They have stolen our joy! That is how a biblical indictment of modern life might go. One is not thinking about a snatch of candy from kids. Something horrendous, a very body snatch. We have seen it all; consciousness bent around grotesquely, a wordless cry arising in the void, like a vocalized painting of Guernica. Surely life was not meant to be like this, we cry, so utterly afflicting, weighing us down. And then the question of task, of good work in the world. We think of the classic Christian ideal of "building the earth," of the common assumption of faith: that providence assigns enough for all, a welcome, a network of services and goods for humans. And, above all, no flamboyant death marking us like doomed

124

sticks for the fire, no death as social method, no redundant death, no death by wanton violence, no death outside the course of gentle nature.

I am trying to say (and the saying is difficult indeed) that the vision of humankind, the simple, truthful sense of who we are offered by the Psalms, is in principle denied by the spirit and drift of the world today. Denied, violated, put at naught, treated with derision, painted for a fool. Whether this has always been true seems to me beside the point; we are here, and now; and here and now the glory of God is under lethal assault. So is our glory, which is to praise, to invoke, to believe, to live and rejoice in the beloved community. Noting that glory, that dignity, I grew to love the Psalms. Day after day, year after year, they purified, blessed, set one moving to a rhythm that was by no means worldly or stereotyped or willful, but lively and tranquil and passionately edgy. To pray the Psalms with even half a heart was to be comforted and discomfited, set in motion, set in stillness, set free, set on edge, led outside, led within.

The sixties came on strong, the war hottened up, the Psalms went with me into that furnace. I remember saying them in the rubble and bomb shelters of Hanoi, in the Baltimore courtroom, finally in Danbury prison. There we sat finally (it seemed fairly final at the time), a group of us, stuck fast for the duration. But not so stuck, as it turned out, that we couldn't be set free. The Psalms were my freedom songs.

Saying the prayers in prison had a certain piquancy. The Psalms were not in the nature of a placebo or a joint (though plenty of both were available, it was a matter of inmate ingenuity or official cataracting). No, in the midst of the sublime public ministries of Nixon and Mitchell et al., the Psalms induced a measure of personal balance, created a world of sense and symbol, an underworld of the spirit really, which had in fact always existed (as the Psalms said in a hundred ways), a world of humans similar to ourselves, who in the grip of mischance and public violence had undergone God, and lived to sing it out. Heightened knowledge for inert knowledge, rebirth for near death. We needed such moments desperately, to put our clutch on them, like a sinking soul a spar. And then, to let go.

Long before I went to jail, my family and friends had accepted the idea that the scripture, more specifically the Psalms, were our landmark, a source of sanity in an insane time. The Psalms spoke up for soul, for survival; they pled for all, they bonded us when the world would break us like dry bones. They made sense, where the "facts"—scientific, political, religious—made only nonsense. For me, the Psalms gave coloration and texture to life itself; gave weight to silence, the space between words that, like the white in a Cezanne painting, intensify form and color, their other side, a sweet cheat, almost a third dimension. . . .

[*The following are two of the Psalms Berrigan translated and commented upon.*]

THEY CALL YOU BLIND MAN: CALL THEIR BLUFF / *PSALM 10*

Lord, why do you stand on the sidelines
silent as the mouth of the dead, the maw of the grave—
        O living One, why?

Evil walks roughshod, the envious set snares
high and mighty the violent ride
Applause for maleficence, rewards for crime
        Yourself set to naught

Eyes like a poniard impale the innocent
Death cheap, life cheaper
The mad beast is loosened, his crooked heart mutters
        Fear only me!

Lord, they call you blind man. Call their bluff

        extinguish their envy

See; the poor are cornered
marked for destruction, grist
        for a mill of dust

        At the bar of injustice
        they tremble, wind-driven birds
        under the beaks and stares
        of the shrouded Big Ones—
        No recourse but you; no recourse
        but your faithful love!

The poem is about a collision between rich and poor. And much more.
God is drawn into the imbroglio. For a down-to-earth, cold-eyed atheism
is in the air; as it invariably is, in spite of all pious protestation to the
contrary, when the powerful decide to show their hand. The psalm dwells
on this point, the difference between faith and incantation, between faith
and religious camouflage. On the one hand, the poem celebrates the
believing trust of the poor, their spontaneous belief that they will be
delivered; and on the other, the neglect, active mistreatment, manipulation,
cold-blooded cruelty of those in power.

The conduct of the powerful is almost invariably a mockery of God.
Nothing more is required, by way of fulfilling the biblical formula for

idolatry, than that the rich be themselves, that is, neglect the poor, live off them, exploit their labor, underpay them, rob them of dignity and hope.

And this sublime, self-deluded charade usually goes on in the midst of the most persuasive cover-up imaginable.

The ultimate deception, of course, occurs in one's own soul, persuaded of the justice of manifest injustice. That achieved, little remains to be done except to institutionalize the lie, introduce it into the structures of public life. Personal crime then flowers in social oppression.

It is at this stage that the oppressor and the prophet collide. A point worth making. In the classical prophets, the attack is mounted not against the personal conduct of the incumbent authority, except insofar as its hypocrisy sets the stage for public injustice. But to prophets, injustice is the point, invariably, mercilessly. The poor are their passion. Set down, defrauded, shunted about, denied a voice in their destiny, reduced to chattels, to money-making integers, the poor are the occasion, not only of anti-human conduct on the part of their masters, but of atheism, of a non-credo, a denial of God.

Small need to point out parallels today. We are witnessing, on the part of the Nuclear Stokers, a massive, even a cosmic rip-off of the goods of the earth. Land fraud, air fraud, sea fraud, space fraud, food fraud, energy fraud. And now the great apocalyptic super-fraud of them all: the nuclear arsenals, the nuclearization so to speak of all things—of the seas, boundaries, air space, land mass. The nuclearization also of consciousness and experience, defrauding us of our right sense of time and space and one another; of that sense of being reasonably in command, of being sensible co-heirs of the past, cooperators in a human present, co-ancestors of the unborn. Today this ordered, integral understanding of our place in the world is thrown hopelessly out of gear by the Inventive Dwarfs.

Many volumes would be needed to pursue the spiritual damage done us, the destruction of right thinking, by the past thirty years of nuclear mischief. A sense of being correctly centered, of being at ease, at home, rightfully in place in the universe, of being at least potentially brothers and sisters under whatever skies—all this is ruthlessly disrupted. We are nuclear within, we break apart. Any hour might be the last hour. Any stranger might be a terrorist. Irritation is the mood of the times. Any disagreement, even the slightest, provokes us beyond measure; the least provocation can mean a wipeout; an ambiguous move at the frontier, a pricking of our thumbs, the Button.

We conduct our business in the world like a sheriff's bully in a frontier town, our Great Equalizer always at the ready. The Bomb looks out of our eyes; we are literally bombed out. The Bomb has replaced our soul. Near zero point of human hope, near infinity point of human pretention.

In the midst of it all, the church, resplendent and witless, like a cock on a dung heap, salutes the "new dawn." What scene will that dawn bring?

What will be left of the good earth? A barren moonscape, a vast cosmic dump? . . .

We may not feel like calling upon God.

We may not feel like calling upon one another.

We may not feel like calling upon our own soul.

We may in fact feel like someone perpetually condemned to walk a Last Mile before execution. Half the horror is getting there.

Or like someone newly dead, still on his feet, going through the robot motions of life. Or like a paraplegic ordered to run the decathalon, or to drag a grand piano across a plowed field, faster than anyone else. To all who live through these or similar nightmares, their daily portion, at least this cold comfort goes out: given the times, such feelings are normal—if anything, they are understated.

Wherefore a group, to be named The Undead Anonymous, is hereby declared in existence. Whose ruling principle is: If you feel dead, waked, buried, disposed of, amortized, the strong possibility is that you are in fact none of these. That you are in fact a dead ringer for the living. Be of good heart. Feeling as you do, undergoing nightmares as you do, you are in a countless company of normal human beings, whose heads are also fogged, heartbeats unsteady, souls shaken. You are alive, you are sane. You should know it.

Prove it to yourself. Make the following simple test.

Call upon God.

Call upon a friend.

Call upon your own soul.

Inquiries invited

THE TRUSTING HEART SHALL PREVAIL / PSALM 31

How great is your goodness Lord
poured out on the one who loves you
Face to face with iniquity
the trusting heart shall prevail

Far from intrigue, from malice
I run to your presence, take sanctuary
in your eyes. Hands aloft, you encompass
a holy tent, a refuge.

The war of tongues, a babble, a rout
      rages, goes nowhere.
        I would dwell
      tongue stilled, mind subdued
       in your holy temple

Come, make me your temple
deep founded, touching high heaven

All you who fear the Lord
    exult, take courage
    come shelter in him!

The beauty of the psalm is in the mouth of the speaker, murmurer, singer, pray-er. The beauty, the wonder, is that we can say the psalm—with all our heart. The trouble is, we have no roof to say it under.

Someone wrote of the Catholic radicals, they have no trouble with the church as such; their trouble is with current leadership. Exactly. And well put, as far as it goes; but what is one to do when the leadership "carries on" with a war establishment, when the Vietnam scandal becomes the post-Vietnam scandal? And this scandal is so nearly universal among the authorities that some of us, for sanity's sake, must stay out in the cold. Outside. Willy-nilly, this is what it has come to—for years and years now.

But you keep on keeping on, praying. The nub: faithlessness on our part is no response to dereliction on theirs.

They held an enormous Mass in Philadelphia during the eucharistic congress; the date was August 6, 1976. They held a Mass to honor the military forces of the world. That was the unutterable scandal, the blasphemy. They dared say the Lord's prayer, Remember me, which brings his saving death to our life. And they forgot. It was not merely that they forgot what date it was, Hiroshima Day. Deeper, beyond deep, in the dark where dry bones lie where they fall. They forgot. They celebrated not His death, but death. It was not a Mass, it was blasphemy. And not a mere handful took part, as though some protested, but all who came to the congress, and several cardinals. That church in procession walked stately toward an altar. And they fell off the edge of the world.

Other Christians stood outside. It was a very old story. Fasting, offering leaflets concerning this weighty matter, this sin of commission (a military commission), this sin of omission, of forgetting, of omitting to be the church.

It was another sorrow in a litany of sorrows. Another lesson (we are slow learners), yet another, in a whole education, years and years in the benches saying to ourselves, No, they can't mean that; or, You probably misunderstood; or, I'll come back next week, things are bound to get better. . . . After a long time, even the retarded (myself) should have known.

Your optimism sounds, even in your own ears, more and more like a graveyard tactic, with a difference. You whistle, but you hang around the grave. Now it is over. No more whistling, no more hanging around.

Which is not to be taken as meaning: No more leafletting, no more standing there, no more fasting, no more speaking the truth. Quite the contrary.

But what has all this to do with psalm 30?

It's a matter of architecture, of tone, of the place the soul desires, thirsts for, hungers for, wants to kneel in; a matter also of faces, Catholic faces, and being able to preach and shrive and bless and give holy bread away. A matter of access, of connection. Of leaving many things, growing out of many things—but never out of the one Thing. A matter of not being literally out in the cold. Of not having to recite a psalm meant to be recited in chorus, in community, in a sacred place—not being forced to recite it, having to summon more faith, a greater faith, than the psalm asks for; which is simply that it be said by believers together in a believing way.

But now the prayer must be said alone, or at least outside. That is the deep wrong, that is awry, that should not be. And for years and years. Where they cannot persecute, they ignore. And thus life goes.

This little psalm, so ingenuous, such a childlike burst of love, opens more life than one can easily bear.

I do not mean to leave it at that. For there are other matters too, not all of them somber; other consolations, other friends. We must hold our hands high over one another, forming a living sanctuary, our protection and canopy, a sacred space, though a sorrowful one.

Let us say the psalm with compassion, for those outside, because their conscience is granted no place inside.

Let us say the psalm, also with compassion, for those who honor violence, and summon to that dishonor the meek and peacemaking Lord. And themselves, and us as well.

UNCOMMON PRAYER, 1978

Dante's *Purgatorio*

It was consequent on long reflection (and an equally long series of actions) that I began my study of Dante. One lives today, trying to imagine our plight, a plight shadowed, first of all, by nuclear event as prophecy. What is God saying to us, what would God have us do, as a seemingly irreversible course leads humanity, like a blindfolded beast, toward the abattoir? Might there be ways of coping, ways which might properly be named spiritual, that is to say, surpassing whatever the politics of left or right might offer? . . .

I began to study Dante in a bilingual edition. Started by setting down notes, phrases, then whole sections. Not a translation by any means, the *terza rima* in English seemed beyond my scope; and in any case a dead form. Another difficulty arose; the events and personages Dante worked into his poem only served to embed large sections of the *Purgatorio* in the thirteenth century.

I had to think about his method, concrete as well as philosophical, political, passionately personal. How might those themes, moods, discourses, encounters be adapted, come alive today?

Dante's Caesarean church repelled me. *Arbiter mundi*, aping the great ones, mourning lost ground, miffed at kings and princes for not playing games of power according to its rules. As though indeed kings and princes and colonels and shahs and juntas could be prodded into secular pacifism (whatever that might be), or rule this world from the Mount of the Sermon. The church on an equal footing with high-handed secular powers? We have different agonies today. And a far less grandiose understanding of who we are vis-à-vis this world; humiliated, "pruned," as John's gospel has it, far less assured, more improvisational, obscurely searching. Christians, I thought, will know what I am groping for. . . .

Dante was a son of the church. This is the great honor I can pay him. By it I mean something quite simple and crucial. He draws clean lines. He knows the gospel and its other face, betrayal; in himself first of all, then in others, including those in high places. He knows the complexity of life in the world, how it sinks some under, bears others along, always uneasily. And he is not bewitched by complexity, ambiguity; he does not make a vocation out of head scratching. No, there are sin and error and foolishness, rancor, ill will, lust. These are not fabrications to keep people in line, names unattached to realities. They are sin. He says so.

And there is redemption; hope beats on, never gives up. As long as time lasts, there is possibility of blessedness, against all hope, against the main chance. It is a word Dante spoke first of all, to himself. And for this I thank him, that he did not exempt himself from the fate of humans, but set himself firmly on the mountain where all must work out the salvation they have betrayed or scorned. He is there, ascending, wondering, doubting, confessing—and judged. One to one he goes, with his friend and teacher, ascending through clutter and darkness to lucid essentials, discovering what a human being might be, a human life, a life worth living. Renewing the symbols that sustain, foster, lend stature, beget clairvoyance and courage. He makes life new, he walks in spite of all, sure footed.

It is called a tradition; it is the stark opposite of a dead religion. Dante knew it; he could not merely inherit such riches, nest in them, live off them. (In this respect, he reminds me of the canny investor spoke of by Christ.) What then to do? He was a poet and a public man; he would move the tradition along, a spider thread from his being, telling, testing as he went.

He called to his side one who had done something like this, long before, Virgil. Because, it seems, he wanted an "opposite number," in Gandhi's phrase. In the manner of the truly great who seek a loving adversary, a friend who will tell the truth, especially the unpleasant truth. Someone unsubdued by leveler Death, someone creaturely. One who had made a like voyage, a world wandered, creator of heroes, and more. In Dante's eyes, Virgil was mentor, moral teacher, guide, a kind of secular saint. Exactly, as things turn out, and with necessary nuances, what Dante became to me.

Dante's was a time, one remembers, that trumpeted its greatness on every wind. It was a time of dazzling innovative art, of the new vernacular poetry. The center was holding; synthesis was the intellectual mode; Christendom turned a confident face on the empire, the world beyond. It could afford to be generous. Were not its glories evident, intact?

And along with all this (as it seems, must be true in every imperial age)—violence. Dante lived with it, was immersed in it. As leader of one warring faction, he inevitably became its victim.

As it turned out, exile was his salvation. (As I learned too, both in 1965 and again in 1970, when I read with bitter relish and a nod of recognition: "How bitter to taste the salt of another's bread, and climb another's stair.")

Still, it seems to me that without the suffering, dependence, wanderings, and, above all, the solitude and study of those nineteen years of banishment, we would have had no *Commedia*.

The imperial stereotype. Florence: Not just a city, more like a state, wars, its own coinage, trade, flag, ambassadors. Above all, wars. And when foreign wars were lacking, internal fighting, bloody conflicts of interests. Does it evoke a tic, recognition? The leading candidates for slaughter in Dante's lifetime (he belonged to one of them) were the Blacks and the Whites.

Florence was a minute image of Rome. Arrangements were not working well; above all, they worked ill for Dante. Still, he thought for a long time that Rome had worked well. He was not granted to see, in other words, that no imperium in history has "worked well"—if by the phrase we mean something approaching the evangelical commonweal; implying access by all to justice, to the goods and services of the realm, public officials who serve instead of battening, no prisons or sanctioned state murder, and so on.

Dante was blind to these grievous shortcomings in his social order. Indeed, in the *Purgatorio* he enshrined the social arrangements of the empire in his esthetic and political vision. He still thought, even in his great poetry, that the church-imperium arrangement was of divine origin, that the destitute condition of the times was due to reparable malice, simony, ego. But that the arrangement was literally "in the nature of things," that it was a divine plan. Alas, we know otherwise.

One is tempted to dwell on this seductive mirage, the imperial plan as mirror of the divine plan. The Bible dissolves it in two ways. First by pointing out the self-destroying forces that lie within every empire, and inevitably bring it down. By concluding, inferentially, that the empire has but one destiny: self-destruction.

Secondly, by insisting that the empire, any empire, is simply an idol. The sum of its energies, structures, gears, fuels, wealth, trade, ideologies, pledges of allegiance, loyalty oaths, armies, cargoes, navies, air forces, marines, secular covenants, and so on—all these lie under the empire of the spiritual powers, they are a hieratic order of death. Christians, who purportedly owe other allegiances, must walk a wary way round these enticing sirens, threats, vows, promises, utopias. Christians are called, not to enlist in the state, but to suffer at its hands.

And to narrow the case to Dante's own, Florence could be expected to "work" no better than Rome, whose unworkability was celebrated in the Book of Revelation. Revelation linked Rome with defunct Babylon, itself linked hand in glove with still older histories of collapse, death. The biblical word is unmistakably clear; but who, in any empire, reads the Bible?

Without pushing things, Florence, and the pseudo-tradition it stands with and for, reminds me of our own times and country. Of Washington, Moscow, Peking. But one should speak of one's own turf—of oneself. Americans, too, have the dizzy, inflated sense of themselves which the demons confer. In our case, too, nagging doubts engender rigid certainties. Material grandeur, media puffing; tawdry though the paradise be, inaccessible to most, still it puts off such questions as Dante raised (but only at a distance, in solitude and suffering). Questions of wisdom, of happiness. Are we happy? We forget to ask ourselves, but faces tell us.

At high level or low, in the empire technique is all. It is the demonic soul of imperial conduct, activity in the world. It is also killingly competitive; in nuclear matters it demands isolation, policing, secrecy. In its service citizens become slaves of Mars.

Dante summoned Virgil, an act of piety, ancestral honor. He did so also, I think, in order to set limits, to declare the boundaries of reality. Virgil indeed guides Dante through that "less cruel sea," up the Mount of Purgation. But, just short of blessedness, Beatrice appears on the scene. And Virgil simply vanishes. He is not suddenly transfigured or canonized. But here, now, nature ends, grace invites. Through Virgil, Dante traces the outer reaches of the possible.

Dante is not dogmatic in all this. He is something infinitely better, rarer. He is a truth teller.

He creates the mountain, a godlike act, and its more or less guilty inhabitants, more or less burdened and blinded, skinny from fasting, immobilized by their past, icy or burning with fever. Each in process of being reborn, restored, healed.

They know him, they converse with him, he is indeed one of them. One of them! Recognition scenes are the poignant heart of his conquest of death, a conquest drawn entirely from the gospel promise. I will not dwell on what this means, that our faith stands in defiance of death; what it might mean to others who dwell in our death-shot century.

In Dante's century, as now, death was an acceptable method—of dealing with enemies, of furthering one's interests, of making a place in the world.

The question is, who will say yes? If we are politically bound, hand and foot, if madmen armed to the teeth pretend to speak for us, to kill in our name—if all this is true (and it is sadly and literally true), then the question is by no means annulled; it grows all the more urgent. Who will say yes? The question rises from the throats of prisoners and the tortured and defamed of earth, innocent, victimized, at the mercy of the powers. Who will say yes?

Dante says yes. Not cheaply, not comfortingly, not with one eye on orthodoxy and another fixated on the pain of the world. But with a whole heart, with all his might, with "two eyes making one in sight," with a courage that dares take into account hell, despair; our fragile, ludicrous, tragic fate. The accuracy of his master image is tested in a most painful and humiliating way; that is to say, it includes him, draws him in, judges him.

My sins. My guilt. My responsibility. My unfinished, indeed self-wounded humanity. My betrayals. My waste of time and grace. And above all and beyond all and beckoning me forward, my hope, which is not mine at all, but gift, grace, calling.

Dante walks there, converses, suffers, pays up. It is all quite simple, direct, concrete, episodic, worldly, here and now. In several episodes things are pushed hard. He meets souls expiating sins he himself has been guilty of. Such moments are cruelly truthful; he is stopped in his tracks. At the terrace of lust he walks the flames, as he tells us, in such agony that "immersion in boiling glass would have spelled relief."

Confessional poetry indeed. Beatrice calls out; the only time in all the *Commedia* when his name is spoken. The lips of transfigured love recognize the poet. But Beatrice is no mere comforter; indeed there are few moments in literature more disconcerting than this one. Beatrice stands before him, a Valkyrie of God, an accuser! In a culture that makes of judgment a dirty word, whose rules decree that no one may be called to accounts — in such a world, the lover who judges, the judge who is lover, these are indeed anomalous. What are we to make of this unfashionable, scriptural, metaphysical sternness?

The episode invites a long reflective look, implying as it does responsibility, forgiveness, power of love victorious over death.

Dante weeps. As a prelude to forgiveness. His tears fall on good soil. Indeed, we are in "another world."

Dante walks among the dead. He arouses wonderment and awe (to us, it is the dead who arouse wonderment and awe) because his flesh and blood are solid, he casts a shadow. He mingles with those souls, commiserates with their suffering, though he knows their suffering is exacted in justice, and so do they. But he mourns, he is one of them. Like a short-term prisoner, he promises to bring back messages to the living. He wants to be found acceptable, to be useful in their helplessness. In every encounter, he is apt to normalize, solidify, verify emotion; the cords of Adam even in that place, bind, hold firm.

Access to the unseen? It is possible, Dante says, but not to pander to comfort, hot or cold; there are to be no ambiguous mutterings in half-darkened rooms. Transactions with the dead, heartbreaking attempts at embraces, all come to pass in broad daylight, in bracing, sun-drenched air. Indeed the geography, height, location of the mountain are matters of great concern. Its measure is taken again and again, at every time of day. Sun and stars are in place. Dante's imagination is exact as a master astronomer's. We must understand that his mountain *exists* — on our planet, in a system of planets, verified, at just such distance from Jerusalem or Rome.

It is one thing to imagine, it is a quite different thing to mystify. In the *Purgatorio* there is no relief from the human condition. That condition, burdened, humiliated, guilty, at once implacable and devious in evil resolve, is everywhere insisted on. Friends say it and enemies: Behold us, we died as we lived. But hear us out, for a mercy greater than malice has intervened.

They show their wounds, they hold up their ravaged faces, beg his intercession and that of the church on earth.

No mystification here. No explaining away of guilt. Dante pays the souls (ourselves) the sublime honor of responsibility; there is lengthy discoursing on this theme. The dead are sinners, they are ourselves. That is to say, they (we) are wounded in our humanity, clouded in understanding, willful and self-deceived as to the truth, resourceful at self-deception. Longing for salvation, shying away from it. Fleeing from that "ragged figure, flitting from tree to tree at the back of the mind."

There was a dualism to be overcome. To those on earth, the dualism of heaven and hell is irrefragable, beyond reversing. They—we. They condemned or transfigured, we on earth, neither buried in torment nor wheeling in bliss. Indeed the dualism here is so strictly in accord with the nature of things, that to dissolve it offends against reality. To accept heaven or hell as images of this world, is to nullify our world.

We see such extremes in our culture: beatitude, despair, flight from reality, flight from responsibility, from the unbearable pain of life. But there is no flight in the *Purgatorio*. Every step is uphill, every step costs and counts. Dante wearies, cries out, grows disheartened, he suffers pain of spirit, remorse. His mind recoils, all but unhinged with grief at the plight of those he has called friends on earth. He cannot understand, must seek counsel. Emotion is drawn out, purified. It is not a dream of reality he invokes. It is reality imagined and undergone.

This is what drew me to the *Purgatorio*, a sense that Dante had dissolved the we—they, this world—other-world impasse. He came upon (created, better) a world whose difference from this world is the difference between the appearance of things and the truth of things. And he said to Virgil (to ourselves): Walk with me. He said to Virgil: Instruct me. And all the while, this cunning spirit is instructing us. To make sense, to make art, Dante had to climb, to risk.

One danger lies particularly close in matters of the spirit: The we-they, the doctrine of several worlds, can easily degenerate into an I-it impasse. Believers, that is to say, can refuse to enter the mountain. They can plant themselves in this world, hold the guidebook, refuse the journey. In so doing, they lose communion with the body of believers, whose vitality, symbols, world understanding, ethic, imaginative sources beckon us on the march.

The great refusal cancels the journey. Then the faith becomes a mere list of dogmas, leaving the will to fend for itself, the emotions frozen. The "I" no longer delights in the "we"; the faith is now a mere "it."

Much ink has been spilled, most of it in vain, around the question of Dante's system of purgatory. Does he offer more than a caricature of human acts, placing lust, anger, and so on, like square pegs in square holes, in a landscape labeled "Seven Deadly Sins"? Can God judge us more lucidly than we judge ourselves? Has not the area of guilt and accountability become a mine field, littered with the corpses of pre-Freudian error? There is, in fact, little that could be called arbitrary about his system. His choice of *seven* (sins, terraces) is an old game of numbers, a symbol of limits; it suggests here (as it often suggests in scripture) a rounding off of life, a longing, reaching for perfection. The seven terraces coalesce in a structure; there, one may observe, enter, grasp the drama of salvation. Parallel structures come to mind: the unities of Greek drama or the plan of an Elizabethean theater. Like the Mount of Purgation, these offer a setting, a geography, a cosmos susceptible to heroic struggle.

Finally the climb levels off, the air clears. Flames of purgation surround those who sing as they endure; their deliverance to the heavenly meadows adjoining their place of torment nears.

On that height we, too, can breath deep, purified, anticipating. On the threshold of blessedness, we look back; the long climb is over at last. Shortly we will stand in a place just short of paradise. There the grandeur, justice, compassion of the Creator is at long last vindicated. Angels have chastened and beckoned us; Beatrice has judged, purged, acquitted. We are at length what we are called to be.

THE DISCIPLINE OF THE MOUNTAIN, 1979

Part Five

ENCOUNTERS, CONFRONTATIONS

The Poet as Observer

I sit like a dunce in the incandescent noon
stool, cap, notes

a liberated blind man
whose eyes bear him like wings
out of night's stinking nest, into this world.

Intellectual vision, reality by definition?
No. The Jesuit mind, a Homer

assembles fleets, sails for its continent
across seas tamed by the ordering governing glance.

But to light on and finger the world, bit by bit
an old woman in the flea market—

junk, onions, ordure. Ingredients and parts.
The old fingers, wise as eyes, come on something. A yes.

THE WORLD FOR WEDDING RING, 1962

Journey from Sharpeville to Selma

Berrigan joined the civil-rights march, led by Dr. Martin Luther King, Jr., in Selma, Alabama, in March 1965; the march reminded him of a similar event in Sharpeville, South Africa, where in 1960 troops killed scores of protesters. Berrigan had visited South Africa in 1964.

One had the sense, rightly or no, of having landed here before. It was not merely the red ground underfoot, swirling in the hot wind, kicking up a red cloud around cattle and people and cars. Nor the earth coming to life again, after winter in July, or winter in January. Nor the plain that ran flat to the horizon in both places, far as the eye could reach; dogwood, magnolias, Spanish moss on the buttonwood and scrub pine. One had seen all this before; but one had seen something more, something that clung to the heart and almost defied the reach of words.

It was in the air. It held the eyes of people to a stranger's eye — too long or too briefly for comfort. It was in the air; it was in the shuffle of the blacks, it clung to the unpaved streets, the open garbage, the children playing in the dirt. It could almost be touched; it was pervasive as memory; something terrifying and obscene. It lingered around the troopers, played and played back from faces too alike to be entirely human. It was death, and violence, and years of terror.

It was the memory of Sharpeville. More than eighty had died in a burst of vicious, pure, unpremeditated violence. It was in the air of Selma; the air bore it like a groan — the memories of some twenty years. Through these town roads, the body of a black man, roped like a venison to the sheriff's car, had been driven into the black area. Go slow — slow. Let them see who's in charge here. It was in the air. Fifteen years ago a black man, arrested "for talkin' back" on the word of a cranky white woman, had been murdered in Selma jail. "An unknown policeman" had entered his cell and shot him. His body was dumped off on his family. No verdict, no investigation. But the town has not forgotten.

It is still in the air. Jimmy Lee Jackson, shot in Marion for defending his mother against a trooper's club, died in Good Samaritan Hospital here. He had powder burns on the skin of his belly. The barrel had been pushed to its closest range, and fired twice. The blacks remembered that night. When they tried to send hearses from Selma to Marion to pick up the wounded, lying untended in the streets, their answer had come from the sheriff's office: Come in here, you'll get what the rest got; I'll dump you in the river.

Could the whites forget, in Selma, or in Johannesburg? In Johannesburg they can, or almost. Once, Sharpeville had been a bitter memory; in '61, the

142

economy was on the verge of a panic. Investors had taken their money elsewhere. There was talk that blood and revolution would follow on the deaths of the blacks. Small countries had begun a boycott; the British Commonwealth had expelled South Africa. But the great powers, and especially the United States, came to the rescue. In one year, 1961, we contributed almost the entire amount needed in foreign exchange to push the trend up once more; some 150 millions poured in to stop the crisis.

The slump was not only eased, it was entirely reversed. By June of 1963, with continued U.S. help, South African gold and foreign exchange reserves had more than tripled, to reach a record high. The boom was on. And no one, not even the hard-headed, cares to say where it will stop.

Time, they say, is a slow healer. Money, one thinks, works faster. One American businessman calls South Africa "tantalizing" to investors. "We know the people and the government, and we back our conviction with our reputation and our dollars."

But money has not come into beleaguered Selma. In the short weeks since blacks and northern whites declared nonviolent war, business has dropped by fifty per cent. And time the healer has not arrived yet, is kept at bay; the false peace is interdicted. The blacks have seen to that; from Martin Luther King to the farmhand who shows up to march on Tuesday with Monday's bandage still bloody on his head. Indeed, the trooper is right when he cries, zooming like a tortured gadfly on his motorcycle from end to end of the marchers: "I've never seen anything like this in all my ——— life!"

Neither has the nation. Neither has the church. Who ever heard of a church, North or South, that has rung, day after day, week after week, with the unending songs, the prayers, the sermons; a church that spilled into the streets a people ready for whatever hell the troopers are ready to bring down on them: dogs, horses, whips, tear gas, billies? What liturgy prepares men and women and children for Lingo and Clark and Connor? What faith arms them by forbidding them arms, tells them to march when they can, to kneel when they cannot, to face the oppressors—maybe even to convert them? The questions are fierce, and for the moment (for white Americans) unanswerable. But the point is clear; the questions are real questions, as real as the broken bones and the blood; as real as the new hope.

Monday, March 15. We came in, thirty-five strong, from New York, in time for the memorial service for Reverend Reeb. We were from Harlem and Manhattan and Brooklyn, blacks and whites, laypeople and priests. Selma was quiet as a mill pond; but the quiet was ominous; the pin had been pulled, the depth charge dropped. Children wandered in the sun, the stores were open, the fresh tourist signs were out: WELCOME TO SELMA . . . SHANNON HOTEL. Then, we approached. Browns Chapel, the reality of Selma hit like a tight fist.

The church was ringed with Clark's troopers. They lounged in the open cars, feet hung out of doors and windows, eyes half closed in the sunlight; helmets, billy clubs, a stereotype of sleepy brutal power; the day of the iguana. Our car circled the church for blocks—no way in. Finally, we parked and walked through.

The church was packed. The TV cameras, the newsmen were there in force, tired out but still there. The nation needed to see this; better, since Sunday, it even wanted to see. A shabby backwater church, that had sheltered and comforted generations of blacks, and had rung with the passion and anguish of a trodden people, was for this week the heart and focus of America. In it, the most astounding ironies were being taken for granted. Black store hands and field workers sat beside distinguished theologians. Hawaiians met New Yorkers, believers shook hands with the unchurched, beatniks sang along with nuns. Men and women who differed in every conceivable respect—faith and race and culture—found themselves bewildered by a sudden unity whose implications went far beyond the unpredictable days they were enduring together. But they knew beyond any doubt that they would never again be the same women and men who had lived Before Selma.

Light by light, individual purpose was fused in the incandescent arc of black courage and black passion. Free-e-e-dom. Free-e-e-dom. They sang it together, the skilled and the ignorant, the neophyte and the victim. Some of them knew what they sang. But the others were learning.

The speeches began. Walter Reuther, an Orthodox Bishop, a Catholic Bishop, two Ministers, and finally Martin Luther King. The words ranged from noble to bathetic, and back again. King's voice was ragged with exhaustion, the strain of vigils and of decisions, the killing round of the weeks, from courts to streets to meetings and back again, with the responsibility of sending the crowds out to face Jim Clark.

One thing was clear. This was the blacks' day. We were, at long last, at their side. But even the newsmen were not sure why we were there. They were not even convinced that we knew why; one of them asked us, in words that were not especially flattering: Why have the Catholics gotten into the act? We were not sure either, in a way that could easily be formulated. But it was something like an ethic of the guts; some things cannot be disposed of, in peace, by moral tics over headlines, even in 1965.

Almost everyone one could think of was there: men and women of concern, theologians, nurses, teaching nuns, writers, rabbis, artists, students. Where were so and so? They were either there (one would meet them or see them in the crowd) or they were on their way or had stopped and gone. And all week long, the vigils, the prayers, the hospitality of the blacks (our money was no good, anywhere), the cheerful faith, the contrast of ascetic purity and puritanism on the rampage, of birth pangs and the desperate lunges of moral death, the swift free calls to prayer and song and march, and the knowledge that slavery hemmed us in—what is the church, anyway? Is it where we came from, or is it here, being created by blacks and their white acolytes?

In any case, it was the black people's day, their week; one might say, their week of creation. They had been conceived and born at Bloody Bridge, at all the bloody crossroads of the nation, weeks and years before Selma. Could they, this week, bring us over that Bridge, to birth? They might; love is a marvelous midwife.

Johannesburg, the black township, Good Friday, 1964. The Gospel of Saint John was read in Zulu. And they crucified Him there; it was about the third hour. . . . The sea of color, the immobile, intent faces, men, women, children, hundreds strong, seated on the earthen floor. What could a white man say to them? what could a white priest say? He could say something surely; he might even say a new thing. He might say that Christ had died for all men and women, even for whites. He could take up his cross, hammered together by fate, propped up, waiting, visible to all. In South Africa, his cross was simply the fact of being a white man with some remnant of conscience. He could say in public, while the Special Branch Police lounged against the walls taking notes, that he was unworthy of his black brothers and sisters; that some day the whites might conceivably leave off being their executioners.

Monday, March 15, Selma. The long memorial service is almost over. Hardly any discomfort is evident; blacks are used to standing, kneeling, waiting; and the whites are learning. The weather outside is Alabama spring time, a frayed and dusty glory. Dogwood and magnolia are coming to flower. The benediction has been pronounced over the memory of Reeb. Flowers bank the speakers' stand. Someone has pinned to the front of the pulpit a drawing from a northern newspaper; it shows a wreath of thorns fastened to a gravestone, the tomb of James Reeb. Martin King has spoken. And then, the announcement comes; the march is permitted by court order. Three by three, in silence, we are allowed by the courts of Alabama to march on the courthouse of Selma. It is to be a memorial march for James Jackson and James Reeb. Prayers at the courthouse are permitted; we can even sing.

Whites and blacks, after all the bitter years, after black heroism and white anger, after Birmingham and Marion and St. Augustine—after all this, both sides are fused together by one fact, a bitter event which neither side wanted but which each side knew in its heart must come to pass. Each side now had a martyr.

For the blacks, the irony is very nearly complete. They have had to wait and wait for the whites—when will they stand with us, or march with us? And the whites have waited for a death, before they could be moved. For the blacks, martyrdom was nothing new at all; it was old as their American history. It had begun with lynchings and disappearances and bodies pulled from rivers. Most of the black martyrs were nameless. But one of them, otherwise obscure and humble, had died in Selma; and Selma, by a convergence of happenings beyond all prediction, had exploded.

The explosion was triggered by a white man's death. The blow had been launched by whites; they had struck down a minister of the gospel. It was a wound with a difference; it lay on the body of the white community.

Time indeed might heal it. Give us time . . . you can't push this thing too fast. . . . But no time was allowed. The blacks granted time no place. They had been clocked too long by whites; Clark and Lingo had had too much time; time for troopers, time for gas, time for Bloody Bridge. The end was there in sight. We started out.

The Gospel of Saint John, in the Zulu tongue, so strange to American ears; sibilants and the clicking of tongues, with only the names Jesus, Mary, Peter, John, coming through. And about the third hour, they crucified Him. . . . A white priest, in the pulpit of the black church; my fellow Christians. He can hardly remember what he had to say to them. But at the end, the veneration of the Cross. A great wave starts forward: mothers with children, young men, the very old. Three priests move among them, holding the crucifix to their lips. And spontaneously, as is the way with Africans, the chant starts; first, as one voice, hardly rising above the sough of bare feet, that sound which above all sounds is like the sea, on a mild evening. The song is the Zulu dirge for a fallen warrior. They are bearing Him homeward to his village after battle. His name is Jesus, great King, black Warrior. Easily, with infinite delicacy and naturalness, the song breaks into harmony; two parts, then four, then eight, as a yolk divides, or a cell . . . Jesus, great Warrior, we mourn you. O the beauty, the youth, the empty place. Who shall plead for us, who shall lift our faces, who shall speak wisdom?

The Zulus have a saying: those who are behind must run faster than those who are in front. Even to the Cross. Even when the Cross is held in white hands. Shall the whites time us, even to the Cross? Do they any longer even know the way?

The strangest thing about the march to Selma courthouse was the utter silence in town. That, and the faces of the troopers. There was a trooper for every marcher, someone said. Almost, but not quite. The three hundred who left the church were joined, like streams to a great river, by those who had arrived outside, and were waiting; some two thousand in all. The town had gone silent, as though a great hand were clapped to its mouth, at five o'clock on a workday evening. Traffic was lined up at corners, storekeepers in their doorways; the troopers' cameras were clicking in the faces of the clergy. (Good to know we'll be in Jim Clark's scrapbook!) But mostly silence. Except that, all along the route, the transistors kept telling us and the nation what it was like, what it could never be like again, in Selma on a spring evening.

The breakthrough had come, irresistible as spring. You could see it, whoever you were, trooper or housewife, white or black. You could hate it like the approach of death, or feel it in your bones like the nudge of Christ on Lazarus — but it was there, for all the world to see. In the dusk around

Courthouse Square (that's Jim Clark's courthouse—but no more, no more) the big TV lights went on in a wink, punctual as dawn, the lights no black had dared hoped to see. The prayers began; for the dead, for the living, for the persecutors. Martin King laid at the glass doorway a purple wreath: "For James Reeb," the crepe said. But at that moment, the worried, porcine face of Jim Clark was peering through the glass. Jim Clark, framed in a burial wreath; beyond the mild ghost of James Reeb, the death of southern power and conscienceless law. For the blacks, it was a moment delicious beyond words; requiescat Jacobus.

In the African reserve, it was autumn; but the autumn had come on so gently it might have been an Alabama spring. Passion flowers and magnolias and wild roses, the last of them. But under the dusty clouds that followed cars and men and women like their shadows, hardly a flower or a blade of grass. We were in the last of the old city reserves, marked by the city for bulldozing. The serpentine alleys, the crazy shacks, were to come down. One thought, It wouldn't take much of a push to bring all this to the ground.

Coming up: a government plan, complete to the last nail and brick. New dormitories for the black city workers, male and female dwellings side by side, housing for some sixty thousand. (But as usual, when the Verwoerd government plans for the Africans, there's a hidden card. The workers are in fact country people, up from the impoverished reserves to seek jobs. Some sixty per cent of the men are married, by conservative estimate; the government understandably supplies no figures. Many have young families started. They leave wives and children behind, and the pass laws lock them in the city. The government is in fact promoting and legalizing the breakup of African families and easing the blow by providing easily available prostitution.)

In the reserve in Johannesburg, everything is inside the fences: the schools, the stores, the church and rectory and convent. They were all to come down. The families would be moved some twenty miles out, into paved streets and brick homes. (The finest in Africa, the government declares. Where else in our continent does each black family have its own home, constructed by the state, with a yard and space for a tree or two? A family can even buy its own home on credit. . . . But a family can never own the land on which the home stands.)

We toured the reserve. Hopelessness, torpor, the crime rate soaring. But the priests are welcome. They are the only whites who can move in and out with a measure of safety or the hope of a greeting, in all this jungle. We returned to the rectory. Out of the darkness of the yard, a man and child emerged. They had waited there for an hour "to see the priest who spoke this afternoon. Everyone is saying, He spoke for us, he said something for us. I wanted to thank him; I brought my small daughter to meet him."

Selma, Tuesday afternoon, March 16. Jim Clark's troopers have raced into Montgomery. A march was undertaken there, and violence has erupted. We in Selma will march also, in sympathy and protest. The wounded are lying in the street of the capital, after a mounted charge. There is a call for doctors and nurses; two nuns get up and leave the church.

Jim Clark has had another frustrating day. Without troopers, he had to keep some hundreds of marchers off the streets, with only his posses and a few men in Conservation Department cars. Baker is not in evidence; he seems to know that Clark cannot do much harm without his bullies. But Clark races up and down Sylvan Street, in front of Browns Chapel, his white Chrysler careening like a dreadnought under fire, stopping the line at one end, then at the other. He swings around to a halt, races from the car ("Man, he'll end up dead; he's too fat for all that runnin' "), confronts the line at the north end; on signal the marchers turn south. Back to the car on the run, down to the other end. But the marchers turn once more, facing center. The line breaks at the middle; those in the center turn at right angles, into the housing project yards. Too narrow for the Chrysler; Clark has to take the long way round. And by then, some are almost to the courthouse. Frantic, sweating, he turns them back.

Into the church again. We pray briefly, a Southern Conference minister leading; We ask You that the black belt may become a belt of light. . . . We stand where the law has been misused, where the innocent have been struck down. . . . Be with us and our leaders. . . .

A young black in overalls speaks to us. "Clark's not going to tell us we can march one day and not march the next. We're going to keep moving. They're bludgeoning people in Montgomery this afternoon, charging them with horses. We're going to reach our courthouse and pray there." Another black approaches the speaker and whispers the news. Clark has the church ringed with police; he's gotten them back into town. "Now this is the worst thing of all. He's trying to keep us in here, against all law. So we're goin' out. We want the priests and ministers to lead; if we're to be beaten, they ought to take it first. Will you go?"

We will. We strike up a song, and start. This might be it.

It was worse, and better, than one had imagined. It may have been all the clerics, the white faces among the black. But there was no charge of the helmeted ring; they stood there, they didn't give an inch; but they didn't move in either. And in Selma, after the past week, that was something new.

In front, the white priest, the rabbi, and the black minister confronted Clark. The newsmen moved close, the TV took it all in; five minutes of passionate exchange, then the decision. A cleric in front turned to the line, spoke quietly, and knelt. Men and women and children went down on knee, as though under the pressure of some sudden wind. The TV commentator said it into his mike, stepping among the crouching figures to get his pictures. But we already knew it: "It looks like another long night in Selma."

CONSEQUENCES, TRUTH AND . . . , 1967

In Vietnam and Laos

In February 1968, Father Berrigan and Howard Zinn, a professor at Boston University, went to Hanoi as representatives of the peace movement; in Hanoi three captured American pilots were released to them by the North Vietnam peace committee "in celebration of our New Year Tet holiday."

Friday, February 9, 1968

At long last, after a week of despair and hope and the cancellation of two planes, we took off from Vientiane to Hanoi at 5:19 P.M. Our aircraft was described optimistically as a Boeing 707; we were told that it was about thirty years old. There survive only three of these marvels on our planet. A fourth crashed on the same run about one year before; no trace of it has ever been found. Our flight was half filled; the complement included both children and civilians, Poles, Indians, and ourselves.

Five minutes after takeoff. The Mekong is below; a vast sprawl of water whose sleepy gods are placated by messy little shrines like pigeon cages along the banks. Like the Mississippi, the Mekong is capable of blindly breaking out in floods. Now, where it crooks an elbow in mid-Vientiane, there lies a great golden bar of sand, like the aftermath of a gesture of creation.

Below, the rice fields, the primitive villages. A misty tranquil day, in a country whose changes in light and temperature are never severe or sudden.

We have been circling the city for ten minutes, gaining our altitude. It is forbidden to move gradually into the air corridor. We must gain altitude and then take off like an arrow.

At 10,000 feet we can still see the huts at the center of the fields; the dikes going outward like cracks in a green crystal. *O doux pays.*

Cumulus clouds, a lonely sunset. "Nature is the imposition of consciousness on fact." The fact for us, as we go to Hanoi, is the maelstrom of violence and death that have stained the country, while we trudged our dusty vacuum and awaited the nod of the powers. But a like scene, viewed from an airliner above the United States or Europe, might induce a reaction of an entirely different order; the contentment of the gods, empery from sea to sea.

The stewardess has just shown us the *"casquettes."* There is one for each passenger in the racks overhead. *"Ce n'est pas drôle—c'est serieux. . . .* Twice we have needed them."

The pilot came along the aisle to chat with us. He had flown the same planes, he said, back in '54. He had been back on this Saigon-Hanoi run for

149

the past two months. He explained that they had radio contact with Hanoi; that we had three hours from Vientiane to make it. Thereafter, the U.S. Navy, with its bombers, and the U.S. Air Force were free to bring us down. There would be a one-hour stop in Hanoi. He recalled how narrow a squeak they had before the bombers came in last October 27; it was announced over the radio that the supersonics were twenty miles away from Hanoi. He landed quickly, just made it.

We asked him about the difficulty of taking off from Saigon with the city in siege since the Tet uprising. He said that ours was the only civilian aircraft to have left; there was still heavy fighting at the airstrip.

The mountains rise to about 9,000 feet; the plane is at about 11,000 feet. The crew wants DC's introduced; there is no pressurization in the cabins of these crates.

Every day, before the bombing sorties, the pilot said, the American flyers are shown the design of this plane and its markings. Yet, he reflected dispassionately, one of these planes was shot down and no remains ever found.

It is now 5:30 P.M. We have crossed the border and are in North Vietnam. Congratulations Zinn, Peacenik, Soul Brother!

There is great interest in us on the part of the French crewmen and stewardesses.

Not yet death. This is a wait longer than Godot, longer than Beckett.

Darkness. The lights are flashing from the ground outside. Howard (my cherished brother and friend, and Old Testament man of heart and guts) is deep in converse, in his delicious fractured French, with a passenger up ahead.

The old craft is shaking in every rivet, like a clay duck before the trapshooters, the war game experts.

How long have I wished to share the common life, to be compassionate with men and women, within the same fear, the same skin, the same trembling and fire and ice, to mourn with the men and women who die and do not wish to die; to weep for the children.

The first lights of Hanoi, 7:15 P.M., the runway. Easy down. The lights of the antiaircraft nest shine full upon us: "just checking, bud." . . .

How to convey the atmosphere, that long and dolorous entrance into the destroyed city; the endless pontoons of the bridges replacing the bombed span; the desolation and patience and cold; the convoys, the endless lines of military vehicles and cars.

As usual the loveliest fact of all was the most elusive and insignificant; we had been received with flowers.

We were ushered, at about 9:30 P.M., into the austere napoleonic deluxe of the "Hotel of Reunification." Supper. We are instructed, "Sleep well." . . .

Saturday, February 10

An air-raid alarm. We went to sleep like children and awakened like adults to the boom! boom!, the guns of an Indian summer, courtesy of our Air Force. Howard appeared at my door, disheveled and primary in the half light, like a runner awaiting the shot, without his socks forsooth. In a few moments we had crossed the garden and ducked into the shelter. Howard was decently covered by a German who placed his own rubber coat over those extensive and defenseless lower limbs.

Later that day, and throughout the week, I could hear the chambermaids in the corridor, singing; the plaintive atonal music with which the meek of heart console themselves for life in the cave of ravening lions. . . .

Friday, February 16

[With the three pilots, Berrigan and Zinn returned to Laos.] The two-hour flight into Laos was uneventful in a way in which every ride of that sort is without issue; or rather, has at its outcome only the issue of survival.

So, too, the entrance on the scene of Ambassador Sullivan, accredited to the United States Embassy in Laos, a man at once ruthless and fascinating — that story also has been told. I should like to add a few reflections that may have the value of an eyewitness account.

My words with regard to the conduct of the ambassador may be of no great import in the larger question of the brutal progress of the war itself. Zinn and I were but one instance in a larger betrayal, whose field of action is the bodies of the Vietnamese people. And yet because a betrayal was wrought upon us, and because both the military, represented by the fliers, and ourselves, of the peace movements, were involved in an extended and even dangerous episode, it seems worthwhile to recall the event, and to reflect upon it here.

We should perhaps be grateful that the outcome was not worse than it was. Treated as we had been by American officials with minimal courtesy, and with a rather obvious effort to remain out of our way, should we not remain content with that? No. Like all resisters, we are afflicted beyond remedy with the idealism of which we read so often in our history, and in the history of political protest in the West. We have not grown used to knavery, and to that species of untruth which lies so near to the truth as to be able to wear its clothing, and to turn upon the idealist its seductive and silencing countenance.

Still, against the ambassador we had, I would think, one great advantage. Men and women of the truth, who constantly search their own motivation and hearts, are perhaps equipped to deal also with that fine art of untruth known to our world as diplomacy. And this may be a clue as to why Sullivan found himself in a much more difficult situation than he could have anticipated. He mounted our plane like a buccaneer; he was governed, I would think, by the expectation of holding us captive to the grandeur of his office and the charm of his personal qualities. No such thing transpired. The five minutes he had perhaps granted himself to hold the press at bay outside, and to win over a rather absent-minded cleric, extended into forty and then to fifty minutes of heated and close discussion. In that hour all of us knew that our mettle was being tested to the utmost. The meaning and momentum of our voyage were at stake—the presence of the three released men in our midst, a prey worthy of steel and will, the clamor of that eagle on the embassy insignia, even now loosing its thunderbolts upon the northern nights, the promises so recently concluded by us, fliers and men of peace, pledges so charged with implication for the future of other men and women, lying so heavy upon the prisoners of the North that their import must yet ring in our ears. All this and more charged the stale air of the grounded craft with drama and danger. And through it all, we could see outside, like the eyes of a jungle night, the lights of the television cameras, a closure of fire and anger and expectation.

What was it to be obedient, what indeed to disobey? This may be the deepest question of the war; it played like a wayward lightning between the fliers, the ambassador, and ourselves on that night. It was a question as old as aerial warfare itself, and much older. But it seemed to us entirely and exactly fitting that the question should be raised in a grounded aircraft, at the edge of an airstrip, itself at the edge of that world which some delighted in calling free—without ever questioning their own unfreedom. "I am an army career man," finally said the ranking officer, the major. "Any least indication of the will of my superiors is a command to me." It was the most ominous sentence I had yet heard in a war whose daily currency was groundless rhetoric, duplicity, body counts, and murderous ideology. Yet I must confess that the sentence also had a kind of untouchable platonic perfection. As an expression of the system from which it issued, the sentiment was virtuous beyond praise. The word was spoken. There remained only what we of the West call, with a clumsy instrumental neologism, its implementation. *Verbum caro.* We issued from the cave of Plato, where all words are indeed an emptiness, to face the world, the times, the purpose, and hope outside. We issued from the cave and stood in the glare of humanity's eyes and instruments, under judgment, under the yoke of the law.

The fliers finished with the press, there on the oil-stained macadam, after a short general statement, delivered in the exhausted monotone of the major. Zinn and I lingered in the background. We were of no interest; the peace had lost its prey. We knew nothing of what was to come, we were desperately in need of sleep and wanted only to get apart and reflect upon the sudden explosion of all our hopes. An attache offered us an embassy car; they wanted us off the scene, once and for all; and I refused, discourteously, as I recall. The pilots strode across the airstrip to their waiting plane. The sleek door of the jet closed upon its burden, as in a children's story the door of a mountain closes upon a piper and the village children. Farewell to the children, farewell!

The newsmen turned about, in our direction.

NIGHT FLIGHT TO HANOI, 1968

Children in the Shelter

Imagine; three of them.

As though survival
were a rat's word,
and a rat's death
waited there at the end

and I must have
in the century's boneyard
heft of flesh and bone in my arms

I picked up the littlest
a boy, his face
breaded with rice (his sister calmly feeding him
as we climbed down)

In my arms fathered
in a moment's grace, the messiah
of all my tears. I bore, reborn

a Hiroshima child from hell.

LIBERATION, MARCH 1968

Statement of the Catonsville Nine

(The following is a press statement released by the undersigned on the occasion described below.)

Today, May 17, 1968, we enter Local Board #33, Catonsville, Maryland, to seize the Selective Service records and to burn them outside with homemade napalm. (The recipe for napalm we took from the Special Forces Handbook, published by the Army's School of Special Warfare at Ft. Bragg, North Carolina.)

As American citizens, we have worked with the poor in the ghetto and abroad. In the course of our Christian ministry, we have watched our country produce more victims than an army of us could console or restore. Two of us face immediate sentencing for similar acts against Selective Service. All of us identify with the victims of American oppression all over the world. We submit voluntarily to their involuntary fate.

We use napalm on these draft records because napalm has burned people to death in Vietnam, Guatemala, and Peru; and because it may be used in America's ghettos. We destroy these draft records not only because they exploit our young men, but because these records represent misplaced power, concentrated in the ruling class of America. Their power threatens the peace of the world; it isolates itself from public dissent and manipulates parliamentary process. And it reduces young men to a cost-efficiency item through the draft. In effect — if not in intent — the rulers of the United States want their global wars fought as cheaply as possible.

Above all, our protest attempts to illustrate why our country is torn at home and harassed abroad by enemies of its own creation. For a long time the United States has been an empire, and today it is history's richest nation. Representing 6 per cent of the world's people, our country controls half the world's productive capacity and two-thirds of its finance. It holds Northern and Southern America in an economic vise. In fifteen years time, economists think that its industry in Europe will be the third greatest industrial power in the world, after the United States and the Soviet Union. Our foreign profits run substantially higher than domestic profits. So industry flees abroad under Government patronage and protection from the CIA, counter-insurgency, and conflict management teams.

The military participates with economic and political sectors to form a triumvirate of power which sets and enforces policy. With an annual budget of more than 80 billion dollars, our military now controls over half of all Federal property (53 per cent, or 183 billion dollars) while U.S. nuclear and conventional weaponry exceeds that of the whole remaining world.

Peace negotiations with the North Vietnamese have begun in Paris. With other Americans, we hope a settlement will be reached, thus sparing the Vietnamese a useless prolongation of their suffering. However, this alone will not solve our nation's problems. The Vietnam War could end tomorrow and leave undisturbed the quality of our society, and its world role. Thailand, Laos, and the Dominican Republic have already been Vietnams. Guatemala, the Canal Zone, Bolivia, and Peru could be Vietnams overnight. Meanwhile, the colonies at home rise in rage and destructiveness. Our black people have concluded that after 350 years, their human acceptance is long overdue.

Injustice is the great catalyst of revolution. A nation that found life in revolution has now become the world's foremost counter-revolutionary force, not because the American people would have it that way, but because an expanding economy and continuing profits require an insistence on the *status quo*. Competitive capitalism as a system, and capitalists in general, must learn the hard lessons of justice, or a country may be swept away and humanity with it.

We believe that some property has no right to exist. Hitler's gas ovens, Stalin's concentration camps, atomic-bacteriological-chemical weaponry, files of conscription, and slum properties have no right to exist. When people starve for bread and lack decent housing, it is usually because the rich debase themselves with abuse of property, causing extravagance on their part and oppression and misery in others.

We are Catholic Christians who take the Christian gospel seriously. We hail the recent Papal encyclical, *The Development of Peoples*. Quotes like the following give us hope:

> No one is justified in keeping for his exclusive use what he does not need, when others lack necessities.
>
> A revolutionary uprising—save where there is open, manifest, and long-standing tyranny which does great damage to fundamental personal rights and dangerous harm to the common good of the country—produces new injustices, throws more elements out of balance, and brings on new disasters.
>
> It is a question of building a world where every man, no matter what his race, religion, or nationality, can live a fully human life, freed from slavery imposed on him by other men or natural forces, a world where the poor man Lazarus can sit down at the same table with the rich man.
>
> The hour for action has now sounded. At stake are the survival of so many children and so many families overcome by misery, with no access to conditions fit for human beings; at stake are the peace of the world and the future of civilization.

Despite such stirring words, we confront the Catholic church, other Christian bodies, and the synagogues of America with their silence and cowardice in the face of our country's crimes. We are convinced that the religious bureaucracy in this country is racist, guilty of complicity in war, and hostile to the poor. In utter fidelity to our faith, we indict religious leaders and their followers for their failure to serve our country and humankind.

Finally, we are appalled by the ruse of the American ruling class invoking pleas for "law and order" to mask and perpetuate injustice. Let our President and the pillars of society speak of "law and justice" and back up their words with deeds. Then there will be "order." We have pleaded, spoken, marched, and nursed the victims of their injustice. Now this injustice must be faced, and this we intend to do, with whatever strength of mind, body, and grace that God will give us. May He have mercy on our nation.

> Rev. Daniel Berrigan
> Rev. Philip Berrigan
> Bro. David Darst
> John Hogan
> Thomas Lewis
> Majorie Bradford Melville
> Thomas Melville
> George Mische
> Mary Moylan

PHILIP BERRIGAN, S.S.J., A PUNISHMENT FOR PEACE.
NEW YORK: MACMILLAN, 1969

The Clock in the Square Reminds Me of Certain Lives

Ineffectuals
chained, reined to time's beaten track—
simulacra all, strangers to action, passion

strike the hour, lurch away
pale as linen
the pharaohs of long refusal.

FALSE GODS, REAL MEN, 1969

Israel, as Presently Constituted

The speech to the Association of Arab University Graduates, referred to in this essay, appears, with responses by Professor Hans Morgenthau and others, in The Great Berrigan Debate (*New York: Committee on New Alternatives in the Middle East, 1974*).

Some two and a half years have passed since I ventured certain remarks in Washington on the Mideast situation.

Everything, it turned out, was wrong with the speech. The tone was awry, the criticism of Israel was inaccurate, clumsy, presumptuous, the audience of Arab students was ill-chosen, the timing was, if not malicious, at least maladroit. I must be either a dim-wit or an anti-Semite. I had followed the irresponsible drift of the American left into a revolutionary maelstrom whose heart was an icy fascism. Or I was cloning the worst historical stereotypes of my church vis-à-vis the Jewish community, from Torquemada to Coughlin.

I began to feel somewhat like Joann Little. At a certain point in her ordeal underground, she tells how she lay hidden under a feather mattress in a southern shack. A hefty sheriff entered to question the householder. In the course of his inquisition, he settled his considerable behind on the aforesaid bed for a long, long session. And Joann, feathered but not tarred, wondered warmly if she would survive this one.

So I, tarred but not feathered, wondered about survival, as the most unlikely bedfellows came to rest — on me. Unlikely, indeed. B'nai Brith had me on their wanted list that year; my hide was up for sale in the pages of *Commentary, World View, Commonweal*, the *Village Voice*, the *New York Times*. I replaced God himself for a time, as a bone of contention in pulpits. I was denounced as "insane" by a high official of the National Council of Churches, was castigated by an Episcopal priest visiting Jerusalem as guest of the Israeli government. At the behest of a liberal minister in midtown Manhattan, I was denied a peace prize. I received hate mail from all over; it included a whopper from a faculty member of the Jewish Theological Seminary. Someone took a count. It appeared that over one hundred articles were written during the following year responding to The Speech; they severally castigated, refuted, called names, speculated on motives base or noble, traced my moral decline and fall, demythologized, in some few cases agreed with the main line of my argument.

All that year the debate raged, fruitbearing, fruitless. At least this could be gleaned (I was becoming an addict to minimal returns) — the skeletons were out of the closet, abroad, in daylight. It would be harder, on this topic, to forbid people to step aside from *parti pris*.

Later, something else happened, worth nothing perhaps. A distinguished American Jew professed himself enraged because I had dared say in print what I repeat here—that I saw no reason to repent my original words. He wrote in a national magazine that, at long last, it was clear that I was exactly what less temperate souls than he had called me—an anti-Semite. I must confess that his words went off in my brain like a delayed mine. So I am now guilty (over and above the original crime) of non-recantation. I ask myself, how double can jeopardy get?

The storm I allude to keeps breaking out, it cannot be stilled, any more than the course of events can be halted. Somewhat over a year ago a small gathering occured in Boston. In the course of what was planned as an off-the-record effort at reconciliation, I had the audacity to say the following: that the State of Israel, as presently constituted, had no future.

I fully intended to explain my words, each word separately and in context, since I had chosen each word with extraordinary care. By the phrase "as presently constituted" I wished to criticize certain aspects of Israeli law and life; the Law of Return, first of all, the colonization of the Golan Heights, the military occupation of the West Bank, the seizure of land, the building of Jewish Quarters in West Jerusalem, the attempts to subdue or assimilate the Palestinian people within Israel.

I wished also to separate out what I took to be two realities. In the first place: a given web of assumptions, an accepted ideology, political and military conduct, modes of authority—all of which constitute "the state." Then, on the other hand, such realities as the consciousness of people, their "mood" at a given time, the continuity or break in their self-understanding, their ethical sense and expression, the myriad ways they choose to present their lives before the world—artistic, religious, intellectual. Thus I believe one can, and should, separate out two realities: "Israel as presently constituted" from "Israel as constituting itself." The two, I believe, are quite different in their political and social reality: the first is an arbitrary structure, the second a spiritual reality in process. The second must question the first; reform, reprove, even replace it.

There was no chance, in Boston, to say these things. Those who had greeted me warmly before I spoke, could hardly bring themselves to listen; the meeting ended in pain and disarray; one distinguished rabbi noisily threw his chair back and left the room with a slam. Reflecting ruefully on all this, I remind myself that history is a better teacher than I will ever be. History is also more abrupt, not to say brutal. Often, its terms are far less generous than I would allow to humans and their structures, Israelis and Palestinians included. In the two and half years since I spoke in Washington, D.C., violating taboos right, left, and center, Jewish and Christian, and in the year and a half since I said roughly the same things in Boston— in that time, events have dealt with Israel in a fashion that makes me look like the tenderest of Jewish mothers. Military, economic, and diplomatic realities have progressively weakened the umbilical connection between Israel and its friends, a connection which many had fondly believed was symbiotic, biophelic, bound to endure. But the connection is now seen in a truer light, a slipshod fail safe arrangement, concocted in benefit of diplomatic and military expediency. Medically speaking, the hodge-podge of wires, tubes, tanks, and hoses kept the patient breathing, without any concern for his life itself; the interest at stake was that of the surgeon's career in the world, his self-image, his cold repute. And even this metaphor puts the matter with maximum optimism; for the tubes may well be pulled out tomorrow and the patient never know why he perished. Dr Kissinger's surgical skills favoring neat and cheap death rather than complex and costly life.

Meantime, to speak of painful internal realities, Israel is being fast transformed into a fortress-state. Inevitably. Insecurity and danger are not ordinarily conducive to political generosity. Within Israel, if there is some tendency to regard Palestinians outside the country as human beings, raising legitimate grievances, this says nothing of the worsening fate of Palestinians within Israel's borders, whether on the Left Bank, in Jerusalem, in Ramallah or Galilee. This state of things must also be regarded as inevitable. The enemy outside the borders, if they are suffi-ciently astute, resolute, and cruel, must be taken into account; they may be hated and hateful, but their voice is magnified a thousand-fold in the first, second, and third worlds. They are heard from, their demands gradually prevail. But the Palestinians within Israel are something else again. In a nation under perpetual trauma, shaken by the underground mutter of violence, domestic Palestinians are regarded as a kind of fifth column, Vichyites, potential internal traitors. So, they must be denied their civil rights; their land must be expropriated; they must be denied political assembly; their villages must be burned; those who are prisoners must be held without trial, even tortured. In such ways, the dream of a democratic homeland turns to a nightmare, a garrison state, a state of siege.

The government of Israel—despite tradition, rhetoric, heroism, skills of survival, liberal initiatives, even a history of martyrs by the millions—today runs a last-ditch race against time. The nearest analogues that come to my mind, also racing against history, against the majority, against humanity itself, are Rhodesia and Southern Africa.

I am impelled to say these things, unpleasant and painful as they are, for the most serious reasons. These reasons can be summed up by saying that in two and a half years my own ground has shifted.

Formerly, even a year ago, I was angry at Israel and overwhelmed by the Palestinian tragedy. I am no longer angry at Israel. I reserve my anger for the mythmakers and kingmakers, Israelis and Americans, who shuttle like voracious locusts between Washington and Tel Aviv, bargaining away the lives of people, upping the military ante, fanning the fires of mythology and fear. I am angry at the American-Jewish establishment who inflate the shoddy political and religious myths—myths that keep foolish Christians at their side. Such Christians, of course, are occupied in repairing historical crimes against Jews by dusting off the oldest sophism in human history: "To Make Peace, Prepare For War." The stated victims of this diabolical ecumenism will be, among others, the Israeli people themselves.

Toward these people, I have no anger today, and only the briefest argument.

It is an argument I and my friends continue to urge with Americans as well. It goes something like this. Since both Israelis and we suffer under abominable leadership, religious and political, and our only salvation lies in resisting—Why do we not resist? In larger numbers, in a clearer voice, in symbolic acts of reconciliation with purported enemies, by breaking iniquitous laws, by preventing land seizures, by protecting and granting sanctuary to the stranger within or outside the gates (who in this case is no stranger at all, but a fellow-citizen of the same ancient land).

That is my argument, an argument between friends, here and in the Middle East, an argument stemming from common respect, a common urgency. But for the Israeli people, for the farmers and workers and students and rabbis, for the children above all, for the mothers and fathers, for the aged who issued from one nightmare only to be pushed into another—for all these, I have only compassion. It is a response which in years past I felt almost wholly toward their opposite numbers—toward the Palestinian people.

Today, when I contemplate Israel, my heart sinks like a stone. Its people are being transformed into the pawns of a tragedy beyond rekoning. Even the word "tragedy" is inadequate to encompass their fate, as the military demigods would enact it; the word confers on their situation a dignity which it cannot in fact claim. Only the clearsighted and free can be the protagonists of tragedy; but of the Israelis I dare use a word denoting mental inertia and moral decrepitude—"pawns." I use the word because I see it verified at home as well as in Israel. It refers to the half-conscious victims of a gathering storm, to the vast majority of people who will never rise to choose their fate. Their fate is altogether in the passive voice; they are spoken for; disposed of. As Americans, they have emerged, inflated and grown amnesic all within the spasm of two hundred years, at the nod of forces they never troubled to understand, or thought to oppose, or opposed with half a heart, too late.

For the people of Israel, it is very nearly too late. Their imperial American masters are growing restive. It is now clear (as it ought to have been clear long ago) that they have no real attachment, whether of sentiment or of altruism, toward Israel. It was no younger Sister Democracy at all. The idea was an illusion, nurtured and huckstered by both sides. It was never seen in such a light, never a partner in redress and political renewal. It was, and remains, to a lesser degree, only a paramilitary outpost, a useful base of "operations."

That usefulness, by now, is nearly past. The American hegemony in the Middle East can be protected otherwise than through Israel. It has become another cost-price item in the imperial marketplace; and the cost has risen beyond reason. Its fate thus is up for grabs; it is, anonymously, humiliatingly, speculated on, along with other former colonial favorites; a reshuffling made imperative either by internal turmoil or the petro-dollar squeeze; Spain, Portugal, Turkey, Greece—now Israel comes up, as they say, "for review." That high-minded hypocrisy, which once disposed of Laos, Cambodia, and very nearly obliterated Vietnam, that same gang of satraps, kingmakers, and king breakers, has decided that the usefulness of Israel is nearly past. To deeper realities, the fate of the innocent, the fate of children, such tactics were always supremely indifferent; now the message to Israel is: "Swim if you can; sink if you can't."

Thus, the tragedy which once hovered over the Palestinian camps has shifted in the rude winds of the world. Israelis know this, if they know anything at all of their own history. Every military buildup, every charade of "secure borders," every effort to terrorize or subdue the Palestinian people, has sown dragons' teeth at its borders, or within its borders. It sowed, repeatedly, fanatically, fatalistically; and armed enemies sprang up. Today, there is no reason to believe that a nuclear force *de frappe* will bring a more benign harvest.

Thus goes the fate of Israel. Tragedy upon tragedy, folly on folly. Foreign "advisers" dumping their witless plans on its benighted leaders, its people increasingly helpless and isolated, embittered, at sea, denied world sympathy, urged on to a hapless heroism by compatriots elsewhere, paramilitarized, taxed to exhaustion, under permanent marching orders, forced to witness in silence the moral outrages once inflicted on its own (now inflicted within its borders by its own authorities, on a people helpless and homeless, as its once were)—what catastrophe! And as if all this were not enough, the threat of another war lies heavy on the land, prepared for, cold-bloodedly stockpiled, taken for granted, by cynical leadership, by advisers, by patrons—there and here.

In conclusion, I offer a conversation I dream of, between Israelis and myself.

Israeli: Where do you go, when there's nowhere to go?
Berrigan: You don't go anywhere.
I. What do you mean, you don't go anywhere?
B. I mean exactly that. You stay put. Which is not to say that you sit there like sitting ducks.
I. Then what in the world do you do?

B. You start making peace where you are. You start listening. You start, as the prophets say, doing the works of justice. You start resisting an iniquitous government—which, in your case, is not only anti-Palestinian, but anti-you as well. (Just as ours is anti-us, anti-decency, anti-human.) You seize for yourself the right to survive, a right which is threatened not primarily by Palestinians at all; but by your own government and ours. You start rejecting interventionist meddlers and their "piecemeal" settlements, their settlements being truly piecemeal; they break you to pieces, they make a meal of you. You start granting to others the human and civil rights you demand for yourself. You start creating safe borders by creating trust across the borders.

I. I see you are full of advice for those on the front lines. Do you have some free advice to offer American Jews as well?

B. My word to Israelis was "start something." To American Jews, it is "stop everything." Stop brokering war and peddling arms. Stop building a Bruederschaft of death in Israel—a death you don't have to endure, only to finance. To put the same thing another way, stop being quintessential Americans first (all your bombs in one basket) and Jews hardly at all.

I. I notice you leave American Christians out of your analysis. Is this your way of saying they've nothing to do with present U.S. policies? Or that they've been converted from anti-Semitism?

B. Not at all. Some Christians are playing what I would call the most pernicious game of all, a post-Christian anti-Semitism. They're working off their guilt about the dead by playing patsy to the powers of death. Their ethic has become a misguided tour through hell; they're perpetual tourists among the dead, indifferent toward the living. They know only one way of proving they improved on their ancestors: the support of the military and economic policies of what is, after all, a rather stereotyped, Western, supermilitarized nation-state. They huff and puff about Israel as a special case. Whereas Israel ought to be accorded respect or contempt on the same basis as, say, Cuba or Rhodesia, Spain or Sweden. The basis of performance. But misguided Christians, like misguided missiles, do enormous harm, purportedly by chance, along the way to their goals. They kill—by misdirection, they say. I say killing is killing, whether by indirection or folly.

I. You don't allow then that Israel, for a hundred reasons, is entitled to be regarded as a special case among the nations, to receive special treatment and help?

B. No nation-state is entitled today to anything more than scepticism. In the case of the Israelis, there is no need to invoke the past in order to arrive at a sane attitude. Let's only say that today, the Israelis are entitled to more compassion than ever. Their leadership, on the other hand, whether religious, military, or political, is entitled only to ever more contempt. So are their patsies, Jews, Christians, whoever, in the United States. We must, in short, resolve to save the Israeli people by making it impossible for present policies to continue.

ISRAEL AND PALESTINE, JULY 1, 1976

Letter to Ernesto Cardenal:
Guns Don't Work

Ernesto Cardenal had helped establish a Christian community on Solentiname Island in Nicaragua. Some members joined the armed resistance to Somoza, and Cardenal issued a declaration of his support for them and the Sandinista Front.

Dear Brother Ernesto Cardenal,

Your account of events in your community of Solentiname has been widely distributed in the United States, especially by the religious press. One translation appended a word: "It is important for us in this country to be able to listen and not to judge this."

Indeed. But at least we can talk together. Please consider what follows, then, as a continuing reflection on matters you have had the courage to open up, and indeed, to act on.

May I also summon a memory or two, as you do so poignantly in your statement? You visited my brother Philip and myself in jail in February of 1977, when we were locked up after a demonstration at the Pentagon. I hope you could read in our faces all your visit meant; a visit from a fellow priest, a poet, a good communitarian, a struggling friend, whose fame was great but whose human warmth was his best gift. Thank you once more for coming to us.

Then there was our first meeting a few years previous, when you brought the art of Solentiname to New York for an exhibition. I had the joy of greeting you, this poet, the intense quiet Latino, known in the southern countries for his sandals and flowing hair and beard, his kindly myopic eyes; known here for his poetry, his courage.

The shadow of Thomas Merton's death lay heavy on us. I think we were seeking consolation in one another's eyes. And we found it.

I am not going to start with the customary disclaimers about your statement. Such are not only superfluous, they verge on the insulting. What Latino, what Yankee doesn't know by now the deadly mutual interests which in Washington prop up the Nicaraguan military government of the Somozas? And who would regard you, an exile, a priest who must now anoint your forehead with the ashes of your dream—regard your convictions, your choices, with anything but the utmost respect? All this is implicit in friendship itself.

I would like to do you a better courtesy, that of taking you seriously:your words, and the actions which by now, I presume, you have taken.

Let me say too that the questions you raise are among the most crucial that Christians can spell out today. Indeed, in your own country, your life raises them. But you thrust them also at us, and rightly so. They are far more than a matter of domestic importance.

There is, first of all, no parallel in America to the violence you describe — whether of the Somozas or the Sandinistas.

What indeed are a few guns, or even a few hundreds guns, in the hands of guerrillas in comparison with the doomsday cache of nuclear horrors lurking in our mountains and bunkers? What reasonable comparison can be made between the sorties of your Frente Sandinista, and the lunar devastation of Vietnam, Laos, Cambodia? On your part, a few deaths, much love, exalted goals. On the part of America — but words fail me.

These things I grant with all my heart. What then nags at me, when I ponder your words? I have some inkling of what you face, what your companions face, the students and workers and peasants of your country. I know that the Somozas, given the leash, could swallow all of you tomorrow. I know that on the same day, the U.S. military could swallow the Somozas who had swallowed you — the mouse within the dog within the python — and hardly feel sated. On the world scale where the stakes are piled high — oil, uranium, laissez-faire larcenies, predatory markets, ripoffs and standoffs; in a world where the superpowers warily circle one another like urban thugs, nuclear firebombs in hand; in such a world, you or your followers, or even your persecutors, count for very little.

You and the Frente, and the Somozas, could disappear tomorrow. Only a minor breeze would stir the papers on the desk of some sub-secretariat of the State Department. A lie or two at a presidential press conference would be your obituary, the Nicaraguan folder transferred to a dead file. The empire, in sum, can take your life, and take your death, and take your theology, and the destruction of your community, and your resistance, all in stride.

I say this in no spirit of cynicism. Merely to suggest that in a way I find both strange and exhilarating, your situation lies quite near the realities of the gospel. It ought not, after all, depress us beyond measure, if the empire finds you and me expendable. That is quite normal and constant in the history of such entities. What is of import finally is whether we are able to salvage something in the open season on humans.

I do not mean salvage our lives; I mean our humanity. Our sense of one another, of compassion — our very sanity.

I hope I am inching toward the contents of your letter. You discuss quite freely and approvingly the violence of a violated people, yourselves. You align yourself with that violence, regretfully but firmly, irrevocably.

I am sobered and saddened by this. I think of the consequences of your choice, within Nicaragua and far beyond. I sense how the web of violence spins another thread, draws you in, and so many others for whom your example is primary, who do not think for themselves, judging that a priest and poet will lead them in the true way.

I think how fatally easy it is, in a world demented and enchanted with the myth of short cuts and definitive solutions, when nonviolence appears increasingly naive, old hat, freakish—how easy it is to cross over, to seize the gun. How easy to conclude: the deck is stacked, first card to last, in favor of the Big Sharks; the outcome of the game, of life itself, is settled before the cards are dealt. Why then isn't taking a few lives (of dubious value at best, torturers, lackeys, police) preferable to the taking of many lives of great value, students, the poor, the victimized and defenseless, the conscientious, those easily identifiable as gospel brothers and sisters? There is, after all, a long tradition of legitimate self-defense.

It may be true, as you say, that "Gandhi would agree with us." Or it may not be true. It may be true, as you imply, that Merton would agree with you. It may be true that Christ would agree with you. I do not believe he would, but I am willing to concede your argument, for the sake of argument.

You may be correct in reporting that "those young Christians fought without hate . . . and especially without hate for the guards" they shortly killed (though this must be cold comfort to the dead). Your vision may one day be verified of a Nicaragua free of "campesino guards killing other campesinos. . . . " The utopia you ache for may one day be realized in Nicaragua: " . . . an abundance of schools, child care centers, hospitals and clinics for everyone . . . and most importantly, love between everyone." This may all be true; the guns may bring on the kingdom.

But I do not believe it.

One religious paper here published your words under the following headline: "When they take up arms for love of the kingdom of God." How sublime, I thought, how ironic. We have had "just" wars of the Right, a long history of blood, the blood of colonials and natives and slaves and workers and peasants. But we are through with all that. Now we are enlightened. We are to have "just" wars of the Left!

So the young men of Solentiname resolved to take up arms. They did it for one reason: "on account of their love for the kingdom of God." Now here we certainly speak within a tradition! In every crusade that ever marched across Christendom, murder—the most secular of undertakings, the most worldly, the one that enlists and rewards us along with the other enlistees of Caesar—this undertaking is invariably baptized in religious ideology: the kingdom of God.

The power of such language we know too well. Religious battle cries induct hearts and minds as no secular slogans can. Religious ideology raises its flag in every nation, even as it denies the final authority of every nation. It offers to transcendent longings a task that is simple and forthright: kill. It offers a slogan that is as immediately tactile and hot as a fired gun: kill for the kingdom. And perhaps most important of all, it offers a way out: out of anger, out of frustration, out of poverty, out of political stagnation, out of the harsh and dreadful necessity of love. God wills it! The kingdom requires it!

Blood and iron, nukes and rifles. The leftists kill the rightists, the rightists kill the leftists, both, given time and occasion, kill the children, the aged, the ill, the suspects. Given time and occasion, both torture prisoners. Always, you understand, inadvertently, regretfully. Both sides, moreover, have excellent intentions, and call on God to witness them. And some god or other does witness them, if we can take the word of whatever bewitched church.

And of course nothing changes. Nothing changes in Beirut, in Belfast, or in Galilee, as I have seen. Except that the living die. And that old, revered distinction between combatant and noncombatant, which was supposed to protect the innocent and helpless, goes down the nearest drain; along with the indistinguishable blood of any and all.

Alas, I have never seen anyone morally improved by killing; neither the one who aimed the bullet, nor the one who received it in his or her flesh.

Of course we have choices, of course we must decide. When all is said, we find that the gospel makes sense, that it strikes against our motives and actions or it does not. Can that word make sense at all today, can it be something more than utopian or extravagant? The gospel is after all a document out of a simpler age, a different culture. It may even be our duty to construct for ourselves another ethic, based on our own impasse or insights or ego. And go from there, with whatever assurance we can muster, amid the encircling gloom.

Or on the other hand, we can bow our heads before a few truths, crude, exigent, obscure as they are. The outcome of obedience we cannot know, the outcome of disobedience we can deceive ourselves about, indefinitely and sweetly. Thou shalt not kill. Love one another as I have loved you. If your enemy strike you on the right cheek, turn to him the other. Practically everyone in the world, citizens and believers alike, consign such words to the images on church walls, or the embroideries in front parlors.

We really are stuck. Christians are stuck with this Christ, the impossible, unteachable, irreformable loser. Revolutionaries must correct him, set him aright. That absurd form, shivering under the crosswinds of power, must be made acceptable, relevant. So a gun is painted into his empty hands. Now he is human! Now he is like us.

Does it all have a familiar ring? In the old empires, the ragged rabbi must be cleaned up, invested in Byzantine robes of state, raised in glittering splendor to the dome of heaven. Correction! correction! we cry to those ignorant gospel scribes, Matthew and the rest. He was not like that, he was not helpless, he was not gentle, he was under no one's heel, no one pushed him around! He would have taken up a gun if one had been at hand, he would have taken up arms, "solely for one reason; on account of his love for the kingdom of God." Did he not have fantasies like ours, in hours out of the public glare, when he too itched for the quick solution, his eyes narrowed like gun sights?

How tricky it all gets! We look around at our culture: an uneasy mix of gunmen, gun makers, gun hucksters, gun researchers, gun runners, guards with guns, property owners with guns. A culture in which the guns put out contracts on the people, the guns own the people, the guns buy and sell the people, the guns practice targets on the people, the guns kill the people. The guns are our second nature, and the first nature is all but obliterated; it is gunned down.

And who will raise it up, that corpse with the neat hole in its temple, ourselves? It is impossible, it is against nature.

Christ asks the literally impossible. And then, our radical helplessness confessed, he confers what was impossible.

Dear brother Ernesto, when I was underground in 1970 with J. Edgar Hoover's hounds on my tail, I had long hours to think of these things. At that time I wrote: "The death of a single human is too heavy a price to pay for the vindication of any principle, however sacred." I should add that at the time, many among the anti-war Left were playing around with bombings, in disarray and despair.

I am grateful that I wrote those words. I find no reason eight years later to amend or deny them. Indeed, in this bloody century, religion has little to offer, little that is not contaminated or broken or in bad faith. But one thing we have: our refusal to take up bombs or guns, aimed at the flesh of brothers and sisters, whom we persist in defining as such, refusing the enmities pushed at us by war-making state or war-blessing church.

This is a long loneliness, and a thankless one. One says "no" when every ache of the heart would say "yes." We, too, long for a community on the land, heartening liturgies, our own turf, the arts, a place where sane ecology can heal us. And the big boot comes down. It destroys everything we have built. And we recoil. Perhaps in shock, perhaps in a change of heart, we begin to savor on our tongues a language that is current all around us: phrases like "legitimate violence," "limited retaliation," "killing for love of the kingdom." And the phrases make sense—we have crossed over. We are now an army, like the pope's army, or Luther's, or the crusaders, or the Muslims. We have disappeared into this world, into bloody, secular history. We cannot adroitly handle both gospel and gun; so we drop the gospel, an impediment in any case.

And our weapons?

They are contaminated in what they do, and condemned in what they cannot do. There is blood on them, as on our hands. And like our hands, they cannot heal injustice or succor the homeless.

How can they signal the advent of the kingdom of God? How can we, who hold them? We announce only another bloody victory for the emperor of necessity, whose name in the Bible is Death.

Shall he have dominion?

Brother, I think of you so often. And pray with you. And hope against hope.

DANIEL

NATIONAL CATHOLIC REPORTER, MAY 5, 1978

Where Death Abounded, Life: St. Rose's Home

I first heard of St. Rose's three years ago, from a friend who had begun working there as an orderly. I was in the usual spinning orbit of teaching, writing, and pilgrimaging to the Pentagon to throw ashes and blood at the idols. Something was lacking; whether true ikons, physical work, or self-testing. I phoned the sister in charge. Could I hire out as a part-time volunteer?

What ensued I like to call, in a modest way, history. I am by no means capable or willing to tell all, nor is there need to. Rather speedily, and in a wonderfully offhand way, I was given a tour of the place; my questions were answered sensibly; it was made clear that if I wished to help I would be welcome.

It gave to ponder, as the French say. Here was a spanking facility humming with compassion and energy, up to the minute in equipment; to it the urban poor came to die; within it the intangible realities of life ("the things which are unseen") were available, abundant. Here, moreover, sisters and orderlies underwent, orchestrated, that Great Day which the spirituals said was "gonna be."

All this struck my earth-bound mind. And there was more, as I was to learn. In payment for such care, such friendship, no money crossed the palm. No guest paid, no one could pay. It was a rule of the order, strictly adhered to. It struck me: here we had a stunning instance of the ethical cemented into natural law. The rule was all but metaphysical: no money. No insurance; no red, white, or blue crosses; no bread from city, state, feds. No payment from any patient or relative, no matter how highly or mightily placed, or how lowly.

I spell out the rule in some detail to show how it spun about in my mind, dazzling. Who could have believed it? It had, I thought, the delicious evanescent aura of the more than human. Then I pondered the phrase "more than human." What in the world could be more than human? The more I pondered, the clearer it became; the phrase meant "simply human." Which is not to deny that the hospital came as a salutary assault on my lowered expectations.

How marred our hopes are! Things which should be available to all inevitably cost a great deal. The few things which are still free of price tags are polluted: air, parks, vistas.

But in any sane scheme of things, that almost unimaginable world that shone on our retinas like a mirage, like the kingdom of God, would not good medical care be free to all?

We were so used to paying up; a cross of gold, as the old orators used to intone; the degradation of the buck, fast or slow, inflated or sound, lies heavy on us. Goods and services became bads and disservices; before the eyes of the poor, they dangle out of reach; and for the rest of us, who desperately tread dark waters, such things are overpriced, begrudged, performed in bad spirit, left to others. What profession today ministers to essential needs, lives up to its own ideals?

Here and there, parochial schools in New York City hold the line. They still do what they once set out to do: serve the poor, teach the children of the poor. Nuns live in the ghetto, poor, standing by. All reports, including secular ones, say the instruction is sound, the children are making it.

Hospitals have fared less well, for a multitude of reasons. The cost of medical care, as is no news to anyone, has soared out of sight. Nineteenth-century orders of women, founded to do basic medical work among the immigrants and poor, have withered before the blight of the buck. Either the (male) diocesan chanceries have grabbed the facilities and "integrated" them into church-state hyphens, or the sisters have given in, done the same sad thing on their own. In either case, the mirage of bigger and better has won over the solid reality of small and beautiful. By now the Catholic hospitals, in any given town, including New York, are a crawling sprawl, big and getting bigger, pledged to roughly the same medical practices, abortion excepted, as their secular counterparts.

In the process, original intentions have all but vanished. Where nuns are present in the typical hospital, they are more apt to be commandeering switchboards or accounts offices than nursing the sick and dying. The services are secularized, with all the ambiguity that implies; so, it goes without saying, are the finances. The poor receive the kind of health care which the state allows or disallows, another function of that bulldozing of existence euphemistically, and despite all malpractice, named "welfare."

St. Rose's Home, for reasons both complex and fascinating, has escaped such attrition. Let me avoid meandering, and simply report that this unique hospital for the dying has hewn to its original line, literally and consistently. The sisters do today what their founder set out to do some ninety years ago; an achievement that strikes one, in the American farce of size, quantity, media puffing, death and dying chic, the stalling of much originality and imagination in the stuck culture—strikes one as either a triumph of plain stubborn vision, or of specially tender providence, or both.

You don't have to be poor in America to die badly. You just have to be dying; the rest is supplied. And by "dying badly," I don't refer to immediate physical care, on which, bad or good, the rich have the usual monopoly.

Let me speak of the obverse, "dying well," as St. Rose's has helped me understand the term. Dying well implies a sense of one's self, a hand on the rudder, a mind that despite rip tides and near swamping is reasonably able to give and take, to read signals and send them out; for the conscious duration, those who die well hold a sense both of anguish and humor, as well as a sense of their plight, discomfort, degree of pain, etc. Such hardy spirits turn the tables, show a good face to others, including family, friends, etc. I recollect the old idea that there is an art of dying, as there is an art of living. And I suspect that the two are more closely joined than is commonly admitted.

Let us take matters further. St. Rose's is a hospital for the dying; but not just for any dying. It is a hospital for those dying of cancer. The dying are, moreover, poor; indeed, poverty is a chief criterion for admission; by presumption, the rich can choose to go elsewhere, and pay as they go.

Such arrangements color the atmosphere of St. Rose's, give the place a special quality, precious to Christian understanding. Let me speak for myself. I belong to an order whose first ideal has been all but obliterated in America (though I am delighted to report that elsewhere, among poor nations and peoples, its spirit flourishes and its tribe increases). Here, the likes of me fight such unlikely battles as, e.g., trying to persuade one of our large universities to disclaim the blood money of the unlamented shah of Iran. And, need I add, I lose the skirmish. Yoked to such bloody helpmeets do we die, in harness to the culture.

With what a sense of refreshment, self-restoring, I came to St. Rose's. Slowly I sensed that an atrophied sixth or seventh sense was coming to life; a sense of recognition. I was awakening to the lineaments of the Catholic; that face which, like the face of Christ, is hideously worked over in America, rendered nearly unrecognizable by a thousand clumsy or malicious hands, our own. Where could one turn in the great city, like the blind, and with the tips of one's fingers touch that face of grandeur, of inner light, wordless, the face of advocate, friend?

I am clumsily shuffling words which the poor and dying have repeated to me, with insistent fervor, a hundred times. What a good place St. Rose's is! Jew and gentile, old and young, streetwise, moneywise, prisonwise—the chorus is remarkable. It converges, in fact, on what the old theology texts used to call an irrefragable argument for the truth. We are in presence of what seems elsewhere, and in many exalted places, to be simply an absence; I mean the church. Hence the shock of recognition; what Chesterton used to call, in despair over language and its shortcomings, simply "the Thing."

Colorless as water, cool rather than perfervid, subtle rather than evangelistic, veiled as befits mystery, skilled in the thousand ways of conveying love, undeclarative, able to hold and let go, smiling and weeping, modest as befits the human condition in extremis. . . .

Dying well, I have suggested, implies dying as one has lived; so does dying badly. One finds that, with a little help, the poor die well. This is an unremarkable observation to anyone who knows the poor; I want to reflect on this.

One begins at the hospital by being silent, observing things. Patients come to us, for the large part, from the lower-income levels of the city. They are the people whom I see on the subway and bus en route to the hospital: the working poor. Now and again, we greet a different guest of the days of the tolling bell — a kind of sub-subway person, a prisoner, an addict, alcoholic, a classic outsider, outside the economy, outside the social contract. In either case, poor or outcast, the people we serve have only the most tenuous handhold on America. They have lived and are about to die at the edge of almost everything that constitutes the Dream: money, profession, opportunity, the upward escalator.

With regard to working people, this fact implies an irony. By and large, their working lives offered true benefits; they were maintenance people, transit workers, supers in apartment buildings, printers, seamen, short order cooks, postal workers, police. As in every great city of the world, they rode the subways in the early morning to, from, long days and nights of labor. Their rhythms, their faces and bodies, especially their hands, remind me vividly of the description of the early morning street scene in Silone's *Bread and Wine*. Spina, the Marxist mystic disguised as a priest, walks about Rome:

> . . . Workmen came trooping along from every side, and there was a beauty in the air that moved Spina deeply, the marvelous beauty of Rome at dawn, when there is no one in the streets but honest people going to work, walking quickly and talking little. . . .

Later the scene changes:

> [Spina] went down the Via della Navicella and the Via Claudia toward the center of the city, in order to see it once more. But the beauty of Rome had faded. The workers had disappeared from the streets, and no one was to be seen now but men in uniform, government clerks, priests, and nuns going shopping. Rome was now a different place.

Later in the morning, the scene is startlingly different:

> And between ten and eleven, when the big parasites began to appear, the hierarchs, the higher officials of the ministries, and the monsignori with their violet stockings, Rome suddenly became odious in his sight.
> . . .

As to our patients, one could not, I think, claim that their slender stake in the Dream had begotten an inspired social or political sense. Hardly. Still, one notices time and again that a life of near poverty, lived close to the bone, a life of relative insecurity, one moreover whose sense of dignity was built on worthwhile work — all this helps one say a good amen at the approach of bell, book, and candle. The moorings that bind these lives to the mainland have never been that firm; now they are slipped with ease.

There is detachment in the air, good humor, even a sense of celebration at times. Folks josh one another, look out for one another; some want to be wheeled about the wards to greet those who are stuck in bed. Up to the final letting go, the prelude is not depression or damp; it is sunny, warm of will.

To grasp something of this, one has to go beyond therapeutic convention. Even if the staff saw the hospital as a kind of mini-*Titanic* heading toward catastrophe (and they do not), it still must be reported that there are no "social facilitators" aboard. People are employed or volunteer, not to daub a presentable cosmetic on the hard face of death, or to whoop things up despite all. We are there to help make life bearable, to make some sense of it, make it attractive as long as it lasts—together. There is respect for privacy, respect for moods and imbalances, a spoiling attention to diet, from kosher to Tipperary Irish. There is an unobtrusive religious feel about the place, which now and again surfaces in sacrament or prayer or plain talk about death; but only on the initiative of the patients. No one is force-fed, whether on religion, psychosemantics, or -antics. Little account is taken, except where suffering or depression require, as to being in or out of purported stages of dying. Things are reasonably lively, sometimes even rambunctious.

There are, moreover, no psychiatrists or social workers on the premises. This information is conveyed here as a mere report; I have never had the impression that such skills are subjects of prejudice. The hospital is simply in another stream. It operates on the principle that work with the dying, though hair-raisingly difficult at times, can be done well by normally endowed people with the heart for it, that the work can be done on a rather modest budget, that ingenuity and inventiveness are the handmaids of skill and will flourish given the chance.

There is a second principle, already alluded to. The sisters feel no need to enlarge what can be done well, only if done small. Adding wings to wings, swelling the staff, more often than not wreaks havoc on the original intent—loving care of the ill. Whose law is that? In any case, Marianne Moore stated it years ago in somewhat different terms: "When excellence is the intent, to add is to subtract." Indeed.

The death managers are likewise absent. This is an inflexible rule in a bending universe. There are no state snoops because there is no state money. It is as simple as that. Freedom from the state is seen as freedom to do one's work. In a deeper sense, it is the freedom of the hospital to be itself, to be other than an instrument of the state, even such a rare instrument as a decent state social service—presuming such a rarity to exist.

All this stubborn grace hatches a *rara avis* indeed. St. Rose's is an institution that calls itself Christian, and deserves to be so called. This, it strikes me, is the best gift of the hospital, whether to the dying or to those who serve them. The Christian sense of things, symbols gently applied for healing, a quintessential skill in foreseeing need or pain—this results in good teamwork, a necessary balance between mourning the newly dead and going on for the living.

And in the city, what a relief!

America, I reflect wryly, is the place where anything can be corrupted. Even (no pun intended) death. Even before the fact.

In 1972, upon release from prison, I taught at Union Seminary for a year. With a start, I noted in the seminary elevators frequent reference to seminars on death and dying. This, while Nixon's savage carpet bombing of Vietnam, the bombing of the dikes, the spoliation of nature, were proceeding apace. And so far as I could learn, not an official or unofficial theological cry was being raised on, say, the death and dying of Vietnamese children.

We corrupt our sense of reality by sentimentalizing it.

Such excess erupts, for example, when we zero in on one aspect of things to the neglect of another; e.g., separating the facts of domestic death (occurring in the course of nature) from the facts of death abroad (inflicted, unrequited.) Thus, it was conceivable during the war that air force officers, in off hours, after successful bombing runs, or as part of their R and R, could attend seminar sessions sponsored by their chaplains on death and dying. The codicils of all this are truly horrific and, in my judgment, go to the heart of matters. That is to say, for war crime one is urged to read "official assignment"; for compassion, "applicable only to the blood line"; for the burning of children, "inevitable enemy casualty." And for theology, read — what?

The abstractions poison the soul, reduce our lives and deaths to market commodities, subject death itself to the technicians of death, whether psychological or technological. It is all, in fact, one: the brutalizing of ourselves, the degradation of language.

I am trying to suggest that we are inevitably sentimental until we become political, especially in matters of life and death. Our understanding, our caring, are summoned to embrace the fate of all, the common weal and woe. And when, at length, our sense of death has reached outward to embrace the enemy, the stranger, the outcast, dissolving petty differences and distance, and declared its peace with all creation — at that point we may claim a human sense that is something more than a threat or a bared weapon.

And in the instance of cancer, such a sense allows us to travel gracefully from fact to metaphor. Better still, to oscillate between the two, touching each pole, the cancer close at hand, the dying across the world; the cancer at St. Rose's, the dying, the perennial dying of the survivors of Hiroshima.

Before the scourge of cancer, our civilization is largely helpless. We are, in fact, in the plight of the original sinner seeking to extirpate original sin. War upon war on cancer (the violent imagery is itself instructive) has been indeed declared and conducted — wars hot and cold. But the forays have resulted, for all their research and money, in ever more cancer.

Indeed, the cancer question widens, fact and mystery, as nuclear technology overshadows it. Thefts of plutonium, hideously inventive engines of mass killings, misuse of resources and talents, dangers of low radiation, a trapped and enfeebled war economy and, above all and permeating all, a spiritual stagnation that forbids us even tentative access to our own faith—these are a few penalties which the care and feeding of nuclear demons wring from us.

For the first time in history, the fate of humanity itself stands on a fail-safe basis, nicely calibrated, weapon for weapon, our side and theirs, a worldwide tension and terror. The question of "who can win" is wiped away by the paw of Mars; who now can survive?

The threat to existence is by no means idly issued. It is, but for an act of God, all but assured of execution, backed by the nicest proof imaginable— weapons apt to consummate the deed. So we live on—on borrowed time. Plain good luck, here and there a sane act of one or another leader drawing back from the verge (as in the Russian response to the Kennedy provocation), terrorism controlled, barely, by the greater terror of nation-states; for some thirty-five years these have given us an illusion of safety, cowering under the iron umbrella of "deterrence."

Deterrence did not deter; it eventually died, to be replaced by the apter gunslinging macho of "first strike." Today we are hostages to leaders who themselves are hostages—to past follies, to new weapons, to bunkers and stockpiles, to national frenzies, to stalking myths, dusted off and set in wilder motion, security, free world, Salt II . . .

I bring this up because something clumsily called the "politics of cancer" presses upon us. St. Rose's Home has become an apt image of our country and world. If a single nuclear device is detonated over any city of the planet (one out of tens of thousands of nukes which lie about the world), those who perish at the flash point may well be accounted lucky. Those who survive will die also, gradually, after mutilation, bloodletting, thirst, nausea, of blood cancer.

Cancer has thus become, as some forty mini-Pentagons across the world testify, a hellish vocation of humanity. Beyond the hospital, the metaphor. Before the catastrophe, the warning. In the race toward oblivion, half the horror is getting there. Day by day, in New York and elsewhere, the poor drop by the wayside, emblems of things to come. The poisoning of air and water and food strikes them down. And in their fate we may read our own.

At present, some twelve orderlies at St. Rose's are Catholic Workers. Several have been jailed in recent years for resisting the nuclear arms race or nuclear energy plants. They bring to the care of the cancer patients a sense of impending showdown, a realism desperately required as an ingredient of compassion, of sanity itself. . . .

Paul Goodman wrote somewhere that his respect for Christians was based on their utterly crazy comprehension of the last day. Perhaps he was right, I am not sure. I think that what we have to offer today is an utterly crazy comprehension of this day, of the day-to-day, of the simultaneous acceptance and taming of the apocalyptic fury. I am not sure the day-to-day is not the last day.

We are indeed, as a hundred rumblings underfoot remind us, stepping gingerly in the mine field of the end of things. This is no news to anyone who walks in prophetic bones; hardly news, certainly not good news. Can we make of a sorry time good news? "I am with you." We must deterrorize the terror, by an act of God, our act.

Let us tell our heart; we will swear our covenant anew. We will hold the hand of the dying. It is an act of sublime trust, of land trust, of water trust, of trust in God, of trust in one another.

The covenant reverberates in the womb; the endangered unborn, surely the "least of these," hear our voice. Please trust us, little ones, we hold your hand.

The covenant reaches into prisons and death rows. Trust us; we do not believe that murder casts out murder.

The covenant says to all: Stand in our circle. We declare that humanity itself is a nuclear-free zone.

God does not walk away from such an oath. Neither would we.

THE CATHOLIC WORKER, JUNE 1979

Swords into Plowshares

On September 9, 1980, the Plowshares Eight, including Daniel Berrigan, entered a General Electric nuclear missile plant in King of Prussia, Pennsylvania, and damaged two nose cones of the Mark 12A reentry missile.

September 9, 1980. We rose at dawn after (to speak for myself) a mostly sleepless night. In and out of dream, in and out of nightmare. The refrain was part nuptial chant, part dirge; the latter theme dominant, the former a minor key indeed. Brasses, kettle drums, and now and again, the plaintive flute in obligato, the cry of an infant in the river reeds . . .

We had passed several days in prayer together, an old custom indeed, as old as our first arrests in the late sixties. We were mostly vets of those years, survivors too, survivors of the culture and its pseudos and counters, survivors of courts and jails, of the American flare of conscience and its long hibernation, survivors in our religious communities, in our families (they have survived us!). By an act of God and nothing of our own, survivors of America—its mimes, grimaces, enticements, abhorrences, shifts and feints, masks, counter-masks. Survivors (barely) of the demons who, challenged, shouted their name—Legion!

We knew for a fact (the fact was there for anyone who bothered to investigate) that General Electric in King of Prussia manufactures the reentry cones of Mark 12A missiles. We learned that Mark 12A is a warhead that will carry an H-bomb of 335 kilotrons to its target. That three of these weapons are being attached to each of three hundred Minuteman III missiles. That because of Mark 12A accuracy and explosive power, it will be used to implement U.S. counterforce or first-strike policy.

We knew these hideous cones ("shrouds" is the GE word) were concocted in a certain building of the General Electric complex. The building is huge: we had no idea exactly where the cones could be found.

Of one thing we were sure. If we were to reach the highly classified area of shipping and delivery and were to do there what we purposed, Someone must intervene, give us a lead.

After our deed, a clamor arose among the FBI and state and county and GE (and God knows what other) police who swarmed into the building. "Did they have inside information? Was there a leak?" Our answer: of course we had Inside Information, of course there had been a Leak. Our

Informant is otherwise known in the New Testament as Advocate, Friend, Spirit. We had been at prayer for days.

And the deed was done. We eight looked at one another, exhausted, bedazzled with the ease of it all. We had been led in about two minutes, and with no interference to speak of, to the heart of the labyrinth.

They rounded us up, trundled us out in closed vans. We spent the day uncommonly cheerful in that place of penitence, in various cells of police headquarters. We underwent what I came to think of as a "forced fast," the opposit : of forced feeding and undoubtedly less perilous to life and limb. Around the corridors of the spiffy new building (we were in GE country, the local economy is 40 percent GE, GE brings good things to life) the atmosphere was one of hit and miss, cross-purpose, barely concealed panic. How the hell did they get into the building so easily? How about the jobs of those of us who were purportedly guarding the nuclear brews and potions?

Lines to Justice Department, Pentagon, FBI were red hot. Why can't you get your act together up there? And what are we to do with these religious doomsayers? Let them go, let them off light, let them off never? Please advise!

About noon another ploy got underway. They loaded us in vans again; back to the scene of the crime. It was like a Mack Sennett film played backward; first you were sped away in Black Maria, then you were backed freakishly into the same doorway. (It devolved later they wanted identification by the employees.)

But they wouldn't talk, so we wouldn't walk.

They carried four of five of us out of the van into that big warehouse room with the bloody floor, the bloody torn blueprints stamped "Top Secret." And then the missile cones, broken, bloodied, useless. No more genocide in our name! And the wall of faces, police, employees, silent as the grave, furious, bewildered, a captive nation.

Under shrill orders from somewhere, the charade was halted. The procedure was illegal. A District Attorney said it might endanger their whole case. Indeed.

So back to durance vile. They locked us up, they kept saying: "Sure we'll feed you, presently we'll charge you." And nothing happened.

By 5 P.M. the more inventive among us were ready to close their eyes, strip their shoelaces, and pretend we were eating spaghetti Rossi in the West Village.

Then something happened. One by one we were led out. Take off your shoes. And (to the six males) take off your pants.

It appeared that, these objects being stained with our blood, they were severely required as evidence.

So, like the bad little boys in the fairy tale, supperless and shoeless, we were led off to our destiny by Stepmother State.

An intuition that we and others have been pondering for a long time grows on us, presses closer.

To wit: in a time of truly massive irrationality, one had best stop playing the old academic-ecclesial game of scrabble, as though merely putting words together could make sense of moral incoherence, treachery, and meandering apathy, could break that spell.

Rationality? Reason? If these were ever in command, they had certainly fled the scene during the Vietnam War. I would be willing to venture that sanity and reason have never sat in the catbird seat again.

In the saddle of power and decision we have instead a kind of "Eichmania" analyzed by Merton, a tightly hierarchical, spiritually captivated, ideologically closed insanity. In it are caught the multicorporations and their squads of engineers and planners, on and up to the highest responsible chairs of command—the Pentagon and White House. All so to speak (so to doublespeak) to "bring good things to life."

And then outward into society the malaise touches all with a leprous finger; meandering apathy, at least as complex an illness as rotten power. Apathy, the natural outcome of such authority so used.

We have evidence of such indifference to moral and physical disaster in other modern societies, societies whose citizens, under whip and lash, or under a rain of bread and a politics of the circus, stood helpless to win the nod of blind, deaf fate, to speak up, to force a hearing.

Such apathy shows face today in our inability to summon resistance against nuclear annihilation. Screen out the horror; a shutter comes down. Best not to imagine what might be, best to act as though the worst could not be.

The phenomenon before the catastrophe is remarkably like the phenomenon after the catastrophe. Many of the survivors of Hiroshima, afflicted with radiation sickness, conceal their illness as long as possible, "act as though" they are not stricken. They go so far as to falsify family history, conceal the fact that they were in the orbit of death on the day of the bomb.

No wonder that today Americans find it more plausible, more conducive to sanity to ignore our nuclear plight, to fight survival in areas where the facts are less horrid, the cards less stacked. Economic woes, job layoffs, inflation—we have enough trouble drawing the next breath. And you with your little hammers and bottles of blood go out against Goliath? Thanks. Good luck. But no thank you.

Blood and hammers. The symbolic aspect of our GE action appealed to some and appalled others. But almost no one who has heard of the action lacks an opinion about it, usually a passionately stated one.

In pondering these passions, so long dormant, newly released, one learns a great deal—not about passions in a void, but about vital capacities for survival, sociability, spirituality.

Some who hear grow furious; some of the furious are Catholics; Catholics also guard us, judge us, prosecute us. This is an old story that need not long detain us.

What is of peculiar and serious interest here is the use and misuse of symbols, their seizure by secular power; then the struggle to keep the symbols in focus, to enable them to be seen, heard, tasted, smelled, lived and died for, in all their integrity, first intent.

Their misuse. How they are leveled off, made consistent with the credo of the state. Thus, to speak of King of Prussia and our symbol there: blood. Its outpouring in the death of Christ announced a gift and, by implication, set a strict boundary, a taboo. No shedding of blood, by anyone, under any circumstances, since this, my blood, is given for you. Blood as gift.

Hence the command: no killing, no war. Which is to say, above all, no nuclear weapons. And thence the imperative: resist those who research, deploy, or justify on whatever grounds such weaponry.

Thus the drama; the symbol outpoured implies a command. Do this; so live, so die. Clear lines are drawn for public as well as personal conduct. Church and state, the "twin powers," always in danger of becoming Siamese twins, are in fact kept from a mutually destructive symbiosis by imperative and taboo. More, they are revealed for what they in fact are—radically opposed spiritual powers, as in Revelation 13. Church can never be state; state is forbidden to ape or absorb church. And this mutual opposition, this nonalignment, this friction and fraying, erupts from time to time in tragic and bloody struggle. The church resists being recast as Caesarian icon. The state, robust, in firm possession, demands that the church knuckle under, bend knee, bless war, pay taxes, shut up. Church, thy name is trouble.

The choices are not large. Toil and trouble or—capitulation. In the latter case all is lost. The symbols are seized at the altar and borne away. Now the blood of Christ, the blood of humans, is cheap indeed; for what could be cheaper than blood the church itself has declared expendable? That blood is now a commodity, a waste. When Caesar speaks, blood may be shed at will, by Christians or others, it makes no difference. Which is also to say: there exists no longer any distinction in fact between armed combatants and citizens, between soldiers and little children. Killing has become the ordinary civil method of furthering civic ends. The sacred symbol of blood, whose gift urged the command "Thou shalt not kill"—that blood is admixed, diluted, poisoned. It is lost in a secular vortex, immensely vigorous and seductive, urging a different vision. Labor is commodity, the flag is a sacred vexillum, humans are productive integers, triage rules the outcome. Finally, a peremptory secular command: "Thou shalt kill when so ordered—or else."

It seems to me that since Hiroshima, to set an arbitrary moment, this debasing of the sacred symbols into secular use and misuse has proceeded apace.

To undo the blasphemy, what a labor.

We have been at this for years—dramatic events, deliberately orchestrated, arbitrary but intensely traditional, liturgical, illegal, in every case wrenching the actors out of routine and community life to face the music, face the public, face the jury.

Is it all worth it? In measure the eight who acted at King of Prussia have already answered the question. At least for themselves, and for one another. One of them said in the course of our discussion, "Even if the action went nowhere, if no one understood or followed through on it, I would still go ahead."

Worth it for ourselves. Each of us had, before the act, to plumb our motives, consult loved ones, care for the future of children, arrange professional and community responsibilities, measure in fact all good things against this "one necessary thing." And decide.

The eight so decided—yes. Such an act must be taken, even though it disrupt almost everything else, call many things in question, inflict suffering on others. The value of the act is thus measured by the sacrifice required to do it; an old and honored Christian idea, if I am not mistaken.

(For us, going as we did in fear and trembling from the Eucharist to General Electric had the feel of the last hours of Jesus, his journey from the upper room to death. We held our liturgy the night before, broke the bread, passed the cup. Light of head, heavy of heart, we nonetheless celebrated by anticipation the chancy event of the following day; and the trial to come; and the penalty. Our logic? the body was "broken for you," the cup "poured out for all."

The logic was not only our own. At one court hearing the prosecutor asked, with more than a show of contempt, under prodding from his chief, who referred to me as "this so-called priest" and "this wandering Gypsy [sic]," "And when did you last celebrate Mass?" I was obviously to be shown up as not only rootless but faithless as well.)

But what of the larger meaning of the action, its value for the church and the public?

Here one must go slow. The value of the act for those who propose it, sweat it out, do it—this is more easily determined. Value is created, so to speak, in the breach, in a decision to gather, unite voices in an outcry, to precipitate a crisis that, at least for a time, will strip away the mask of evil.

But I know of no sure way of predicting where things will go from there, whether others will hear and respond, or how quickly or slowly. Or whether the act will fail to vitalize others, will come to a grinding halt then and there, its actors stigmatized or dismissed as fools. One swallows dry and takes a chance.

There was one sign that our action touched a nerve. A hasty attempt was made on the day of the action itself to discredit us through a dizzying list of charges. Ideology, panic, and special interests combined to barrage the media and the public with a verdict before the verdict — more violent crazies had gone on a rampage. The charges included assault, false imprisonment, reckless endangerment, criminal mischief, terroristic threats, harassment, criminal coercion, unlawful restraint. Talk about overkill! We sat in court, transfixed, gazing on our images in the crazy mirrors of the state fun house.

It takes a large measure of good sense to stand firm at such moments. People gifted with our nefarious history must remind themselves that at King of Prussia, hammers and blood in hand, we set in motion a lengthy and complex drama. One should speak perhaps of three acts.

The first act belonged in the main to us, an early morning curtain raiser, the action underway. In a sense the adversaries have not yet appeared; only a few subalterns act on their behalf, in their name: the guards and police and employees. But GE has not yet turned on its voltage. No official appears in justifying garb to bespeak the ancient myths, to invoke sacro-secular outrage at the violation of a holy place, property off bounds, the shrine accessible only to initiates. (Antigone has buried her brother's body, but Creon has not yet flogged his way to condemn her.)

Then a second act opens. It marks the marshalling of forces of law and order, the invoking of daemons of natural law, secular karma.

Anger, retaliation are in the air, the gods of property buzz furiously overhead. The actors all but tear up the script of act one; and assault is mounted on the earlier reliance on "higher law" or "con-science." Behold true conscience, behold the highest law of all, the law by which all citizens must live, the law that is our common safeguard against anarchy!

So in the manner of Shakespeare or Pirandello or Sophocles, act two is a kind of play within the play. The audience is bewildered, thrown off guard. It had read a certain kind of admirable moral truth in the face of the young woman Antigone (in the faces of a nun, of a mother of six, of a lawyer, a professor, a seminary graduate — faces like the credentials of moral worth) — now it hears another kind of truth. This is not the truth of "symbolic action," which from a legal point of view is always murky, easily discredited, and reaching troublesomely as it does into dark existence (the forbidden burial of a brother, the breaking and bloodying of icons) must be exorcised, discredited — by measured, relentless argument.

The argument, of devastating force, in ancient Greece as today, I call that of the Great If.

The example of Antigone, the example of the eight, is deliberately magnified, made stark. Behold their act, performed under clerical guise, under the guise of virtue. Behold their act, as viewed by the state, the guardian and interpreter of public morality. (What an unconscious and ironic tribute is paid the defendants here, as though in the court itself, the state were erecting stone by stone a monument to the conscience it so fears — and so magnifies.)

In any case, citizens and believers, whatever divagations of spirit they were beckoned toward by the conduct of the protagonists, by their age or condition or credentials (above all, by their dark probing symbols) — all this is brought up short and abrupt. You are in court, this audience, as extensions of the jury, who are in effect extensions of the judge. You are not here to indulge in murky existential probings, but to consider the letter of the law and in your hearts to approach a verdict. . . .

Finally, act three. Many scenes and changes; the great world, a time between events (action/trial), the agora, a courtroom, the many places where people discuss, argue, make up their minds and unmake them again, slowly or with speed come to a conclusion, the knotting of the action.

In court, the argument of the Great If is relentlessly pursued. The crime of the eight is segregated from the world, the faces of the defendants, mirrors of conscience, are hooded. The inert symbols, hammers, empty bloodied bottles, lie there, tagged, soulless, mere items of evidence. They are relics of moral defeat, emblems of legal punishment; as such, the prosecutor will refer to them with disdain and handle them with distaste. They will be compared, subtly or openly, to the tools of safecrackers, to bloodied knives and guns. What If such implements became the common tools of so-called conscience? What If all citizens, under whatever itch of notoriety, took up such tools (like the soiled hands of Antigone, heaping foul dust on her brother's body) against the law of the state? How sordid a venture!

In the course of this act, the classic Greek formula is verified; the purging of pity and fear.

These must be purged, for pity and terror get in the way of spiritual change. They are obstructive emotions; to be taken seriously, no doubt, but strictly as preliminary to the main event.

That event, in a large sense, is destined to occur neither on stage nor in the court. It is rather the unending passionate pursuit of moral good, the righting of injustice, the ousting of death; the reordering of an ethical universe and of its social and political forms.

But in order to be purged, pity and fear have first to be aroused.

How acute the Greeks were! In the first days following our action, friends invariably spoke of their forebodings, their dread of the harsh sentences that undoubtedly would befall us, their fear that our action would be ignored or misconstrued.

Pity and fear. The pity narrows emotional largesse, the fear spreads out inordinately, claims all minds. Fear of the future, fear for children bereft of parents, fear of the state and its legal savageries . . .

One emotion is too narrow, the other too diffused. Neither finally is useful; that is to say, neither serves to heighten the truth of the universal predicament (which is not defined by prison sentences, but by nuclear annihilation) — or to grant hints and leads as to a way out.

I must inject here a message from the jails of Pennsylvania. If the eight have insisted on anything, it is that their trial and imprisonment are not the issue at stake. Pity for them gains nothing. Neither does fear for them or for their children and spouses. The eight go their way, a way meticulously chosen and after much prayer. But the issues they raise will continue to shadow their lives and vex their hearts. It is the corporate crimes of General Electric, the race toward oblivion that this monstrous entity both fuels and illustrates.

Finally, what drove us to "such extremes"?

To reach the truth, one must turn from Creon to Antigone; from the prosecutor, in our case, to the gospel.

In America, in 1980, it could hardly be called useful to the common weal or a mitigation of the common woe that a group of religious folk enter a megadeath factory — in vain proof that they are in possession of some kind of magical counterforce.

Why then?

Let us say merely because they hungered for the truth, for its embodiment, longed to offer a response to its claim on us. That even through us, an all but submerged voice might be heard, the voice of "God not of the dead, but of the living."

From our statement: "In confronting GE, we choose to obey God's law of life, rather than a corporate summons to death. Our beating of swords into plowshares is a way to enflesh this biblical call. In our action, we draw on a deep-rooted faith in Christ, who changed the course of history through his willingness to suffer rather than to kill. We are filled with hope for our world and for our children as we join this act of resistance."

THE CATHOLIC WORKER, OCTOBER-NOVEMBER 1980

On Bombing Libya: A Letter

June 6, 1986

Dear Cardinal Bernardin,

I was abroad at the time of the Reagan attack on Libya. On return I heard a disturbing rumor that you had "justified" the assault. Unfortunately I haven't been able to track down more than a quotation in the current *St. Anthony's Messenger*. Consequently, I must proceed on admittedly incomplete information. Even on that basis, I judged it better to write you of my distress.

You are quoted as saying that "the evil of terrorism must be confronted." I am wondering what such a statement could possibly mean. Is it an invitation to consider the nonviolent example of Jesus and Gandhi and Dr. King? Or is it a code expression of approval for the horrors loosed on women and children? If you mean the former, it should have been said clearly. If the latter, I can only hope you have second thoughts, or perhaps even nightmares. I speak as one who cowered under the unimaginable horror of American bombs in Hanoi in '68.

Further you are quoted: "the administration sought to make what it judged a proportionate response to Libyan-sponsored violence." Please enlighten me as to whether the nonviolent Christ justifies the "proportionality" of bombing children, women, the ill — anyone.

Further, whether such justification itself can be, so to speak, biblically justified — in light of say, the Sermon on the Mount.

Further, and no matter what the provocation offered by an adversary, whether a Christian basis can be offered for such violence. No matter if the provocation were the most monstrous of crimes, even the execution of Jesus. I seem to recall in this regard, a statement of the Subject of execution, to the effect of "Father, forgive . . . " Or is the citation inept, or the original plea irrelevant?

Further, whether the justification, if accurately reported, befits, considering that the present administration is guilty of the perennial terrorizing of Nicaraguan peasants.

And finally, please enlighten me as to the following; on grounds of what ordination or mandate, do we Christians justify the violence of any government, anywhere in the world, in any conceivable case? I had imagined that given the inevitable violence of governments, it was our business to cast a wary eye on their bombs, their rhetoric, their enmities, and perhaps also, on their efforts to enlist religion in the blessing of bombers.

Not to try your patience beyond endurance. May I ask whether the statement attributed to you, does not in fact weaken or extinguish the light bishops might cast on nuclear terror? I have a haunting sense that it does. I raise the question because that light has been all but extinguished in my mind. And I am commonly assumed to be a Christian of good will.

Given your implied approval of the bombing, if true, it seems to me that the hope you express by way of conclusion, is of small value. Mr. Reagan has won his main point with you. He and his bombers can bow heads piously, in the prayer that "current tensions and hostile acts will not escalate," etc. etc.

Such tensions and acts will of course escalate, inevitably. There is an ancient saying to the effect that "those who grasp the sword, etc." I had presumed we Christians were capable of taking fair warning seriously, and seeking another Way.

If you or I could imagine drawing a dying child from the rubble of Tripoli and holding it in our arms until it expired, our moral clarity would be wonderfully sharpened. We might be blessed with the gift of tears. We might awaken to that other Way.

I write as a Christian under a three- to ten-year sentence for resisting the violence of our government. My sister-in-law is in prison. Christians are paying up, severely. Father Carl Kabat, eighteen years. Helen Woodson, fourteen years. And many others. We wonder.

May the blood of the innocent enlighten us all.

DANIEL BERRIGAN, S.J.

Part Six

ON TRIAL

The Trial of the Catonsville Nine

INTRODUCTION

The trial was finished, the judge's gavel had pounded us into true shape, and the thing was done, lost, given over, run like veins aground; in the shape of the body, in the shape of man.

The facts of the case are perhaps known by now. "An F.B.I. agent estimated that at least 600 individual draft files were in the two huge wire baskets carried by nine defendants from local board number 33 in Catonsville, Maryland, on May 17, 1968, and set afire in a parking lot" (A.P. Wire). The trial evidence brought forward a more modest figure of ruin: some 378 files. In any case, the damage was something more than symbolic, as the judge insisted several times. The damage exceeded $100, and the prosecution proved it to the hilt. So our crime stood under a Federal statute.

The trial of the "Catonsville Nine" was held in a Baltimore Federal court, October 5-9, 1968. A verdict of guilty was returned against each defendant on each of three counts: destruction of U.S. property, destruction of Selective Service records, and interference with the Selective Service Act of 1967.

In composing this book, I have worked directly with the data of the trial record, somewhat in the manner of the new "factual theater." As I understand it, that form requires essential adherence to the letter of a text (in this case, some twelve hundred pages, supplied to us by the court stenographer). I have been as faithful as possible to the original words, spoken in the heat or long haul of the trial, making only those minute changes required for clarity or good sense.

In condensing such a mass of material, it was predictable that a qualitative change would occur, almost by the law of nature, as the form emerged. And this of course was my hope: to induce out of the density of matter an art form worthy of the passionate acts and words of the Nine, acts and words which were the substance of the court record.

It was not however a matter merely of a record. It was a matter for us of life and death. For each of us, the spring had wound tight in the weeks of discernment and scrutiny and long, patient sharing which preceded Catonsville. There was a danger that intensity and passion would be dissipated in the routine of the trial itself, in the obeisance paid to legal niceties and court routine, in the wrangling and paper shuffling which threatened to obscure the firmness and clarity of the original deed.

This work had but one purpose therefore: to wind the spring tighter.

I have reduced all the principals of the trial, with the exception of the defendants, to anonymity. The defense counsel, who are our friends, will not be chagrined by this treatment. The judge and prosecutors have their own kind of fame, elsewhere. It is extremely dubious that I could do anything to add to it. Where evidence overlapped due to common experience (Philip Berrigan, Tom Lewis), or where special circumstances intervened (Marjorie and Tom Melville, the only married couple in the group), I have altered the text in accord with what I understood to be dramatic exigency.

The tone of that exigency is of course more easily sensed than described. How to convey the tenderness of Marjorie Melville, the gentle simplicity of John Hogan, the anguish of Tom Lewis, brought into court from jail each day, remanded to jail at the end of each exhausting session? The air of the court was charged with grandeur, with damnation, with bathos. Spite, blindness, danger, gentleness, the interplay of wit and dim wit, an overriding sense that here, in one place, almost against our will, by choices that bore us headlong, the tragic ingredients of the war were being pressed into a single concentrate. Was it named hemlock?

It was my impossible, almost despairing, task to attempt to evoke something of all this.

Six months before the short journey to Catonsville, I had gone half way around the world to Hanoi, on a mission to repatriate three American prisoners of war. I had cause to remember, after our crime, the virtue commended to us by our hosts in North Vietnam. It was strangely enough that of patience. "A revolutionary virtue," they called it — those men who of all men of our century should by rights know. And I have questioned myself in the year since our trial; is it possible, having endured a Federal trial and, six months later, a state trial (held in despite of double jeopardy), enduring a limbo of travel restriction and limitation of speech — is it possible that in being more patient than the warmakers, we might become peacemakers? We could only try. We could be patient with the judge, with the prosecution, with the Federal marshals, with one another (we would learn the cost of that); patient also with the students who marched for us, who went home from our trial fervent and turned around; and then promptly forgot or repudiated us within a few months.

Cornell, where I had been teaching and counseling for two years, came quickly to its own torment, after sharing to some degree in mine. The students who traveled to Baltimore by the hundreds in October put us down sharply a few months later: our style, our nonviolence, our religion. The spring of 1969 brought the hour of decision closer to home; the atmosphere was hottening up, a torrid zone. The war that had no end, the police repression, the immobile, marmoreal establishments (those Maginot Line Eminences!). And then the response: seizure of a building, hit and run, anger, inner division, threat of sabotage. The *Cornell Sun* (no tongue of revolution it!) saluted my *hutzpah* a few days before the trial. But by June, I was old hat.

My brother Philip said, when we talked of these things: "There is no one way, there are as many ways as there are people or communities. It is up to us to pursue our way as best we know how, and to respect theirs."

His remark had a Buddhist flavor. About methods in such times as these, no one knew. We improvised our lives as we went along. To be sure, we had certain insights, having to do with community and nonviolence. We had come upon them in the course of a long loneliness, a long exposure, a long defeat, as conditions worsened around us, and the light sank lower.

But we could be reasonably sure of one thing, in the midst of great and general perplexity. That is to say, we had not sleepwalked toward Catonsville, nor toward the trials that followed. We went into court as we had gone into the draft center—wide awake, neither insane nor amnesiac.

And that might be something, that might offer something. We had had no part in social madness. We knew (how simple and crucial a thing) our own names, where we came from, why we were on trial, the direction we had chosen to follow. We knew who our brothers and sisters were, and what our duty was to them; all the truths denied to American consciousness, by wars running hot and cold, and by peace, another word for war. We knew who we were; we could at least claim that. We had not dismembered our brothers and sisters on a universal autopsy slab. And having no part in that murderous operation, perhaps we could re-member humankind, perhaps we could surgically and lovingly put it together—according to the image of God, according to the law of life, by which the healer is healed in the very act of the healer's art.

Yet an ominous sense of the future weighs upon me, as these words go to press. The war continues, inexorably. Will this record, the first of its kind to be published since the war began, also be the last? It well may be. The time of taking risks and submitting before the judicial system is drawing to a close. The war machine, which has come to include the court process that serves it, is proving self-destructive. The courts, like the President (two, three Presidents), like the Congress, are turning to stone. The "separation of powers" is proving a fiction; ball and joint, the functions of power are fusing, like the bones of an aged body.

Indeed it cannot be thought that men and women like ourselves will continue, as though we were automated heroes, to rush for redress from the King of the Blind. The King will have to listen to other voices, over which neither he nor we will indefinitely have control: voices of public violence and chaos. For you cannot set up a court in the Kingdom of the Blind, to condemn those who see; a court presided over by those who would pluck out the eyes of men and women and call it rehabilitation.

SUMMER 1969

CONTENTS

1

THE DAY OF A JURY OF PEERS

DEFENSE

With regard to jury selection, we wish to make one brief statement, your honor. The defendants will not participate in any way in the selection of the jury. That will be a matter between the court and the U.S. attorney.

JUDGE

You do not wish to have the benefit of striking out names you object to?

DEFENSE

We do not wish any strikes whatever. We are abstaining completely from the jury selection.

JUDGE

Very well. All I am going to do is to be sure I get the names. I am now going to do a little housekeeping. Bring in the prospective jurors. Swear them in.

(*The prospective jurors are brought in.*)

Members of this panel, in this case the United States government, by indictment, has commenced a prosecution against nine defendants. The indictment charges in three counts the following offenses:

That the defendants did willfully injure and commit depradation against property of the United States; did willfully and unlawfully obliterate records of the Selective Service System, Local Board No. 33 located in Catonsville, Maryland; and did willfully and knowingly interfere with the administration of the Military Selective Service Act of 1967, by removing and burning the records of Local Board No. 33 located in Catonsville, Maryland, and by disrupting the official activities at the location of the Local Board No. 33.

The indictment further charges that the defendants aided and abetted one another in committing these alleged offenses.

Each of the defendants has pleaded innocent to these charges. Accordingly, the burden of proof is upon the government to prove the guilt of any of the defendants beyond a reasonable doubt. Now I want to ask each of the prospective jurors some questions.

Mr. Starlings, what is your position?

JUROR

I work for the National Security Agency.

JUDGE

Do you feel that your position in the government would make it difficult or impossible for you to do equal justice between the government and the defendants in this case?

JUROR

No, sir.

JUDGE

You may step down.

Mr. Jones. You served in World War I?

JUROR

Yes, sir. I was in the Army, American Expeditionary Force, World War I.

JUDGE

Have you been active in the American Legion or other activities since? Have you taken any position with respect to protests against the Vietnam war? Have you taken any public position on that war?

JUROR

No, sir.

JUDGE

You may step down. . . .

Mrs. Kilmurray, you say that at one time you worked for the Department of Defense?

JUROR

That is right. I was the Chief of Position Classification at the U.S. Army at Edgewood Arsenal.

JUDGE

Do you feel that your experience in that job would make it impossible, or would make it difficult, for you to do equal justice between the government and the defendants in this case?

JUROR

No, I do not. . . .

JUDGE

You may step down.

Mr. Seidel. I believe that you answered "yes" to the question that you had served in the Armed Forces.

JUROR

Yes, sir. It was in the Second World War.

JUDGE

Have you taken any position, any public position, with respect to the war in Vietnam?

JUROR

No, sir.

JUDGE

You may step down. . . .

Mrs. Smith, you answered, I believe, that you are now working for the Federal government?

JUROR

Yes, as a management analyst with the Army.

JUDGE

Is there anything about your job, or anything about your experience, or any other reason at all, which you feel would make it difficult for you to do impartial justice between the government on the one side, and the defendants on the other?

JUROR

No, sir. . . .

JUDGE

You may step down.

Mr. Buchanan, you were, I believe you said, in the military service at some time?

JUROR

Yes, sir.

JUDGE

During what conflict was that?

JUROR

The Korean War and the Cuban crisis.

JUDGE

Do you feel that your experience in the service would make it difficult for you to do equal justice?

JUROR

No, sir.

JUDGE

You may step down.

State your name, sir.

JUROR

My name is Eric Smith, Jr.

JUDGE

Mr. Smith, you say that you are the branch chief of the Department of Defense at Fort Meade?

JUROR

Yes, sir.

JUDGE

Are your duties classified, or can you tell me what the branch chief does, what you do?

JUROR

I am an industrial engineer in charge of construction and space allocation for the National Security Agency and the Department of Defense.

JUDGE

And you served in the Armed Forces heretofore in one of the conflicts?

JUROR

I have served in the Armed Forces, yes, sir, during Korea.

JUDGE

Would your experience as a former Military Policeman make it difficult for you to decide this case fairly?

JUROR

No, sir, I don't think it would influence or bias my opinion . . . .

JUDGE

You may step down.

Mr. Austin, you have served in the military?

JUROR

World War II for three years, 1942 to 1945, in the U.S. Navy.

JUDGE

Do you know of any reason why you would not be able to decide the case solely on the evidence?

JUROR

No, sir. I am a very conscientious person.

JUDGE

I hope all the jurors will be. You may step down. . . .

Mr. Raymond Steer. You have served, I believe, in the Armed Forces?

JUROR

I started with the 29th Division here at Fort Meade, and I switched to the Air Force.

JUDGE

Does anything in your experience make it difficult for you to do justice in this case?

JUROR

No.

JUDGE

You may step down.

Mr. Johnston, have you served in the military service?

JUROR

I was in the Army, yes, sir.

JUDGE

What branch?

JUROR

Well, I was on active duty in the Army, then I was in the Army Reserves, and I was at the rank of Sergeant E–5 when I got out.

JUDGE

You may step down.

Mr. Bergman, you have a contract with the government, is that right?

JUROR

Yes, sir. With NASA.

JUDGE

And you also were in the Armed Forces?

JUROR

Yes, sir.

JUDGE

Is there anything about your experience in the Army which would make it difficult for you to do justice between the government on the one side, and these defendants on the other?

JUROR

I do not believe so.

JUDGE

Are you prejudiced in any way, for or against the defendants, and the position they have taken?

JUROR

Well, I believe I have already formed an opinion, sir.

JUDGE

I think we have run into difficulties here. You may be excused. . . .

Mr. Fanzone, you have been in the Armed Forces?

JUROR

I served three years in the U.S. Army, from 1961 to 1964.

JUDGE

Would anything make it difficult for you to do equal justice here?

JUROR

No, your honor. . . .

JUDGE

Mr. Davis, you have served in the Armed Forces?

JUROR

Yes. I was in the U.S. Navy in World War II, between 1943 and 1946.

JUDGE

Would anything in your experience in the Navy, or since, make it difficult for you to do equal justice between the government on the one hand, and these defendants on the other?

JUROR

No, sir. . . .

JUDGE

You may step down.

Are the government and the defense ready to have the jury sworn?

PROSECUTION

The government is ready.

DEFENSE

We are ready.

JUDGE

Swear the jury.

(*Whereupon the jury was sworn and seated.*)

2

THE DAY OF THE FACTS OF THE CASE

WITNESS

We had just come back from lunch. A gentleman came up the steps. I looked at him, and I said: "Could I help you, sir?"

Before I could say anything else, all of these people came in.

I asked them not to come in. I begged them not to come in the office, but they did.

I was so confused and upset at that point. They utterly terrified us. We were just terrified.

Of course, they immediately went to the files. I noticed one gentleman was carrying a trash burner.

I begged them not to take the files. I begged them. One of them went right over to the files, and I could see him read the label on the 1−A Qualified drawer.

He just emptied all those sheets right into the trash burner.

I begged them and pleaded with them, but it was to no avail, and I might say that I have never been treated with such bad manners in my whole life, and with such disrespect or uncharity.

JUDGE

Strike it out. The defendants are not being tried for their manners.

PROSECUTION

What happened after they emptied the drawers?

WITNESS

I took hold of the trash burner, and I tried to pull it away, but I could not get it away from them, naturally. And in the scuffle I cut my leg and my hand.

Then they ran down the stairs. I followed to the edge of the building and saw the fire, and I came running back up, and I said to the girls: "My God, they are burning our records."

PROSECUTION

And the 378 files taken would include all information necessary to draft young men?

WITNESS

That is right, everything that concerns a man.

PROSECUTION

What effect on the functioning of Local Board 33 has the incident of May 17 had?

WITNESS

It has given us a tremendous amount of work, and it certainly has inconvenienced our boys.

PROSECUTION

Have you yourself done any work in restoring those files?

WITNESS

I would estimate that in the general reconstruction, getting the papers from the Armed Forces, making lists, reconstructing the cover sheets, writing them all up again—all of this—I would estimate that, myself, alone, I have spent at least eighty hours. The other clerks spent about forty hours working with me. We also had three supervisors from State Headquarters working for three weeks.

PROSECUTION

Have you finished reconstructing these 378 files, as of today?

WITNESS

No, sir.

DEFENSE

Mrs. Murphy, at the time of the action about which you testified, what did the several people who came into the office say to you?

WITNESS

There was a lot of conversation: "We don't want to hurt you. We have no intention of hurting you." Some of it was about the war in Vietnam; that this is not a good war, and that we shouldn't be there. One of them said: "You send boys away to be killed." Father Philip Berrigan told me he didn't want to hurt me, and I am sure he meant it.

DEFENSE

Can you remember this having been said: "Don't fight." "We don't mean you any bodily harm." "You are helping in the deaths of American boys."

WITNESS

That is right. Yes, I remember that, sir.

DEFENSE

When you speak of an injury you received, would that be an injury for which you treated yourself with a Band-Aid?

WITNESS

Well, I went to the doctor, really, because it was—I suppose it was maybe, superficial. But I was very, very, very, very much upset. Mental anguish, I had.

DEFENSE

Would you conceive that the prime purpose of the files, and the work you do, is to serve the government?

WITNESS

Yes, sir, the Army of Defense. I am part of the Army of Defense.

DEFENSE

Mrs. Murphy, did not some of the defendants while in jail send you flowers and candy?

PROSECUTION

Objection, your honor.

JUDGE

We are not trying the manners of the defendants, neither their good manners nor their bad manners. We are trying a specific charge.

DEFENSE

No more questions.

3

THE DAY OF THE NINE DEFENDANTS

PHILIP BERRIGAN

    I am a member of a family including six boys
All of us were born in Minnesota
My father was railroading out there
and he married my mother   who was a German immigrant
I think perhaps some influence on my life
came from these days
Minnesota was pioneer country
We lived on the Iron Range
Most of the people were Scandinavians   Finlanders
Swedes and Norwegians
I remember my older brothers telling at great length
of the struggles they had
to survive in the bitter winters
We were poor
I remember the depression years very well
I think those years had some bearing
on the inclination my life was to take
I think this is true of my brother Dan as well
and other members of our family
We lived with people
and accepted them as they were
During the depression years I remember my mother
welcoming people from the road
There were many men in those days traveling the roads
impoverished and desperate
Even though we did not have too much to eat
she never refused them
This made an early and deep impression upon us

DEFENSE

    Will you indicate what your early education was?

PHILIP BERRIGAN

    I come from a devout Catholic family
our early years were more or less stereotyped
All six boys went to parochial school
about two miles away

We had to walk both ways and pack our lunches
We were educated by nuns
in a rather harsh and authoritarian environment
We graduated from a Catholic high school
I went to work and tried
to save a little money to go to college
I was inducted into military service
after one semester of college
I underwent training in the Deep South
first in Georgia and later in Florida
and North Carolina
I was perceptive in a dim sort of way
noticing the conditions of Black people
in the rural areas where we trained
I noticed
and remembered
the dire poverty we encountered
One time when we were out on maneuvers
we happened to be trying out the rations
that would be fed us overseas
The climate was very humid and oppressive
and we were famished
at the end of the day
We came upon some Black people
who were selling whole chickens for $1 apiece
We had some money along
Five or six of us
bought chickens and ravenously ate them
Then a white boy came along
grinned at us   Said we had been eating
not chicken   but buzzard

DEFENSE
Did you experience any of the war in Europe?

PHILIP BERRIGAN
I spent about a month
in the British Isles
I saw the devastation of cities
a result of the great German air raids
Bristol   Coventry   Sheffield   London
I think I should add
in all candor
I was an enthusiastic participant in World War II—
in contrast   of course to my present attitude
which arose because of the influence of people
who have surrounded me

DEFENSE

What happened after your discharge from military service?

PHILIP BERRIGAN

I entered the Society of Saint Joseph
for training
toward the priesthood
I lived with Black seminarians
I learned from them
in a graphic way
what it means to be Black
in this country

DEFENSE

Where did you go after ordination?

PHILIP BERRIGAN

To New Orleans to teach
in a Black high school

DEFENSE

Did you participate in the social struggles then going on in the South?

PROSECUTION

Your honor, how long are we going to go on?

God forbid we should be twenty years without a rebellion. What country can preserve its liberties if the rulers are not warned from time to time that their people preserve the spirit of resistance?

THOMAS JEFFERSON
"LETTER TO GENERAL WILLIAM S. SMITH
NOVEMBER 13, 1787"

PHILIP BERRIGAN

Very early   in New Orleans
I became deeply involved
in the civil rights struggle
We did voter registration work
We worked with the poor
in the slums of New Orleans
We tried to provide
some sort of bridge
between the Black and White communities
We tried to attack racism at its roots
We tried to open minds a bit

JUDGE

We are not trying the racial situation in the United States, nor are we trying the high moral character of this witness.

PHILIP BERRIGAN
> At any rate
> I began to investigate
> what was called the Cold War
> I began to study
> how nuclear weapons were engineered
> and gotten ready for "duty"
> on both sides

—————————

FRANZ
> *The century might have been a good one, if man had not been watched*
> *from time immemorial by the cruel enemy who had sworn to destroy him;*
> *that hairless, evil, flesh-eating beast—man himself.*
>
> *Perhaps there will be no more centuries after ours. Perhaps a bomb will*
> *blow out all the lights. Everything will be dead—eyes, judges, time.*
> *Night. O tribunal of the night, I have taken the century upon my*
> *shoulders and have said: I will answer for it. This day and forever.*

SARTRE: THE CONDEMNED OF ALTONA

—————————

There was a loosely formed group
of peace people
operating on the campuses
I did some work with them
after President Kennedy's assassination
When the bombing of North Vietnam started
we began a peace organization
We were doing very unsophisticated
and unthreatening things
in those days
We were trying to get a forum on the war
trying to get people to listen
But I remember the fierce opposition
even to this
Anyone who spoke out against Vietnam
was apt to lose his coattails
I lost mine
I was transferred to Baltimore
by my superiors
because of my peace activity
The Catholic community in Newburgh
where I had been teaching
was distraught by what we were doing

I was ordered by my superior to keep silent
But then Pope Paul
spoke at the United Nations
I considered this a mandate
to open my mouth again

DEFENSE
What was the nature of your peace activity in Baltimore?
PHILIP BERRIGAN
We always tried
to gauge our activity
in terms of the reality of the war
We started with prayer vigils
with meals of reconciliation
with a few tentative marches
in downtown Baltimore
We began to demonstrate   at military bases
We went to Fort Myers   Virginia
(Fort Myers is the home
of the Joint Chiefs of Staff)
We tried to contact men
like General Wheeler
and General Johnson
former Chiefs of Staff of the Army
to tell them of our concerns
to sit down with them
citizen to leader
The military were immune
from any citizen influence
They were a law unto themselves
General Wheeler ignored our letters
So we went to his home
and demonstrated outside
We were forced to leave
We came back in a month's time
and were forced out again
The third time   we were forcibly ejected
Apart from these attempts
I also tried continually
to keep in touch with the Congress
I made a proposal to Senator Fulbright
suggesting it might be a good thing
to investigate the war
in light of the moral opinion of the nation
We planned to bring a team
of theologians   to testify

before the Foreign Relations Committee
Fulbright was partial to the idea
but he never had political leverage
particularly from the churches
so of course our idea died aborning.
At Christmas of 1967
I also spent two hours
with Secretary Rusk   I went to his office
with another clergyman
We discussed all aspects of the war
He was very gracious
but he did not tell us anything
he had not said before
and that was not enough for us

DEFENSE

Are there any books that influenced your thinking on the war in Vietnam?

PHILIP BERRIGAN

I was influenced by my reading
on both sides of the question
I have read all the authors
on the Vietnam war
including those who wrote
in support of the war

DEFENSE

I would like to have this book, *In the Name of America*, marked for identification. Father Berrigan, I show you Defendant's Exhibit No. 5. And I ask if you have read this book?

PHILIP BERRIGAN

Yes I have

DEFENSE

Did this book influence your thinking as to the legal aspects of the war in Vietnam?

PHILIP BERRIGAN

Yes it did

DEFENSE

I want to make a formal proffer. The book *In the Name of America* has to do with the reasonableness of the defendants' view.

JUDGE

The government has agreed on the sincerity of his views.

DEFENSE

The government did not agree as to the reasonableness of his views.

JUDGE

In that case, I must question the prosecution. Does the government contend that the reasonableness or unreasonableness of the defendant's view has any bearing on the issue of intent? You had better think that over carefully. . . .

(*The prosecuting attorneys consult.*)

PROSECUTION

Your honor, we say that a reasonable man could have the defendant's views. . . .

DEFENSE

Your honor, the defense has scored a capital point. This is the first time in a trial of this nature that such an admission has been made by the government. But we shall return to this matter later. . . .

Father Berrigan, I ask you: did there come a time, then, when you began seriously to consider civil disobedience?

PHILIP BERRIGAN

Yes   I came
to the conclusion
that I was in direct line
with American democratic tradition
in choosing civil disobedience
in a serious fashion
There have been times in our history
when in order to get redress
in order to get a voice   vox populi
arising from the roots
people have so acted
From the Boston Tea Party
through the abolitionist and anarchist movements
through World War I   and World War II
and right on
through the civil rights movement
we have a rich tradition
of civil disobedience

DEFENSE

Now, the action for which you are being tried here was not the first such action you were involved in. To state it briefly: seven months earlier, in October 1967, you along with the defendant Thomas Lewis and two others not present poured blood over Selective Service records in the Baltimore Customs House.

PHILIP BERRIGAN

We were prepared
for the blood pouring
because we had practiced civil disobedience
in Virginia
In fact my brother and myself
had practiced civil disobedience for years
by signing complicity statements

in support of draft resisters
So four of us took our own blood
and when the equipment for drawing our blood
broke down   we added animal blood
We attempted to anoint these files
with the Christian symbol of life and purification
which is blood

DEFENSE

Will you explain why, with a jail sentence staring you in the face, you felt
impelled to act again at Catonsville?

PHILIP BERRIGAN

Neither at the Customs House   nor at Catonsville
do I wish my actions reduced
to a question   of acquittal or conviction
Rather I   and all of us
desire to communicate
with the bench   with the prosecution
with our country
We have already made it clear   our dissent runs counter
to more than the war   which is but one instance
of American power in the world
Latin America is another instance   So is the Near East
This trial is yet another
From those in power we have met
little understanding   much silence
much scorn and punishment
We have been accused of arrogance
But what of the fantastic arrogance   of our leaders
What of their crimes against the people   the poor and powerless
Still no court will try them   no jail will receive them
They live in righteousness   They will die in honor
For them we have one message   for those
in whose manicured hands   the power of the land lies
We say to them
Lead us   Lead us in justice
and there will be no need to break the law
Let the President do   what his predecessors failed to do
Let him obey the rich less   and the people more
Let him think less of the privileged
and more of the poor
Less of America and more of the world
Let lawmakers   judges   and lawyers
think less of the law   more of justice
less of legal ritual   more of human rights

To our bishops and superiors we say
Learn something about the gospel
and something about illegitimate power
When you do   you will liquidate your investments
take a house in the slums   or even
join us in jail
To lawyers we say
Defend draft resisters   ask no fees
insist on justice   risk contempt of court
to jail with your clients
To the prosecution we say
Refuse to indict
opponents of the war
prefer to resign   practice in private
To Federal judges we say
Give anti-war people   suspended sentences
to work for justice and peace
or resign your posts
You men of power   I also have a dream
Federal Judges   District Attorneys   Marshals
Against the War in Vietnam
You men of power   you have told us
that your system is reformable
Reform it then
and we will help
with all our conviction and energy
in jail or out

DAVID DARST

I was not in the room
when the files were taken
Perhaps I could be called
the lookout man
If anyone came to stop us
I was to hurry in
and let the others know
One might have called it
a Bonnie and Clyde act
on behalf of God and humankind

DEFENSE

Do you recall the substance with which the records were burned?

DAVID DARST

They were burned
with a kind of crude napalm
We made it from a formula

in the Special Forces Handbook
published by the School for Special Warfare
at Fort Bragg

———————

*The recruit is led through candles to the image of a saint. His blood is drawn
and sprinkled on the effigy. He then takes an oath and is required to carry
out a murder.*

MAFIA HANDBOOK

———————

In emergencies, napalm is made in the following manner.

GREEN BERET HANDBOOK

———————

We did not use all the ingredients called for
We made a very crude form of napalm
consisting of two parts gasoline
one part soap flakes
Nor did we cook our mix into a jelly
We left it in liquid form
so we could pour it on the files
We felt it was fitting that this agent
which had burned human flesh
in the war in Vietnam   and in many other places
should now be poured on the records
which gave war and violence
their cruel legitimacy

DEFENSE

Would you explain your intent in acting at Catonsville, other than
destroying the files?

DAVID DARST

First of all to raise a cry
an outcry   at what was clearly a crime
an unnecessary suffering
a clear and wanton slaughter
Perhaps this is similar to the case
of a man in his home who sees a crime
someone is being attacked outside
His impulse   I think   his
basic human impulse
is to cry out   to call for help

Dear people of Camardo, I appeal to you for understanding and forgiveness.

I tried to save what could be saved. It was not possible for me totally to prevent the terrible deaths.

I do not want to defend myself. I can only abandon myself to God's judgment.

I resisted the orders without success. Could I not then have refused to carry out the order with my last breath, without heed to the most extreme personal consequences?

BISHOP DEFREGGER OF MUNICH

ON HIS WARTIME ROLE IN EXECUTION

OF ITALIAN VILLAGERS

That was one intention
an outcry that   hopefully
would stop the crime
I saw being perpetrated
Another intention was
to halt the machine of death
which I saw moving   and killing
In the same way perhaps
people in Czechoslovakia
when tanks invade their country
throw bricks into the wheels
of the tanks
and sometimes a puny effort
stops a tank
This was my hope
to hinder this war
in a literal way
an actual physical way

DEFENSE

Do you have any other basis for the intent you have described?

DAVID DARST

An outcry against the fact
that our country can spend
eighty billions a year
chasing imaginary enemies
all around the world
I was living last year
in a poor ghetto district
I saw many little children
who did not have enough to eat

This is an astonishing thing
that our country
cannot command the energy
to give bread and milk
to children
Yet it can rain   fire and death
on people   ten thousand miles away
for reasons that are unclear
to thoughtful men and women

DEFENSE

Did your religious belief have any influence on your decision?

DAVID DARST

Well I suppose my thinking
is part of an ethic
found in the New Testament
You could say
Jesus too was guilty
of assault and battery
when he cast the money changers
out of the temple
and wasted their property and wealth
He was saying
It is wrong to do what you are doing
And this was our point
We came to realize
draft files are death's own cry
We have not been able
to let sacred life
and total death
live together quietly within us
We have cried out on behalf of life
The government has chosen
to see our cry
as anarchy and arrogance
Perhaps real anarchy lies
in the acts of those
who loose this plague of war
upon a proud people
in face of a great and burning doubt
This doubt cries to heaven
Our cry too goes out
in the name of life
Men and women around the world hear   and take heart
We are one with them   We believe that today
we are at a joyful beginning   We are together
and we are not afraid

PROSECUTION

You have said elsewhere that draft files have no right to exist. Do you believe that slum properties have no right to exist?

DAVID DARST

Slum properties I would say
have no right to exist

PROSECUTION

Would you symbolically burn down slum properties?

DAVID DARST

How could I
symbolically burn down slum properties?
(*Commotion in court. Laughter from the audience.*)

JUDGE (*Gavel. Anger.*)

If we have any more demonstrations, we are going to clear the court-room.

•

THOMAS LEWIS

Let me speak of an experience
that has bearing on why I am here
As you recall   some years ago
there were civil rights demonstrations
at Gwyn Oak Park   here in Baltimore
The issue was the right of Blacks
to use the park
I went there   to do some sketches
of the demonstrations
When I arrived
they had just arrested some clergy
You know I had a feeling
that I should be where they were
I was slowly drawn into things
I picketed for awhile
But I was in no position psychologically
to consider civil disobedience
Later I became active
in the Catholic Interracial Council
and in CORE
I was slowly being educated
in the realities around me
My schooling went forward
with my experience
In a sense   I could have been called
a very conservative person
coming out of high school
going into art studies

It is a shocking thing
walking a picket line
for the first time
sensing the hostility of the people   the White people
particularly when we went to suburbia
to demonstrate for open occupancy

DEFENSE

What first motivated you to become interested in the issue of Vietnam?

THOMAS LEWIS

Well there were many factors
It is unfortunate
reflecting on it now
In Christianity   we are taught
that all people are a human family
Yet I was not profoundly moved
about Vietnam
until my younger brother was there
an immediate relative
Of course
in a Christian sense
one's family is much more broad
than the immediate family
The war helped educate me
I began to read and go to lectures
about the war
Of course   on an artist
the visual impact of the war
is immediate

DEFENSE

What opinion did you come to, with respect to the war in Vietnam?

THOMAS LEWIS

I came to the conclusion
that the war
is totally outrageous
from the Christian point of view
But it is not enough   to say this
You know   those terms
have become almost meaningless
The war is outrageous   unChristian
and it is a great deal more than this

DEFENSE

On the strength of these beliefs, did you then engage in peace activity?

THOMAS LEWIS

Yes   after the speech
of Pope Paul at the U.N.
a group of us

began what we called
the Interfaith Peace Mission of Baltimore
We were a group of concerned people
attempting to express to others
what we felt about the war
We began with a peace vigil
at one of the churches here
We prayed for peace
in response to the invitation
of religious leaders throughout the world
We followed this with a walk
demonstrating visually
our hope for peace
Things progressed   We had visits
with Maryland congressmen and senators
We wrote letters to them   and delivered them
personally   in Washington
We met with silence
from all of them
We met
with hostility and apathy
One of the vigils in Washington
was at the home of McNamara
another was at the home of Rusk
Particularly Rusk indicated
his lack of concern
He said it was not his job
to deal with moral matters
He said
to the clergymen in the group
that it was their responsibility
to deal with the morality of the war
We did not need his homilies
We had been doing that for years
So we turned toward the military
We engaged in conversations
with the military hierarchy
They accepted no responsibility
for the direction of the war
The responsibility was not theirs
They were just taking orders

JUDGE

You said "no response." You mean they did not do what you asked them
to do, is that it?

THOMAS LEWIS

No response your honor

We were standing there   We were speaking
on behalf of the suffering
We were speaking as Americans
We were proud to be Americans
Yet we have representatives in Vietnam
who do terrible things in our name
We were saying to the military
This is wrong   This is immoral   This is illegal
And their response to this was
they were only obeying orders

JUDGE

But they did respond to you, did they not?

THOMAS LEWIS

It was an atrocious response

DEFENSE

You are an artist, are you not?

THOMAS LEWIS

Yes sir

JUDGE

We are not trying his ability as an artist.

DEFENSE

Would you indicate, Mr. Lewis, where your work has been exhibited?
And what prizes you have won?

JUDGE

This has nothing to do with the issue. We are not trying his ability as an
artist.

THOMAS LEWIS

So be it
I then moved into civil disobedience
This is a legitimate form
of social protest   It is well documented
in Christianity
Civil disobedience was practiced
by the early Christians
The spirit of the New Testament deals
with one's response to others
and with a law that overrides
all laws   The one law
is the primary law of love and justice
toward others
As a Christian
I am obligated
to the primary law of brotherhood and sisterhood
Men and women have responsibilities not only

to their immediate family
but to the world.

JUDGE

Yes, you have said that.

THOMAS LEWIS

So I made a decision to protest
This protest involved
the pouring of blood
a strong indictment of those records
Blood   in biblical terms
and in contemporary terms
is a symbol of reconciliation
related to the blood
that is being wasted in Vietnam
not only American blood
but the blood of the Vietnamese
We acted   Father Phil Berrigan   Dave Eberhart
Reverend Mengel and myself
in Baltimore in October of 1967
For that I received a prison sentence
of six years in a Federal penitentiary

DEFENSE

After the conviction, and while you were awaiting sentence, you also
engaged in the Catonsville action, did you not?

THOMAS LEWIS

Yes
It was the response of a man
a man standing for humanity   a man
a Christian   a human being
seeing what was happening   not only
in Vietnam but beyond Vietnam
There was a difference   in my mind   between
the two protests
The draft records
on which we poured blood
were records of the inner city
the ghetto areas
Part   of the protest
was to dramatize that the war
is taking more cannon fodder   from the poor areas
than from the more affluent areas
The symbolism was perhaps clearer
in the second case
We used a contemporary symbol   napalm
to destroy records

which are potential death certificates
They stand for the death of the men they represent
men who are put in the situation
where they have to kill
But beyond this
napalm manufactured in the United States
is part of our foreign aid
We supply weaponry
to more than 80 countries   We have troops
in more than 40 countries   These troops
are backed up with our weaponry
So I was speaking not only of Vietnam
I was speaking of other parts of the world
The fact is
the American system can flourish
only if we expand our economy
in these other countries
The fact is
we produce more goods than we are capable
of consuming   We must have new markets
We must bring our industries   our way of life
into Vietnam and Latin America
We must protect our interests there
But we asked at Catonsville
Whose interests are these?
Who represents the interests of Latin America?
Who represents the interests of Vietnam?
I was well aware
that in civil disobedience
you take an action
you stand   you are arrested
you attempt to express your views
you are prepared   to take the consequences
The consequence to me w
as a six-year sentence   for pouring blood

GALILEO

*If only I had resisted, if only the natural scientists had been able to evolve
something like the Hippocratic Oath of doctors, the vow to devote their
knowledge wholly to the benefit of mankind! As things now stand, the
best one can hope for is a race of inventive dwarfs who can be hired for
anything. . . . I surrendered my knowledge to those in power, to use, or
not to use, or to misuse, just as suited their purposes.*

BRECHT: GALILEO

I was aware too that
if I became involved in Catonsville
I would be summoned once more
for trial   This is the trial
and a greater sentence may follow
I was fully aware of this at the time
It was a very thoughtful time
In a sense   it was a choice
between life and death
It was a choice between
saving one's soul and losing it
I was saving my soul

OPPENHEIMER

We have spent years of our lives in developing ever sweeter means of destruction; we have been doing the work of the military, and I feel it in my very bones that this was wrong. . . .

I will never work on war projects again. We have been doing the work of the devil, and now we must return to our real tasks. . . . We cannot do better than keep the world open in the few places which can still be kept open.

KIPPHARDT: IN THE MATTER OF J. ROBERT OPPENHEIMER

PROSECUTION

Did you consider that others like you might hold a view about Vietnam that was contrary to yours?

THOMAS LEWIS

Well that has happened
as we all know   I don't see
any of these people in jail
I don't see any of these people suffering
as we are suffering

PROSECUTION

That was not my question. That was not my question.

THOMAS LEWIS

I don't see any of these people
in prison
What do these people represent?
such people
are defending their economic interest
They are defending
their personal interests

They are gaining because of the war
The whole weaponry industry is enormous
because of the war
The Sentinel Missile System
would not be possible if it were not for this war
Who are gaining from the war?
They are an elite minority
who are very wealthy
But what is happening to the poor
in this country?
I am not trying to
belabor the point

PROSECUTION

I think the question could be answered yes or no, could it not? Yes or no,
were you aware that it was against the law to take records from the
Selective Service, and burn them?

THOMAS LEWIS

I wasn't concerned with the law
I wasn't even thinking about the law
I was thinking of what those records meant
I wasn't concerned with the law
I was concerned with the lives
of innocent people
I went in there with the intent   of stopping
what the files justify
The young men
whose files we destroyed
have not yet been drafted   may not be drafted
may not be sent to Vietnam for cannon fodder
My intent in going there
was to save lives   A person
may break the law to save lives

JUDGE

If these men were not sent, other people would have been sent, who
would not otherwise have been sent, would they not?

THOMAS LEWIS

But why your honor
Why this?
Why does it have to be like this
You are accepting the fact
that if these men are not sent
other men will be sent
You are not even asking
what can be done
to stop this insane killing

what can be done
to stop the genocide
what can be done
to stop the conditions in Latin America
You are not dealing
with these things
You are accepting this
as in Nazi Germany
people accepted the massacre
of other people
This is insane
I protest this

PROSECUTION

Your honor, I move that all of this be stricken. I don't know how long he
is going to continue.

THOMAS LEWIS

How long?
I have six years Mr. Prosecutor
I have lots of time

BECKET

It is not for me to win you round. I have only to say no to you.

KING

But you must be logical, Becket!

BECKET

*No. That isn't necessary, my liege. We must only do — absurdly — what we
have been given to do — fight to the end.*

JEAN ANOUILH: BECKET

THOMAS MELVILLE

I am Thomas Melville   priest
In August of 1957
I went to Guatemala
My work there was the work
of any Christian minister
trying to teach the people
the truths of the Christian faith
I was not there very long
when I felt I was getting
a little ahead of myself
The material circumstances of the people —
I hesitate to use the word "poverty"

they were living
in utter misery
So I thought   perhaps instead of talking
about the life to come
and justice beyond
perhaps I could do a little
to ameliorate their conditions
on this earth
and at the same time
could give a demonstration
of what Christianity is all about
So we decided we would join
the revolutionary movement
knowing that perhaps
some of us would be killed
Myself   Marjorie my wife
who was a nun at the time
John Hogan   and five others
joined in this agreement
We were all finally expelled
by the American Ambassador
who was recently assassinated
I know you are bored by this

JUDGE

Nobody is bored by this, it is an extremely interesting story. But we
cannot try the last ten years in Guatemala.

•

MARJORIE MELVILLE

I am Marjorie Melville
wife of Thomas Melville
We first met in Guatemala
We were trying to find out
our role as Christians
Was it to see people's needs
and get involved
or were we to say
Well   this is too difficult
It is too hard to know what to do
Do we stand back
or do we go in
on the side of the people   and say
What can I do to help?
We were in anguish

trying to figure out what to do
with people who needed our help

THOMAS MELVILLE

I put up the title of the church property
so we could get a loan
(without the permission of the Bishops)
I got into trouble for it   I signed the loan myself
There was simply
no organization in the country
that would help the people

JUDGE

We are not trying the state of Guatemala. We are not
trying the Church in Guatemala.

MAJORIE MELVILLE

I had been living
a very sheltered life
in Guatemala City
I never went out
I dealt only with the parents of school children
Then I took a course
in Christian social doctrine
I went into the slum areas
I began to understand   and to show the students
what life in Guatemala City was about
Through working with the students
I began to realize
my country's involvement in Guatemala
Every time we asked for help
for very simple projects
like putting water in a village
or setting up a cooperative
we found that funds were not available
Money was always available
but only in areas
where the peasants
were in active despair   Money was available
so they would stay quiet

THOMAS MELVILLE

Under one government
land that belonged to the United Fruit Company
was distributed to peasants
But a later President   Castillo Armas
took the land from the peasants
and gave it back

to the United Fruit Company
There were about 3000 people who did not want to move
off the land
They were killed or moved forcibly
off the land

JUDGE

We are not trying the United Fruit Company.

THE UNITED FRUIT COMPANY

When the trumpets had sounded and all
was in readiness on the face of the earth,
Jehovah divided his universe;
Anaconda, Ford Motor,
Coca-Cola, Inc., and similar entities;

the most succulent item of all,
The United Fruit Company Incorporated
reserved for itself: the heartland
and coasts of my country. . . .

Then in the bloody domain of the flies
The United Fruit Company Incorporated
unloaded, a booty of coffee and fruits
brimming its cargo boats, gliding
like trays with the spoils
of our drowning dominions.

PABLO NERUDA

THOMAS MELVILLE

I went to the President
Ygidores Fuentes
to ask for land for the people
He had 80 national plantations
He was giving them to his political cronies
He was very courteous
but he said there was
no land for these peasants
They did not have capital
They did not have know-how to work the land

JUDGE

We are not trying the government of Guatemala, nor the Catholic Church
in Guatemala.

MARJORIE MELVILLE
The group of students I was working with
chose a name
which in English means "Crater"
because they felt that our spirit
should be like a volcano
which erupts forth love for men and women

---

*The United States should not worry about communists in Latin America.
The communists are no longer revolutionaries. But the Americans should
worry about the Catholics, who are.*

FIDEL

Our superiors
got a little nervous
about our desire   to work with the peasants
and they thought it would be better
if we left the country
before the thing got too big

---

*The world expects that Christians will speak out loud and clear, so that
never a doubt, never the slightest doubt, could arise in the heart of the
simplest man.*

*The world expects that Christians will get away from abstractions and
confront the blood stained face which history has taken on today.*

*The grouping we need is a grouping of men resolved to speak out clearly
and to pay up personally.*

CAMUS: THE UNBELIEVER AND THE CHRISTIAN

We were asked to leave Guatemala
in December of 1967
We went to Mexico
trying to help the peasants
and student leaders
who also had been expelled
Their lives were in danger
Being associated with us put them in danger
In fact I found out
that their names
were on the Secret Police lists
and they would have been murdered

as 4000 people had been murdered
in the last 2 years
It is impossible to describe that

JUDGE

Well, we are listening.

THOMAS MELVILLE

Eighty-five percent of the people of Guatemala
live in misery
You don't live in misery
perhaps that is why
you don't worry about it
They live in misery
because two percent of the population
are determined
to keep them that way
These two percent
are aligned with business interests
in Guatemala
especially with the United Fruit Company
The United States government
identifies its interests
in Guatemala
with the interests of American big business
and with the Guatemalan two percent
who control the country
So if any peasant movement
does not conduct itself
according to their wishes   that is to say
if such a movement
is not completely ineffective
they start screaming
"They are communists!"
and begin executing these people

JUDGE

You mean to say that the United States government is executing
Guatemalans?

THOMAS MELVILLE

Yes   your honor

JUDGE

Has the United States government sent troops into Guatemala?

THOMAS MELVILLE

Yes   your honor

JUDGE

When?

THOMAS MELVILLE
   At the end of 1966
   and in January of 1967
JUDGE
   And you say that the United States executed people there?
THOMAS MELVILLE
   Yes   It was reported
   even in *Time* magazine
JUDGE
   Well, we are not trying the series of Guatemalan revolutions.
THOMAS MELVILLE
   No   the court
   is quite busy   trying us
   We wanted to participate
   in the revolutionary movement
   We knew it would not look good
   if an American priest or nun
   were killed in Guatemala
   by American Green Berets
   We wanted to complicate things
   for the United States in Guatemala
   because we did not want to see a slaughter
   there   like the one in Vietnam
   There are all kinds of communists
   in Guatemala   beyond doubt
   I was accused of being a communist
   Good people who want a piece of land
   are accused of being communists
   Thousands of them have been killed
   in the last few years
   and I wanted to stop that
MARJORIE MELVILLE
   I did not want to bring
   hurt upon myself
   but there comes a moment
   when you decide
   that some things should not be
   Then you have to act
   to try to stop those things
   On my return
   I was very happy when I found
   other people in this country
   concerned as I was
   I know that burning draft files
   is not an effective way

to stop a war   but
who has found a way
of stopping this war
I have racked my brain
I have talked to all kinds of people
What can you do
They say yes   yes
but there is no answer
no stopping it
the horror continues

THOMAS MELVILLE

We wish to say lastly
why we went to Catonsville
Americans know
that their nation was born in blood
we have expanded our frontiers
and pacified the Indians
in blood

MARJORIE MELVILLE

The creature of our history
is our country today
The history we create today
will form the minds and hearts
of our children tomorrow

THOMAS MELVILLE

I hear our President   confuse greatness with strength
riches with goodness   fear with respect
hopelessness and passivity with peace
The clichés of our leaders
pay tribute to property   and indifference to suffering
We long for a hand of friendship and succor
and that hand
clenches into a fist
I wonder how long we can endure

MARJORIE MELVILLE

We wash our hands in the dirt of others
pointing to the invasions or atrocities of others
certain that our own invasions and atrocities
are more excusable   because more subtle
though indeed far more devasting

THOMAS MELVILLE

We ask this court and this nation today
Will you acknowledge our right
to work for change?

MARJORIE MELVILLE

We do not ask for mercy   we do not ask that history
judge us right   That is a consolation
for more visionary souls than ours

THOMAS MELVILLE

We ask only that Americans
consider seriously   the points
we have tried to raise

MARJORIE MELVILLE

If they do this   we have been successful
our act has been worth the expense   the suffering

•

MARY MOYLAN

I went to Uganda in 1959
I worked as a nurse-midwife
I also went on safaris
I trained students in nursing
I taught English to secondary school girls
While I was in Africa
I took courses
in African history and anthropology
I was working at Fort Portal
up near the Mountains of the Moon
In the summer of 1965
American planes   piloted by Cubans
bombed Uganda
supposedly by accident
This made me very interested
in our foreign policy
and exactly what was going on
Finally
a serious conflict developed
between myself
and the Administrator of Hospitals
I said that I loved Fort Portal very much
but there were several things I must object to
I felt that the Africans
should have more responsibility
Much of our role   seemed to be
to provide a white face in a black community
I also felt that the students
should have broader training than they were getting
There was a large government hospital
right down the road

It could use our help
The administrator broke my contract
and asked me to leave
I stayed in Uganda for two months
so that I could tell the people
why I was leaving
When I returned home
I became director of the Women Volunteers Association
in Washington D.C.
Through my involvement in Washington
it became obvious to me
that we had no right to speak
to foreign countries about their policies
when things at home were in very sad shape
I was aware of
the militant black community in Washington
It became obvious that "law and order" is a farcical term
In instances which I know of
the law was broken by the government
In fact justice for a black person
is just about impossible
It became obvious to me
that our politicans are right
Our foreign policy is indeed
a reflection of our domestic policy
In Washington a black youth
was shot by a white policeman
A verdict of justifiable homicide
was handed down
I remember too
a protest staged by a young leader
who had a juvenile record
A southern congressman then read
into the *Congressional Record*
this man's juvenile record
This is absolutely forbidden   by law
It was pointed out to the congressman
that his procedure
was illegal   His answer was
I did it once and I will do it again
I think when you see
the imperatives placed on you
by such events at home
by the lives
lost in Vietnam

lost in Latin America and in Africa
then it is time to stand up
This is what it means to be a Christian
that you act on what you say you believe
This is what
Christ meant when He lived
We have not only to talk
but if we see something wrong
we have to be willing
to do something about it
This is my belief
As a nurse
my profession is
to preserve life
to prevent disease
To a nurse
the effect of napalm on human beings
is apparent
I think of children and women
bombed by napalm
burned alive by a substance
which does not roll off
It is a jelly
It adheres
It continues burning
This is inhuman   absolutely
To pour napalm
on pieces of paper
is certainly preferable
to using napalm on human beings
By pouring napalm on draft files
I wish to celebrate life
not to engage in a dance of death

———————

In dark corners I have heard them say
how the whole town is grieving for this girl
unjustly dealt, if ever woman was
for glorious action done

ANTIGONE: SOPHOCLES

———————

•

DEFENSE
Mr. Mische, you worked in Latin America for four years?

GEORGE MISCHE

Yes   I worked in Central America
and in the Caribbean
I organized labor groups
housing programs   land programs
We would work up   through the grass roots
I would submit our proposals
to Washington for approval
I went to Latin America
with the idea
that the Latins would be there
waiting at the boat to greet me
because I was an American
That is the naîveté we have   I guess
until we arrive overseas
Then I realized
how wrong I was
We were not only not welcome
now and then we had bricks
thrown at us
This confused me   but
after I became involved
at a higher level
I started to understand
why bricks were thrown at us
I was working in two countries
where revolutions had taken place
I should not say "revolution"
I should say "coup d'état"
military overthrow of governments
Two democratically elected governments
were overthrown by the military
with Pentagon support
At that point   I felt I could not
in conscience go on with this work
because John Kennedy had said
we would not deal
with military dictatorships
At the overthrow of democracy
we would stop all military support
and all economic support
We would withdraw our people
to force the leaders
to return to democracy
Well   when I saw the opposite occur
I resigned   This reversal of things

had most impact on me
in the Dominican Republic
That was such a tragedy
as to be unbelievable
A man like Trujillo
ran that country   for 32 years
When someone dared talk
about social change   or social reform
they would go into his house
take the head of the family   out of the house
cut off his penis
put it in his mouth
cut off his arms and legs
drop them in the doorway

PROSECUTION

I have to object. I am trying to be patient. I would suggest that we get to
the issues.

GEORGE MISCHE

I am trying to speak
as a human being   to the jury
who I hope are human beings
and can understand us
Will the jury dare to deal
with the spirit of the law
and the issues we are talking about
If not   we can expect
no peace   no solutions
only disorder and riots
in our country   and in the world

---

*The streets of our country are in turmoil. The universities are filled with
rebelling, rioting students. Communists are seeking to destroy our country;
Russia is threatening us with her might.*

The Republic is in danger; yes, danger from within and without.

*Without law and order, our nation cannot survive. We shall restore law
and order.*

ADOLF HITLER

DEFENSE

Mr. Mische, after you left the Alliance for Progress, what did you do?

GEORGE MISCHE

I came back to the United States
and went around this country

I talked to university students
I talked to religious groups
I talked at businessmen's clubs
I spoke to 80 Catholic Bishops
As a Catholic I apologize to you
for their cowardice
I asked them
since they have $80 billions worth of property
and ten times as much in investments
If they were really to live
in the spirit of the stable
in which Christ was born
then why not get rid of the buildings
give them to the poor

PROSECUTION

Your honor, may I object again?

JUDGE

We are not trying the Bishops of the United States.

GEORGE MISCHE

It seemed to me that the war in Vietnam
was illegal   because only Congress
can declare a war
The President cannot legally
take us into a war
We should never have let him
He should be on trial here today
In the peace movement
one of the most powerful things I knew of
was Philip Berrigan's first trial
for the blood pouring
A six-year sentence
for pouring blood on files
Men walk our streets
spilling blood continuously
and they walk free
I also had a feeling   a strong feeling
about what happened in Germany during the last war
my father was from Germany
The United States in 1945
supported the Nuremberg trials
I thought   that was the finest precedent
this country ever set
I said   Good   You are right
All of us Christians
share the responsibility

for having put those Jews
in the ovens

ACCUSED #12

Your Honor
I would like to explain that
every third word we heard
even back in grammar school
was about
how they
were to blame for everything
and how they
ought to be weeded out
It was hammered into us
that this would only be for the good
of our people
In leadership school
we were taught above all
to accept everything
without question
If anybody did raise a question
they were told
What is being done
is done strictly according to the law
Your Honor
we weren't supposed to think for ourselves
There were others around to do our thinking for us

WEISS: THE INVESTIGATION

If this was true
then it is also true
that this is expected of me now
as a Christian
Because the Vietnamese people are crying out
Stop the bombing   Stop the napalming
Stop the death   day in and day out
But now
we want to forget the precedent
we set in 1945
There is a tendency to say
That was another country   another time
It is said
in times of crisis

We cannot make black and white decisions
Everything is gray
That is the problem
It is easy for us on Monday morning
to tell how we should have played
Sunday's game
We say that it is too complicated
It is too obscure
So nothing happens
The violence continues
I felt that the crisis
this country is in
needed something drastic
something people could see
But the act had to be nonviolent
We were not out to destroy life
There is a higher law we are commanded to obey
It takes precedence over human laws
My intent was to follow the higher law
My intent was to save lives   Vietnamese lives
North and South American lives
To stop the madness
That was the intent

PROSECUTION

Is it your position that those who take a view contrary   to yours are
insane?

GEORGE MISCHE

No sir   you did not hear
I was trying to say
that the style of one's action
must coincide with the style of his life
And that is all

•

JOHN HOGAN

I have something of a comparison
an analogy
If there were   a group of children
walking along the street
returning home from school
and a car
came down the street
out of control   even though
there was a driver in that car
If I could divert the car
from crashing into those children

I would feel an obligation
to turn the car from its path
Of course the car is property
and would be damaged
It is even possible
something would happen
to the individual in the car
But no matter   I would be thinking
ten times more of those children
than of the driver of that car
And I know too
if I were driving that car
and it were out of control
I would hope
and pray to God
that somebody would smash the car
so that I might not destroy those children

DEFENSE

If there were, Mr. Hogan, one phrase in which you could sum up your
intent in going to Catonsville, how would you express it?

JOHN HOGAN

I just want
to let people live
That is all

JUDGE

I did not hear it.

JOHN HOGAN

I said
I want to let people live
That is all

●

DEFENSE

What was the impact of the act of your brother Philip Berrigan when he
poured blood on draft files in Baltimore?

DANIEL BERRIGAN

I began to understand
one could not indefinitely obey the law
while social conditions deteriorated
structures of compassion breaking down
neighborhoods slowly rotting
the poor despairing   unrest
forever present in the land   especially among
the young people
who are our only hope   our only resource

My brother's action helped me realize
from the beginning   of our republic
good men and women had said no
acted outside the law
when conditions so demanded
And if they did this
time might vindicate them   show their act to be lawful
a gift to society
a gift to history
and to the community
A few men and women
must have a long view
must leave history to itself
to interpret their lives   their repute
Someday
these defendants may be summoned
to the Rose Garden and decorated
but not today

DEFENSE

Could you state to the court what your intent was in burning the draft files?

DANIEL BERRIGAN

I did not want the children
or the grandchildren of the jury
or of the judge
to be burned with napalm

JUDGE

You say your intention was to save these children, of the jury, of myself, when you burned the records? That is what I heard you say. I ask if you meant that.

DANIEL BERRIGAN

I meant that
of course I meant that
or I would not say it
The great sinfulness
of modern war is
that it renders concrete things abstract
I do not want to talk
about Americans in general

JUDGE

You cannot think up arguments now that you would like to have had in your mind then.

DANIEL BERRIGAN

My intention on that day
was
to save the innocent

from death by fire
I was trying to save the poor
who are mainly charged with
dying in this war
I poured napalm
on behalf of the prosecutor's
and the jury's children
It seems to me quite logical
If my way of putting the facts
is inadmissible
then so be it
But I was trying to be concrete
about death   because death
is a concrete fact
as I have throughout my life
tried to be concrete
about the existence of God
Who is not an abstraction
but is someone before me
for Whom I am responsible

DEFENSE

Was your action at Catonsville a way of carrying out your religious
beliefs?

DANIEL BERRIGAN

Of course it was
May I say
if my religious belief is not accepted
as a substantial part of my action
then the action is eviscerated
of all meaning   and I should be
committed for insanity

DEFENSE

How did your views on the Vietnam war take shape?

DANIEL BERRIGAN

My views on war and peace
arose in me slowly
as life itself
pushed hard and fast
I should like to speak of
5 or 6 stages   in my development
I was invited to South Africa
around Easter of 1964
There I had about two weeks
of intense exposure
to a segregationist police state
At one meeting in Durbin

I remember   the question being raised
What happens to our children
if things go so badly
that we have to go to jail?
I remember saying
I could not answer that question
not being a citizen of that country
but I could perhaps help
by reversing the question
What happens to us and our children
if we do *not* go to jail?
2   I visited eastern Europe twice
in 1964
meeting with Christians in Czechoslovakia   Hungary   Russia
This had bearing
on my development   I was coming to realize
what it might cost to be a Christian
what it might cost
even at home
if things were to change
in the direction I felt events were taking
even then
In the summer of 1965   I went to Prague
to attend the Christian Peace Conference
This was a kind of breakthrough
For the first time   a Catholic priest
sat in that vast assembly of Christians
from all over the world   from Marxist countries
from India   from Africa   from the east and west
talking about things
that diplomacy and power and the military
were not talking about
That is to say
How can we survive as human beings
in a world
more and more officially given over
to violence and death
I think the imperceptible movement
of my conscience
was pushed forward by that experience
3   I returned in the summer of 1964
and was assigned as editor and writer
at a magazine in New York
named *Jesuit Missions*
I was quite convinced
that the war in Vietnam

would inevitably worsen
I felt that a cloud
no larger than a man's hand
would shortly cover the sky
In the autumn of 1964
I began to say no to the war
knowing
if I delayed too long
I would never find the courage to say no
In that year
I underwent a kind of bootcamp
in the "new humanity" becoming a peaceable man
in a time of great turmoil
New York was not an auspicious place
to be a peaceable Catholic priest
Cardinal Spellman was living
He had always supported American wars
He believed   I think this states his thought
that the highest expression   of Christian faith
was to bless our military
By his Christmas visits
to our foreign legions
he placed official approval
on our military adventuring
I had to say no to that too
I had to say no to the church

Gentlemen:

Since we are among those pagans who take declarations seriously, we must ask you as declared Christians, certain questions. . . .

Should you not stand up and denounce with all the righteousness and pity and anger and charity and love and humility which your faith may place at your command, the political and militarist assumptions now followed by the leaders of the nations of Christendom?

Pagans are waiting for your answer. You claim to be Christians. What does that mean as a public fact?

C. WRIGHT MILLS: A PAGAN SERMON

---

4   Finally
in the autumn of 1965
I was exiled from the United States
to Latin America

JUDGE
   What do you mean, "exiled"?
DANIEL BERRIGAN
   I was sent out   your honor
   with no return ticket
   As one of my friends expressed it
   sending me to Latin America was a little like
   tossing Br'er Rabbit into the briar patch
   I visited ten countries in four and a half months
   from Mexico to Southern Chile and then
   up the western coasts
   I discussed American involvement
   in the political and social scene of those countries
   I spent time with the students   the slumdwellers
   with whatever government officials would talk
   as well as with church leaders
   In Mexico   a student said to me
   We hate you North Americans   with all our hearts
   but we know   that if you do not make it
   we all come down   we are all doomed
   I arrived in Rio in January of 1966
   in the midst of devastating floods
   In the space of a single night
   the rains came down with torrential force
   whole towns collapsed
   people and shacks fell into a stew of death
   I remember the next morning
   slogging through the mud
   in the company of a slumdweller
   who was also a community organizer
   He looked at me and said
   My friend   millions for war in Vietnam
   and this for us
JUDGE
   What? Are you saying that the United States government caused the
   flood?
DANIEL BERRIGAN
   I think   the fact
   was a bit more subtle than that
   I think he was saying
   the resources of America
   which belong in justice
   to the poor of the world
   are squandered in war   and war preparation
DEFENSE
   Now may I ask about your writings and publications?

PROSECUTION

What difference does it make how many books he has written?

DEFENSE

I show you the book *Night Flight to Hanoi*. Will you outline the circumstances out of which this book was written?

DANIEL BERRIGAN

5   The book marks
the next stage   of my development
In January of 1968   an invitation came
from the government of North Vietnam
Professor Howard Zinn and myself
were invited to Hanoi
to bring home   3 captive American airmen
For me to go to Hanoi
was a very serious decision
I believe   I have always believed
that the peace movement must not merely say no
to the war
It must also say
yes to life   yes to the possibility of a human future
We must go beyond frontiers
frontiers declared by our country or by the enemy
So I thought it would be important
to show Americans
that we were ready to risk our lives
to bring back American prisoners
because we did not believe
that in wartime
anyone should be in prison
or should suffer separation
from families
simply   we did not believe in war
And so we went

What crime have I committed, I keep on asking?
The crime of being devoted to my people.

HO CHI MINH: PRISON DIARY

In Hanoi I think we were the first Americans
to undergo
an American bombing attack
When the burned draft files
were brought into court yesterday
as evidence

I could not but recall
that I had seen in Hanoi
evidence of a very different nature
I saw   not boxes of burned papers
I saw parts of human bodies   preserved in alcohol
the bodies of children   the hearts and organs and limbs
of women

EVIDENCE FOR THE PROSECUTION

The boxes of paper ash
The size of infant caskets
Were rolled in on a dolly,
Heaped there like cord wood
Or children after a usual
Air strike on Hanoi.
I heard between heartbeats
Of Jesus and his hangman
The children's mouths mewing
For the breasts of murdered women
The blackened hands beating
The box of death for breath.

DANIEL BERRIGAN

---

teachers   workers   peasants   bombed
in fields and churches and schools and hospitals
I examined our "improved weaponry"
It was quite clear to me
during three years of air war
America had been experimenting
upon the bodies of the innocent
We had improved our weapons
on their flesh

JUDGE

He did not see this first hand. He is telling of things he was told in Hanoi, about some things that were preserved in alcohol.

DANIEL BERRIGAN

French   English   Swedish experts   doctors
testified
these were actually the bodies
whose pictures
accompanied the exhibits
The evidence was unassailable

The bombings
were a massive crime against humanity
The meaning of the air war in the North
was the deliberate systematic destruction
of a poor and developing people

JUDGE

We are not trying the air war in North Vietnam.

DANIEL BERRIGAN

I must protest the effort
to discredit me on the stand
I am speaking of what I saw
There is a consistent effort
to say that I did not see it

JUDGE

The best evidence of what some "crime commission" found is not a
summary that you give.

DANIEL BERRIGAN

So be it
In any case we brought the flyers home
I think as a result of the trip to Hanoi
I understood the limits
of what I had done before
and the next step that must come

Calamity has tempered and hardened me and turned my mind to steel.

HO CHI MINH: PRISON DIARY

On my return to America
another event
helped me understand
the way I must go
It was the self-immolation
of a high school student
in Syracuse New York
in the spring of 1968
This boy had come to a point of despair
about the war   He had gone
into the Catholic cathedral
drenched himself with kerosene
and immolated himself in the street
He was still living a month later
I was able to gain access to him
I smelled the odor

of burning flesh
And I understood anew
what I had seen in North Vietnam
The boy was dying in torment
his body like a piece of meat
cast upon a grille
He died shortly thereafter
I felt that my senses
had been invaded in a new way
I had understood
the power of death in the modern world
I knew I must speak and act
against death
because this boy's death
was being multiplied
a thousandfold
in the Land of Burning Children
So I went to Catonsville
and burned some papers   because
the burning of children
is inhuman and unbearable
I went to Catonsville
because I had gone to Hanoi
because my brother was a man
and I must be a man
and because
I knew at length
I could not announce the gospel
from a pedestal
I must act as a Christian
sharing the risks and burdens and anguish
of those whose lives were placed
in the breach by us
I saw suddenly   and it struck with the force of lightning
that my position was false
I was threatened with verbalizing
my moral substance out of existence
I was placing upon young shoulders
a filthy burden   the original sin of war
I was asking them to enter a ceremony of death
Although I was too old
to carry a draft card   there were other ways
of getting in trouble with a state
that seemed determined upon multiplying the dead
totally intent upon a war

the meaning of which   no sane man could tell
So I went to Hanoi
and then to Catonsville
and that is why I am here

DEFENSE

Did you not write a meditation to accompany the statement issued by the
nine defendants at Catonsville?

DANIEL BERRIGAN

Yes sir

DEFENSE

Would you read the meditation?

DANIEL BERRIGAN

Certainly
"Some ten or twelve of us (the number is still uncertain)
will if all goes well (ill?) take our religious bodies
during this week
to a draft center in or near Baltimore
There we shall   of purpose and forethought
remove the 1–A files   sprinkle them in the public street
with home-made napalm   and set them afire
For which act we shall beyond doubt
be placed behind bars for some portion of our natural lives
in consequence of our inability
to live and die content in the plagued city
to say 'peace peace' when there is no peace
to keep the poor poor
the thirsty and hungry thirsty and hungry
Our apologies   good friends
for the fracture of good order   the burning of paper
instead of children   the angering of the orderlies
in the front parlor of the charnel house
We could not   so help us God   do otherwise
For we are sick at heart   our hearts
give us no rest for thinking of the Land of Burning Children
and for thinking of that other Child of whom
the poet Luke speaks   The infant was taken up
in the arms of an old man whose tongue
grew resonant and vatic at the touch of that beauty
And the old man spoke: this child is set
for the fall and rise of many in Israel
a sign that is spoken against
Small consolation   a child born to make trouble
and to die for it   the First Jew (not the last)
to be subject of a 'definitive solution'
And so we stretch out our hands

to our brothers and sisters throughout the world
We who are priests to our fellow priests
All of us who act against the law
turn to the poor of the world   to the Vietnamese
to the victims   to the soldiers who kill and die
for the wrong reasons for no reason at all
because they were so ordered by the authorities
of that public order which is in effect
a massive institutionalized disorder
We say: killing is disorder
life and gentleness and community and unselfishness
is the only order we recognize
For the sake of that order
we risk our liberty   our good name
The time is past when good men and women may be silent
when obedience
can segregate people from public risk
when the poor can die without defense
How many indeed must die
before our voices are heard
how many must be tortured dislocated
starved maddened?
How long must the world's resources
be raped in the service of legalized murder?
When at what point will you say no to this war?
We have chosen to say
with the gift of our liberty
if necessary our lives:
the violence stops here
the death stops here
the suppression of the truth stops here
this war stops here
Redeem the times!
The times are inexpressibly evil
Christians pay conscious   indeed religious tribute
to Caesar and Mars
by the approval of overkill tactics   by brinkmanship
by nuclear liturgies   by racism   by support of genocide
They embrace their society with all their heart
and abandon the cross
They pay lip service to Christ
and military service to the powers of death
And yet   and yet   the times are inexhaustibly good
solaced by the courage and hope of many
The truth rules   Christ is not forsaken

In a time of death some men and women
the resisters   those who work hardily for social change
those who preach and embrace the truth
such men and women overcome death
their lives are bathed in the light of the resurrection
the truth has set them free
In the jaws of death
they proclaim their love of the neighbor
We think of such men and women
in the world   in our nation   in the churches
and the stone in our breast is dissolved
we take heart once more"

DEFENSE

Nothing further.

4

THE DAY OF SUMMATION

DEFENSE

Your honor, the government's concession this morning, with reference to the reasonableness of the views held by these defendants, has, in the opinion of the defense, made it unnecessary to call expert witnesses.

Since the government concedes that reasonable men and women can hold that the war is illegal, unconstitutional, and immoral, the proffered witnesses no longer have any relevance to this case.

PROSECUTION

Your honor, I want it understood for the record that I don't accept his use of the word "concession." If we accept the version of the defense, they would have it believed that the government feels that any person who thinks the war in Vietnam is illegal would be insane. We never took this position, so there is no concession to make.

DEFENSE

Your honor, I might indicate that the government has never before publicly made the statement that was made in this court today. There is a great difference between saying that "a person is insane to hold these views," and saying, "a reasonable person can hold these views."

JUDGE

The government certainly is not conceding that those views are correct, and the court will have to rule on those was a matter of law. And that is the test case that you want.

DEFENSE

I am making the record clear. The argument now is not the correctness of the views, but whether a reasonable person could hold them. . . .

JUDGE

At any rate, the defense has its test case. Now I ask: Is the government ready to begin the final argument?

PROSECUTION

The government is ready, your honor.

May it please the court and members of the jury. It is now my responsibility to attempt, in summary fashion, to review with you the evidence that has been produced in this courtroom.

First of all, I want it clearly understood that the government is not about to put itself in the position—has not heretofore and is not now—

of conducting its policies at the end of a string tied to the consciences of these nine defendants. This trial does not include the issues of the Vietnam conflict. It does not include the issue of whether the United States ought to be in the conflict or out of it.

The government quite candidly admits that the position these defendants took is reasonable — as to the fact that the war is illegal, that it is immoral, that it is against religious principles, that any reasonable person could take that view. We do not even say that a person has to be insane to have the views that they have. No, we don't say that.

But this prosecution is the government's response, the law's response, the people's response, to what the defendants did. And what they did was to take government property and throw flammable material upon it and burn it beyond recognition. And that is what this case is about.

There are people, it hardly need be pointed out, who rely upon the files in Local Board No. 33 in Catonsville.

Suppose you were to acquit these people on the only basis possible, in view of everything they have conceded? Acquit them, that is, although they did those acts with the intention of hindering the Selective Service System and of burning the files and records. Suppose that because of their sincerity, their conscience, their religious convictions, they were entitled to be acquitted in this courtroom?

If these people were entitled to be acquitted by virtue of their sincerity and religion and conviction, then according to the same logic, should not the person who commits any other crime be also entitled to acquittal?

We also heard about unpleasant things happening, or about to happen, in other areas of the world. Among these nine defendants, there are four or five justifications floating around. One defendant is upset about one ill in the world, and that justifies his going to Catonsville. Another is upset about another ill in the world, and that justifies her going to Catonsville. And so on. The possibilities are infinite. There could in fact be fifty defendants, each upset about fifty different supposed ills in the world. And each one of them could say: This is why I violated the law.

Ladies and gentlemen of the jury, the government has never contended that this country is perfect, that it is without flaw, without ills and problems and failings. To assert that would be absurd.

But I would suggest to you that, to the extent that this country has problems, those problems will be solved. We will progress. We will get better. The country will get better.

But our problems are not going to be solved by people who deliberately violate our laws, the foundation and support for an ordered and just and civilized society.

It is your sworn duty to assert, by finding the defendants guilty, that our problems will not be solved, but will be increased beyond imagining, by people who deliberately violate the law under which we all live.

Whatever commandment the prisoner has disobeyed is written upon his body by the Harrow. This prisoner for instance (the officer indicated the man) will have written on his body: HONOR THY SUPERIORS.

KAFKA: THE PENAL COLONY

DEFENSE

Ladies and gentlemen of the jury, this is an historic moment for all of us — for the judge, the jury, the counsel, the defendants. Undoubtedly, a great measure of personal reflection is required, even to begin to appreciate the meaning of this trial for us who participated in it.

As for those who did not, only the passage of time can tell whether the events of this courtroom will strike responsive chords both in our country and around the world.

I must beg your leave to inject a personal note. In law school, I was repeatedly warned never to identify too closely with prospective clients. Perhaps under other circumstances, this might be considered sound advice. But as your honor acknowledged during the trial, these are not ordinary clients; and this is hardly a run-of-the-mill prosecution.

For myself, I must confess with more heartfelt pride than I could adequately describe, that in the course of this litigation, I have come to love and respect the men and women who stand before this court. Like them, I make no plea for mercy. I dare not tarnish the transcendent witness they have given, in an attempt to persuade this court to bend in their direction.

Still, there are some things I must say if I am to remain faithful to my obligations as a lawyer, as an American, and as a human being.

The court has agreed that this is a unique case. It shares the historic meaning of other great contests of law. The trial of Socrates was not merely a question of a man sowing confusion and distrust among the youth of Athens; the trial of Jesus could not be reduced to one of conspiracy against the Empire.

In a parallel way, there are overriding issues at stake in this case; I hope to bring them to your attention, within the limits the defense is allowed to touch on.

In the first place, we agree with the prosecutor as to the essential facts of the case. The defendants did participate in the burning of records.

You must have understood, because it was pointed out here, that the Selective Service System is an arm of the Federal government, for the procurement of young men for military service, as decided by the authorities of the United States.

In other words, such young men are to be used, as one defendant said, for cannon fodder, if the government so dictates.

It is not a question of records which are independent of life. We are not talking about driving licenses or licenses to operate a brewery. We are speaking of one kind of records. No others so directly affect life and death on a mass scale, as do these. They affect every mother's son who is registered with any Board. These records stand quite literally for life and death to young men.

The defendants did not go to Catonsville to act as criminals, to frighten Mrs. Murphy, or to annoy or hinder her. They were there to complete a symbolic act (first of all) which we claim is a free speech act. And secondly, they were there to impede and interfere with the operation of a system which they have concluded (and it is not an unreasonable belief, as the government has told you) is immoral, illegal, and is destroying innocent people around the world.

The defendants weren't burning files for the sake of burning files. If they were, I would not stand in this court to defend them. They burned the files at Catonsville for two reasons, both of which they admitted:

They wanted, in some small way, to throw a roadblock into a system which they considered murderous, which was grinding young men, many thousands of them, to death in Vietnam.

Also, they wanted, as they said, to reach the American public, to reach you. They were trying to make an outcry, an anguished outcry, to reach the American community before it was too late. It was a cry that could conceivably have been made in Germany in 1931 and 1932, if there were someone to listen and act on it. It was a cry of despair and anguish and hope, all at the same time. And to make this outcry, they were willing to risk years of their lives.

The government has conceded that the defendants were sincere, it has conceded their truthfulness. The government has also conceded that it is reasonable to hold the views held by the defendants as to the illegality of this war.

So we come to the only issue left for you to decide: whether, in your opinion, they are guilty or innocent of crime.

I want to point out to you, in some detail, a case which offers parallels to this one, a case which affected the character of American history, some two hundred years ago. The defendant was a printer, Peter Zenger by name; he was accused of seditious libel. Andrew Hamilton, the defending lawyer, spoke the following words in the course of the trial (it seems to me that they are of point here).

"Jurors are to see with their own eyes, to hear with their own ears, and to make use of their conscience and understanding in judging of the lives, liberties, and estates of their fellow subjects."

Ladies and gentlemen of the jury, that is what we are asking you to do.

JUDGE

You are urging the jury to make their decision on the basis of conscience. This morning, I said to you that if you attempt to argue that the jury has the power to decide this case on the basis of conscience, the court willinterrupt to tell the jury their duty. The jury may not decide this case on the basis of the conscience of the defendants. They are to decide this case only on the basis of the facts presented by both sides.

Put simply, the court said, the right to be tried by a jury of one's peers . . . would be meaningless, if the judge could call the turn. . . . In the exercise of its function, not only must the jury be free from direct control of its verdict, it must be free from judicial pressure, both contemporaneous and subsequent.

U.S. COURT OF APPEALS, REVERSING
THE CONVICTION OF DR. SPOCK

DEFENSE

I would like to say to the jury: I am appealing to you, as Andrew Hamilton appealed to a jury, to consider all the facts of the case before you.

All the words, writing, marching, fasting, demonstrating —all the peaceable acts of the defendants, over a period of some years—had failed to change a single American decision in Vietnam. All their protests had failed to prevent a single innocent death, failed to end the anguish of napalm on human flesh, failed even momentarily to slow the unnatural, senseless destruction of men, women, and children, including the destruc- tion of our own sons—a destruction wrought in the name of a policy that passes all human understanding.

Perhaps in the last analysis, this cataclysm of our times can be understood only in the lives of a few people who, for one moment, stand naked before the horrified gaze of their fellow human beings.

Anne Frank did this for six million Jews. And it may be that the thousands of American and Vietnamese ghosts created by this war can best be spoken for by three small children who crouched in a Hanoi air raid shelter, before the compassionate eyes of an American priest.

He saw in these children, as many of us saw in Anne Frank, the waifs spawned by an incomprehensible and savage war; a war that envelops and affects each of us, and makes us partners in the common tragedy which brings me before you.

Perhaps in this poem by Daniel Berrigan, who stands in judgment before you, some understanding of the truth of things can come through.

"Imagine; three of them.

As though survival
were a rat's word

and a rat's end
waited there at the end

and I must have
in the century's boneyard
heft of flesh and bone in my arms

I picked up the littlest
a boy, his face
breaded with rice (his sister calmly feeding him
as we climbed down)
In my arms fathered
in a moment's grace, the messiah
of all my tears. I bore, reborn

a Hiroshima child from hell."

JUDGE

The jury may now begin their deliberations.

(*The jury files out.*)

Now then, let the defendants or their counsel be heard from. Have I said something I should not have said, or left unsaid something I should have said?

DEFENSE

Your honor, the defendants have requested to be permitted to say something to the court.

(*Whereupon, at this point, the following proceedings were had.*)

5

THE DAY OF THE VERDICT

JUDGE

I want to hear the defendants. I do not want to cut them off from anything they may want to say. Mr. Melville, will you begin?

THOMAS MELVILLE

Your honor, we feel that the overriding issue in the case has been obscured by the treatment given us. If our intention was to destroy government records, we could very easily have gone in at nighttime and taken the files out and burned them.

As it was, we went in the middle of the day, and, after burning the files, waited for fifteen minutes until the police came, to give public witness to what we did.

Our intention was to speak to our country, to the conscience of our people.

Now, during these few days we have been in this court in an attempt to speak to the conscience of the American people. We feel that the twelve jurors have heard all kinds of legal arguments, which I suppose they must hear. But we feel that the overriding issue has been obscured. You have sent the jury out — to judge whether we committed the acts which we admitted from the beginning that we had committed.

JUDGE

The jury are not the representatives of the American people. Also, nobody has cut you down on the evidence you wanted to present. You have made your case in public.

It is quite true that I have not submitted to the jury the question you would like to have submitted, in a way you would like. I have told the jury if they find that you intended to burn the records and hinder the draft board, then it was immaterial that you had other good purposes. And it was immaterial how sincere you were and how right you may ultimately be judged by history.

I am not questioning the morality of what you did.

I disagree with the theory of law which you are presenting and which was argued very eloquently by your counsel, as far as I would permit him to do it. I cannot allow somebody to argue something which is entirely contrary to the law. That would be to ask the jury to disregard their oath. I cannot allow that.

If you had gone to Catonsville and taken one file under some token arrangement, you might have had something to argue. But you went out and burned 378 files, according to your own admission. And every one of you, I think, said that you did it in order to hinder the operation of the draft.

I am not questioning the highness of your motive. I think that one must admire a person who is willing to suffer for his beliefs. But people who are going to violate the law in order to make a point must expect to be convicted.

THOMAS MELVILLE

Your honor, we are not arguing from a purely legal standpoint. We are arguing to you as an American, with your obligations to society, to those jurors as Americans and in their obligations to our society.

If it is only a question of whether we committed this act or not, we feel it would be better if the jury is dismissed. We can save ourselves a lot of time and money by receiving an immediate sentence from you.

JUDGE

Mr. Mische next.

GEORGE MISCHE

My question, your honor, concerns conscience. Did you tell the jury they could not act according to their conscience?

JUDGE

I did not mention conscience.

JUDGE

I said this to the defense: If you attempt to argue that the jury has the power to decide this case on the basis of conscience, the court will interrupt and tell the jury of their duty.

COURT RECORD

I did not talk about conscience. I do not mind saying that this is the first time the question of conscience has been raised in this court.

GEORGE MISCHE

But was the jury told they could not use their conscience in determining —

JUDGE

I certainly did not tell them they could disregard their oath and let you off on sympathy, or because they thought you were sincere people.

DANIEL BERRIGAN

Your honor, we are having great difficulty in trying to adjust to the atmosphere of a court from which the world is excluded, and the events that brought us here are excluded deliberately, by the charge to the jury.

JUDGE

They were not excluded. The question —

DANIEL BERRIGAN

May I continue? Our moral passion was excluded. It is as though we were subjects of an autopsy, were being dismembered by people who wondered whether or not we had a soul. We are sure that we have a soul. It is our soul that brought us here. It is our soul that got us in trouble. It is our conception of humanity.

But our moral passion is banished from this court. It is as though the legal process were an autopsy.

JUDGE

Well, I cannot match your poetic language.

(*Applause from the audience.*)

Any further demonstration and the court will be cleared. And I mean that, the whole crowd.

Father Berrigan, you made your points on the stand, very persuasively. I admire you as a poet. But I think you simply do not understand the function of a court.

DANIEL BERRIGAN

I am sure that is true.

JUDGE

You admitted that you went to Catonsville with a purpose which requires your conviction. You wrote your purpose down in advance. Your counsel stood and boasted of it. Now I happen to have a job in which I am bound by an oath of office.

If you had done this thing in many countries of the world, you would not be standing here. You would have been in your coffins long ago. Now, nobody is going to draw and quarter you. You may be convicted by the jury; and if you are, I certainly propose to give you every opportunity to say what you want.

DANIEL BERRIGAN

Your honor, you spoke very movingly of your understanding of what it is to be a judge. I wish to ask whether or not reverence for the law does not also require a judge to interpret and adjust the law to the needs of people here and now. I believe that no tradition can remain a mere dead inheritance. It is a living inheritance which we must continue to offer to the living.

So it may be possible, even though the law excludes certain important questions of conscience, to include them nonetheless; and thereby, to bring the tradition to life again for the sake of the people.

JUDGE

Well, I think there are two answers to that. You speak to me as a man and as a judge. As a man, I would be a very funny sort if I were not moved by your sincerity on the stand, and by your views. I agree with you completely, as a person. We can never accomplish what we would like to accomplish, or give a better life to people, if we are going to keep on spending so much money for war. But a variety of circumstances makes it most difficult to have your point of view presented. It is very unfortunate, but the issue of the war cannot be presented as sharply as you would like. The basic principle of our law is that we do things in an orderly fashion. People cannot take the law into their own hands.

DANIEL BERRIGAN

You are including our President in that assertion.

JUDGE

Of course, the President must obey the law.

THOMAS LEWIS

He hasn't though.

JUDGE

If the President has not obeyed the law, there is very little that can be done.

GEORGE MISCHE

And that is what this trial is all about. . . .

DANIEL BERRIGAN

Your honor, you have referred to the war question as one which may be either political or legal. Suppose it were considered as a question of life and death. Could that be appropriately raised here?

JUDGE

Well, again, that is poetic speech. I am not sure what the legal proposition is. I understand why it seems a matter of life and death to you. Of course, the war is a matter of life and death to all boys who are in it. It is a matter of life and death to people in Vietnam.

MARY MOYLAN

Your honor, I think you said previously that you had a great deal of respect for the law and the Constitution of the United States.

I would like to call this respect into question, if you are unwilling to do anything about a war which is in violation of our legal tradition and the United States Constitution.

JUDGE

Well, I understand your point. But I cannot appoint you either my legal or spiritual adviser.

GEORGE MISCHE

We have people from the peace movement here. Will you, then, allow them to file in your court, calling into question the entire Vietnam war; and will you be willing to review the charge in its entirety? Whatever decision you make then can be submitted to the Supreme Court.

JUDGE

But you have to have a case—

GEORGE MISCHE

You have to break a law first.

JUDGE

—that can be brought in court.

GEORGE MISCHE

You have to break a law. It seems that, before we can get a judge to face the situation, you have to break a law, as Dr. King found.

JUDGE

If you had gotten legal advice, I am sure you would have been advised that there are better ways to raise this question than the way you raised it at Catonsville.

THOMAS LEWIS

Your honor, one question:

I have been called an honest and just man in this courtroom. I appreciate that. But the reality is that I leave this room in chains. I am taken back to prison. How do you explain this?

JUDGE

Good character is not a defense for breaking the law. That is the only way I can explain it.

DAVID DARST

Your honor, the instructions you gave to the jury bound them to the narrow letter of the law. And a verdict according to the spirit of the law was strictly prohibited.

It is my feeling that the spirit of the law is important, particularly in American legal tradition and in American life. It is the spirit which counts.

JUDGE

I am not God almighty. I did what the law required me to do. All we can do is our best. . . .

PHILIP BERRIGAN

Your honor, I think that we would be less than honest with you if we did not state our attitude. Simply, we have lost confidence in the institutions of this country, including our own churches.

I think this has been a rational process on our part. We have come to our conclusion slowly and painfully. We have lost confidence, because we do not believe any longer that these institutions are reformable.

JUDGE

Well, if you are saying that you are advocating revolution —

Whenever the ends of government are perverted and public liberty manifestly endangered and all other means of redress are ineffectual, the people may, and of right ought to, reform the old or establish a new government. The doctrine of nonresistance against arbitrary power and oppression is absurd, slavish, and destructive of the good and happiness of mankind.

CONSTITUTION OF THE STATE OF NEW HAMPSHIRE,

ARTICLE 10

PHILIP BERRIGAN

I am saying merely this:

We see no evidence that the institutions of this country, including our own churches, are able to provide the type of change that justice calls for, not only in this country, but around the world.

We believe that this has occurred because law is no longer serving the needs of the people; which is a pretty good definition of morality.

JUDGE

I can understand how you feel. I think the only difference between us is that I believe the institutions can do what you believe they cannot do.

PHILIP BERRIGAN

Our question remains: How much time is left this country, as our casualties inch upward, as Vietnamese casualties mount every day? And nuclear war is staring us in the face. That is the question we are concerned about: human survival.

JUDGE

I assure you I am concerned about your question, for my grandchildren, as well as for everybody else. It is a serious thing.

GEORGE MISCHE

Change could come if one judge would rule on the war. If one judge would act, the war could not continue as it does.

JUDGE

I think you misunderstand the organization of the United States. One judge ruling on it would not end the war. Each judge must do his best with what comes before him. . . .

DANIEL BERRIGAN

We want to thank you, your honor; I speak for the others. But we do not want the edge taken off what we have tried to say, by any implication that we are seeking mercy in this Court. We welcome the rigors of the Court.

Our intention in appearing here after Catonsville was to be useful to the poor of the world, to the Black people of the world and of our country, and to those in our prisons who have no voice.

We do not wish that primary blade of intention to be honed down to no edge at all by a gentleman's agreement, whereby you agree with us and we with you. We do not agree with you, and we thank you.

JUDGE

All right.

DANIEL BERRIGAN

Could we finish with a prayer? Would that be against your wishes? We would like to recite the "Our Father" with our friends.

JUDGE

The Court has no objection whatsoever, and rather welcomes the idea.

*(Whereupon, at this point in the proceedings, those who wished
to do so stood and joined in prayer.)*

JUDGE

(After 1 1/2 hours) I have just received a note from the foreman. The jury
has concluded its deliberations and is ready to report its findings. The
jury will come in now, and the clerk will take the verdict.

There must be no demonstrations from the audience. If there are, I
may clear the room, or I may instruct the marshal to take appropriate
action with respect to any recalcitrants.

*(Whereupon at this point the jury was brought into the court-
room, and the following proceedings were had.)*

THE CLERK

The taking of the verdict in Criminal Action No. 28111, the United States
of America against Philip Berrigan, Daniel Berrigan, Thomas Lewis,
James Darst, John Hogan, Marjorie Melville, Thomas Melville, George
Mische, and Mary Moylan.

Members of the jury, what say you: Is the defendant John Hogan
guilty of the matters whereof he stands indicted?

THE FOREMAN

We find John Hogan guilty.

THE CLERK

Members of the jury, what say you: Is the defendant Marjorie Melville
guilty of the matters whereof she stands indicted, or not guilty?

THE FOREMAN

We find Marjorie Melville guilty.

THE CLERK

Members of the jury, what say you: Is the defendant Thomas Melville
guilty of the matters whereof he stands indicted, or not guilty?

THE FOREMAN

We find Thomas Melville guilty.

THE CLERK

Members of the jury, what say you: Is the defendant George Mische
guilty or not guilty of the matters whereof he stands indicted?

THE FOREMAN

We find George Mische guilty.

THE CLERK

Members of the jury, what say you: Is the defendant Mary Moylan guilty
of the matters whereof she stands indicted, or not guilty?

THE FOREMAN

We find Mary Moylan guilty.

THE CLERK

Members of the jury, what say you: Is the defendant Philip Berrigan
guilty of the matters whereof he stands indicted, or not guilty?

THE FOREMAN

We find Philip Berrigan guilty.

THE CLERK

Members of the jury, what say you: Is the defendant Daniel Berrigan guilty of the matters whereof he stands indicted, or not guilty?

THE FOREMAN

We find Daniel Berrigan guilty.

THE CLERK

Members of the jury, what say you: Is the defendant Thomas Lewis guilty of the matters whereof he stands indicted, or not guilty?

THE FOREMAN

We find Thomas Lewis guilty.

THE CLERK

Members of the jury, what say you: Is the defendant James Darst guilty of the matters whereof he stands indicted, or not guilty?

THE FOREMAN

We find James Darst guilty.

A MEMBER OF THE AUDIENCE

Members of the jury, you have just found Jesus Christ guilty.

    *(Commotion in court. Similar outbursts from other members of
      the audience.)*

JUDGE

Marshals, clear the courtroom.

    (Whereupon, at this point the courtroom was slowly cleared.)

JUDGE

Now, is there anything further that the government or the defendants wish brought to the attention of the court?

DANIEL BERRIGAN

We would simply like to thank the Court and the prosecution. We agree that this is the greatest day of our lives.

THE TRIAL OF THE CATONSVILLE NINE, 1970

To the Actors, from Underground

To the Actors

This is Father Dan Berrigan speaking from the underground. Your playwright is in good spirits on a beautiful day. I am thinking of you all and of the important event about to be launched by you on our behalf. As I set down these few reflections, I've just finished three months of this absurd underground existence. I don't know exactly what lies at the other end but am convinced that I had better go forward as far as I can.

What specifically would I have to say to you of the cast? I think I've already expressed my feeling about the play to Gordon [Davidson] a few months ago. We all share a certain hope that the Catonsville play might speak to people, might bring them to a more accurate, realistic, and painful sense of things. At the same time we wish to release a capacity of hope and joy. This was the spirit in which we carried off our Catonsville caper, and faced its consequences—consequences which indeed have enlarged since then.

Let me say that in the course of the last five years I have felt a very special hope in regard to Americans. This strange hope grew out of the befouled and violence-ridden atmosphere in which young people were coming into adulthood. At the same time, this atmosphere exerted special pressures, heated things up, and hastened maturity; as a result in certain cases, I saw moral changes of enormous import and quality occurring in these young lives. I saw communities arising very quickly; I had a feeling that such teams or caucuses or communities, connected with an acute political point of view, would offer some clue for the rest of us. And I felt that we had better keep experimenting in this regard, for everything had to be created from whole cloth. It seemed almost as though each of us had been lowered from on high into our existence on wires; we touched ground, the wires were then cut by some hand and there we were. There was a new way of getting born in the world which was special to Americans.

I am speaking of special circumstances, the enormous cultural ferment and the long genetic period of the cold war. Out of the worst came, at least in some measure, the best (and this may be true of our drama, too). Obviously we are unable to reproduce the European experience arising out of religion, or nationalism, or an anti-form of those. Our experience is a rupture of continuity, a little bit like the first morning of the creation of the first man. He rubbed his eyes in the world and awakened, as though there had been no one before him; he was marked by an enormous optimism, as though there had been no failure and no wounds before, as though everything remained to be done, as though almost anything could be done, because he is putting hand and brain to the world for the first time.

The youngest of our members was David Darst, who exemplified Adam awakening in the world. The first man, filled with candor and a sense of surprise and thanksgiving; he proceeded to work as though he bore no shadow, as though everything were possible, as though indeed he was the man who was to make it actual. So this young David lived his life, brought this spirit to us, and died.

The rest of us were enormously more dragged and harried by the experience of the real world. In varying degrees we had covered many continents, many cultures, lived among many peoples, and experienced the blood-ridden fate of humankind in the twentieth century. So we came to Catonsville with a sense of ourselves and of the world which was neither sour nor disenchanted; still we had passed over that invisible line that Blake calls innocence, into experience. We were singing a different song from David's.

We might recall with a certain envy groups that have arisen in the past years: the Living Theater, the New Theater. We think in their regard of a common discipline, a common view of the world, a common politics, and above all perhaps of a common linking love that grants them an exciting, innovative character. I don't know whether or not this is possible in America except for short periods and small numbers of actors. Maybe we're stuck with short-term efforts, being faithful to a sense of the moment heating things up in our lives and imaginations. Thus we may be able to reproduce some sense of the depth, inwardness and communality that arises in a slower social scene over longer periods. I am speaking again especially of the European dramatic experience and European teams.

It would of course be remarkable if we came to understand that a strong political sense is a clue to making sense of men and women. Much of the stuff that goes by the name theater on and off Broadway has no politics, no real expression in face of the world, is sprayed with the false front of frivolity, amnesia, anomie. Certain productions that are making a great deal of money are infantile in regard to the real world; they contribute only to the public amnesia that afflicts people with dread of the real world. Such work closes the vicious circle in which drama helps retard the moral sense of humankind, certainly a vicious turnabout from the classical intention of the theater.

How do we help Americans get born, get going, get growing, get moving toward recovery of intention, recovery of what the Greeks would call the true way, the true road, as expressed in Ocdipus? But it seems to me that actors, with moral passion and bodily gestures, are in a certain place with regard to the spirit. That is to say, they are exerting pressure against the outer darkness. They are creating and communicating light around their bodies, the light of the human spirit. They are saying something that others are saying in prison and in the underground and in exile and indeed in death. So to be onstage is to be a rather special person these days, to be human in a unique way, to be saying something unique to others. So the connection between resistance and the theater ought to be pondered not merely by actors but by the relationship they strive to establish with their audience as well as by the kind of audience they attract.

You may know that in April of 1970 I made my escape from Cornell surrounded by fifteen thousand students and many FBI agents. The happening occurred during the course of a weekend in celebration of resistance, and especially of the Catonsville Nine. The supposition was that we were all going to jail that weekend. What is delicious in retrospect is that I made my escape through a dramatic troupe, the Bread and Puppet Theater, borrowing one of their large, marvelous puppets of one of the twelve apostles. I proceeded out of the hall bobbing underneath this tremendous papier-mâché and burlap figure, got into a panel truck, and away.

I think it was a metaphor of how one may make an escape into a deeper underground, almost in a Greek mythological sense, into a deeper reality through drama, in such a way that one's escape may become, from another point of view, a return. Theater is not escapism. I am trying to say it is the exact opposite of that. It requires shedding everything that cannot be contained within the strict limits of the definition of human being. One offers this definition by standing in a circle of imaginative protection; the actor's function becomes both the tightening of crisis and the facing together of the consequence of crisis. I would think that in such a way a link is closed between what you are doing onstage and what I am trying to do in the underground. That is to say, we are dramatizing from different points of view, different points of visibility, the teasing and testing aspects of drama. We are hottening things up where we are and then extending our reach so that we are not the only ones saved; so that others get in and under and away with us. It seems to me this makes sense in relationship to the Catonsville play. I cannot imagine an actor entering such a furnace of moral resolve as Catonsville was for us, without changes of a rather serious order occurring within those taking part and those witnessing the act. At least I would hope this would be true.

I wanted to wish you all well and to say that I will be present with you in spirit. So will all the Catonsville people including, I am sure, our dear David, who shares in a special kind of immortality for having desired it so passionately.

AMERICA IS HARD TO FIND, 1972

Part Seven

IN EXILE, UNDERGROUND, IN PRISON

To Limbo and Back:
A Latin American Exile

In November 1965, Father Berrigan was sent to Latin America by his Jesuit superior, on orders from Francis Cardinal Spellman; after considerable public controversy, Berrigan returned to the United States in March 1966.

Cuernavaca, Mexico

The important thing was not that injustice had happened *to me*. The important thing was that injustice had occurred at all; that injustice was still possible — an evil of this kind, the defeat of good work, the silencing of truth. This bit deep. But the purification of evil was the most important thing of all; first of all in myself — neither bitterness nor vengeful thoughts, nor even malingering around the idea of personal vindication. The desire for purification must advance into the possibility of creating purity in others, and especially in systems of authority which had become the persecutor, and in that measure were impure.

To turn others toward peace: One does not walk out of that vocation in walking across a border. Not even when one is forced across. For one cannot be forced out of his or her own peace, nor out of the making of peace. One can only be forced by the hand of God into another ambiance, another opportunity. In this sense, one is forced into the realization of what is always struggling to be born in the church, of what cannot be brought to birth without a struggle. The intelligence of Christ so often took up this theme; in death, in new birth, in new age of humanity, in new quality of life.

Unity is always cheap in the beginning. We are born into it; we inherit it. Such unity is a grace, a foothold. The falsity comes when we live off our inheritance without trading in it, without giving it away, or starting anew. In such a case, the bloodline becomes a curse, the inheritance a slavery.

To the degree that life becomes conscious, it becomes charged with responsibilities. And becomes universalized. And yet more and more concrete. *Pax in parvis et in multis.* And conversely. The irresponsibility and regression implied in "leaving history to form itself" — or in leaving history to others, or assailing it with the stereotypes of one's own betrayals of truth.

We seek a morality which builds itself from a convergence of values—lives press in on us and we are powerless to remain unconscious of them. They pour out on us their cries of lives betrayed, sold, neglected. To construct a conscience from such lives, from the living.

A time of war judges the time of peace that has gone before, and the quality of those who built the peace. Were they truly peaceful women and men, or were they sunning themselves along a wall they had not helped to raise? To go along with such a peace is very like going along with war.

The price of a false peace is as high as the price of a hot war. In fact, the cost of the first amounts to exactly the inevitability of the second.

A time of division, of misunderstanding, and of friction, may well seem the least auspicious time of healing or of reconciliation. And yet, when love is in question, the opposite may also be true. The worst of times may be the best of times.

Those who have been evicted from their normal community may well be "the least of these"—the least qualified to speak of peace and unity. And yet the opposite may be true: A testing of spirits may reveal that the worst have something in their favor, something to offer others.

A time of war may be the least favorable time in which to speak for peace. Much is against it; frenzy, conflicting loyalties, and newly inflamed fears drive passions forward with a boiling intensity. Who will have the energy and staying power to confront the times, even to create a countercurrent, a kind of temperate Gulf Stream, choosing its own mysterious direction, maintaining its own temperature?

One must accept the ironies of life and take up the tasks of life. Disgraced or not, foolish or wise, living in ill times or good, we are what we are, we are where we are. The actual world is our only world. We must go forward; we must accept all that people say of us, however painful or unfair it be. The times allow for no delay. Life grants us no space for idleness, regrets, the pursuit of illusions. The work of peace must go on, in hardiness and steadfast good humor. We must consent to being ourselves, to being the unworthy vessels of God's word, to working with others, to the slow inching forward of compassion and hope.

What is the task before us? It is as large as life itself, and remains so even when times of crisis or war narrow it to the compass of a needle's eye, to a simple *no* to war and violence. If we must pass through the needle's eye, must take an unfrequented road, still our journey must not be solitary or capricious. It must be a journey with others and for others. It must form the largest possible company which is commensurate with a good conscience. It must include those who agree with us wholly, those who disagree in part, those who confront us with unwelcome alternatives. All are our sisters and brothers; it is their task as well as our own. We journey toward humanity. We all hear the same cry in the darkness — the wounded and the violated, the neglected poor, the victims of our history, those in whose destruction we have had part.

A time of exile may be the worst of times to assert our solidarity with others, with our nation, our church, our brothers and sisters across the world. Let there be no romanticizing about the enchantment lent by distance. Exile is a terrible burden, a terrible weight. Even when understanding and welcome and new tasks are offered to those of us exiled, the fact remains that our lives have been terribly dislocated; we are thrust into a life for which we are grossly unprepared. We must abandon those who had depended on us, rightly or excessively. We must put aside our efforts to construct something rational and ongoing, a vision of life which drew on local community and circumstance, a vision of peace to which war itself was ironically contributing. But sometimes all this is disrupted. We will have some day to pick up the pieces; indeed, we have no real assurance that we can ever do so with those persons whose thought and example were part of the passionate fabric of our hearts.

This is the hardest thing of all: to accept an impasse, a problematic, the dead end reached by life as one has known it. In such a situation, which is my actual one, there can be no solution, in the proper sense of the word. Life, with the values and opportunities and joys one had known, has ground to a halt. Life has become crisis, and the crisis is insoluble, humanly speaking. Or at least let me say, Whatever resources or ingenuity I can summon offer me no present way out.

Or rather, only one way leads out. It offers not a solution at all, or a logical outcome. It offers no more than today offered, no more light, no more understanding, no healing. Almost no hope at all — at least not in the ordinary sense of the word.

What form, then, will life take, since it must take some form, supposing that one is to go on living? I can only say: The shape of my life, broken by human hands, must be formed again by other hands. I can see no other way; the problematic must yield to the mystery.

The mystery of the Cross. It is the mystery of this war, which has destroyed so many lives, including the moral lives of those who destroy. A war that has now reached perilously into my own life and destroyed its former shape, deflected its energies, disrupted its friendships, made of my life an occasion of division instead of the sign of unity I had hoped for.

An acceptance of the presence of mystery implies a lucid understanding of one's self and of others. One cannot claim to master life so long as he or she is ignorant of life. The obsessive longing for peace at any price, the willingness to barter valuable men and women for the cheap grace of good order, the dread of responsibilities implicit in friendship—all these are germane to the mystery I speak of. They are the ingredients of the cup of life itself—not, indeed, the only ingredients, since life is a rich vintage and offers but love and joy and heroism as well as other things. But we must speak of *this* cup, the taste of its contents presently on our lips. And the taste is that of gall, so extremely, so purely and outrageously bitter that one can perhaps conclude that no human ingenuity could have devised its essence. It is a vintage of God—or of Satan. Or, absurdly, of both.

So there is a problem of evil, and there is a mystery of evil. The first is a product of history, explainable to history, assuaged to a degree, within history. Its nature is not of formal interest to me. Or let me at least say: Such evil could not create me as a human being any more than it could destroy me as a human being. It can awaken energies or render them lax and lazy. Its omnipresence can arouse compassion or despair. It can send my hand to my pocket or send me on a conventional religious mission. It can command gestures without content. But its power over me goes only so far, only so far into my eyes or skin or soul as to leave them intact, neither greatly offended nor painfully awakened. I remain what I am though a beggar is before me, though an accident occurs down the street. I sit in the sunlight; I continue with my dinner. My moral life takes its food and drink, hears and sees and breathes the air of the world, evacuates its poisons. I remain a good intellectual animal, an approved domesticated specimen, a moral neutral. I deal inoffensively with the world; it offers me no reason for acting as anything but its colorless civil servant.

But the mystery of evil! Not a problem raised to the Nth degree. Nor a tag put arbitrarily on life simply because life has suddenly grown too big for my resources. A problem does not differ from a mystery because the problem has no evident answer, or is pure enigma.

The gesture proper to a problem before one is the taking up of a plumbline or calipers. Proper means are chosen and put resourcefully to work. But the gesture proper to mystery cannot be termed a hopeless lifting and falling of one's hands! Indeed, if the workings of our spirit were visible we would see a response to mystery as something parallel to the summoning of a person's body before an obstacle. *Fides quaerens intellectum*. We want to *know*, whatever the case. In the first, that of the problematic, we wish to apprehend, to take the world to ourselves. In the second, we wish to submit before a world which we confess is larger than our resources. Problems are made for us in order--through their largeness and scope and puzzle once confronted—to make us more fully ourselves. Through solutions we enter into wider, and richer, implications of our universe. So, more surely, we enter into ourselves by way of the real world; into our own bodies which are world bodies; into a future which we are able to bring nearer to ourselves, to declare as our own, and so to make over into a true present.

But mystery? A will exists, which declares itself in a Human Being like us, to be a Will of love, of concern. This Will has its design in the world, is immanent in the world. But it is not subsumed, not seized on by the world. Indeed, this Will brings the world to a term that no confluence of history, no concentration of energy or genius or human love could imagine—much less bring about.

So the end of the problem is, at least in degree, an "arrival": A human being is in outer space; a disease is controlled; a theory is vindicated. But before mystery, we stand perpetually before an invitation so merciful, in fact, that our submission before it as well as our powerlessness to possess it, is our greatest dignity. To stand under that waterfall whose music is the promise, "More, I will give more!"

It is a cliché that history is always renewing with surprising events, that the truth is a matter to be lived, to be made present in persons and communities. One way of doing this—one among many—is to speak the truth. Which is not always possible, or even expedient. Or even, let it be added, valuable. One recalls the intemperate, insistent, all-disclosing kind of truth that leaves men and women unmoved, leaves them only more stubbornly where they were.

But to *live* the truth! Another matter entirely. So different a matter, in fact, of so different an order, that it raises questions of truth to another plane, sheds upon them an altogether unexpected radiance, grants them a new parabola of experience upon which to draw. To be concrete: Is it better, in defense of the truth, for us to be in community in New York exploring with others the questions that animate us, drawing on the resources concentrated there to protest evil, to uncover the alternatives of life? Or is it better to be thrown back upon one's self abroad, leaving our past like a diminishing wake, a memory that is freshened only by occasional flutters? It is hard to answer. Perhaps it is useless to attempt to answer. For if either activity is valid as a human contribution, it must be true that both the range of life is in fact being extended, and that we are living the truth for others. We are not wasting or violating life in either circumstance; nor are we turning selfishly or surreptitiously to our own ends.

The call to live the truth, rising from the pages of the Gospels as well as from one's own being, thus can act in two complementary ways. It can chasten and subordinate one's activity to the good of others, and it can act in order to interpret misfortune. The first is the task of conscience as reproof and limiting power of spirit upon egoism. The second is conscience as consoler. In both cases, we are speaking of the activity of the spirit of truth.

"It is sad not to see any good in goodness" (Gogol). It is at least equally sad not to see any evil in evil. In both cases we are speaking of a consciousness that is fearfully alienated from its proper world function. That function is the making of history, which "walks upon two legs" or falls flat. But which must go forward with humankind.

Perhaps from a historical point of view, this is what we are living through in the church, a spasm away from love back to the iron breast of law, which is at once mother and destroyer. As mother, offering a haven against the pain and threat of experience—two arms which purport to be the arms of God. But in reality, a destroyer; the dark prison of the womb, the return to which is a mortal danger to humankind. A historic misreading of the text of history as God has actually communicated it: "I am not in your iron idols— I am in humankind."

The response of churches during wartime is instructive. It usually parallels the mentality of a nation at war. As such, it represents a betrayal of the God of history—a falling back upon a profoundly stereotyped, acquisitive morality—unassailable by reason, unassailable also by the alternatives that actual life is always offering to the living. Once such a "morality" is in command, and is presumed to be in possession, beyond criticism or assault, literally anything is possible against "the enemy." And the first victims of such action will, in the nature of things, be the community of violence itself—will be destroyed more thoroughly than its enemies, or even its prophets. Humankind cannot exist in a form of life that takes violence for its first method. For such violence is waged against itself. The first fact of its obituary is not that it has reduced the world to ashes— it is that the giant perished by suicide.

Humankind is redeemed by Christ from the power of the law, from abstract ideals, from merely human goodness, from laissez-faire morality, from illusions of omnipotence, from reliance on technique as a way of controlling human lives, from pseudospiritual jots and tittles, from the evil power of creating propaganda and the evil slavery of submitting to it, from Hitler and Stalin, from statism and racism, from communism and capitalism, from cold and hot wars. Thus far and further: the liberation offered by Christ. And further—even as far as history reaches, as far as its unborn contaminations can reach. But the question remains: How many men and women, how many Christians, desire this kind of freedom? It remains, as far as history has taken us, a gift suspended in midair, a fruit never plucked. Or by only a few.

For the sake of abstract ideals, one can always become the executioner of the living. This is the history of humankind B.C.—and very nearly the history since. The *trahison des clercs*—the revolution crushed by "good men."

When the church yields before the ideology of the state, classifying men and women as enemies and remaining silent before methods of wholesale slaughter, it in fact moves perilously near to disbelief. It no longer proclaims its faith in the God who converts hearts to God's justice. Equally it ceases to believe in itself as church. For to be church is to be sinner, subject to God's forgiving and renewing love. But to consent to war, to cease to speak for the innocent, is to connive in such monstrous guilt as places the church itself beyond God's forgiveness. So in the Vietnam War, no official voice of the American church has yet condemned the indiscriminate bombing of the innocent, the torture of prisoners, the burning of crops, or the suspension of civil liberties.

To oppose our present war on such grounds is justifiable, and, as we believe, expedient. But it is by no means the whole ground open to discussion. Even if not one civilian were killed, not one person reduced to beggary, not one person maltreated, and if somehow the fabric of social life remained intact through the years of war—and all these hypotheses lead us further into the absurdity of a claim that modern war can be just—many grave questions would remain. And the gravest revolves around this war as a paradigm of history. Does social change take place in these ways, under such leadership, by such methods, vitalized by such ideology? Is this our way into the future, for Asia and for ourselves? Or is the war not rather an historic abortivus, something whose birth may perhaps have been proper to nineteenth-century colonial history, but whose horror has been transplanted and forced into birth in the twentieth century?

Human beings are forbidden to kill. But they step into uniforms, are handed weapons, and commanded to kill. We have here a kind of walking into Alice's mirror, the ugly change that takes—that overtakes—human beings once they assume their history. But are human beings required to be in history in such a way? For an eventual good, for moral or cultural reasons, can they be required or even allowed to kill? Do they express their solidarity with life, with the defense of life, by dealing out death? A most painful question. And one to which the past can give only the most unsatisfactory of answers. For the fact remains that once we have granted everything possible to the wars of history, once we have called them beneficial or inevitable or conducive of greater good than evil—after all this, we must still insist that the argument has little or no bearing upon present facts, for our past, as a history of war, presents really no alternatives to us.

We simply do not know what peace could have done, or peaceable arrangements, or the ingenuity of men and women who would have chosen peaceable change instead of violence. In the large print of history, we know only what violence accomplished. And even a history of violence is not so totally evil as here and there not to bring about some human benefit. But the question remains: What would methods of peace and compassion have wrought in circumstances where only war was wrought? What if the implications of the Sermon on the Mount had been realized, at a given period? Do we really know what might have been the alternatives to the Versailles Treaty if the Christian message of peace had been heard at the time of that treaty? Would the alternatives to unconditional surrender perhaps have saved Germany from its fatal response to Hitler, made it unnecessary to crush all other hope by demands of unconditional surrender, the dismemberment of its industry, and the impoverishment and humiliation of its people?

Thus, when we presume to judge our history something is always left out. The history itself is mutilated. We can measure our progress toward humanism or Christian life only by what data we have — which is to say, by the fury or comparative mercifulness of our wars. And this, by and large, is the history of the church, in an analogous sense. In the world, fluctuations of violence; in the church, long periods of consecrated violence. The other alternative, which we might call a concrete and living faith in Christ, is almost totally absent. Its social effects therefore lie beyond analysis; they have never germinated.

The history of war makes large claims for itself. Berdyaev, for example, repeats the claims with no particular attempt at analysis, and has little sense of what he is implying: "War has been the source of the lofty virtues of courage, honor, loyalty, chivalry, and nobility." This is an obvious recalling of the mythology of the Middle Ages. But what of these virtues, as the vision of the New Testament might have elevated them to a pure scheme of life? And what of the uncounted thousands whose destruction was the price paid for the exercise of such virtues?

It is not so much the presence of a world of sin that renders Christ inadequate or utopian in history. It is the presence of sin, concretely and historically, in Christians themselves. The defenders of the necessity of war, drawing on the history of war, inevitably regard the Sermon on the Mount from this point of view; if war is a historical necessity, it must follow that a kingdom of peace is purely eschatological. Which is to say, not merely that such ideology is in fact unrealizable, but more — that its existence depends radically on a further intervention of God, a day which no human resources can prepare for or bring to pass. But such reasoning is a highly specious use of the gospel. The truth is that no history, however massively moving in one or another direction, can nullify the act of God, already brought to pass in Christ Jesus. The Kingdom is announced in the presence of God's son; a visible, active, audible reality, a body of believers, a kingdom of peace, of justice, and of love. Granted that such a group has not succeeded in converting the world to the ways of peace. But neither can the world declare, nor can a worldly church declare, that the peaceful work of the Kingdom is null and void, that every decision to submit to violence rather than to exercise violence, has not been a guarantee of the Lord's continued presence in time—an intervention of such constancy and power that, against it, violence could never quite possess the earth, never entirely claim humankind.

Insofar as the regime of the law is vigorously outside the regime of grace, attempts to return to the law and its methods amount to a rejection of Christ. The *sensus ecclesiae* is important and normative here. People know when the church is working violence on them. They know because once more it is being preached that "man is made for the Sabbath," that the church has come "to be served, not to serve," that "the outside of the cup and the plate" are to be kept clean for public view. And men and women know this more acutely when one among them, or many, lie untended in the ditch.

When faith in God is alive, there are no alternatives to humanity; neither state, nor ideology, nor cultural idolatries—nor, indeed, church. There is, after Christ, only humanity. We Christians can have no quarrel with that. Or if we have a quarrel, our objections have the absurdity and invalidity of reproaches against God.

When we begin to wonder what has happened to the former "signs and wonders" that marked the beginnings of the church, we can conclude that God has withdrawn from humankind, which is really an accusation that God has reneged on his own promise. Or we can conclude that God has drawn closer to humankind, has sealed his promise afresh. I had rather opt for the latter. The great contemporary signs of God are the lives of men and women who speak up, and who die if necessary, for others. If this is an overhumanized version of things, it is the Incarnation which must stand trial for it. But religious faith, too, is on trial before the world, and the accusing judge is not on Sinai; he stands in the eyes of the undefended and violated, "the miner whom he shot down, the slave in the camps, the legions of persecuted throughout the world"—the litany of suffering that Camus knew so well. There can be no more armchair artists while men and women are being broken on the wheel of life. And no armchair Christians either.

The truest joy of Christians is to know that their lives serve; to know even obscurely that something is building up within them; to sense that an obscure fidelity, moment by moment, act by act, has brought them to where they stand at present. In apparently haphazard or brutal circumstances, they can witness in their lives some larger creation than their lives had prepared for; a mysterious beginning of a race which is at length fit for the world—fit for here and now, and for eternity. Something larger than themselves! And exhilaration in all that is—in the midst of all that is apparently defeated and broken. An exhilaration, a gift to others, a life that shows when all is weighed in the balance, something left over, something available for others.

Suppose we were to disappear from the human landscape, in the sense that no merely inherited signs of our life on earth existed. To give up a history which is in so many aspects false, in what it is pretending to say, or persuading itself that it is saying. We must admit that a rather large percentage of what we are doing could disappear without any real damage to humankind. But force the same question further: What if the "Christian message" itself were silent for one generation? When the question is put in such a way, we perhaps come to the real point — which is that Christ might then have a chance to be heard, without the corruption of false signs offered by those who are irresponsible inheritors of the pure Word. . . .

Lima, Peru

Human indignity attains another meaning here, and inevitably, by way of contrast, men and women give another meaning to human dignity than we are used to. How can those who honor themselves allow others to be dishonored? We saw, coming in from the airport, the smoldering, stinking *favellas* — half garbage heap, half dump — where thousands of families live what may, with a kind of satanic jocoseness, be called life. "And he fed the pigs, and would wish to have eaten the husks of pigs" (St. Luke). "Man, living among brute beasts" (St. Ignatius).

Wallace Stevens could see beauty in a city dump. But the place he saw was transfigured by moonlight, and he condemned no one to live with what he wrote of. But what happens to people who are condemned to live and die in the places we have seen? And, more to the point, what happens to the chiefs of society, who allow such conditions to prevail; indeed, whose power of place depends exactly on the existence of such places? To all appearances, the twenty First Families of Peru seem far indeed from the fate of Job. They are neither stricken by God, nor driven by frenzy to curse God. They exemplify what is in many cases a kind of blasphemy and a kind of judgment of God, for they are "good Catholics." Of the import of that, we shall see hereafter.

We have heard of a bishop in a poor diocese who asks $175 for a wedding in the cathedral. He wears a train some sixty feet long, never appears in the slum areas, and is known to live with a certain insistence upon personal comfort. We concelebrated this morning in a parish church where the pastor read the bishop's Lenten letter to his people. His words spoke much of heaven and more of hell, and urged, among other virtues, that Christians "be resigned to the social condition in which they were born." This in a diocese where Indians from the mountain areas live on ten or five cents a day and chew coco leaves to immunize themselves from cold and hunger. The people were also urged strongly to fast and pray. For many of them, nature and feudalism had already conspired to ensure the first benefit. And no bishop could teach them the second, so long as the Church itself invested in their misery.

We spent most of the day in the Monton slum. I suddenly came from great perplexity into a kind of peace. Sick at the stomach, eyes smarting from the smoke of spontaneous combustion arising here and there and settling in a pall upon the whole area. Was the peace a spurious one? In any case, it was as though God were trying to say:

> Try to understand that these conditions are a Biblical condition. They are joined to the life of Job, of Jeremiah, to the death of Isaiah and the death of Jesus. Try to understand further that my hidden mercy is never less hidden than here. Try also to understand that I have led my people as pioneers to this place, as a desert encampment, to form in them the fiber of heroes — steadfastness, freedom from illusion, isolation from the corrupt possession of the earth, love, and detachment. Understand also that you are led here for this purpose: to know in such a place as perhaps nowhere else that a future is being formed for you and others. In these people, in the few who share their fate, a new exodus is under way, a new form of death which always precedes birth.

In the eyes of a young priest, weak from illness, reflecting for all who could see the rewards of the Beatitudes, I seem to see what was meant by the Apocalypse: to stand where one must stand, to plant the landmarks by which the unborn will be enabled to walk (Rev. 2: 1, 9, 19).

JUBILEE, JULY 1966

Letter to the Weathermen

The Weatherman was a radical and at times violent splinter group of the Students for a Democratic Society.

Dear Brothers and Sisters,

This is Dan Berrigan speaking. I want to say what a very deep sense of gratitude I have that the chance has come to speak to you across the underground. It's a great moment when I can rejoice in the fact that we can at last start setting up a dialogue that I hope will be a continuing thing through the smoke signals, all with a view to enlarging the circle of those who realize that the times demand not that we narrow our method of communication but that we actually enlarge it if anything new or anything better is going to emerge. I'm talking out of a set of rough notes and my idea was that I could not only discuss these ideas with you but possibly publish them.

The Cold-War alliance between politics, labor, and the military finds many Americans at the right end of the cornucopia. What has not yet risen in them is the question of whose blood is paying for all this, what families elsewhere are being blasted, what separation and agony and death are the other side of that coin of the realm — the connections are very hard to make, and very few come on them, and many can hardly imagine that all being right with America means that very much must go wrong elsewhere. How do we get such a message across to others? It seems to me that that is one way of putting the very substance of our task. Trying to keep connections, or to create new ones. It's a most difficult job, and in hours of depression it seems all but impossible to speak to Americans across the military and diplomatic and economic idiocies — and yet I think we have to carry our reflection further and realize that the difficulty of our task is the other side of the judgment Americans are constantly making about us. This determination to keep talking with all who seek a rightful place in the world or all who have not yet awakened to it, this, I think, is the revolution, and the United States perversely and negatively knows it, and this is why we are in trouble. And this is why we accept trouble, and ostracism and the fear of jail and of death, as the normal conditions under which decent men and women are called upon to function today.

Undoubtedly the F.B.I. comes after people like me with guns because deeper than their personal chagrin and their corporate machismo, which is a kind of debased esprit de corps since they always get their man, there was that threat that the Panthers and the Vietnamese had learned so well as a reality. The threat is a very simple one because we are making connections, political connections, religious and moral connections, connections with prisoners and Cubans and Vietnamese, and these connections are forbidden under the policies which J. Edgar Hoover is greatly skilled both in enacting and in enforcing. They know by now what we are about, they know we are serious. And they are serious about us. Just as with a mortal fear for the last five years they have known what the Vietnamese are about and the Brazilians and the Angolese and the Guatemalans. We are guilty of making connections, of urging others to explore new ways of getting connected, of getting married, of educating children, of sharing goods and skills, of being religious, of being human, of resisting. I am speaking for prisoners and exiles and that true silent, deathly silent majority which is that of the dead and the unavenged as well as the unborn, and I am guilty again of making connections with you.

By and large the public is petrified of you. There is a great mythology surrounding you—much more than around me. You come through in public as another embodiment of the public nightmare which is menacing and sinister and senseless and violent: a spin-off of the public dread of Panthers and Vietcong, of Latins and Africans, and the poor of our country, of all those expendable and cluttering and clamorous lives who have refused to lie down and die on command or to perish at peace with their fate, or to exist in the world as suppliants and slaves.

But in a sense, of course, your case is even more complicated because your choice to rebel is not the passionate consequence of the stigma of slavery. Yours is a choice. It's one of the few momentous choices in American history. Your no could have been a yes, and the society realizes it because you had everything going for you. Your lives could have been posh and secure, but you said no. And you said it, moreover, by attacking the very properties you were supposed to have inherited, a very amazing kind of turnabout.

The society, I think, was traumatized. What to do with Vietcong or Panthers had never been a very complicated matter, after all. We jailed them or shot them down or brought in the National Guard. But what to do with you—this indeed was one hell of a question. There was no blueprint and no answer. And yet this question, too, was not long in being answered, as we learned at Kent State. That is to say, when property and the question of its survival come up close, the metaphor is once more invariably military. It is lives that go down. And now we know that even if those lives are white and middle-class, they are going to be in the same gun-sights.

The mythology of fear that surrounds you is exactly what the society demands, as it demands more and more mythology, more and more unreality to live by. But it also offers a very special opportunity to break this myth that flourishes on silence and ignorance and has you stereotyped as mindless, indifferent to human life and death, determined to raise hell at any hour or place. We have to deal with this as we go along; but from where, from what sort of mentalities, what views of one another and ourselves? Not from an opposite window of insanity or useless rage, but with a new kind of anger which is both useful in communicating and imaginative and slow-burning to fuel the long haul which is the definition of our whole lives.

I'm trying to say that when people look about them for lives to run with and when hopeless people look for hope, the gift we can offer others is so simple a thing as hope. As they said about Che, as they say about Jesus, some people, even to this day, he gave up hope. So that my hope is that you see your lives in somewhat this way, which is to say I hope your lives are about something more than sabotage. I'm certain they are. I hope the sabotage question is tactical and peripheral. I hope indeed that you are remaining uneasy about its meaning and usefulness, and that you realize that the burning down of properties, whether Catonsville or in the case of Chase Manhattan or anywhere else, by no means guarantees a change of consciousness, the risk remaining always very great that sabotage will change people for the worse and harden them against further change.

I hope you see your lives as Che saw his, that is to say mainly as teachers of the people, conscious as we must be of the vast range of human life that still awaits liberation and education and consciousness. If I'm learning anything it is that nearly everyone is in need of this and therefore in need of us, whether or not they realize it. I think of all those who so easily dismiss and whose rage against us is an index of the blank pages of their real lives, those to whom no meaning or value has ever been attached by politicians or generals or churches or universities or indeed anyone, those whose sons fight the wars, those whose wages are drained away paying for the wars, those who are constantly mortgaged and indebted to the consumer system, and those closer to ourselves, among fellow students who are still enchanted by careerism and selfishness, those who are unaware that the human future must be created out of suffering and loss.

How shall we speak to our people, to the people everywhere? We must never refuse, in spite of their refusal of us, to call them our brothers and sisters. I must say to you as simply as I know how, if the people are not the main issue, there is simply no main issue and you and I are fooling ourselves also, and the American fear and dread of change has only transferred itself to a new setting.

This, I think, is where a sensible, humane movement operates on several levels at once if it is to get anywhere. So it is saying communication yes, organizing yes, community yes, sabotage yes — as a tool. That is the conviction that took us where we went. And it took us beyond, to this night. We reasoned that the effect of our act could not be to impede the war or much less to stop the war in its tracks. God help us, if that had been our intention, we were certainly fools before the fact and doubly fools after it, for in fact the war went on. And still we undertook sabotage long before any of you. It might be worthwhile just very quickly reflecting on some reasons why. We were trying first of all to say something about the pernicious effect of certain properties on the lives of those who guarded them or died in consequence of them. And we were determined to talk to as many people as possible and as long as possible afterward, to interpret and to write, and through our conduct, through the appeal, through questioning ourselves again and again, finding out where we were, where we were going, where people might follow.

My hope is that affection and compassion and nonviolence are now common resources once more and that we can proceed on that assumption, the assumption that the quality of life within our communities is exactly what we have to offer. I think a mistake in S.D.S.'s past was to kick out any evidence of that as being weakening or reactionary or counterproductive. The mark of inhuman treatment of humans is a mark that also hovers over us. It is the mark of a beast, whether its insignia is the military or the movement.

No principle is worth the sacrifice of a single human being. That's a very hard statement. At various stages of the movement some have acted as if almost the opposite were true, in that we get purer and purer. More and more people have been kicked out for less and less reason. At one period of the past, way back, the result of such thinking was another of the religious wars, or wars of extinction. At another time it was Hitler; he wanted a ton of purity too. Still another is still with us in the war against the Panthers and the Vietnamese. I think I'm in the underground because I want part of none of these, whatever name they go by, whatever rhetoric they justify themselves with.

When madness is the acceptable public state of mind, we're all in danger, all in danger for under the heel of former masters as under the heel of new ones.

Some of your actions are going to involve inciting and conflict and trashing, and these actions are very difficult for thoughtful people. But I came upon a rule of thumb somewhere which might be of some help to us: do only that which one cannot not do. Maybe it isn't very helpful, and of course it's going to be applied differently by the Joint Chiefs of Staff and the underground group of sane men and women. In the former, hypocritical expressions of sympathy will always be sown along the path of the latest rampage. Such grief is like that of a mortician in a year of plague. But I think our realization is that a movement has historic meaning only insofar as it puts its gains to the side dictated by human dignity and the protection of life, even of the lives most unworthy of such respect. A revolution is interesting insofar as it avoids like the plague the plague it promised to heal. Ultimately if we want to define the plague as death, and I think that's a good definition, the healing will neither put people to death nor fill the prisons nor inhibit freedom nor brainwash nor torture its enemies nor be mendacious nor exploit anyone, whether women or children or blacks or the poor. It will have a certain respect for the power of the truth, which created the revolution in the first place.

We may take it, I think, as a simple rule of thumb that the revolution will be no better and no more truthful and no more populist and no more attractive than those who brought it into being. Which is to say we are not killers, as America would stigmatize us, and indeed as America perversely longs for us to be. We are something far different, we are teachers of the people who have come on a new vision of things. We struggle to embody that vision day after day, to make it a reality among those we live with so that the people are literally disarmed by knowing us, so that their fear of change, their dread of life is exorcised, and their dread of human differences is slowly expunged.

Instead of thinking of the underground as temporary or exotic or abnormal, perhaps we are being called upon to start thinking of its implication as an entirely self-sufficient, mobile, internal revival community, so that the underground may be the definition of our future. What does it mean literally to have nowhere to go in America or to be kicked out of America? It must mean to us—let us go somewhere in America, let us stay here and play here and love here and build here, and in this way join not only those who like us are recently kicked out also, but those who have never been inside at all, the blacks and the Indians and Puerto Ricans and Chicanos, whose consciousness has gone far under the rock.

Next, we are to strive to become such men and women as may, in a new world, be nonviolent. If there's any definition of the new humanity, the humanity of the future, it seems to me that we do violence unwillingly, bar exception, as instrument, knowing that destruction of property is only a means and keeping the end as vivid and urgent and as alive to us as are the means so that the means are judged in every instance by their relation to the ends. I have a great fear of American violence, not only out there in the military and the diplomacy, in economics, in industry and advertising, but also in here, in me, up close among us.

On the other hand, I must say, I have very little fear, from firsthand experience, of the violence of the Vietcong or Panthers (I hesitate to use the word violence), for their acts come from the proximate threat of extinction, from being invariably put on the line of self-defense, but that's not true of us and our history. We can simply say from outside the culture of these others, no matter what admiration or fraternity we feel, we are unlike them, we have other demons to battle.

But the history of the movement, in the last years, it seems to me, shows how constantly and easily we are seduced by violence, not only as to method but as to end in itself. With very little politics, very little ethics, very little direction, and only a minimum moral sense, if any at all, it might lead one to conclude in despair: the movement is debased beyond recognition, I can't be a part of it. Far from giving birth to the new humanity, it has only proliferated the armed, bellicose, and inflated spirit of the army, the plantation, the corporation, the diplomat.

Yet it seems to me good, in public as well as in our own house, to turn the question of violence back on the true creators and purveyors of it, working as we do from a very different ethos and for very different ends. I remember being on a television program recently and having the whole thing thrown at me, and saying—look, ask the question in the seats of power, don't ask it of me, don't ask me why I broke the law, go ask Nixon why he breaks the law constantly, ask the Justice Department, ask the racists. Obviously, but for Johnson and Nixon and their fetching ways, Catonsville would never have taken place and you and I would not be here today, just as but for the same people S.D.S. would never have grown into the Weathermen or the Weathermen have gone underground. In a decent society, normally functioning for its people, all of us would be doing the things that decent men and women do for one another. That we are forbidden so to act, forced to meet so secretly and with so few, is a tragedy we must live with. We have been forbidden a future by the forms of power, which include death as the ordinary social method, by having rejected the future they drafted us into and having refused, on the other hand, to be kicked out of America, either by aping their methods or leaving the country.

The question now is what can we create. I feel at your side across the miles, and I hope that sometime, sometime in this mad world, in this mad time, it will be possible for us to sit down face to face, brother to brother, sister to sister, and find that our hopes and our sweat, and the hopes and sweat and death and tears and blood of our brothers and sisters throughout the world, have brought to birth that for which we began.

Thank you and shalom.

DANIEL BERRIGAN, S.J.
VILLAGE VOICE, JANUARY 21, 1971

Rehabilitative Report:
We Can Still Laugh

In prison you put on your clothes
and take them off again.
You jam your food down
and shit it out again
You round the compound right
to left and right again.
The year grows irretrievably old
so does your hair burn white.
The mood; one volt above
one volt below survival,
roughly per specimen, space
sufficient for decent burial.

PRISON POEMS, 1973

A Piece of Advice
to a Young Prisoner

When they own your smile, I reminded
The next man in the stripsearch line
They own your balls. Nothing in the
Constitooshun requires handing over
That silk purse to the anti-
Ecologicals. GIMME growls the
mercenary paw. IN A SOW'S EAR growl
Back. It might not be gracious but
By God it's clear, as Confucius say.
And where soul, grit and growl are
In the breech, the bag,
You'd best be clear or
J. Edgar's leer
Will hitch up
In dishonor of your
Broke and entered
Crotch
A big notch.

PRISON POEMS, 1973

We Used to Meet for Classes. Sometimes It Was Ecstasy, Sometimes Blah

The big claims of the powerless are not notably more interesting
than the big claims of the powerful. The first inspire pity
   the others, fear. Together they make a parody
of the tragic. Now and again in our prisoners' class
   someone, a new arrival or a loquacious con man
takes over. Pushing his big claim up front
   a rickety cart laden with dubious "goods," slightly tainted
   virtuous side upward.
He would die, in sum, for this or that. (I forget what)
   Our fingers drum. The words of dead heroes
twitch in our hands like a struck face.

Like torches stuck in the ground, a night encampment
an unwearied courage; thought plays, light and shadow cross
   a mad general flays the air
A mad president charts, premises, promises. A seductive
   foreshortening
of the long march.
   "Take over—revolution—consciousness 3." Eyes cloud.
Have heard it all before, have heard it all
   before, heard it all, all before
before

PRISON POEMS, 1973

Prison Journal

January 23, 1971

Every time someone opens a door. Every time someone locks a door, unlocks a door. Every lineup for food, laundry, coffee at the company store. Every say-no behind every right (or left) turn. You may not do the opposite. The four limits of the compound; the guards' eyes, faces, jaws. The purpose renewed. The quiet battle. The will unassailed. Every bad news of every day — when was it we last had good news? Every sweating, wrung minute, toward dawn; the growing measure of an event which will have no heroic or noble outcome in this world. Every prayer, every effort to praise that God who is silent; to praise Him because He is silent, to praise Him although He is silent. To serve His honor in a darkening world, which honors only death.

Every search of the person, who is, according to our faith, sacred. Every ignoble transaction of the person, betrayal of the person, thieving, lying, betraying, putting one's own well-being first. Every sin, here also, against a community of persons, which must be born here, as in a lying-in hospital of the future.

Cheerfulness, Joy, Peace. Hardly won, hourly assailed, even here. The discouraged, the lost. Those who give up, by buying the pernicious public values. Those here for the wrong reasons, returning to the world for the wrong reasons, to do the wrong things with their lives.

The anguish of husbands and fathers. The hunger of faces, during visits; of hands and eyes, under the scrutiny of the guards. The artificial and artful and contrived scarcity of love, as a public resource, an energy available to all who would live, would live for others; who have begotten children and made love, and now are forbidden the presence of the fruits of their love.

Relationships awry. The necessity of silence, to preserve the little of integrity or health that exists in fact. The renunciation of wrong hope, wrong love, wrong words. The encompassing power of a silence in which God is free (He must be free) to bring the future into being. The forgiveness which is silent, which admits even the transgressor, the oppressing overlord, into the ambit of one's life, concern.

Freedom from distraction — most of all from the distraction which is a vitiated form of life itself, in combat with the true life promised by the Savior. A whisper: embrace me, I will comfort and strengthen you and make the time pass; so you will "do good time."

Time as punishment: do your time! Time as reward, responsibility: redeem the time! Human beings as (official) slaves of time, walking the treadmill: earning "good time."

"Any time is your time" (Jesus). No action, no passion, no heroism, no reward, no "other." Time as the envelope and atmosphere of selfishness. "My hour is not yet come"—His death will be the choice in which new life is contained and bestowed.

The wrecks, the hopeless, the diminished, the perennial children, the defeated, the bargainers, the betrayers . . . Over them all: the owners, the oppressors, the 9 to 5 keys with their legs, arms, eyes attached. The rattling of keys, the approach of power, the owners of bodies and spirits, the slave masters—and their slaves.

January 26

The situation at work (in the dental clinic) has been ludicrous in the extreme; something out of Gogol or Kafka. They first took on two extra clerks, thus putting others on the sidelines, there being little enough work for two, let alone four. Then last Friday, they summarily fired everyone but me. When I demanded an explanation, was told there was a minor scandal on the part of one, another has snitched, etc., etc. I was saved because I was not of their ilk, presumably. I "gave the clinic a tone!" Imagine that. Then today I learn in this breeding house of rumor that I was to be dumped also but was saved by the captain, who didn't want another *cause célèbre* on his lily hands. Prosit! By inference another bubble is burst—that my work there is of any real value to them . . . but is it? I read betimes, but try to take the technical side of things seriously, as much as I may, reflecting that the work is a real service to the inmates and I am responsible for a decent job. The enervating realization is that one is powerless—absolutely so, in such circumstances as we are in, that all decisions as to survival etc. come down from above, no inmate is worthy of being consulted about any decisions. One is an inmate in the same sense exactly as a mental patient or a terminally ill person would be. One's life, work, etc. are in no serious sense in one's own hands. The disintegrating effects of all this are evident in everything from the men's faces to their habitual conduct and demeanor. They are not allowed to give a damn—so they do not.

There is little to be gained by striving over all this. It is more fruitful simply to do one's best and leave the rest to God. Or at least so I have decided. We are walking on extremely thin ice. Our civil suit for rights of prisoners has been denied; six are indicted, the rest of us are co-conspirators, our friends generally are in disarray, stunned by the swift descent of ruin. We are just slowly picking up the pieces and evaluating the personal loss, recovering from the first shock with the help of a few who have appeared at our side.

This P.M. our class was "visited" for the first time by two officials—an ominous move, in view of the past weeks. We shall have simply to see what occurs and take our soundings accordingly. But the time ahead will not be easy. Philip will be taken off for arraignment, maybe an attempt will be made to transfer him permanently. There is so much anguish to taste, so much power and autonomy and time in the hands of the government officials, who have not even the threat of elections to deter them—at least a year, possibly two, in which they can cut their murderous swath—at home and abroad, and no resistance to speak of. The war seems to be absorbed into the natural organism, like a foreign body or an illness—it festers there, but life drags on somehow. And meantime we are entirely in their power, except for the slight deterrence of public interest—much waned in fact since recent accusations against us. We go on, carrying a great weight of personal opprobrium, discouragement, etc. I can't remember when I felt life to be such a burden, so cheapened, so bereft of joy and hope. Yet one goes on— a compound attitude—partly out of habit, partly out of purpose. At least a few of us must survive, if not intact, at least recognizably *here*, and ourselves.

Most of the publicity has done great damage, reinforcing public suspicion of us as idealists turned to madness. Some would like to believe otherwise, and make gestures in our direction. But it is all disheartening in the extreme. I feel as though a blade were being held to our throats, we helpless as animals to turn it aside. Prayer in a spirit of faith is almost, it seems, no prayer at all. I felt this most acutely when the Quakers came to pray with us. They are good and sincere but so bright and cheery and caught up in their unassailed lives as to make us feel all the more acutely our alienation from the common middle life of America. They do not seem to sense what we are enduring—nor do they show in any real way a will to share our suffering. We pray and believe nonetheless—alone, or with a few, here and there, who are tasting the gall of life at their own lips.

Most days I am stupefied by the fact that locks are turned on me, by the noisy days and nights around me, by the atmosphere of distraction and abandonment to iron fate, by sleeplessness, by the uncertain future which casts so thick a shadow. Most of all by the sufferings of Philip which I share to the hilt—mostly because I do not yet share them. I am learning what it must mean to be his brother. I die of it.

We have Mass together and I cannot scrape together a single thought— whether of acceptance, aversion, hope, response. Stand there like a vertical corpse, take the bread and wine, empty as a plank, dry as a stone. My whole being, the open throat of a man who has died of thirst, who has no succor in this world—whose only justification for existing at all is that he believes, and so stands there. Let the Lord make of it what he will—nothing at all, or someday, a man. But after such days and nights one must surely count death as dearest friend. Except that I could not die without Philip, or apart from his fate. Will he ever know how I love him?

January 28

I am setting this down with my new pen, presented (with a matching pencil) to Philip and myself this P.M. in virtue of "our fine work with the education of the inmates." The atmosphere was a little chilling, the air of a posthumous award for "service to the party." Or at least so it seems to me. There are very few here from whom I would wish to receive anything, in truth.

The atmosphere, if one lets oneself dwell on it, is terrifying for political prisoners. One becomes literally the sport of any fleeting rumor that happens to be in the air—like a poison. E.g., that one prisoner, whom indeed we have no reason to trust, has already agreed to testify against Philip in court. He confronted him, by my advice. It was for that fellow's salvation, as I saw it. Can he hope to live with himself if such a rumor be true? One reads every day of trials where informers supplied the heart of the evidence against the charged—much like the atmosphere of *Hope Against Hope*, which I am reading in horror. There is so little conscience anywhere and most are willing to trade their souls for a bit of time off their sentences. To keep a diary such as this one is an act which would be impugned as a crime. No wonder one's sleep is troubled, feeling to the heart the shadow that lies over us all. Practically all the prisoners drug themselves with the same diet they trade on outside—commissary and TV, and some meretricious reading. . . . One resolves in face of this to continue his diet of prayer, reflections, and reading and let the chips fall where they may. Someone sent me a poem by Neruda written while he was on the lam; he lived to be an old man, now is ambassador to France—but what will our future be like? The clouds are inexpressibly dark for us and our friends—and we know nothing of the other side of what we must simply suffer through, trusting in God that we are standing where men and women must stand—if there are to be any left in the world. . . .

March 4

Woke to the sense, washing over like a tide, of being in jail; how many days! And thought of all 750 men here, all awakening from the neutrality of sleep, its free-floating geography—one might be literally anywhere. To be in jail—stirring and moving into that depression of spirit which seizes on one before he is fully in command, lowers its harness on him, restricts, enfeebles the movement of his mind, puts him at rigorous distance from family and friends, orders him about, decrees that this day will be like every other day—the worse for being a day added to the crushing burden of the days. . . . So that awakening is another hiatus in the vast toothless, tasteless yawn of existence-without-choosing-one's-existence. Purgatorial. The hard task of making virtue out of a necessity that grinds one down . . . Some of this I feel for myself, all of it I feel for the others, especially for those with families and wives; the loosening of ties, the enforced distance from love.

I wonder if in purgatory one would be able to make necessity a virtuous choice. Sometimes I am able to walk—head high, breathing the prayer for all of us that we would keep alive in our hearts the flame that first brought us to Catonsville. . . .

The difficulty of writing anything down at the end of the day. Turning to reading almost as a narcotic, a way out, through the experiences and lives of others—out of the fact that we are living and experiencing so little for ourselves.

Caught, as I feel, between Zen as a vice of laziness, letting literally anything happen to myself; and on the other hand, forcing the hand of life, wrenching it to one's own "uses," as though to endure all this had no value in itself, because one was quite literally bankrupt and had nothing to offer others, the future, the brothers and sisters outside. . . .

I was demeaned by a crude hospital official who made a cruel pseudo-humorous crack, and then went his way, after other prey no doubt. Stood the humiliation for some five minutes, realizing I would be unable to live with myself if I let it pass. Sought him out in his office, told him face to face what I thought of such a crack. He relented, apologized, followed me back to the clinic to apologize before the others as well. End of the matter except I believe I set up a legitimate line between the humiliation of being an inmate and the gratuitous humiliation dumped on one by an inferior spirit playing hobs with the feelings of a powerless man. . . .

In course of a conversation with another assistant, spoke heatedly of "g.d. idiots" making war policy. He registered dismay at my language. "Though you're a convict I respect you as a priest etc." I was unable to concur with the basis of his "respect" and advised reading of the imprecatory Psalms and Old Testament prophets, whose language is scarely of the boudoir or sacristy. Religion is politesse. I say, a plague on it. So it goes.

The men are out late tonight breaking up the ice after a hailstorm that tore apart, at one blow, the false promise of an untimely spring. Across the compound in A and O, men are showering, reading, playing ping-pong. There is a semblance of order and discipline.

With inquiring eyes, priests, lawyers, friends, editors come to seek out our life. We are as exotic as birds or beasts in a big city zoo—or terminal patients in a hospital. How do we live? What is the day like? What do we eat? What is our work? Do we brothers get to see one another, to talk, to share? Indeed, what seems killingly ordinary from the inside (peacocks lead the life of rather mangy barnyard cocks after all) has about it the subtle glow of the caged and captured gorgeous bird, brought gingerly from afar. . . .

We rise about 7:30. Sometimes I manage a cup of cocoa and coffee, missing breakfast habitually, manage also to say a quick prayer, a Psalm perhaps, straighten the bed, dress, wash, get to work by 8 or 8:05.

The clinic! The morning can bring any bit of comico-tragedy, and usually does. Every Tuesday we give a quick, thorough checkup to the new arrivals, as part of their medical induction. Then the day: cleaning sinks, sweeping, X rays to be taken, developed, mounted; helping at the chair, mixing filling material, sterilizing instruments—there is no end to it. But there is an end; the periods of quiet over cups of coffee at mid-morning—to me the most typical moments of the day—a prisoner's day. The eyes of a convict go dim with memory, men lean out a window (barred) offering a rare expansive view of the countryside, memory or expectation turn one to the past or future—or a cloud of despair descends, the present, the accursed present. . . . We cross the wintry yard and line up for the midday chow—some 750 are served a nourishing, varied, generally tasteless meal, from 10:45 to 12. (The food is like the religion is like the discipline is like the tenor and atmosphere of time—everything tastes like everything else; i.e., things that should have distinctive odor, gusto, moral, sharp outline, should spur or start reactions, chains of thought, sensibility, spurts of love or aversion— nothing tastes like nothing. We are in prison.)

Back to work by 1, roughly to 4 P.M. Eat by 5. First count of day at 5:30—the hour when the zoo keepers render account of the bodies whose lockup is the rationale for the employment of some hundreds of key-bearing, goose-stepping custodians of private and public weal, the retention behind bars of menaces like myself. So on and on. Two nights a week to classes in Great Books. One night, if not prevented by putrefied offerings, to movie. Several nights to reading indoors or walking the geological squirrel cage outside. So, dear reader, to a turn of exercises, to Psalms, to bed.

At least for the duration of this present long haul; as innocent, though not nearly as dispirited, as a molting captive dove. Indeed, Picasso would have to draw me in mid-flight even here, striking fire from feather and beak. . . .

July 4

—A long silence here is due to my efforts to get in and out of death. I shall be (in fact am) heard from again.

—Half of life they say is patience. I know that now, in my game. The other half is impatience.

—On June 9 I was taking a dental checkup, consequent on the cracking of a cuspid a few days before. The doctor had begun with a routine injection; five minutes of waiting, then he wanted to know, as I had winced under the drill, was I still in pain? I was (obviously). He filled another needle holder and injected me again, this time on the outside gum. . . . Thus began, in a sense, a comedy of errors that was to turn in very short order into something very near tragedy for your correspondent. The second needle; it was like shouting the right infernal word over Mount Etna, it was a match tossed into tinder.

The dentist wandered off to allow the potion to take its course. He even called me over to help with an impression for dentures. I wandered over, feeling vaguely dizzy, unwell; comforting myself as usual with the formula of the "unchoiced," i.e., so who feels good in a place like this? Not I certainly . . . Back to the chair and in some minutes, about two I think, into a faint, into shock, into massive paralysis of lungs. An hour's tense and turbulent effort followed, to keep me moored this side of the Styx.

I was curiously in and out of the happening; detached, at times "floating above," struggling like a blue baby the better part of an hour to make it, to keep breathing. I remember the dentist picking up my hand, which was icy and blue and stiffened, shaking his head with disbelief, pointing to my feet, which were not about to go anywhere, ever; just look at this.

They were free to. So was I. When they rushed me across the hall for oxygen, I recovered enough balance to begin saying a few prayers.

Close as all this was to the final curtain, I remember it as a curiously secular event. Which is to say, there was nothing baroque, gothic, or Byzantine about it. It was strictly twentieth-century tawdry; sweaty, brutal, racing against time.

I could look up from where I lay into the impassive spider face of a crawling wall clock, thus knew how long how long at every moment to wrap up a life, to keep it unskeining. Mine.

Philip was finally there and I reached up and kissed him and as I recall told him not to worry: it would be all right. For once, right. It was that very nearly total confidence in the good upper left-hand breast pocket convenience bequeathed to me (and to all six of us) by Dad-o. He would have reserved a bottomless imperial contempt for any invasion of "heart trouble" into the linear anatomy. Harrr-rumph! When he died, it was with sound heart and lungs, going under totally and grandly, like Atlantis or the one hoss shay.

How curious it was, a few hours later, to breathe again without wrench or strain! How curious to breathe at all! I felt as though it were the miracle of the end of days; as though every insect and lowly flower were conspiring with me in this miracle, renewed with every instant, the gentle rise and fall of the recumbent, all but human form of the universe. I lay there spent, all eye, all ear, skinless as a heart; was this a second birth? It was the nearest I would come to it in all the years of life.

They diagnosed "massive allergic shock." It was like most of life today, unpredictable as lightning or wildfire.

The difficulty, as I glance back, was not with dying, which was a fairly simple affair, rather in the course of things, like a self-conscious eclipse or the gobbling of a smaller fish by a larger mouth. . . . The difficulty is getting one's customary clothing back on, getting back to life, getting enough of that sweet and vanishing air to keep one on the move. . . .

So here I am on the compound, dumped back into time; as the Buddhists would say, for recycling. All is wheel. I have bowed out of the dental office. I am afflicted with gout in the right elbow and the neck, with a hernia in the esophagus. Grave medicos put heads together in my presence and cluck commiseratingly about my deteriorating frame. When my oval ivories loosen in their sockets from now on, I shall flock to the leaves as though tasting, foretasting, dramatizing the onset of death. . . .

July 13

Reading Fischer's Gandhi in the prison yard, I reflect on his great "fast unto death" in '32. On his mysteriously correct sense of the time to act and the time to be silent . . . and reflect on how clogged and drugged my own life is, like a rat in a drainpipe, unable to go backward or forward, immobilized between yes and no. An uncertain note . . . Did Gandhi ever feel like this, and suffer from it? I think of the difference between his dignified deliberate willingness to die, with all India holding its breath, and my lying on a prison cot one month ago, gasping like a wrung chicken for the air of all four winds after an absurd medical mischance. What a distance we have come!

P.M. — I was so shot full of pain, cortisone, weakness, and malaise of spirit that I wept tonight for some fifteen minutes, calling upon an absent one, so near a nobody as to be no relief, no opposite number to the *horror vacui*. Dried my tears, which at my age are hardly even wet, and went down to our class on the lawn — to work through two hours of that struggle toward rebirth that vindicates, so rarely, the name "education." It does not frighten me even that I find it impossible to keep a more even keel in this place. I know the Psalms too well to expect to go about in an iron mask. And my personal resistance to personal death is much lower than when I came here — too much has happened to maintain that constant good humor I once could rely upon — for myself as well as for others.

Someone brought me a flower from Block Island.

We are still fighting, on many fronts, the battle of the media — saving, when we can, the lorn media masters, committed unto gnashing of teeth and the undying worm to the word that (they say) saves.

LIGHTS ON IN THE HOUSE OF THE DEAD, 1974

Part Eight

CELEBRATIONS

Its Perfect Heart

It was November: an invisible fire
freshened the heart of the grey-blue heron
that had drifted and loved contented
on mild streams, among summer dwellings and children.

But what aroused it powerfully
that it shook earth like a disease, pettiness and location,
to set breast against wearying universal air?

Now while dawn streams upward from fields
or early stars send man to fireside
still it labors above him, by day and night
starting the sunrise, shadowing the red leaning moon;

sufficient, remote from the longings of men
as they look aloft: vowed to greatness
and powerfully steered by its lodestone, its perfect heart.

Time without Number, 1957

Song
(from Jacopone Da Todi)

In my morning prayer
I saw *love* written
upon every creature

men on their foreheads
trees on their leaves
houses on their walls.

Christ has flowered in man's flesh
let human nature rejoice!

THOUGHT, WINTER 1964

Invitation to a Trial

Friends,

A month or so ago, I asked Sister Corita to design an invitation to the trial of the Catonsville Nine. Corita, who consents to almost anything, agreed to this one too. Then we had second thoughts. It occurred to us how expensive it would be to send, absolutely first class, our invitation to all those hundreds who have made the past months bearable, and who by their friendship would make even federal prison a form of freedom.

It is practically impossible for Corita, as everyone knows, to produce a design of less than four delectable colors. It is also beyond our financial resources to do justice to her rainbow imaginings.

Therefore (as judges love to say) we have judged it would be more in accord with (1) our poverty, and (2) the poverty of our brothers and sisters throughout the world, to send this letter instead. It is written in strict black and white, inviting all our friends to the proceedings in Baltimore on Oct. 7 and following. We would like to commence on that Monday morning with a worship service for peace in St. Ignatius Church, on 720 North Calvert Street. From there, we will march to the courtroom in time for the opening of proceedings at 10 o'clock. Those who wish to do so are invited to wear black armbands in honor of the American war dead, and white headbands in honor of the Vietnamese war dead. But whatever you wear, come in joy, as a sign of life. We will welcome you in the same spirit. . . .

We promise all who come a good time in the company of love and courage, "legal" proceedings that will blow your mind and open your heart, . . . a defense proceeding that defends you, a prosecution that prosecutes you. What more could one ask, after Chicago, before Nov. 5? We think you know what we mean. As the Lord once said (we paraphrase, with apologies to the sacred writers), "We go to prepare a place for you."

Finally, I dedicate a poem to all we love, who understand that a poem is always personal, always an invitation. Please be invited, personally, and read as you run toward Baltimore.

> Peacemaking is hard,
> hard almost as war.
> The difference being one
> we can stake life upon
> and limb and thought and love.
>
> I stake this poem out
> dead man to a dead stick

to tempt an Easter chance—
if faith may be
truth, an evil chance
penultimate at last

not last.
We are not lost.

When these lines gathered
of no resource at all
serenity and strength,
it dawned on me—

a man stood on his nails

an ash like dew, a sweat
smelling of death and life.
Our evil Friday fled,
the blind face gently turned
another way, toward life

a man walks in his shroud.

DAN BERRIGAN, S.J.
FOR THE CATONSVILLE NINE

COMMONWEAL, SEPTEMBER 27, 1968

West Side Story

A Broadway hash joint, a Puerto Rican
short orders *2 burgers with cheese,*
2 without; onions, ketchup

in 4 minutes flat, with style, verve, and
a rare smile in a sour borough.

Far from Gracie Mansion and the gentle Sheep
Meadow. He hasn't smelled roses in years

but he wears them. While
nightmares hustle like rats
a night's undoing
                          he feeds modestly
(a few inferior loaves, a few
greasy fish) the city poor.

Winner? we have no other.
In a bad time, blessed
are you, for blessing me.

Fᴀʟsᴇ Gᴏᴅs, Rᴇᴀʟ Mᴇɴ, 1969

Eucharist

7 A.M. trial day,
courtesy of Warden Foster,
the San Jose vineyards
and a common baking shop

we took
in a workman's cracked cup
at a slum table

prisoners' pot luck

SELECTED AND NEW POEMS, 1973

Skunk

The only fauna admitted
to the widespread country zoo
(every animal in his natural
habitat, no visible bars)
was an unloquacious
bumbling skunk.
He crept in under the full moon
like a moon thing, eyes
dazed, moonstruck. Limped
along unhandily, as though
on 5 feet or 3, footsore.
Looking for what?
We wished
he would breathe deep
as an ancestor, metamorphose
10 times his size
piss high as a Versailles fountain
his remarkable musk perfume.
We didn't want additional
prisoners, even dumb ones.
If they must come, atavistic,
mystical, then let them be
spectaculars, trouble-
shooters. O skunk, raise
against lawnorder, your grandiose
geysering stinking *NO*!

PRISON POEMS, 1973

On Torture Road: Kim Chi Ha

(A REVIEW OF *TORTURE ROAD*, BY KIM CHI HA)

What can one person do? The question, as put today, has a desperate ring;
like a blow on the liberty bell, it gives off a cracked note. What can one do?
Two hundred million people, asking the question with whatever overtones — despair, anomie, futility, fear — become two hundred million
cracked voices, a cacophany, a chorus in hell.

Something more, a different voice, is needed to make a bicentennial that
will ring true. A Dostoievskian purification, maybe. Or a rebirth. The
agony that shares the agony of the world; more, that admits our solidarity
in guilt; a prelude to sight, a postlude to two centuries of blindness. This is
where Kim Chi Ha comes in. We have had poets; we have had prisoners; we
have had a few who brought the two together. But in the current bloody
wave of Big Brotherhood, we have not had a poet like this one, a recidivist,
seized and tortured again and again, tried and tried again, always charged
with the same crimes — crimes of the tongue, misuse of the pen. He was
sentenced to death; sentence was rescinded; he is about to be tried once
more. Was ever a sharper sliver imbedded in the finger nail of the mailed
fist?

Finally, it should be said, we have not had such a Catholic resister as
Kim, one who so clearly embodies the healing, the heroism, the chutzpah,
the lyrical and tragic, the mask of grotesquerie — and perhaps most important of all, the spinal courage, the articulated, stalking, indomitable **no**
which today is the chief ingredient of that vocation. Quite a human. Quite
a Christian.

ARTISTS UNDER FIRE

Kim Chi Ha also writes poetry. The "also" is of import to anyone who seeks
the sources of such a life. But in a sense, the "also" is redundant. How could
the Christian life be anything but an art? And how could that art sustain
itself under the fiercest attack, unless it were drawing on the grace of a
spiritual tradition? It seems to me Kim is summoning energies every
Christian has available, to be savored or neglected, recouped or stifled. His
poetry is his state of grace; but the grace is under pressure. In New York
recently, we welcomed two prisoners back from hell. One of them, an
Iranian poet and editor, had been tortured in the prisons of the shah.
Another, a distinguished Ukranian mathematician, had spent seven years in
a Moscow psychiatric hospital, where he had been injected, browbeaten,
experimented on. Evidently, by their deportment on release, by speaking

out again, these men were showing more clearly than any medical opinion could, how their spirit had won over the commissars and colonels.

These were among the few lucky ones; they survived. Kim Chi Ha has not yet come out; chances are that he will not. It is important, in consequence, that Americans connect with such spirits as his, not like parasites seeking an injection of greatness, cheaply bought, but in deep trouble of spirit, realizing first of all that, in large measure, America makes the fate of such prisoners inevitable.

A question arises; why do such people, honorable spirits, persons of front rank achievement and undoubted courage, get locked up? In a sense, the reason lies in the meld of genius, the moral edginess, the out of step minds, the hearts that nurture the fire. Why seek further? Their trouble is their humanity; they die of it.

THE WEIGHT OF WORDS

In Kim's case, as in that of the Iranian, one is struck by another element of trouble, something about the power of the word, spoken or written, polemic or poetry. Indeed a suspicion arises that in many countries, the word has an impact that is very skillfully dissipated in the "free west."

In our culture, the word, trivial, outrageous, laden with genius, is usually heard with a yawn, a wink, a tic of agreement or dissent, a shrug. In any case, with a switch of channels. A word is an image on a cave wall; it is replaceable instantaneously by another image. It is a kind of mirage, it promises what it cannot deliver, it conceals everything it should come out with, the real message is the invisible one.

How to explain the widely differing weights granted to words in different political and cultural climates? One at least knows that the differences exist, to a degree that gives serious pause, and offers clues to weighty matters indeed. It is commonly assumed that in America one can write practically anything, say practically anything — hard porn, big claims, political absurdities, highly placed lies — and get away with it. One can even try to speak the truth; one is heard and not heeded. One discusses, debates, publishes (if lucky); the words get lost. One sees his or her words vanish into thin air.

A notable contrast! In South Korea, a poet writes a few lines — and the junta leans forward, all ears. He is arrested, rigorously judged, condemned. How can this be? Why are speech and writing charged with political and religious lightning? Why must the poet's mouth be bloodied, his teeth caved in?

A GIFT OF BREAD

I read somewhere a story that offered me a clue. It concerned a village baker, who for some period of time neglected his work, passed whole days in silence, kept to himself. Evidently he was pondering some deep affair, kept jealously to himself. Doctors were consulted; after observing him, they assured his family there was no need of treatment; he would in all likelihood recover on his own. Which indeed happened, or seemed to. One bright morning, the baker opened his shutters. He had passed the night at his ovens; the loaves were placed proudly in his window. But, when he unlocked his doors, an unexpected twist; he stood not behind the counter, but in the doorway. In his hand were some leaflets. The message, it appeared, was a blockbuster. The baker wrote that since bread was obviously meant for hungry people, and since the hungriest people had no money to buy, henceforth his bread was not for sale. It was to be given away.

All day, the shop was inundated by the poor, as might be expected. The shelves were emptied. The baker's family was confounded; the doctors came running. They seized the leaflet, shook their grey polls, ordered the baker locked up indefinitely in a mental hospital.

Thus far our story. To me, it said something regarding the mysterious fate of the poet Kim. The baker could be tolerated (by his family, by medicos) as long as he merely thought his rambunctious thoughts, kept them under his baker's cap. But when he began to act! When the word of the gospel came to light in his mind—that was the flash point. At that moment, the organized, hyphenated insanity of state-medicine-family-economics, began to move in. Our friend had crossed a line. He was no longer manageable, a well-intentioned churchgoing integer (what another prisoner would call a "good cog in a lock step"). Giving away bread? Where would such things stop?

Consequences. They fell on the baker like an avalanche.

The story concludes beautifully. The author wrote, "Our Master, who was also a baker of sorts, also suffered the consequences of His gift of bread to the poor." Amen.

POLITICAL IMAGINATION

Evidently the poet Kim also reached a point of no return. His prison diary is an infinitely moving pot-pourri of nightmare and insight, vision and horror. At one point, he writes, he touched "the height of artistic vision . . . a glittering zenith of wholeness of human values and sublimities. . . . I began to feel as though I were in touch with the mystery of the spirit. . . ." Another phrase occurs to him, as he gropes to express the clarity that flooded his soul. He writes of "the power of political imagination."

This I take to be the heart of the matter, his self-understanding, his predicament. He is in trouble; he knows why; better, he imagines why.

Kim is dangerous to the political powers because he has come upon another way than theirs, other resources, other grace, true community. In a burst of agony, under their clubs, in degradation and torture, he has discovered what Buber calls the power "to imagine the real world." In doing so—in seizing on that reality of nonviolence and peaceableness of spirit, of resistance to tyranny, the veritable flowering of the kingdom of the heart— Kim has dealt a twist of the knife in the rotten vitals, the sewer of damnation, the **No Exit** of commissars, torturers, shahs, nuclear tinkers, czars, and all their adoring legions of obedient cogs. Power indeed, political imagination indeed!

No idle dream either. Kim is in prison, under torture, sentenced to death at least once; proof enough of his resolve, and the uneasy respect of his captors. "The power of political imagination," I translate the admirable phrase to say. The imagination is no transmitter of cheap dreams; neither is it a storehouse of drugs, or a fabricator of fantasy. It is not a way out of the pain of the world. It is rather a self-directing power of turning human life around—in the direction of the human. It is the human power to judge the inhuman, from the soul outward, into the public arena. It is self-purifying; it calls one to account—for time wasted, for self-indulgence, for cultural surrender.

It stands under judgment, and it judges. Thus surrounded by "a pack of dogs" (as the psalmist writes), clearly judging the bestial conduct of others, it cancels judgment in order to allow the persecutor space in which to repent. (Father forgive them; they know not what they do.)

Such insight is a gift; it cannot be concocted or even deserved. Further, it must be followed through, acted on, realized. And precisely here is the rub. Enacting what one has once seen (given the ersatz "real" world of executioners and victims) is a bloody business indeed. Nothing imagined unless embodied! The one who believes this is dangerous to the Caesarian state. He gives bread away. He seeks, works, endures, on behalf of something that does not even exist—a public structure that (to paraphrase Peter Maurin) would make it easier for men and women to be ecstatics.

So Kim begins. In the pit of unlikelihood, at sea level of survival, in the dungeons and interrogation centers of the crushers and melders, he verifies his vision. He tests it out on his own flesh. More, he sends scraps, messages to the living, about "the power of political imagination." The messages are bloodstained (his own blood), they are also postmarked (a warning), **hell**.

ALONG THE TORTURE ROAD

The ironies have to be brought up close before they can be seen for what they are, something more than interlocking gentleman's agreements. This is what the political imagination does. It introduces, one to another, what Mao calls "the contradictions." The adversaries are invited to shake hands, not in order to resolve the unresolvable, but as prelude to honorable combat, in which the character, soul, historic validity, of each will be illumined, in conflict, chaos even; and finally, a burst of light, a higher resolution.

I ask myself; what is the widest contradiction I know of today; what is the widest split in the human soul? I think it is exactly the one Kim speaks

of in his prison diary. It is the one which gunfire, nuclear fire, wars on
poverty, wars on cancer (wars on humans), military rape of the cosmos, all
grandiosities of academe and church—all these have served only to widen,
bless, maintain, beef up, police. But never to bridge or heal.

Kim writes of the contradiction, the split—and then the unity:

> I felt these words were deeply carved into the bottom of my heart like
> red hot brands. Yes, "the power of political imagination," the wedding
> of politics and art in the highest sense of the words. It is not an absurd
> relationship.
>
> Unity. Yes. At last, I have bridged the gap in a single leap—between
> my mass movements, political activities, and artistic creation—the gap
> that had driven me insane for so long. The definitive answer to this
> enigma has been presented to me through the torture road. An
> extravagant, extravagant moment. At that time, I muttered to myself,
> "I thank you," and these almost unspeakable words, "I am honored."

Volumes could be written, from many perspectives, on the insight so
bloodily won, so artlessly offered. Let me point out one immensely
important sentence; Kim insists that the "power of political imagination"
comes alive in him only "through the torture road." The condition of
awakening is the electric clash between utmost degradation and the riding
spirit. Simple as that. Let the engineers of cheap change take notice, drug
purveyors, instant salvationists, those who offer sinister short cuts to
ecstasy. And let those of us who love to mess about in the same vile alchemy
also take warning. There is blood on the road which Kim travels. It is not
the low road, it is not named Good Intentions. Its only recommendation is
this—it leads otherwhere than to hell.

Need one add that in the case of Kim, the virtue of torture road is not
that it is tortuous, but that it is a road? That is to say, along such a road,
laid out, designed to be the only road, the iron clad one, the imperial one,
the guarded one, one creates alternate routes. In this sense, politics, the
politics of compassion, of resistance, of legitimate self-love, is itself an
exercise of the imagination.

BRINGING THE KINGDOM

One stubbornly recurrent symbol of this act is a biblical one; one cannot but
think of it when Kim writes of his awakening. The ultimate political form
of things which the Lord imagines, under many images, is the Kingdom:
seed, jewel, great banquet, tree, harvest, inner harmony, eventual world
harmony. In any case, a community suffused with love, the transfigured
structure of a twice born humanity.

Kim dreams of this. More, following the biblical injunction, he suffers in
order to bring it nearer. He is grounded in this world (who more so than a
prisoner?)—at the same time, he is released from its gravity. He tries and

fails, tries and succeeds, always with the understanding that both outcomes are provisory, that another chapter is yet to be written, another age carries it on. Still, he is never demoralized, moving in circles, chasing a will-o'-the-wisp in vainglory or despair. He knows the outcome of things, in hope, knowing "all manner of things will be well." And for the present he insures, as far as he can, as long as he can, that things at least will be less unwell.

What a word he offers us, what a stretched irony, what a cry from the rack—a fetid cell in Seoul, a poet who announces the immanence of the Kingdom! More, he verifies his word with those indispensable virtues which are the squared blocks of the Kingdom—courage, good humor, staying power.

The Kingdom? Immanent? Normally, we slog along, doing what we can from day to day, out of a dogged persistence, none the less admirable for being not at all ecstatic. We do what we can; only in the rarest moments do we gain hints of other vistas, other rhythms. We long for the good, reach toward it, are grateful for its presence in those we love and work with. Unless we are fools, we spend little time casting heroic runes for ourselves; we have taken our own measure; better than any tyrant, we know our own limits.

At the insular end of human development, overcome frequently by the suffocation of hope, forever put off, deceived, treated like vagrants or children (by vagrants and moral children), elated and put down by false messiahs, we feel shamed, cheated before our own souls. This is the bicentennial mood, a wintry discontent in July. (As I write these words, a procession of worthies gathers before a congressional committee, in Washington, assuring the members that violence is inevitable on July 4. The mirror game goes on.) We have scarcely an inkling of what the good life, in the sense our history speaks of it, our Bible speaks of it, might consist. The church offers a few paltry clues, the state none at all—quite the opposite. In both cases, the vocation of the word is the vocation of the speaker—blah.

Yet, we would like to be "doers of the word," not as those "vainly beating the air." We are sick of cheap charisms, one-track radicals, political card sharps. It is our epitaph; we have tried everything, every nostrum, drug, quick cure, instant improver, ardent consumers as we are. Traveled every road. Reached a dead end.

Every road except one?

Ragged and frail, a sorry figure staggers along torture road. Scarcely making it, bloody, marked by the stigmata of his resolve, he keeps on keeping on.

For Christians it is an old story, an old road. By now it ought also to be a well-traveled one. That it is not, that Kim goes it alone, that Christians are not crying out at this crime (at so many crimes, multiplied across the bloody face of the earth), this too is an old story. (This week the Vatican is sweating out a last ditch effort to "defeat communism" in the national elections.)

Kim goes on, he "stands far off" from assimilation; he refuses to be squared off into a paving stone; he tests his stamina, sends us crudely scrawled maps. He seeks—in dreams, ironies, oppositions, fantasies, broadsides, parables, nightmares, satires—what the political imagination might forge, by way of a future, by way of the human, along torture road.

REFLECTIONS ALONG THE ROAD

A few reflections occur, in conclusion. I pray that they, and the words of this essay, may not be entirely unworthy of the vistas Kim Chi Ha has opened.

—A "politics of imagination" is necessarily modest, in scope and method. It avoids the inflation of spirit so common to those who are possessed by the machine, who want change fast, want it new, want it cheap, want everyone to change (it goes without saying) except themselves, want human betterment (whatever that means) but want to lose nothing. The impasse, the horned dilemma. Its outcome—no change, except for the worse.

—"The honor of dishonor." Pauline, Nietzschean, Maoist, the ironies have to be explored, weighed, given space, heard from, suffered over; otherwise one falls between stools—sour spiritism, rampaging activism; either one, the payment of tribute to Caesar. The old saw, "everyone wants to go to heaven, nobody wants to die." Exactly.

—Sam Melville wrote from prison, shortly before he was murdered. The subject was ecstasy. Ecstasy in Attica? The idea is so close to madness as to make one suspect he too came on a new breakthrough, like Kim's. We would like to have safe places in which to levitate. Prisoners have other news for us. No levitating, except by crucifixion.

—Ecstasy, along with everything else, can be bought and sold. Witness the drug czars, and their coterie of gurus. It always ends in a corner, not on an open road. The corner marked "fascism."

—In time of deluge, everything becomes an item in a fire sale, a water sale, a garage sale. Marked down, damaged. Religion too. Normally part of the culture, it is also part of the catastrophe, victim, victimizer. Discounted. Except, the religion of Kim.

—From Marx, "Bourgeois revolutions advance gradually from success to success; their dramatic effects keep piling up; people and things seem illuminated by diamond-like fires. Ecstasy is the permanent state of society. But these revolutions are short lived: they soon reach their apotheosis and then a wide depression takes hold of society. . . . "

—From a document circulating in Latin America (IDOC 06597), "If the experiences of the charismatics had been authentic, they would have already passed from the stage of disciples to that of apostles—those who are sent. They would have committed themselves to just causes, giving the hungry to eat, and the thirsty to drink, struggling for the liberation of the captives, and most of all, allying themselves with the poor of this world who cry out for better wages, and whose cry, according to James 5, has reached the ear of God."

— Jesus, "This is my command to you: love one another. If the world hates you, it hated me first, as you know well. If you belonged to the world, the world would love its own; but because you do not belong to the world, for that reason, the world hates you. Remember what I said: A servant is not greater than his master. As they persecuted me, they will persecute you; they will follow your teaching as little as they have followed mine. It is on my account that they will treat you thus, because they do not know the One who sent me" (Jn. 15, 17).

— Kim: "The death sentence was proclaimed. Both Kim Byong-Kon and I laughed. Byong-Kon began his last statement: 'This is an honor . . . ' What in the world does that mean, 'an honor'? What is this all about? . . . Are these the words of saints? Are we saints? . . . Can we who know their barbarism too well, flirt with the luxury of sarcasm? No it is not that. What do these words then mean? We at last conquered our terror of death."

Thus the ecstasy, which like life itself has no purpose beyond itself, which was prepared for along that road named Torture, bears its fruit. It conquers the fear of death. In so doing, it conquers death itself.

— Ecstasy gives the tortured one back to the living. He is the only one worthy of being trusted with the world, with life itself, with children, with the poor, with the holy and human. Such a one is Kim. The others join the executioners, or fall into despair, and so join the victims. In any case, lose the third way; no third eye.

— Almost everyone believes that the removal of some person, some class, some "problem," would clean up the world. Mister Clean is always bigger than human; he sees further than you or me, a kind of transhistorical Warmaker on Dirt. Trouble is, his definition of dirt tends to get all inclusive; today armed with a nuclear aerosal can, he has a new gleam in his eye, "Why, let's clean up everybody, while we're at it!"

— It goes without saying that, armed with a like immaculate obsession, the jailers and torturers of Kim believe that his removal would clean up Korea, making it safe for Sani-flush, Kleenex and Coke. In this they are, of course, correct.

— The above mentality and skill is ambidextrous; it functions equally well, right or left. Once death is adopted as a social method, human lives become strictly unnecessary, except insofar as life may be, here and there, slightly more "useful" than death. Thus death proliferates, even under the ideology and aegis of life. The right invokes the ideology, so does the left. It all works, the machinery moves on, in the same old way. One day the slogan is law and order, the next it is revolution. And innocent people die, are tortured, are exiled, degraded, under the mad cross fire. They are never consulted, it goes without saying, regarding their fate.

THE CATHOLIC WORKER, JULY-AUGUST 1976

Ezra Pound: A Season in Hell

A REVIEW OF *EZRA POUND:*
THE LAST ROWER, A POLITICAL PROFILE,
BY C. DAVID HEYMANN

THERE are no short cuts around Ezra Pound. Artist, freak, madman, good hater, macho, *il miglior fabbro*, lord of word and image, friend of the great and fender of the fallen, exile, victim, vile haranguer—and finally, master of the sacred silence. He forged the American experience, fitted it to his finger like a wedding band, wore it to a watery grave. *Homo Americanus*, working the dream for all its worth, both sides of the street, both ends of the world, within, without, yin and yang, fame and degradation. Were these the sources, these oppositions, never reconciled? Call them a clue.

I remember sitting on Danbury ice, reading Pound on Chinese ideograms, so intrigued I'd copy the images, cut them from soap erasers and stamp them in color on letters home. Anything to liven up the house of the dead. I read the Cantos again and again, the masterful one on usury:

> with usura. . . .
> no picture is made to endure nor to live with
> but is made to sell and sell quickly
> with usura, sin against nature,
> is thy bread ever more of stale rags
> is thy bread dry as paper,
> with no mountain wheat, no strong flour [Canto XLV]

And years before, I'd come on a small volume of his essays; this one on money, how the dollar and its ancestry had abstracted people from the land, alienated their work. It must have been one of his better efforts; I don't remember any loud arguments, only that it seemed to make sense. Especially since I had read somewhere, about the same time, that the late middle ages introduced a money economy, and then the church also began to lock up the Bread of the eucharist. Locked banks and locked tabernacles—that made no sense at all, except as twin devices to keep food from people, land from workers, salvation from this world.

Pound thought art was a saving act. It was as simple as that. He was a Pelagian through and through. He came up through the culture, anointed (self-anointed, inevitably) to remake things, ride them under hobbledehoy, armed with untouchable innocence, a big head packed with talent—and no conscience.

Yet immediately as I write this, I know I must modify it; he was far from dead to generous impulses, a sense of common needs. Some of the instances are well known. He borrowed and plagued and begged for others. He cared for Eliot and got Frost published (a thankless venture if ever there was one). He rammed poets down the craws of editors, started magazines on his own, got money somehow for ventures that were bound to go unappreciated, unread. And all the while, he gave not a spit for personal comfort, income, lived poor, at the edge.

It all makes the outcome more foolish, unclear, a waste.

At what point did all this decency go awry, what bent the soul of this clairvoyant, what fueled the hatred? He said toward the end, in one of his spates of anguish, "USURY; I was out of focus, taking a symptom for a cause. The cause is AVARICE." Was the fault just that, magnified, extended a thousandfold; never in his life had he been spiritually in focus, his ego creaturely before reality. Was he Kierkegaard's classic esthetic soul, taking vengeance on others, on the world, for not being like himself, malfocused, out of joint?

In any case, what followed was pure shame: radio broadcasts during the second war on behalf of Mussolini, fawning letters to the Big Brute. And above and beyond all credence—the anti-Jewish hatred.

Maybe the truth was (many have thought so) that he was rootless, that he gave not a damn about America or anyplace else—or anyone else. And being so, willful, bereft of loyalty, touching nothing as native, holding no one dear, mesmerized by his heady ideal society—always ancient, never verifiable, China, Languedoc; appalled also by the horror of a world drifting toward another round of slaughter, traumatized, the classic shadow of the Problem of Evil falling on him, freezing him; like the crudest redneck alive (or the most refined intellectual alive, it makes small difference in such matters), Pound went hunting for scapegoats, the favorite sport of purported innocents, domestically or foreignly.

And paid for it.

He was never one to keep his opinings under a bushel. The madder they were, it seemed, the more generously he must spout. The more they were beamed abroad, the more outrageous, sour, irrational they became. It was an early lesson in someone's Law of the Media, to wit; The more you talk, the less gets heard. Or (in wartime parlance): He who spouts, gets sunk.

Indeed. It was the time of that distant, second world war; fought on the curious assumption that at long last, all the devils of history had coalesced in one; and that one scotched, on the run. Once he was downed, once that deranged falsetto was silenced (so the theory went, fervently peddled by states and state churches), all God's people would find themselves breathing free, exorcised. And forever. No matter that we had learned the demon's methods too well in the very act of dealing with him; Dresden, the fire storms over the cities, Hiroshima finally. No matter that the eumenides were smiling a subtle smile, were drawing closer, a pursuit of the furies. There was to be no end to innocence; even murder would not heal it.

Did Pound see events in such terms, as he raved and yelled on Italian radio, denouncing, berating, stirring his hot pot of scurrility, making less and less sense, grown windily mad on his own nostrums? Had he gone witless at sight of a truth that could not be looked on, a Medusa? It may be so; it may not. In any case, one did not have to love America in the infantile way America demands, when it declares war and enlists all grown minds — one could resist such nonsense, as many in fact did. And yet, in so resisting, one need not fall into the arms of the Great Bear, shuffling at the end of a Nazi leash. Nor praise folly. Nor serve it. Nor philander to it. Nor sell one's soul. All of which is precisely what Pound did.

Thus the pathology named, at least in the official indictment: treason. In normal times, that noose lies slack on the ground, half hidden, all but forgotten, an animal trap out of season. War puts a hand to the rope, draws it in, ever so slowly.

Pound undoubtedly thought himself in the clear. He was living abroad, he was self-contained, angry, he had assurance, success, the brassy tongue of the "definitive solver."

He broadcast what he pleased, he thought himself in the clear. But he had, in fact, set up his foolish project in the exact center of a lethal circumference. With scarcely a whisper, it was closing, a garrote. He was repatriated, at the war's end.

All manner of legal jockeyings got him declared mentally incompetent to stand trial. As matters turned out, the move was somewhat less than brilliant. It resulted in a twelve year stint in the third circle, St. Elizabeth's Hospital, in Washington:

> where the dead walked
>   and the living were made of
>   cardboard

[CANTO CXV]

The war ended; with it came a demand for unconditional surrender. That savage outcome must perforce include all those who, in one way or another, by resisting, by fleeing, by refusing, had given a species of aid to the enemy. Pound's crime was notorious. Now he stood at the bar named Justice.

He had been "mentally unhinged" for a long time; which is to say out of touch, out of mind, self-consumed, envious. Then the breakthrough; he lit on a brilliant univocal solution. Mark well the "enemy"; so cunning, so well implanted in consciousness and the peoples' confidence as to be all but invisible there, even named, rewarded as benefactor. Hunt it down, cut its throat. Finally he put on its skin for his own. Thus the game's progress, from goat hunter to scapegoat.

He stood in court, quavering, slack headed, without focus. A weird logic had ordered his repatriation, in fetters. The reasoning went like this: First drive him mad, then declare him mad.

In Pisa, after his capture, they put him "in a specially constructed, grilled 'security cage,' heavy duty air strip welded over galvanized mesh. Pound called his cell the *gabbia*, gorilla cage. Like the others (reserved for men about to be executed), it measured six feet by six. . . . A tarpaper roof provided little shelter from sun or rain. By night a special reflector poured glaring light into his cage alone. He slept on the cold cement floor. He was fed meager rations once a day. His toilet was a tin can." For three weeks he was in the cage; for five months more, under scarcely better conditions in the Detention Training Center, maintained for the toughest army criminals.

On November 18, 1945, they brought him home. He was thrown into the District of Columbia jail, a noisome Civil War relic, a place at once cruel, unusual, and punishing. (I remember well its superior facilities; they included roaches, rats, mad fellow prisoners, a noise factor such as to addle the most collected wits, extreme filth, hot and cold temperatures, absolute isolation.) No wonder Pound appeared in court looking like a loosely strung puppet.

> Nor can who has passed a month in the death cells
>   believe in capital punishment
> No man who has passed a month in the death cells
>   believes in cages for beasts

> [CANTO LXXXIII]

"Pound's women" appear in Heymann's book in exactly that crude macho guise; i.e., Pound's women. Indians in Americanized history, Palestinians in the *New York Times*, Namibians *passim*, TV Indians. There is a cruel consistency in Heymann's method; like a Fellini camera, he moves so close to his subject as to get swallowed. All that decadence (all that Poundage on the hoof)—is the method a moral comment, is it stroking, is it holding its nose, is it smiling behind a mask?

Pound married, early in life. One might have thought the event, among other things, was a political act, therefore within the ambit of "a political profile." Not at all. He married (thus far Heymann; or thus far Pound) as he might have bought a toothbrush, an overnight convenience. Who Dorothy Shakespear was, what were her attitudes toward war, money, Jews, literature, vorticism, cubism, or Pound, we are not told. Did these things matter? Did they matter to Dorothy, to Pound, or to Heymann because of Pound? We are not told.

Olga was a concert violinist, Pound was—Pound. He was already married, when Love Took Over. Of Dorothy's antecedence, nothing. The silence is in line with the biographer's method (of Dorothy's consequences— nothing). She yielded, whether with grace or fury, to the onslaught of a "great goddess," "a dream passing over the face in the half-light," "the line of the cameo." The portent's name was Olga Rudge, but the effluence is of course Pound's, the inflationary sweep of the rake on the rove.

Then there were children; and for awhile, a *menage à trois* (or *cinq*, depending on the count). But the presence of children seemed never to have registered. Pound's mind was in another direction; he spelled it "kulcher," despising it while he paid for it. Like a woman.

When he treats of Dorothy or Olga, Heymann seems to put on Pound's spectacles. From that moment he is as myopic as Pound himself, of the damage wrought, the debts owed. (He has thoughtful moral comment on every other failing of Pound.) But what about this sentiment, concerning Dorothy Pound toward the end of her life?: "And Dorothy Pound, still a picture of Attic grace, lived half the year in Rapallo near Ezra, the other half in England near her son. Somehow she too had jumbled her life. . . . " One wonders at the "somehow"; one puzzles over the "jumble." No light is offered. Pound's women were, in fact, startlingly like Pound's Jews. Except that, the world being what it is, half ridden, half unconscious, his anti-Semitism became an international scandal. Where he stood on women, how he used women, went by the board.

He was no Dante, he was never able to finish the Cantos. The reason is as much hidden in ourselves as in him. About hell, we have some ideas, and about purgatory a few others, having been there. On the subject of heaven, we are uncommonly mute.

It has been your habit for long to do away with good writers.
You either drive them mad, or else you blink at their suicides

Or else you condone their drugs, and talk of insanity and genius,
But I will not go mad to please you.

[SALUTATION THE THIRD, 1914]

He very nearly did. Or perhaps did; if not to please, then to spite. And the government replied in kind; it declared him non compos, sent him off to a warehouse to play booby for the rest of his mortal life. That failing, falling once more into sanity (Catch 22), he was to be fetched back to court, compos and all.

All the world loves a madman. Or so it seems. The world flocked to Pound, chained at the center, a rare and pampered panda. The pilgrimages even had religious overtones. Il maestro had joined the company of immortal bedlamites, he was declared insane by an ordaining structure which refused to bear with the cranky brawling genius on a flagpole, messing the flag. . . .

There was an element of self-justification, even a search for healing, in the visitors. Writers habitually flock together, migrate, teach, write, claim their cash and medals; but all this is no more than rite and rote. Pound offered them something more; he had broken from the wheel, had very nearly broken his head. *There* was the excitement, there he sat amid the debris, the books, the interminable notes and projects, a broken king in a madhouse alcove. He was the very type and ideal of romantic hero, he had done it all, he had circumnavigated, braved the Horn, and come back. Mad? In his madness lay his method, every distinguished hand extended, crowned him anew.

Twelve years. Denounced, segregated, locked up, he produced or reworked, or enlarged ten books, at least six of them absolutely irreplaceable. *The Unwobbling Pivot, Personae, Selected Poems, Guide to Kulcher, The Classic Anthology Defined by Confucius, The Women of Trachis.* He wrote feverishly, unevenly, for magazines in the U.S., England, Australia, innumerable political tracts, editorials, letters, manifestoes. Mostly, they were the work of the old pitchman — edgy, browbeating, scurrilous. Friends kept his name green; there were poetry readings, tributes, literary criticism, birthday commemorations.

In his account of the years in St. Elizabeth's, Heymann disposes of Dorothy Pound in the following ineffable passage:

Another muse, this one permanently displaced, was the Maestro's wife. Dorothy Pound visited St. Elizabeth's nearly every day for twelve years. Her husband's confinement forced her to live in the drab and rundown neighborhood surrounding the hospital. . . . She seemed to exist only for her husband, one visitor remarked, and as a result suffered almost without respite. Yet for all her selflessness she was terribly naive. . . .

Was there ever an apter dismissal of the Woman As Appendage? "She was terribly naive"; no explanation is offered. Indeed, as in the case of slaves, delinquents, minors, and the insane (except the insane great), none is required. She was required only to follow her fate; her biology, as they say, was her destiny.

For twelve terrible years, while the mandarins beat a path to the door and laid down their tributes, while the politicized literate and the illiterate pols made of him their Cause, this "terribly naive" woman took dictation, bore with the volcano's huffings, posted letters, typed poems and prose, kept the lifeline humming. She scrounged her own life, a life of sorts, out of a dustbin. She camped out in a hovel near the hospital, bereft of every comfort, evidently in the hope (we are not told her hope) that Pound would someday be released. He was — because of her.

Still, this woman simply did not count. No one has written her life story, she never composed an heroic stanza, never hated a Jew nor played footsy with Fascists. For twelve years she stood by, lived in silence and service, the shade of a ragged wild-eyed shade. She deserved better of life; better of Pound, better of his biographer. But Pound after all was a genius; and she, alas, only faithful, only a woman.

Is Pound's treatment of women a clue (maybe *the* clue) to his political fascism? Heymann never raises the question.

Fascism, violence as social method, such things hang together, adhere in certain minds. Not only in Hitler, but in many intellectuals, artists, true believers, those who, according to every Catalogue of Advantage, should know better. So should we all. So should have Ezra. Which reflection might give pause to the hardiest spirit, armed with weighty credentials from whatever Center of Enlightenment. *Pace* Ezra and his stoned promethean mind, and lest we make of him an example of The One Who Had Everything But Unaccountably Went Wrong, the following chastened reflection is offered. It was not the Southern California admen or the Texas hustlers who concocted our very own Vietnam war. It was the academics from our classic citadels, the abominable architects who streamed into D.C. to set things right. ("Things" being translated, that little war that simply had to get bigger before it could get better.) They were the best and the brightest, they waved their bloody blueprint in the dawn's early light, they pushed us, punch drunk, into ten years of horror. Let not our Ezra be over-blamed, let him not be called the solitary curse of our line. There are more of him. There always are.

Of all that spotty deranged life, a season in hell, the closing did him most honor.

I had never before thought of silence as a form of atonement. Heymann implies, and I think rightly, that Pound saw it so; that at some point toward the end, he took a great vow; simply to shut up. And thus to repair in measure that lifelong excess, the more piled upon more and signifying nothing, the violation of Greek middle ground. Had he read the Letter of James on sins of the tongue? Its cadences would have pleased him. But far beyond the esthetic, his soul would have twisted in recognition:

What a huge stack of timber can be set ablaze by the tiniest spark! And the tongue is in effect, a fire. It represents among our members the world with all its wickedness; it pollutes our whole being; it keeps the wheel of our existence red hot, and its flames are fed by hell. . . . No man can subdue the tongue. It is an intractable evil, charged with deadly venom. We use it to sing the praises of our Lord and Father, and we use it to invoke curses on our fellows who are made in God's likeness.

No more turmoil, no more aggrandizing, no more hatred. He cut out his tongue, he cauterized his soul.

It was the closest he would come to that Paradiso which always escaped his pen.

Those last years! Tortured, yet strangely resilient, mournful, self-blaming, yet on occasion moved to tears by a gesture of tenderness; he made a classic of his taking off.

He had conquered both fame and infamy, his own crimes and the world's bloody rejoinder. Out of his moral depth for most of his life, floundering in ignorance, anger—now he trod water, a twice born creature. The transformation transformed those around. He had been a puzzle for so many years, a labyrinth of false turns, tortured contradictions, a cul-de-sac of a soul. Now he was transfigured; his face wore the inscrutable sublime mask of a mystery.

One of those who came to visit was Allen Ginsberg. (I had seen Allen in action before, and since. In New York, in 1974, a fervent ecumenical effort was underway to have me tossed out of the universe. A prize had been offered; then at the end of a string, pulled away. The War Resisters League offered a consolation packet. Allen offered to present it, and a poem to boot. I'll not soon forget the calm, goodness, depth of the man. And one remembered how years before, during the Chicago Convention frenzies, he had turned the lions around; how the beleaguered followed his chant OM, how he slowed pulses, made peace.) He arrived to visit Pound in Venice, October, 1967. Old Silent warmed to him as the days went by. Allen proved as skillful as the other in the dance of silence. Allen walked with the old man, they played records and listened together, Allen sang his Blake songs.

Then the silence broke, a torrent, tears—was it paradiso or purgatorio? "The intention was bad. . . . That's the trouble—anything I've done has been an accident. Any good has been spoiled by my intentions, the preoccupation with irrelevant and stupid things. . . . But the worst mistake I made was that stupid, suburban prejudice of anti-Semitism. All along, that spoiled everything."

Not everything was spoiled. Amen.

The Whale's Tale

I have a man inside me
like the universe.

It all seemed like the most natural thing in the world. To begin with, a day of utmost beauty. I was steaming along on my own, a cloudless blue sky, the sea trackless and shimmering; an impressive argument for, so to speak, the providence of God.

Then, with shocking suddenness and no prior consultation, a storm overhead. Well, I reflected swallowing hard, what, after all, is a storm to me. It merely heightens the joy and variety of the course—like running through a great forest instead of a mowed field. Blowing and spinning, sending up clouds of steam, I plow along, in wonderment at the harsh grandeur of the primary weather. Waves that break and form again, momentary cliffs; I leap off one, carried along on the tip of another, the waters in perpetual ecstasy, forming, dissolving, taking shape, breaking up. So caught up in life, the waters like ecstatic dancers, moment by moment tossing aside, assuming their guises.

Then, like a thunderclap, ahead of me, trouble.

A ship wallowing and limping along, half its yards sheared away.

What a scupperful of fools, I snorted, out on such a day. They have all the earth for their own, what more do they want?

But for all my annoyance, cursed with my great heart I kept drawing near, alongside or in her wake; though it was hard work, indeed, keeping that tortured mote in view through so monstrous a vortex.

In regard to them, I know only one law; when things are bad, there's worse to come. As though a ship in distress weren't enough to contend with, there's the sailors. With them, you never know what's going to happen, once folly takes over. I've seen them scuttle a perfectly sound ship and leap into the void in sieves one tenth the size of the decks they jump from. They pray to their gods, you see them shivering and yelling on deck, on their knees no less—and you know it; anything can happen. I've seen them dance around in a frenzy, then break off, break away, leap over-board, deck, then air, sea, never loosening their grip on one another.

Now I was closer. They were praying all right. The marathon was on. I pulled nearer.

Kneeling in a circle on a deck, a poor water-soaked bundle in their midst; they were attending to it with the ominous devotion that always precedes some horrible move, something religious. Three of them picked him up, unresisting (he was probably religious, too). The others stood there in the fury of wind, the storm coming at them horizontal, demons tossing brimstone in their faces. Arms raised, faces a concentrated horror, they stumbled toward the railing of that foundering scow, imprecating, the unresisting bundle dragged along. A burial at sea, they were burying him alive!

Oh I know their ilk, they and their gods. Why should they give a sou about one another? Their religion forbids it.

They threw him over, to hell and gone.

And I caught the bundle of misery neatly on a fluke, tossed it forward to a flipper.

Held him up there, like a newborn babe, eye to eye. Who was this castaway? A prophet?

When that suspicion dawned, I almost pulled in my life-saving equipment and let him go down. Trod water there only half believing my eyes.

How'd I know who he was? I didn't for certain. But in our line of work, and given our age on earth, the chances were overwhelming. We're always being called on to save their chestnuts. The bestiary of providence — whales, porpoises, ravens, lions, jackasses even. Prophets loud as thunder on the saving word, short as sticks on consequences. No, they rush forward, despise the anger, danger, bad-mouthing, death even. Onward Christian soldiers! That's their disease, it's called glory.

Well, there I was, this morsel of misery on the end of my flipper, blinking back at me like the day of his birth. Storm blowing doomsday, rising and falling in unison, a mad madrigal. A prophet, I knew it. It could only be.

They all look — how to put it? — like the half-drowned cat that just swallowed the half-dead canary. Not exactly living, better off than dead. He sat there hanging on, a steady look, a mouse in a cat's cradle. He knew all along I'd be hanging about, just waiting for the sublime privilege of plucking him from the sea; that salvation look, unmelting, unto himself, beyond circumstance.

I saw it in his eyes. When they tossed him into the drenched air like a corpse in its canvas — he didn't care a whit! That's what his look said, louder than words. He didn't care; there might be nothing between him and salty oblivion, or there might be a whale's right arm to pluck him out of the sea.

Why should he care? There was always an option. Savior whale, killer sea, that wasn't all there was. I shouldn't get overbearing. What greater privilege for a mere whale anyway, than to save the Lord's anointed?

Of course, we're supposed to be at their beck, snatching them from ruin. By such a neat arrangement they wipe out at a stroke the heroism, the coolheadedness, the near miraculous benignity, of our vocation. And in the process, canonize their own vagaries. Behold, the Lord's handpicked can do no wrong!

This one wasn't exactly jaunty, though. After all, he'd had a shakeup, his future was uncertain. But he was confident! Neck deep in innocence. He hadn't lived long enough to realize what a triphammer life is, beating you out of one shape, into another.

His first adventure; he was like an infant tossed between playful adults. Younger than I, by a century or so, no beard, eyes too big to qualify for the world. He looked more like the captain's boy than the captain; all the harder to reason with.

Well, this was the conversation that followed, I swear it.

By no means repenting his situation, he began: "Good day, sir." Oh he was cool. Here we were only half in this world, a small chip on the back of a large one, both caught in a tidal wave, and he wished me a good day, sir!

—I thank you for your service this day. You have saved me from a watery end. (Which minus the cliché was the naked truth.)

—Blameless as I am, I was tossed overboard by heathen sailors. They know no better, as you are aware, being worshipers of false gods. (Couldn't resist rolling out his big guns on me, perched a half-inch from the abyss as he was, totally dependent on me for the salvation of his limbs. Improve me he would!)

—You may be sure you have won a great blessing by your saving action, he blared.

—You have preserved a servant of the true God, who rewards and punishes according to our service and his good pleasure. Blah blah. A fundamentalist to the end. Drowned he might be, or near it, from his chattering teeth to his blue toe nails. But his tongue? Limber to the end.

Did I call it a conversation? People like him don't hold conversations, they rent auditoriums, even the open sea and its tempests are not safe from their great lungs. What could I do, but blink in disbelief and take my medicine like the good beast I am?

A pause in his confabulations, while he gathered breath from the winds. I interjected, the first sensible remark of the exchange.

—And what would you suggest we do now? The question was not for him at all; it was addressed to the only sensible being in sight—myself.

What was I to do? Land him safe on some distant shore, a polyp on a platter? But we were nowhere near a shore; in the full rage of the sea, God had let go of him, midway, so to speak, between unwelcome sky and bottomless wave. Jonah could point his prophetic finger where his fancy pleased: north, east, south, west, go here, run there, it was all equidistant; he was nowhere. We wouldn't make it; or more properly, he wouldn't. Not soaked and frozen in the extremities and half gone with hunger as he was.

Now with such serious issues at hand, I didn't like his preaching, finding it among other deficiencies redundant, badly composed and untimely. But that doesn't mean, let me add, that I'm theologically hostile. How could I be, plunged as I am in a watery world that even a blind shark could see is more laden with design than chance?

We whales have been around a long time. We may not have leather lunged prophets to tell us the cosmic score. Maybe we don't need them. Nor, might I add, do we on occasion, carve them into sections, cast them overboard in storms, or crucify them to trees.

Anyway you learn patience. Take life as it comes, step by step. Granted for a moment God signaled to me that morning; follow such and such a ship, they're making gull fodder out of my chosen, and I want it stopped. Granted God set the compass and synchronized the clocks. (Granted on the other hand, God also set the barometer plunging.) I'm willing to waive the argument because the moment is a pressing one; viz, I've got the *Vox Dei* hanging on to me as though I'm the everlasting arms. Now what do I do?

Obviously, he's in no state to make a suggestion worth listening to; and hearken as I may, I hear no divine voice twitching at my ear lobe, telling me the next move.

So what *is* to be done?

There's not a moment to be lost. He's got a look in his eye like a poster on a picket line; WHALE STEAKS FOR JESUS! (Did you know, by the way, we have bigger brains than they do?) I can all but read his next thought; no great feat, he gives it away, sitting there, counting off on his fingers the proofs for the existence of God most apt to win a waterlogged pachyderm to the one true way.

I had enough. Pursed my lips a bit, leaning in his direction, as though rendered thoughtful by his wisdom, about to share a confidence out of earshot of the almighty.

And took him in like a smelt. Swallowed. He went down easy. . . .

JONAH, ARE YOU DOWN THERE?

He heard me all right. We're among the few mammals who can reverse their voice box. This unique gift of inward rumination is granted for just such occasions, when we've suddenly had to swallow a prophet for his own good.

JONAH—ARE YOU . . . ?

O I knew he was there. You see, we can also reverse our eyesight, in order to check on inward operations, so to speak.

Oh, he wasn't fooling me with his silence. I could see him crouching in a corner of my guest suite, in a low mood I judged. I couldn't see his face too well, he being too miffed even to light the candle I had thoughtfully provided on a shelf. (Along I might add, with basic survival foods, central heating, a soft wall to wall membrane; even, if he required sleep, a folded lap rug. These perquisites snatched from a shipwreck some years before, never ingested or eliminated in view of just such a contingency.)

Ingratitude, in face of all this forethought, these Class A accommodations? You get used to it.

JONAH . . . !

He's humiliated, he's confused. No wonder he's withdrawn. Imagine, a whale for weathervane, world mother, lifeboat—providence! All his choices are gone. The planet's given him up; he's overboard. No one wants him, no one gives a damn.

I'm in charge. That comes down hard on the prophetic spleen.

No idea where he's going, how he's to get there. No sailors, no compass, no captain. No night, no day. No wonder he's unstrung, sleepless, pacing up and down, up and down my guts. Or tossing himself into a corner in a snit. I'm not his proper environment, he's lost all vim, stopped composing sermons. Even given up converting me—the last thing to go, their flagrant apostolic fervor. Well.

Sleep then, Jonah!

Sleep my son, my child.

My whole being, my breast, my womb is for you.

Sleep Jonah in the belly of a paradox. Now you need have no purpose, nothing to prove, nowhere to go.

You may, as of now, stop talking, stop planning, stop thinking. The God who thinks of you has no need of your thought. The God who loves you has no need of your love. The God who upholds the universe has no need of your strength.

Why should he? Are you then to hold him up?

Sleep Jonah, in a motion that is no motion, in a direction that is no direction. Does the unborn child order its mother about, when to sit, when to eat, when to go forth, what words to speak? Be still, then, and know that I am God.

There will be a time perhaps (perhaps!) when these things will be proper, in accord with right reason. But only when you have been born again; if, indeed, you are to be born, which event is not in your devising either.

Be still, Jonah, sleep at last. (He sleeps at last.) In the belly of your savior, in the perilous, fathomless sea, where salvation is a miracle and death is most likely—sleep.

Let me whisper to you, prophet, maker, doer, voyager, weaver of words, serious browed one, rambunctious, moody one. There is one greater than you, and he is silent. There is one who encompasses you, and he lets you go. There is one named Hope, and he casts you overboard. There is one named God and his servant is—a whale.

Embryo, sleeper, mote, pin prick, blind eye, pretender, blusterer. Sleep awhile, awaken and rub your eyes; then perhaps he will summon you.

Until then, I bear you through the pathless sea. Another than you plans for you, another than you breathes for you, another than you loves you, another than you sees before and after, yesterday and tomorrow. While you lie there, ignorant of where you come from, where you might be going, indeed, of who you are.

Who am I, you will ask on awakening, as your eyes open, as the light floods in, as you walk the earth once more. As over you floats, and then entwines, over shoulders and arms and legs and close about your head, the cloak of import, the cloak of office, the cloak so ample you must stand upright in order to wear it properly, and walk about to show it to best advantage, and speak sonorously to draw attention to its splendor. Why, this is my cloak, I am Jonah the prophet, man of the truth, man burdened with the world's weight, the world's sin, the world's error. And you will twitch your mantle, impatient for time lost, you world-encompassing man, and make a noise in public once more, and breathe deep while the people cry; Jonah, the prophet of the most high is in our midst; hearken to him, repent!

And you will forget the days and nights you passed in the belly of a whale, in the belly of absurdity, in the belly of birth.

You great man! Only remember; once for a space you shuddered on the tip of a mortal dilemma out of which you were drawn by no power of your own, by no word of yours, by the unlikely flipper of a whale.

Sent to save you.

No archangel.

Not Providence.

Not a prophet.

Not God.

Behold! A wallowing insensate ugly fog-hued oversized paradigm of the inscrutable ways.

He wakens
in me
my son, Jonah.

A BOOK OF PARABLES, 1977

A Visit to the Book of Kells and a Walk in the Park

A kick of wind
like the left hind leg
of the ghost of a dog
lickety-split
the brown leaves go

then
leaves lie quiet
the wind chases itself
elsewhere.

Under glass, in Met museum
this day I saw
a bird of paradise
outspread
the grandiose, grotesque
book of Kells.

Come wind, let us die easy
come book, let us live forever.

UNPUBLISHED, CA. 1982

The Strange Case of the Teacher Who Practiced What He Taught

Indeed, in our age they talk about the importance of presenting Christianity simply; not elaborately and grandiloquently. And about this subject they write books, it becomes a science, perhaps one may even make a living of it and become a professor. But they forget or ignore the fact that the truly simple way of presenting Christianity is—to do it.

KIERKEGAARD,"FOR SELF EXAMINATION"

On May 10 of this year [1982], several of our family embarked on a rather unusual journey. Great travelers all, especially those of us who undertook this latest trip, we had severally gone off to seminaries, embarked for war, traveled abroad for studies, voyaged to every hamlet and corner of America. But this was something else, even for us.

In his sixty-third year, with a joyful and even nonchalant air, our brother Jerry, professor of English literature, was turning himself in to federal prison. We set out on Monday from Syracuse to deliver the prisoner into the iron embrace of holy mother state, at the prison camp in Allenwood, Pa. The sentence; three months. The crime; destruction of something called government property. Or more properly; the pouring of human blood on the Pentagon.

Considerable local interest surrounded the crime and punishment; a local citizen was to be sentenced on his own turf. In the courtroom, the three brothers, seasoned felons all, sat amid spouses, children, friends. The judge was a former colleague of mine at the Jesuit Le Moyne College. Averting his eyes, manifestly in great discomfiture of spirit, he did his thing. Legal punctilio was observed to the letter; even with a slight bend backward toward courtesy. Jerry was allowed to address the court. He did so briefly and pointedly, with rare grace and a kind of total moral recall which one comes to associate with such occasions, such defendants. Briefly, he recalled the nuclear facts of life, the world reduced to a shack teetering on the cusp of a universal, monstrous destruction.

He drove the facts forward like a drover of slow-witted cattle. He had gone to the Pentagon because, among other reasons, it was impossible to teach what one did not practice. It was intolerable to call oneself a teacher of literature, and at the same time, to push the elegant illusion that all was well in the world, that literature created its own ambiance, a superior world of imagination, mercifully spared bloodstained actualities.

332

Or, in another sense, a sense nearer the bone and marrow, it was intolerable that Christianity should be presented to one's own children as though rote memory said it all. As though he, the parent of four, could present Christianity as a matter of private virtue, a cottage industry of good works humming away. Or as though liturgy in the home, the rhythms of the ritual year, grace at table, periodic prayer, retreats—as though these summed up the matter,—a religion of regular order, esthetics, good taste instead of faith.

And finally—and this was the hardest question of all—whether given the nuclear stampede toward Armageddon, —whether he could live Christianity today only by ministering to local needs, feeding the hungry at Unity Kitchen, serving at the men's night shelter. Whether he could simply conclude that such activity sufficed, sealed one's Christianity with the blessing of Christ on "works of mercy."

If I could work a bit of metaphoric violence on a Gospel story, it seems to me that my brother is somewhat like the rich young man who came to Christ, seeking "what was yet lacking." Incurably and morally inquisitive, he put a dangerous question to One not given to slamming doors on mettlesome spirits. In my brother's case, the story had a far different outcome. He posed the question and received his answer. Then he proceeded, not to walk away, with a bent nose and the dogged look of one who had sought the truth and unhappily came on it.

Jerry went for the truth; then he proceeded to act. Such an astounding proceeding is known in the great world as asking for trouble—and getting it.

This is our brother, relatively unsung and (as of now) relatively uncursed as well. On the day of his sentencing it struck me that he had broken through the tabus of academe in somewhat the manner Philip and I had had to break through the tabus of the priesthood.

Priests do not burn draft cards, we were once sternly advised. Nor do tenured professors commonly trek to the Pentagon, asserting, in an untidy and even shocking manner, their objection to the engineered end of the world. Such things simply are not done. There are civilized rules binding those admitted, after long apprenticeship and multiplied scrutiny, to the Groves, the Good Life guaranteed, the Officers' Club. Certain assumptions are in force, all the more rigorous for being implicit. Like these: One's turf is one's own; a professor, by definition an expert, leaves military and political matters to other experts. Or again, literature (or theology, or sociology, or mathematics, it makes little difference)—these are inherently apolitical. Or again; one does not bring up unpleasant or frictive matters in public. Professorial sociabilities are often pursued drink in hand, amid inconsequential chatter and internal gossip. The French, who are apt for almost any unmentionable subject, have a word for this: one of them, Julien Benda, has even written a book about such arrangements. It is called, impolitely enough, *la Trahison des Clercs* (The Betrayal of the Intellectuals). It is a cruel historical scrutiny of the conduct of French academics in periods of public crisis. The moral is startlingly consistent: don't count on them.

Any and all claims attached to academe, regarding superior moral discernment or development, are universally false. My sense of things in America is not notably different from the French report. It is rare to find, in theology departments for example, that scripture or a given religious code, is considered binding, or a call to faith. Theology, like every other discipline, is often considered an object of competence, not of faith; dry grist for the mill. Religious traditions, which have historically nourished heroes and saints, are treated as matters of "specialty," "expertise." Their outcome in a given instance is nothing like a unitive conscience, political sense or passion, wisdom. None of these. But a small-minded, cold-fish attitude toward the world, any world but one's own; and one's own world tight and small as a worry bead in the palm.

The above is commonly referred to as "value free" intellectual life. Value free, if one is allowed comment, only in the sense that it is an invitation to self-interest, fastidious, even disdainful toward the common life of people. More, in America, many academics hang out their shingle; available for the big deal, the multicorporate sellout to war research, warmaking government, the big bucks attendant on the big bang. Not without reason are some academic functionaries plucked easily from campuses, transplanted to State or Pentagon. Their roots are shallow enough. It is all one.

One of these, a renowned Catholic college president, was advanced recently to the board of directors of General Dynamics, manufacturers of the Trident nuclear submarine fleet. When I dared voice reservations regarding the arrangement, she said to me with disdain, "Really, you and your friends have no conception of the many gifts and functions open to the Body of Christ." Well, no.

I draw a harsh picture here, but perhaps no harsher than the reality. I believe that in achieving criminal status in America, my brother has focused a light, for those who can withstand the glare, on one of the unaccountable hypes of our culture; academe. In so doing, he also, and as if by inadvertence, put his own privileges of tenure to uniquely good use. His college cannot now quite dispose of him. To assimilate him to its values has proven impossible; to amputate him violates the rules by which drones and workers alike flourish. The rules must be applied, even to such specimens as he; tenured he is, tenured he must remain, even in federal pen.

In so acting, he stands very nearly alone. We are light years removed from the '60's; the campuses have only of late, and then desultorily, begun to object to nuclear arms (and that, only when dismayed at the drying up of government largesse). Meantime, cupidity, game playing with imperial power, recoiling from social responsibility (especially in the cities, where universities often batten on urban land seizure) tax free, "value free,"—the campuses have raised self-interest to the level of high art.

The Catholic campuses offer little relief. One cannot but marvel at the gap between religious rhetoric and public conduct. It could even be argued that on the matter of pretension to a higher moral code, the Catholics come off worse than their secular counterparts. It is probably no news that the showcase Catholic universities boast prestigious theology departments, even while the military march on their commons. The incongruence of this is, as they say, instructive to the seeking mind. Military presence, military instruction, maneuvers; and then the word of God. In uneasy conjunction? Inducing second thoughts in those responsible? Subject to campus debate? Not at all, in my experience — or hardly ever.

I recall that in the past years, I have been invited to the campuses of at least five religious orders, including my own: Vincentians, Holy Cross, Franciscans, Benedictines, Jesuits. On each campus, theology looms large; on each campus also, ROTC. The Big Buck stalks the Little Book, all but slams it shut. The theologians who consider such matters to be morally grotesque are few and far between. There occurs, so to speak, in contravention of the ancient Easter hymn, no life and death wrestling between the adversaries named Life and Death. Indeed not. The two, reconciled at last, lie in one bed, a discreet bundling board between. Half dead, shall we call them? In any case, only half alive.

A mantle of religio-secular rhetoric (to keep the figure) discreetly veils the scene. Each university has its founding hero, its favorite **fioretto**, its chatter about "charisms." Money is as unmentionable as an obscenity on an undertaker's tongue; it is also omnipresent, a god with an itching palm. At St. Bonaventure's, the Franciscans celebrate the 800th anniversary of St. Francis; with, if one may be pardoned, flying colors. The Jesuits recall, as one of their favorite stories, how St. Ignatius, signaling his conversion from a life of violence and oat-sowing, hung up his sword before the shrine of the Queen of Peace. The Benedictines display PAX as their family motto. The President of University Number One hurries about the world, making peace in the grand manner. And the Vincentians, founded by a saint who ransomed slaves and harbored street folk — one could go on. On each of the campuses, the military is ensconced, peddles its wares, offers military scholarships. No matter what the name of the order, no matter who the founder. One might conclude, were one not cognizant of the coverup, that all Catholic universities were conducted, founded, funded, ideologized, by a single hard-headed western male realist, in whose head guns and butter, Eucharist and uniform, rested easy.

Here are a few course offerings from one such (Jesuit) University.

MS 103. American Military History. Military history from colonial wars to Vietnam. Emphasis is on military leadership, the principles of war, and development of military art.

MS 202. Concepts of Military Operations. Application of the principles of warfare by small unit leaders. Principles of offense and defense at the squad level to include tactical formations and battle drill.

MS 302. Tactical Operations. The role of the company commander
and subordinate leaders during tactical operations. Planning and
execution of small unit offensive and defensive maneuvers.

I dwell on the above, since these campuses were, for better or worse, the
matrix out of which my brothers and I issued. What we learned there, what
we had to unlearn at some cost, is perhaps by now becoming clearer. To be
unlearned above all else was the assumption, fostered in a thousand subtle
ways, that the military in any of its forms, could cohabit easily with
Christian faith; or indeed, to push matters further, that the military could
be reconciled with literature, or with any subject or discipline consonant
with a humanist, let alone a Christian, vision.

At long last, America is beginning to stir from its psychic numbing.
There arises an inchoate, half-formed fear, the military is our great danger;
the enemy of life itself. In spite of this, in ignorance of this, Catholic
universities slumber on. They stubbornly protect, justify, welcome, inte-
grate, the military. I cannot, alas, report that the reasoning behind this
lamentable incongruity could be called Christianly persuasive. Mostly, the
reasoning comes to a set of frivolous clichés, free floating ideology, the
tooting of a bugle around the flagpole, all designed to muffle the clink of
avarice. Here is an example, by no means unique:

> I do not believe we can escape our responsibilities as citizens,
> Christians or humans by divorcing ourselves from that segment of
> society which has been given the task of defending our way of life.
> . . . For the severity of the task they have been charged with, isn't it
> better that these officers be educated in the values espoused
> by_____ University, rather than at a secular university uncon-
> cerned with philosophy, ethics, religion or global concerns?

Enough said.

When a situation becomes intolerable to one's sense of justice, one's love
of children, one's dream of the beloved community—then one speaks up, or
acts up. This, I take it, is no great thing, but a simple rule of thumb, if
moral survival is taken seriously. One should be able to make sense of one's
own face.

Yeats writes in a lovely verse that he "sought the face I had / before the
world was made." My brother the teacher, along with others, including my
friends of the Plowshares Eight, the mother of children, the lawyer, the
student, the missioner, the theologian—they seek perhaps a face fit to resist
the end of the world. In seeking such a countenance, will they perhaps come
on the face of the Suffering Servant, the face of God?

THE CATHOLIC WORKER, AUGUST 1982

Denise Levertov's Prose

(A REVIEW OF *LIGHT UP THE CAVE,* **BY DENISE LEVERTOV)**

The hallmark of Denise Levertov's prose is something so simple and elusive as clear-eyed common sense. In the nature of things, so esoteric a virtue has not been grandly rewarded. Common sense? mainline writers along with their multicorporate pushers, have stampeded toward the rainbow named Avarice; others have shown a sorrowful, even despairing obsession with the Confession That Bares All.

Levertov is aware of the implications here, destructive as they are of political understanding and writers' craft. And of life itself, as in writers who have constructed a game called despair; and played it, bullet to head.

She takes up such matters, despair, anomie, political indifference, matters which most writers today prefer to keep decently out of sight and mind. She analyzes despair and its practitioners, and those who justify it as a resource. And by a parallel right instinct, she avoids the rapacious rush to trivialize life, to bring it in line with a desperate and trivial culture.

She is that rara avis, a poet, a political writer, very much a woman. These are the poles of her art as of her existence. She stays close to essentials, and the resolve, in the best sense, has paid off. Her writing remains wonderfully contemporary, it walks with us, illumines the journey of conscience that began in civil rights days and continues on into the eighties and the antinuclear struggle.

She charts the essentials; how we grew, what mistakes we made, how we failed one another, what gains and losses percolated, boiled over. And perhaps, most important, how we've grown, and into what. (*We* being the phalanx of ages, backgrounds, hopes, tactics, that started marching in the fifties and continues till now.)

There is a measure of courage required to march and be arrested. And there is another sort of courage, intelligence, and discipline implied in setting down a record of the march, the arrests, the meaning of it all. Their tone, excitement, verve! In the lives of most who take part, there is no comparable taste of the lost American art known as community.

Her essays thus hearten young and old alike; they are a diary of our neglected soul. Norman Mailer did something like this in the sixties; but since those heady days and nights, he, like most such marchers and writers, has turned to other matters. (I remember half seriously writing Mailer in 1980, announcing that we of the Plowshares Eight were prepared to name him the chronicler of our crime and punishment. He responded by sending a [small] check to the defense committee. Otherwise, no taker.)

Levertov is still marching, still recording the march. There are dazzling skills here; they start in the feet, rhythmically implanted in mother earth, and make their way, mysterious, tingling, into hand, fingers, pen. It begins with courage, a continuity of courage, a cold stream in the temperate larger stream of soul. Robert Frost's contrary stream, headlong in one direction when the rivers of a given time, and the voice of those rivers, would have us believe that "all is well."

"All is well" was the siren voice of the seventies. That the word was a lie, a blockage of soul, a numbing that threatened to turn us shortly dead—this seemed to penetrate almost no one. Many writers were ensconced on campuses where moral insolvency and bonhomie went hand in hand. A very few made it big, with what came to be known as "blockbusters." (The term, one recalls, referred to the largest of the prenuclear bombs of World War II.) Others joined the urban working class, one met them driving cabs or doing short order cooking or cleaning or acting as security guards. A few came and went in academe, an adjunct job here and there, hewers of wood and drawers of water so to speak, untenured and unrehabilitated. They published where they could in little magazines and presses, counted themselves lucky to publish at all.

But at the same time, writers like Levertov kept to the themes, kept to the marches, kept being arrested. The big sleep was on, but some were awake through the seductive night. The questions kept them awake. Were humans, any humans, going to make it through the century? Would there be a next generation? Were we intent, as a people, on bringing down the world, and if so, by what authority, in whose name? Who was the enemy anyway? Why was all the mad intemperate talk (winnable nuclear war, limited nuclear war) coming from one side, ours; and all the talk of mitigation, dread, disarmament, coming from the "enemy"?

The questions, until recently, kept being ignored. So did the questioners, including the questioning writers like Levertov. I presume that this is her history, as it is of a few others. She tells of that comatose decade, the seventies, almost as though it hadn't existed. She marches, keeps something alive, is personally dispassionate. There was work to be done, that was all. It little mattered that the work was despised or ignored or neglected. It was simply there, as evil was, as the world was; as hope was. She is passionate only about the issues, life or death. In this she, so to speak, turns the cultural method on its head. That is to say, American writing in the seventies, both prose and poetry, was disproportionately passionate about the self, and correspondingly numb (passion not being in large supply) toward the public weal and woe. Thus was a natural balance thrown out of kilter.

In insisting on this balance, and thus restoring it, Levertov reminds me of Paul Goodman; in political sanity, in large scope and interest, in intellectual clarity—and especially in moral unabashedness. I think of her, as I recall him, unashamed to be old fashioned and patriotic, calling the country to accounts, being (horrors!) "judgmental" toward morons and rogues in high places, linking her work to spirits like Thoreau, Emerson, Hawthorne, Melville, Mother Jones, John Brown, the Quaker chroniclers—and, in our lifetime, to the incomparable Martin Luther King and Dorothy Day. Moralists, poets, activists, pacifists, abolitionists, prolabor, propoor, prohuman, these formed her history, as ours, if we can but rise to it; living it, rising to it, testing its native decency against the manifest social indecency of war, piratical economics, hatred of the poor, racism, nouveau riche clowning, the mad mutual rhythms of waste and want.

I have not so much as mentioned the richness and scope of her literary criticism. *Multum in parvo*; the entire book is beyond praise. I think of how, in a sane time, such a book and those which preceded it, including poetry, short stories, literary essays, social criticism, would form a university course entitled something like: A Renaissance Woman of the Late Twentieth Century. But this is dreaming; it would mean crossing jealous frontiers, violating "expertise."

Meantime, for those who come on this book, there is much to ponder, much to learn. Since these essays were published, several of her themes have grown, imperceptibly and ominously, like stalactites aimed at the heart of things. The despair for instance, which she analyzes so acutely, a point of departure for a debased theory of "art at the extremes"—despair has spread, become the national mood, from sea to shining sea. Its articulations, symbols, justifications are all about, infect everything; grab and run economics, chic selfishness, parasitic evangelism. Not merely a few poets are cultivating it, but the public at large, its institutions, those who read, those who manage, the image makers. Fear at the heart; a heart of darkness, frivolity at the surface.

All this being our predicament, political responsibility, resistance, together with the recounting and pondering and exemplifying—these can no longer be viewed as a choice in a range of choices. Our options, as they say, are no longer large. The eye narrows (the choices narrow), when we look (when we refuse to look) into the medusa mirror—the Mark 12A for example, a first strike nuclear warhead, destroyed by eight of us in September 1980. Or when in nightmare, there slides toward us head-on the monstrous pirana, a nuclear submarine named Trident. Its prey we know. Knowing, we may choose to do nothing; which is to say, to go discreetly or wildly mad, letting fear possess us and frivolity rule our days.

Or we may, along with admirable spirits like Denise Levertov, be driven sane; by community, by conscience, by treading the human crucible.

THE AMERICAN BOOK REVIEW, JANUARY 1983

Journey to Block Island:
In Memoriam

Anthony Towne and William Stringfellow (Bill, in the poem) lived on Black Island, Rhode Island, where Daniel Berrigan has been a frequent visitor for many years.

i
ANTHONY TOWNE

Anthony, great bearded bear of man.
At some point
he laid aside use, misuse, urban frenzies
follies, pride of place. Resolved
like a Stonehenge circle, simply
to be. I thought
this deliberately useless man
is image of a useless God.
Teach us so; You who die and live
in the great bearded image of Yourself.

Bill wrote to me in Berkeley:
We'll bury Anthony's ashes on your return.
A dazzling dervish nor'easter, rain
striking like blue nails. Bill and I
two faulty frames, dug a small grave.
We lowered the box
no larger than a jeweler's casket shrining
a jeweled time piece. His heart stilled.
Scripture readings, silence.
Hear the rain drum *mean time! mean time!* the peaceable
echo in nature, of that stilled heart.
Then, Bill commanded
in a voice tears and rain together commandeered:
Now we shall face the house; presumptuous death
held sway awhile, shall oust him. We turned
against malignant huff and puff.
And Bill intoned; every jot and title
of ancient exorcism. We shivered in our bones
under the driving downpour, prayer books dissolved

to illiterate oatmeal. I thought
what demon worth his salt
would flee comfortable hearth and hutch
for devilish weather?
Dignum et justum. Prayers said,
two hefty islanders
dragged across streaming lawn a four foot whaler's anchor
leaned it crossways over Anthony's grave.
Anchored now. Hope befits
ashes. Anthony anchored above the sea. Hope starts
when worldly hope, flesh, assertive bones
works, pomps, pride, place, rule of thumb
religiosities, merits, prevailing clamors, all, all
rendered, reduced, ash. This ash, verily
ash of the body of Christ, humbly melded
with worm and clod, shall serve
to save. Anthony, Christ, salvage the shipwreck world.

About our business went, after death's
hiatus, breathing again. The dead were houseled
the living had their house. Grief turned in time
in turning time, to temperate mourning. Pages
by grief defaced, grew legible once more.

---

ii
JOHN LEARY, 1958–82

Rare spirit, rare,
Harvard College had not his peer.
"An award for drowning do gooders," he joked
when honors came his way.
Now a face shines
on water, as though an angel
shone momentary there. And we weep,
letting go.
Memory, keep him,
memory, never the less.
Summon in bread and wine
primary acts. The Lord's death
barely to be borne
must be, must be. That necessity
I take for discipline, a bell rope
ringing changes, fast, furious
must be! must be! in dead hands.

Imagine John Leary came
seeker and seer to this cottage
before the world broke
his untameable heart.
Imagine his short run
ended
at this land's end.
Murmuring his Jesus prayer
at last he knew
all that is knowable
though the world's brutish will
break like sticks or bones
noblest hearts first.
At wit's end, at such ending
of promise, sweetness, surmise
fantasy takes hold
John Leary at cliff side
life's headlong venture
by no means stalled.
John Leary, child
of air, earth, fire—
his Jesus prayer
come true at last, vision
consumes belief like a straw.
In his element at last
he follows the walker of waves.

BLOCK ISLAND, 1985

Not Feeling Poetic

Not feeling poetic these days. Where's it gone, that state of the art called human?

State of the heart. Not feeling poetic. No wonder. A war on the human.

When the bombers nose southward toward Tripoli, they're blasting — poetry.

When the contras make havoc across borders (waste, confusion, incoherence), they and their mentors leave behind — the bones and limbs of dismembered poetry.

They prowl the night (those night-ridden faces) hot on the trail of — poetry. The poetry of murmurous children, the poetry of peasants. Poetry of a new light in the eyes, a forbidden light, an incandescence of soul. Quench it!

Poetry of the Sermon on the Mount, of the Magnificat. All those forbidden songs of hope rising from ashes. Quench it!

Can't abide it! Shoot it, knife it, disappear it, rape it.

Done. Day after day.

Who in the world can feel poetic?

Nevertheless. And in spite of. And against all odds — I give you (give one another!) — poetry.

Or at least; an edging toward, some equivalent, some near thing. Like this; not giving up, not giving in, not nodding agreement like dumb metronomes of fate.

Can this be our best, this near poetry, this little more than — non prose? this non conformity, this prelude and preparation?

Let us consider our beginnings; which were, we are told, somewhat more aspiring. As though someone (there is not yet someone) — someone prayed, say on the fifth day of creation; "Tomorrow, please make a human. More; make another human. Let us then, under the first moon of all, sing out our first hours like nightingales, throat to throat, glory to glory. Casting a rainbow of poetry on the astonished night."

Thus far dreams, new starts.

For now, perhaps we can only make do, not give up, come together in the bleak firelight, make what sense we can of it all. Dwelling as we do, in pre dawn, that darkest blink of night which seems for a horrid moment, like the blinding of the eye of day.

No great achievement. But something. At least we don't ape the horrid prose, we keep intact the code of the nearly lost.

Nearly found? the prisoners sing by heart, like the soul's secret open-sesame; "No one owns us, no one buys us, no one silences us." They set that vow to music, a plaintive hum, a plain chant arising from a tomb.

Prisoners, disappeared ones, madres, dismembered bones gleaming like phosphorus in the waste lands,—(and Christ the gleaner of this holy wheat)—sing out, sing out; "I am here, I am with you all days, we are one!"

I hear this unquenchable poetry of survival. I hear it, it prevails, even on the winds of a firestorm.

It will decompose, into sweet compost of song even the vile prose of hell.

UNPUBLISHED, JUNE 1986

A Buddhist Chants His Epitaph

To have, to hold
is all the rage —
Turn a blank page
let go, let go.

UNPUBLISHED, CA. 1987

Works by Daniel Berrigan

BOOKS

Time without Number. New York: Macmillan, 1957.

The Bride: Essays in the Church. New York: Macmillan, 1959.

Encounters. Cleveland: World Publishing Co., 1960.

The Bow in the Clouds: Man's Covenant with God. New York: Coward-McCann, 1961.

The World for Wedding Ring. New York: Macmillan, 1962.

No One Walks Waters. New York: Macmillan, 1966.

They Call Us Dead Men: Reflections on Life and Conscience. New York: Macmillan, 1966.

Consequences: Truth and . . . New York: Macmillan, 1967.

Night Flight to Hanoi: War Diary with 11 Poems. New York: Macmillan, 1968.

Love, Love at the End. Parables, Prayers and Meditations. New York: Macmillan, 1968.

False Gods, Real Men: New Poems. New York: Macmillan, 1969.

Trial Poems: A Poet, a Painter, with Tom Lewis. Boston: Beacon Press, 1970.

The Trial of the Catonsville Nine. Boston: Beacon Press, 1970.

No Bars to Manhood. New York: Doubleday, 1970.

The Geography of Faith: Conversation between Daniel Berrigan, when Underground, and Robert Coles. Boston: Beacon Press, 1971.

The Dark Night of Resistance. Garden City, N.Y.: Doubleday, 1971.

America Is Hard to Find. Garden City, N. Y.: Doubleday, 1972.

Absurd Convictions, Modest Hopes: Conversations after Prison with Lee Lockwood. New York: Random House, 1972.

Jesus Chirst, with Gregory and Deborah Harris. Garden City, N. Y.: Doubleday, 1972.

Selected and New Poems. Garden City, N. Y.: Doubleday, 1973.

Prison Poems. Greensboro, N.C.: Unicorn Press, 1973; also New York: Viking Press, 1974.

Lights on in the House of the Dead: A Prison Diary. Garden City, N. Y.: Doubleday, 1974.

The Raft Is Not the Shore: Conversations towards a Buddhist/Christian Awareness, with Thich Nhat Hanh. Boston: Beacon Press, 1975.

A Book of Parables. New York: Seabury Press, 1977.

Uncommon Prayer: A Book of Psalms. New York: The Seabury Press, 1978.

Beside the Sea of Glass: The Song of the Lamb. New York: The Seabury Press, 1978.

The Words Our Savior Gave Us. Springfield, Il.: Templegate Publishers, 1978.

The Discipline of the Mountain: Dante's Purgatorio in a Nuclear World. New York: The Seabury Press, 1979.

We Die before We Live: Talking with the Very Ill. New York: The Seabury Press, 1980.

Ten Commandments for the Long Haul. Nashville: Abingdon, 1981.
Portraits—Of Those I Love. New York: Crossroad, 1982.
The Nightmare of God. Portland, Or.: Sunburst Press, 1983.
*Steadfastness of the Saints: A Journal of Peace and War in Central and North
      America*. Maryknoll, N.Y.: Orbis Books, 1985.
Block Island. Greensboro, N.C.: Unicorn Press, 1985.
The Mission: A Film Journal. New York: Harper and Row, 1986.
To Dwell in Peace: An Autobiography. San Francisco: Harper and Row, 1987.
Stations (with Margaret Parker). San Francisco: Harper and Row, 1988.

FILMS

Holy Outlaw, 1970.
The Trial of the Catonsville Nine, 1973.
In the King of Prussia, 1982.
The Mission, 1986.

RECORDINGS

America Is Hard to Find, 1972.
The Trial of the Catonsville Nine, 1973.

A Note on Secondary Sources

The principal biographical studies are Francine DuPlessis Gray, *Divine Disobedience* (New York: A. A. Knopf, 1970), and John Deedy, *"Apologies, Good Friends": An Interim Biography of Daniel Berrigan, S.J.* (Chicago: Fides/Claretian; and Mystic, Conn.: XXIII Publications, 1981). A comprehensive listing of books and articles, both primary and secondary sources through 1977, appears in Anne Klejment, *The Berrigans: A Bibliography of Published Works by Daniel, Phillip, and Elizabeth McAlister Berrigan.* (New York: Graland Publishing, Inc., 1979). This indispensable book includes an informative introduction as well as a chronology for the years 1921–76.

Permissions Acknowledgments

Reprinted by permission of Abingdon Press:

"Of Priests, Women, Women Priests, and Other Unlikely Recombinants," from *Ten Commandments for the Long Haul* © 1981 by Abingdon Press.

Reprinted by permission of *American Book Review*:

"Denise Levertov's Prose."

Reprinted by permission of *The Catholic Worker*:

"The Strange Case of the Teacher Who Practiced What He Taught," "Swords into Plowshares," "On Torture Road: Kim Chi Ha," and "Where Death Abounded, Life."

Reprinted by permission of *Commonweal*:

"Invitation to a Trial."

Reprinted by permission of *The Critic*:

"Ezra Pound: A Season in Hell" and "Death and the Bishop."

Reprinted by permission of The Crossroad Publishing Company:

"Thomas Merton" (originally "The Monk"), "My Mother" (originally "The Mother"), and "Dorothy Day" (originally "The Woman"), from *Portraits: Of Those I Love* © 1982 by Daniel Berrigan.

Reprinted by permission of Doubleday, a division of Bantam, Doubleday, Dell Publishing Group, Inc.:

"To the Actors, from Underground," from *America Is Hard to Find* © 1972 by Daniel Berrigan.

"Eucharist," from *Selected and New Poems* © 1973 by Daniel Berrigan.

Excerpts from *Lights on in the House of the Dead* © 1974 by Daniel Berrigan.

Reprinted by permission of Harper & Row, Publishers, Inc.:

"A Whale's Tale," from *A Book of Parables* © 1977 by The Seabury Press.

"Dante's *Purgatorio*," the introduction to *The Discipline of the Mountain: Dante's Purgatorio in the Nuclear World* © 1979 by The Seabury Press Inc.

"Cassocks," from *The Mission* © 1986 by Daniel Berrigan.

Excerpts from *Uncommon Prayer* © 1978 by The Seabury Press Inc.

Reprinted by permission of *Israel & Palestine Monthly Review* (5 rue Cardinal Mercier, 75009, Paris, France):

"Israel, as Presently Constituted"

Reprinted by permission of Katallagete (Box 2307 College Station, Berea, Kentucky 40404):

"Open Sesame: My Life and Good Times" © Katallagete INC.

Reprinted by permission of the National Catholic Reporter (P. O. Box 419281, Kansas City, Mo. 64141):

"Letter to Ernesto Cardenal: Guns Don't Work"

Reprinted by permission of *The New York Review of Books*:

"Inside and Outside the Church" © 1971 Nyrev, Inc.

Reprinted by permission of The New York Times Company:

"Each Day Writes" © 1957 by The New York Times Company.

Reprinted by permission of the Putnam Publishing Group:
   "Catholicism and the Intelligence," from *The Bow in the Clouds* © 1961 by
   Daniel Berrigan.
Reprinted by permission of Radix Magazine:
   "Living in the Shadow of Egypt: Reflections on Isaiah."
Reprinted by permission of *Spirit:*
   "The Sistine Chapel."
Reprinted by permission of *Thought:*
   "Credentials" © 1957 by *Thought*; "Song (from Jacopone Da Todi)" © 1964 by
   Thought.
Reprinted by permission of Unicorn Press (P. O. Box 3307, Greensboro, NC 27402):
   "We Used to Meet for Classes, Sometimes It Was Ecstasy, Sometimes Blah,"
   "We Will Now Hear the Word of God from Each of Our Beloved Chaplains,"
   "My Father," "Skunk," "A Bit of History," "Rehabilitative Report," and "A
   Piece of Advice for a Young Prisoner," from *Prison Poems* © 1973 by Daniel
   Berrigan. "Journey to Block Island: In Memoriam," from *Block Island* © 1985
   by Daniel Berrigan.
Reprinted by permission of U. S. CATHOLIC (published by Claretian Publications,
   205 W. Monroe St., Chicago, Illinois 60606):
   "To Limbo and Back: A Latin American Exile."
Reprinted by permission of the Village Voice and the author:
   "Letter to the Weathermen" © 1971.

*Every attempt was made to locate those who held permissions for the works in this
book.*